Search Engine Positioning

Fredrick Marckini

Wordware Publishing, Inc.

Library of Congress Cataloging-in-Publication Data

Marckini, Fredrick.
  Search engine positioning / by Fredrick Marckini.
    p.   cm.
  ISBN 1-55622-804-X (pb)
    1. Web sites--Design.   2. Search engines.   3. Metadata   4. Electronic
commerce.   5. Cataloging of computer network resources.   I. Title.

  TK5105.888 .M362   2001
  025.04--dc21   2001025833
                                                          CIP

ISBN 1-55622-804-X
10 9 8 7 6 5 4 3 2 1
0104

All inquiries for volume purchases of this book should be addressed to Wordware Publishing, Inc., at the above address. Telephone inquiries may be made by calling:

(972) 423-0090

Dedication

To my mom and dad who raised me to believe that literally anything is possible if you put your mind to it. Preparing this book challenged that belief system to its very core, yet validated it in the end.

Contents

Contents

Contents

Acknowledgments

In 1997 I wrote Secrets to Achieving Top 10 Rankings, which later became #1 Web Marketing: Achieving Top 10 Rankings in Internet Search Engines. Back then my company consisted of a computer, a banquet table, and me in my bathrobe typing away in the second bedroom of my Weston apartment to complete the first book in just under eight months. There were no phone calls from clients (I had just one), no employees needing my attention, no reporters asking for quotes, and no vendors calling on me. The first book wrote itself. Today, iProspect is a much larger organization and my time is split between many competing interests.

Search Engine Positioning did not write itself. It was the labor and participation of more than a dozen dedicated professionals that made this book possible. It is with the greatest humility that I must acknowledge that while I wrote or contributed to most of the chapters, I served as an executive editor of sorts directing the research and writing of a large team of folks who brought this book together. I have been humbled by the experience, and by their commitment to the project, their unbelievable dedication to our firm, and to the quality and consistency of their work product. Without the following people, this book would not have been published.

First and foremost, I must acknowledge Dr. Amanda Watlington, iProspect's Director of Research, without whom this book would not have been completed. I cannot overstate the value and quality of the research and writing Dr. Watlington contributed to this book.

Deborah Hickey, Manager of Marketing and PR; Brian Kaminski, Client Services Manager; Matthew Meier, Research Analyst; Rob Murray, President; John Tawadros, Director of Client Services; and John Kaiser, Vice President Business and Legal Affairs, all worked tirelessly, dare I say doggedly, to make this book a reality.

The following iProspect employees also contributed their time and skill to the research, writing, and editing of this book: Susan Closky, Chad Coury, Ron Domenici, Matthew Evans, Brandon Huck, Kevin Michaluk, Christina Mulhern, Jason Pacheco, Ben Perry, Sage Peterson, Amy Pignatiello, Lynn Roberts,

Johanna Rodriguez, George Smith, and alphabetically last but certainly not least, Colleen Stephan.

Special Thanks

Catherine Seda, Vice President of Online Promotions for SiteLab International in San Diego, California, and a noted speaker on search engine advertising, for her fantastic chapter, "Buying Advertising on Search Engines."

Ali Brown and the fabulous team at AKB & Associates (www.akbwriting.com), the world's best copy writing and editing company (in this author's humble opinion), for dressing up and editing down my writing without hurting my feelings too much.

Reviewers

The following good people generously contributed their time to proofreading the final draft of the book. Their backgrounds are varied — some have search engine positioning backgrounds, some are vendors or partners, and others are current or past iProspect clients; all are friends:

Gina Allemand, Jim Byrd, Sue Decker-Blake, Ann Dufresne, Diana Georgeou, Susan Goodson, Detlev Johnson, Stephen Kelly, Sir Adam Norton, Carey Oster, Rick Ralston, Curtis Roderick, Kim Scheer, Marshall Simmonds, Robert Skelly, Frank Sousa, Joe Sousa, Dr. Chad Stearns, Jim Stob, and Brent Winters.

And to anyone whose name was inadvertently left out, thank you, too! This was no one-man job; it was a team project involving iProspect staff, customers, vendors, and advisors, in short, all of our closest friends. Thank you all for your help. I am in your debt.

Intro:

Search Engine Positioning

hen I first started in the search engine positioning business, so many advisors and friends told me that this industry would not last that I almost started to believe them. They said the search engines would not "allow" us to exist, and that they would eventually find ways to prevent us from being effective. That hasn't happened, and I do not expect that it ever will. Five years later, the company I started out of the second bedroom in my Weston, Massachusetts apartment now flourishes as iProspect.com. So long as there are billions of documents being indexed by relatively few search tools, companies that work their way to the top of the list will benefit most. And as long as there are billions of publicly accessible documents, companies like ours will have work.

What I have found most interesting about this business is the symbiotic relationship between search engine positioning professionals and the search engines. While, like any profession, there are those practitioners who will do anything to get ahead, most of us perform good work of considerable value to the clients we represent. And, in turn, this work benefits the Internet community at large.

Most people venture onto the Internet to solve a "search problem." If the Web site that would best satisfy the intent of their query does not contain any targeted keywords in any of the places where search engines would look for them, that document will not be presented to that searcher. If that document exists on the Web site of one of our clients, it most likely **will** be found by someone using a search engine. Therefore, the activity of search engine positioning benefits the searcher, the search engine, and the Web site itself. In fact, the reason our industry exists at all is that a Web site will gain little ground in being found in a search engine by simply following the tips that the engine posts on its submission pages. Why is this? The search engines do not want to reveal their proprietary ranking methodologies for fear that the unscrupulous will abuse that knowledge. That's their right, as it's our right to include relevant keyword phrases in the metadata and on the viewable page of our clients' Web sites so that they produce higher search results.

It is not, as articles in the trade and business press have attempted to characterize it, an "escalating online arms race." This is not "Spy vs. Spy." It is one industry responding to the realities created by another, and responding, usually, in such a way that benefits all involved. However, reporters love controversy and controversy sells newspapers and magazines. On many occasions I've been asked to discuss search engine positioning in terms of "us against them." In each instance, I simply refused to sling mud. We are fighting every day to communicate to the world the legitimacy of our industry, and I will not contribute to an article that seeks to marginalize what we do. Search engine positioning has emerged as a legitimate, highly valuable, and, dare I say, necessary, component of every online marketing campaign. There's no need to resort to sensationalism to attract attention, especially since most search engine positioning service companies have more business inquiries than they can answer.

It's important to note that the search engine positioning industry was born of a software tool, WebPosition, that could only be downloaded from the Web and was not sold in stores. For this reason, among others, the practice of search engine positioning was "home-grown" — with companies literally springing up out of garages and spare bedrooms. This was a start-up business category that didn't exist before a few years ago in any fashion. As a result, search engine positioning started as a classic "cottage industry" that is just now growing up. Many of the practitioners were Web pioneers — home-based entrepreneurs, self-taught through newsletters and books like this one. And regrettably, many of these home-based pioneers are willing to say anything to trade press, believing in the ever-popular "any press is good press" adage. As these companies age, they'll learn the folly of that belief. Press coverage that makes a mockery of our industry category and scares away established bricks-and-mortar companies is detrimental to our very survival. Until then, iProspect will continue to evangelize about the need for, the value in, and the legitimacy of this industry we call "search engine positioning."

Listen up, folks: Search engine positioning is here to stay. Like other professions, it has its own skill sets and tricks of the trade, and like most professions, it's beginning to take on the form of a true discipline. It has noted leaders, its own body of principles, a recognized methodology, refined techniques, and its own language. But what it lacks is a community of discourse — a shared understanding of its tenets and how to best implement them. This book aims to be just that — a compendium of information for the aspiring search engine positioning professional. To provide the information needed to "top the charts" and attain top 10 to top 30 rankings.

Like its predecessors, our first two books — *Secrets to Achieving Top 10 Rankings* and *#1 Web Marketing: Achieving Top 10 Rankings in Internet Search Engines* — this book will share "secrets" and useful insights for both the experienced practitioner and the novice alike. We hope you enjoy the fruits of our labor — the written compilation of our five years of consulting experience as the world's leading search engine positioning practitioners.

Part 1:

Understanding Search Engines and Search Engine Positioning

Part 1:

Chapter 1:

The History of Search Engines and Search Engine Positioning

he practice of *search engine positioning* did not exist back in 1990 when Alan Emtage, a student at McGill University in Montreal, developed Archie — the first search engine. From Archie's birth to the launch of Raging Search by AltaVista in February 2000, the development of search engines has been driven by: 1) the rapid growth of the Web and 2) the need to find valuable data hidden in its massive volume of more than five billion documents. This unfathomable amount of available information has also spawned the need for Web site owners to develop methods that improve their site's visibility and enhance a search engine's ability to find it. Search engine positioning is the exciting new discipline that comprises these methods. (In the interest of saving space and syllables, we'll refer to search engine positioning as SEP from this point on.)

In late 1996, I discovered my "killer application." When I performed a query in Excite, I was stunned to discover that a simple search for the phrase "car parts" yielded some two million search matches. It seemed intuitive that the higher up a Web site was found on the search matches, the more people would click on that listing and visit the site. Higher rankings meant more traffic. Eureka! My million-dollar idea was born! I would write a piece of software that would perform a query in the major search engines, spider down the results page, and tell the user where the Web site ranked — positioning software.

As far as I knew, there was no such application at the time. There was a popular submission Web site called Submit-It.com, which would submit your site to numerous engines. This was then followed by several software programs that emphasized how many engines they could submit your site to. (A totally irrelevant factor, by the way, as we'll later explain how many peripheral search engines exist solely to capture submitters' e-mail addresses to spam them.) These programs did nothing to help you achieve high rankings in search engines. Even if you got listings, you could be hundreds of pages down in the engine user's search results. (This prompted me to coin the phrase "Because submitting to search engines is just NOT enough!" for my client, FirstPlace Software, makers of WebPosition, which still graces every edition of their *MarketPosition* monthly newsletter.)

I became so excited with my new software idea that a few months later I quit my job, wrote a business plan, and set out on the Web to figure out how to write a software "spec" for such a program. One afternoon, while visiting a Web site for this research, I saw an alarming banner ad: "Software That Checks Your

Web Site's Rank in Search Engines Free Trial Download of WebPosition Agent. Click Here!"

"Just great!" I thought to myself. "Someone beat me to it!" I clicked on the link, downloaded WebPosition Agent, and installed the trial version. To my amazement, the software was better than anything I had even considered developing. It offered robust reports, clever features I hadn't thought to include, and a very simple and friendly user interface. I knew instantly that I'd been beaten. In a moment of clarity, I thought, "Well, if I can't beat 'em, maybe I can join 'em." I picked up the phone and called the company's founder, Brent Winters, who was also its lead software developer. Brent's home-based company, Innovative Solutions and Technologies (IST), Inc., in Joplin, Missouri, had launched WebPosition Agent in 1997. (His company is now called FirstPlace Software, Inc.)

The creation of WebPosition Agent was a landmark accomplishment in the field of SEP, because before its introduction, companies had no choice but to measure their search engine rankings by hand — engine by engine, keyword by keyword — literally performing keyword queries and then reviewing the search results, squinting at screen after screen in hopes of finding their site's URL. It could take someone 30 hours per week to measure a Web site's ranking on just 10 keywords over 10 manual searches. Although several automated submission tools were available, rank measurement software did not yet exist. WebPosition was the first. This pioneering software literally created the entire SEP industry. (Not only will you hear about this software throughout this volume, you'll get detailed instructions on how to incorporate it into your search engine optimization campaign.)

After Brent and I had a few conversations, he asked me to review a marketing letter he wanted to send to all of the people who had downloaded the trial version of WebPosition Agent that would serve to convince them to buy the product. He e-mailed it to me and asked me what I thought. I told him I thought I could improve it. I rewrote the letter and e-mailed it back to him. He told me that he loved it, thanked me, and then sent me another marketing piece he hoped I would review. Once again, I reworked the letter and sent it back. And again, he loved it and thanked me. This went on for about two weeks without any discussion of fees when he asked if I would provide marketing support and manage all of the public relations for WebPosition. There I was, working out of my home, and invited to be the agency of record for the company that produced WebPosition Agent. I was elated. The working relationship between our companies grew strong and successful.

About three months later, I was informed that everyone who had downloaded WebPosition Agent was asking the company what they could do to increase their rankings in the search engines. With WebPosition Agent, they could easily check their rankings, but how could they improve them? They were desperately in need of clear, valid instructions on how to "optimize" their Web sites to achieve search engine visibility. Brent turned to me and asked if I would write such a guide. I explained to him that writing a guide to search engine optimization techniques was actually part of my original business plan, and that I was already planning to write it. He commissioned me to complete it, and some months later I delivered the first complete instructional guide to SEP, titled *Secrets to Achieving Top 10 Rankings.* The guide, now in its fourth revision, continues to be distributed with WebPosition software (Brent's company dropped "Agent" from the product name after protest from a company that produced a product called Position Agent), and all of the product Help files are taken verbatim from this guide. As a result of writing the guide, I became recognized as an authority on SEP and sought after by those who needed to increase their search engine visibility.

My company, then called Response Direct, Inc., began to accept SEP clients. Now, some five years later, we've changed the name to iProspect.com and boast the largest full-time staff of SEP professionals of any SEP services company. Today, iProspect.com represents some of the biggest names in consumer goods, pharmaceuticals, dot-com companies, electronics, telecommunications, and financial services. We've demonstrated that SEP is an important element of any online marketing campaign. Our client roster demonstrates that Web sites in nearly every industry benefit from SEP. iProspect.com has become a fast-growing and hugely successful services company, and we owe it all to WebPosition software, before which the practice of SEP was not a practical application.

The first person to actually investigate what caused Web sites to attain higher ranking in search engines was a former newspaper graphics reporter, Danny Sullivan, a journalist-turned-Web designer. Danny went on to become the general manager of Maximized Online, a Web design company where he honed his HTML and Web site design skills. Maximized Software, the parent company of Maximized Online, eventually decided to close down its Web design business, but one of its clients asked Danny to remain on their project. Danny Sullivan launched Calafia Consulting (www.calafia.com), and his consulting practice was born. In April 1996, after a customer complained to Danny that his Web site could not be found in WebCrawler, he set out on a research mission to better

understand how Web sites were listed and attained rankings in the major search engines. Danny wrote and published an online treatise titled *A Webmaster's Guide to Search Engines,* which later evolved into the search engine mega-site Search Engine Watch (www.searchenginewatch.com). The site launched on June 9, 1997 — coincidentally, the very same month WebPosition was introduced.

Search Engine Watch has become the Drudge Report of the search engine industry. It's often the first to post inside information on search engine partnerships or why a particular search engine is banning a specific SEP tactic. In addition to its news-gathering and reporting functions, the site tracks Webmaster techniques, alliances, stock and investor information, and any number of other tidbits on search engines and their use, all of which can be found nowhere else. It is unequivocally the most important site on the Web for SEP and for those interested in learning about search engines. Bookmark this site and refer to it at least weekly.

Search Engines: The Wonder Years

As search engines and directories have increased in number, sophistication, and complexity, so too have the art and science of search engine positioning. Existing search engines and directories are constantly changing their search algorithms and striking new alliances, and new search engines are emerging. This book will give you up-to-date information specifically about positioning for each of the major search engines and directories that are currently referring visitors to sites.

This chapter will give you a simple overview of the history of the development of search engines for the Web. Because SEP has developed in concert with the search engines, knowing the origin of many of the algorithms, rules, and procedures that circumscribe the discipline will make the landscape easier for you to navigate.

Search engines have evolved from academic and research tools with intriguing names like Archie, Gopher, Veronica, and Jughead to some of the most-visited sites on the Web (still with novel names like Yahoo!, AltaVista, and Google). Originally designed by scientists to find information across small networks, these tools have evolved tremendously. Today, they are used by millions of consumers looking for information as well as vendors and products in the burgeoning world of e-commerce. A brief review of the history of the search engines and their contribution to search technology as it relates to SEP will provide a backdrop for the discussion in later chapters on how to position a Web site so that it appears (ranks) within the first three pages of search results.

And, as we'll be emphasizing again and again, if your Web site is not found in the top 10 to 30 matches of the search engine's results (the first three pages of search matches), your site will be as effective as a billboard in the woods. No one will find it, and no one will come.

1990-1993: The Early Entrants

In 1990, before the World Wide Web as we know it even existed, Alan Emtage at McGill University created **Archie**, the first search tool. Back then, the primary method for sharing data was through anonymous FTP (file transfer protocol) of files stored on FTP servers. These files were frequently stored on FTP archive sites where individuals could deposit and retrieve files for sharing. However, there was no method for searching these FTP servers and their archives, and many of the servers had just a few files available. To locate a file, the researcher had to know its exact server address — very inconvenient.

Emtage altered the landscape permanently when he designed Archie to search the archive sites on FTP servers. He initially wanted to call the program "Archives," but the confines of Unix syntax forced him to shorten the name to Archie. Short, catchy names have typified search engines ever since.

Archie used a script-based data retriever to gather site listings of anonymous FTP files and gave users access to the database through an expression matcher. The development of a database with searchable results from multiple anonymous sources paved the way for the search tools and massive databases we use today.

Archie was so popular for finding files on FTP sites that other researchers began developing tools for searching other types of available electronic information. In the early 1990s, many plaintext documents were available on Gopher servers, where they could be retrieved and read anonymously. (Many Gopher servers are still available today, but Web servers have eclipsed them in popularity and use.) In 1993, the University of Nevada System Computing Services group developed **Veronica**. This search device was similar to Archie but searched Gopher servers for text files.

The problem with Veronica was that it didn't group the results it returned in any way that gave users an understanding of the possible content of the pages. The results returned for Java could just as easily be for code as for coffee. This surfaced a problem that still bedevils search engine developers today —

how to provide searchers a context for interpreting search results. Resolving this problem lies at the heart of many of the search algorithms in use to this day.

Soon after the development of Archie, the comic strip family was complete with the entry of **Jughead**, a search tool with functionality similar to Veronica. But the information tidal wave of the Web would soon blow away all three comic characters.

In 1989, Tim Berners-Lee at the European Laboratory for Particle Physics (CERN) invented HTML (Hypertext Markup Language), which allowed users to structure pages that could include images, sound, and video along with text. With its hyperlink capability, HTML made it easier to link together documents from different servers. Then the Web tidal wave really hit with the development of **Mosaic**, a browser that could take advantage of this functionality. A team of developers at the National Center for Supercomputing Applications (NCSA) at the University of Illinois developed Mosaic and made the browser available for free across the Internet, in accordance with NCSA regulations.

This led to the rapid development of the Internet as we know it today. With the ability to include images, sound, and video clips in easily viewable hypertext, HTML and the Web rapidly replaced Gophers and FTP file repositories.

In June 1993, Matthew Gray of MIT launched the first "spider" robot on the Web. The **World Wide Web Wanderer** was designed as a research tool to track the size and growth of the Web. At first, it simply counted the rapidly growing number of Web servers. It was later modified to capture URLs into the first searchable Web database, the **Wandex**.

The Wanderer created quite a stir because early versions of this spider (and similar research spiders) were able to quickly overwhelm networks and create network performance degradation. Because the spiders could make multiple document requests in a short period of time, they acted as if a large volume of users had all logged in at once. In the limited bandwidth environment of the early Web, this created huge problems. Unless the spidered server could handle this traffic, a rampant spider would quickly overwhelm it. Early spiders frequently visited the same site multiple times in a single day, creating serious havoc.

The problems created by Wanderer and other early spiders led to the development of informal protocols for "polite" spidering — still observed by search spiders combing the Web today. A polite spider spaces its requests to a given server at least a minute apart so as to not overwhelm it. It identifies itself so that, if there is a problem, the owner can be contacted, and it also avoids redundant accesses to the same site. For additional information on robots and spiders, visit WebCrawler's Web Robots FAQ at: http://info.webcrawler.com /mak/projects/robots/faq.html.

In October 1993, Martiijn Koster, who is now a consultant software engineer with Excite, developed **ALIWEB** (which stands for Archie-Like Indexing of the Web). Koster had three goals in developing ALIWEB:

- Reduce the effort required to maintain the index
- Make searches easier
- Reduce the strain on the infrastructures

His design recognized that the rapid growth and development of the Web rendered manual indexing impractical and required a scalable solution that could operate in the Web's environment.

ALIWEB did not use a Web-walking spider, but instead relied on the Webmasters of participating sites to post their own index information for each page that they wanted listed. Unfortunately, ALIWEB required that Webmasters submit a special indexing file. Many Webmasters did not understand how to develop these files, and as a result, the database grew more slowly than those developed by robots. The solution was the development of foolproof input/submission mechanisms. Submission pages designed to make it easy for Webmasters to submit URLs to search engine databases have remained a fixture of search engine growth ever since.

Koster's design also called for a search and indexing system that could interpret META information (HTML tags placed in the head section of a Web site, provided by document originators for enhancing the indexing and searching functions). By using keywords and META information, providers could decide how their material should be best indexed. ALIWEB gave Webmasters their first opportunity to use META tags to position their sites on a search tool. (We'll discuss the role META tags play in SEP in Chapter 6.)

By the end of 1993, programmers were rapidly answering the call for developing newer and better search technologies. These included the robot-driven search engines **JumpStation**, **World Wide Web Worm**, and the **Repository-Based Software Engineering** (RBSE) spider developed by NASA. JumpStation's robot gathered document titles and headings and then indexed them by searching the database and matching keywords. This methodology worked for smaller databases, but not for the rapidly growing Internet. The WWW Worm indexed Title tags and URLs.

JumpStation and World Wide Web Worm did not sift the results in any way. They would simply deliver a large number of matches. RBSE, however, spidered by content and included the first relevancy algorithm in its search results, based on keyword frequency in the document. Keyword frequency, Title tags, and URLs are all still leveraged by SEP professionals.

1994-1998: And Along Came a Spider...

By 1995, the original 200 Web servers had grown exponentially. This huge growth created a fertile field for search developers, who sought better ways for searchers to find information in the ever-growing database and created the popular search engines of today. This growth in capabilities and popularity also paralleled the rapid expansion of the number of commercial browsers available and of Web usage.

Between 1994 and 1998, new technology for browsing was introduced and popularized. The introduction of Netscape and Microsoft's Internet Explorer added a user-friendly point-and-click interface for browsing. This, coupled with the broad availability of computers with Web connectivity, democratized the Web. It left the halls of academe forever and moved into offices and homes around the world.

During this same period, the sales of computers outstripped the sales of televisions in the United States for the first time in history. All that stood between these PCs and the Web were modems and connections. (By 1995, the commercial backbones and infrastructure to support the Web were firmly in place, and NSFNET, the original Internet, simply retired.)

In the development of search tools, 1994 was a very busy year: during these 12 months, Galaxy, WebCrawler, Yahoo!, and Lycos debuted. The first to launch in January was **Galaxy** — the oldest searchable directory (www.galaxy.com). The original prototype was associated with the Manufacturing

Automation and Design Engineering (MADE) program, funded by DARPA (the federal government's Defense Advanced Research Projects Agency). Galaxy was developed by a consortium of technology companies to provide large-scale directory support for electronic commerce, and it was administered by the Microelectronics and Computer Technology Corporation in Austin, Texas. This directory links documents into hierarchical categories with subcategories — a familiar organizational strategy today. Prior to getting listed in Galaxy, sites had to submit their information which was then individually reviewed. In May 1999, Galaxy merged into the Fox/News Corporation's properties and remains at its own URL. It still lists sites and claims its goal is to provide a "gateway to the best of the Web."

WebCrawler was originally a research project of Brian Pinkerton in the University of Washington's Department of Computer Science and Engineering

(CSE). It was initially a single-user application for finding information on the Web, but with a big difference: the user could search the entire text of the site, not just the URLs.

Persuaded by his fellow students, Pinkerton built a Web interface for WebCrawler and on April 20, 1994, issued the first release of the tool with information from over 6,000 different Web servers. Because of its exciting full-text search capabilities, WebCrawler (www.webcrawler.com) enjoyed a rapid growth in popularity — by that October, it was handling almost 15,000 queries per day.

By January 1995, WebCrawler's success was quickly overwhelming the capacity of the Department of Computer Science and Engineering's resources. It was the heaviest user of the CSE network and became so unstable and overloaded that its daytime use was not possible. America Online (AOL) purchased the WebCrawler system in 1995 and moved it to its network in March of the same year. In 1996, AOL sold WebCrawler to Excite. AOL has subsequently replaced WebCrawler for its searches; since August 1999, it's used the Inktomi search infrastructure for its own NetFind. Today, WebCrawler exists as a separate brand of Excite.

In April 1994, David Filo and Jerry Yang, two doctoral candidates at Stanford University, developed **Yahoo!**. It started out as just a collection of pages with links to sites that interested the founders. As more links were added, Filo

and Yang developed more sophisticated ways to organize the data into a searchable directory. Originally, these searches were done using a simple database search engine.

The first version of Yahoo! resided on Yang's student workstation, "Akebono," while the search engine was stored on Filo's computer, "Konishiki." Both computers were named for famous sumo wrestlers. (Yahoo! has certainly become the sumo wrestler of search engines.)

In early 1995, Marc Andreessen, co-founder of Netscape Communications in Mountain View, California, invited Filo and Yang to move their files over to larger computers housed at Netscape. The move to these powerful computing capabilities led the way for the rapid development of Yahoo! (www.yahoo.com).

"The Wanderer," the original directory that captured only URLs, made it difficult to find information not explicitly contained in a URL. By including more detailed descriptions, Yahoo! greatly improved the effectiveness of this directory-type search. With the addition of Web searches from Google, Yahoo! now provides Web searchers both the convenience of a directory structure and the search capabilities of a spider-based engine. Today, Yahoo! is the top-referring site for searches on the Web. This attests both to its usefulness and its popularity with searchers.

Yahoo! led the way for the transformation of search retrieval methods to focus on trying to most clearly match the user's intent with the database. There is now typically no assumption that the user has a specific file or document in mind when embarking on a search — he or she is assumed to be looking for an answer to a search mission. One or more documents might satisfy a single search problem.

Other directories, including Lycos and NBCi, include Web search results in addition to their directory listings. These additions are part of the increase in functionality that has marked the competitive search landscape in recent years. Directories have come to resemble search engines, and search engines now increasingly resemble directories. Furthermore, in an attempt to increase the size and improve the searchability of their databases, search engines and directories today display information derived from multiple data sources. Therefore, it's important to understand the basic technology and the databases that are the source of the results.

In November 2000, Yahoo became the second major directory to limit its free submission option. Sites wishing to be listed in the commercial areas of the directory must now use Yahoo's $199 "Business Express" service.

On July 20, 1994, **Lycos** debuted with a directory of 54,000 documents. Named for the wolf spider, this search engine was the product of Michael

 Mauldin's work in the computer labs at Carnegie Mellon University in Pittsburgh, Pennsylvania. Lycos (www.lycos.com) brought new features to Web searching including ranked relevance retrieval, prefix matching, and word proximity matching — elements that still figure prominently into the algorithms of many current engines. An SEP professional must be part linguist and part information technologist to interpret how these elements contribute to site visibility.

Lycos not only had a more sophisticated search algorithm than its predecessors, but it also very rapidly grew in size. In August 1994, it had already
spidered and indexed 394,000 documents, and by January 1995, the catalog
encompassed 1.5 million documents. By 1996, when Lycos went public, it had
ballooned to 60 million documents — more than any other search engine at that
time. On May 16, 2000, Spanish telephone giant Terra bought Lycos for $15.5
billion in stock. Today, Lycos is primarily a directory through its partnership
with the Open Directory, a public and free source of directory listings staffed by
volunteers whose database is made available to sites who wish to use it free of
charge. Until June 2000, Lycos had used Inktomi as its back-end database provider. It then struck a deal to power its Web searches with the Norwegian
search provider FAST.

The rapid growth of the early search databases fueled a race among the
search engines that still continues. Today, there is ongoing competitive pressure
among the search engines to lay claim to having the largest database. This race
for size has set in motion many of the alliances, combinations, and fusions that
characterized the end of the decade. Although many of these alliances and partnerships are outlined in this chapter, they are so complex, numerous, and
confusing, that we also outline them in other chapters as they relate to each
specific engine. Because these alliances affect the positioning tactics used for
each engine, ignore them only at your own risk.

In baseball, some games are defined by a few "big innings" with lots of hits
and runs. 1995 was the big inning for the development of spider-based search
engines. During that year, Excite, Infoseek, AltaVista, and MetaCrawler all
made their debuts. SavvySearch was also developed the same year but not com-
mercialized until 1997.

Excite was originally developed by Architext Software. Six California
entrepreneurs — Mark Van Haren, Ryan McIntyre, Ben Lutch, Joe Kraus, Gra-
ham Spencer, and Martin Reinfried — decided
in February 1993 to create a software tool that
would help manage information on the
Internet. Their product, Excite Search
(www.excite.com), combined search-and-retrieval with automatic hypertext
linking to documents. It also included subject grouping and automatic abstract-
ing algorithms that can electronically parse an abstract from the Web page.

In October 1995, Architext launched Excite and the company grew very
rapidly. By April 1996, when it went public as Excite, Inc., the company had a
staff of 65. Later that year Excite acquired search competitors Magellan and

WebCrawler. Since it joined forces in 1999 with @Home Network to form Excite@Home, Excite has grown into a formidable media company that SEP professionals must consider in their site promotion campaigns. Current company information indicates that Excite@Home is looking forward to providing services for wireless Internet, the next information delivery wave. For a time, AOL used Excite's search engine results for its own engine. If you had a high ranking in Excite, you also had a high ranking in any search launched from aol.com. AOL recently replaced its Excite-driven search results with search matches from Open Directory, which is covered later in this chapter.

Infoseek was founded in 1994 and launched its first search tool in February 1995 at www.infoseek.com. This search engine's big break came in

December 1995 when it became the default search engine for Netscape. (Previously, Netscape had used Yahoo! for its NetSearch.) This was a big coup for Infoseek. Its technology

was not revolutionary, but it was unique enough to receive a patent in September 1997. Infoseek combined many functional elements seen in other search tools such as Yahoo! and Lycos, but it boasted a solid user-friendly interface and consumer-focused features such as news that rapidly made it a favorite. Infoseek went public in June 1996.

What made Infoseek a favorite among SEP professionals was the speed with which it indexed Web sites and then added them to its live search database. There was a time during most of '97 and '98 that Infoseek boasted 10-minute indexing. You could submit a site to Infoseek and literally learn how your site ranked only 10 minutes later. The obvious benefit was that you could revise your page, change the keyword concentrations, resubmit it, and see how your changes improved or hurt your rankings. Many SEP techniques were developed by companies like ours during this golden period when Infoseek flaunted its ability to instantly update its index.

Today, Infoseek is scarcely visible. In November 1998, it consummated a deal with Disney to buy Starwave, a Disney property. In return, Disney took a 43 percent share in Infoseek. When the **Go Network** was launched in January

1999, Infoseek was the search tool for this Disney brand. In July, Disney took control of 72 percent of Infoseek, and the search engine brand became an increasingly less distinct element of the Go Network. Whenever you used the search

function within any property of the Go Network, you were actually using Infoseek. In December 1999, the Go Network announced its intent to focus its site (www.go.com) on entertainment. At the end of 2000 Disney indicated its intent to refocus from search and probably shut down the search engine by March 2001. Instead, GO.com has relaunched using search results from GoTo. Today, every search match displayed by GO.com is a paid ranking from GoTo. GO.com "monetized" their search results after laying off virtually all of their staff. The Infoseek saga points out that search properties and technologies are valuable Web businesses. With search engines' ability to bring large volumes of ad-viewing traffic to a site, they rapidly have developed economic lives quite independent of their functionality. The SEP professional needs to keep an ever-watchful eye on the changing relationships that drive the search market.

In December 1995, **AltaVista** came online. Originally owned by Digital Equipment Corporation (DEC) and its successor, Compaq, AltaVista (www.altavista.com) was powered by powerful DEC Alpha servers. AltaVista met the velocity and capacity challenges faced by other search engines head-on. Although blazing speed was its true hall-mark from the outset, AltaVista introduced many unique features that made it an almost instant success.

AltaVista was the first search engine to use "natural language" queries. Before this point, if a searcher typed in a sentence such as, "What is baking powder?" he or she would get back millions of documents containing "what" and "is." Instead, AltaVista's search engine delivered documents based on an algo-rithm that parsed the sentences for meaning. Today, natural-language searching is a prominent search engine feature. Ask Jeeves, which debuted in 1997, is well known for using this feature, but AltaVista was the first to use it.

AltaVista also provided searchers with many advanced search options such as the use of Boolean operators (and, or, if, not, etc.). These operators let searchers refine and limit their searches — a valuable addition for power users. To assist novice searchers, AltaVista was the first engine to add a link to helpful search tips below the search field. (Today, most engines provide this feature either at or near the search box.) With a combination of blazing speed and a user-friendly interface, this engine rapidly became a user favorite. Today, AltaVista is a separate company controlled by CMGI.

For SEP professionals, AltaVista offers a unique and critically important function: You can search for all of the sites that link to a particular URL. Anyone can use AltaVista to find out how many Web sites point to theirs, or their competitors'. This is particularly useful given the large number of search engines that consider link popularity in their ranking algorithms. Many search engine marketing professionals rely on the link-checking feature of AltaVista for information on this key component of SEP.

Developed by Erik Selberg, a graduate student at the University of Washington, and Oren Etizioni, an associate professor there, **MetaCrawler** debuted in June 1995. MetaCrawler (www.metacrawler.com) was the first metasearch

engine and paved the way for other metasearch engines such as SavvySearch, Ask Jeeves, and Dogpile. These engines launch multiple queries to other search engines simultaneously and then reformat the results onto a single page. MetaCrawler was originally licensed to Netbot, Inc., and in 1997 was brought under Go2Net with their purchase of Netbot.

SavvySearch (now www.search.com), developed at Colorado State University by Daniel Dreilinger, was designed to search the databases of 20 search engines and directories at once. It would then display the results a few engines at a time. Today, SavvySearch is the property of CNET and claims to present results from searches of over 200 search engines and directories.

Inktomi and **HotBot** were the products of government-sponsored research. In 1994, the Advanced Research Projects Agency (ARPA) made a

grant to Eric Brewer, a professor at the University of California at Berkeley. The grant was to study how to use clustered inexpensive workstation computers to achieve the same computing power as expensive supercomputers. Brewer focused on creating a search application and built powerful search technologies that made use of the clustering of workstations to achieve a scalable and flexible information retrieval system.

In February 1996, Brewer and graduate student Paul Gauthier founded Inktomi (www.inktomi.com). Named for the mythological spider of the Plains Indians that brought culture to their people, Inktomi remains a power player in search infrastructure. Today, Inktomi powers searches for HotBot, AOL Search, NetFind, ICQ, MSN Search, GoTo, NBCi, and other search engines.

HotBot, powered by Inktomi, and initially licensed to *Wired* magazine's Wired Digital, was launched in May 1996. Using Inktomi's technology, HotBot (www.hotbot.com) was able to rapidly index and spider the Web, thus developing a very large database within a very short time. The HotBot spider was able to index 10 million pages a day, a huge achievement in 1996. In October 1998, Lycos bought Wired Digital and HotBot became a Lycos property.

More recently, other search engines including Google and FAST have employed similar technology for harnessing the power achieved through clustered workstations to create large scalable search engines.

The Next Generation — Specialized Hybrids

The astounding commercial success of the early entrants into the search marketplace has fueled the growth of numerous new engines seeking to be the next Yahoo!, Lycos, or Excite. Each new entrant has sought to differentiate itself from the rest of the search market through innovative technology, a unique business proposition, a novel user interface, or the sheer size of its database. There is no doubt that many of these search properties will remain players in the search arena, but others may take hold and develop large enough followings to challenge the market shares of the current search favorites Yahoo! and AltaVista. You must keep a constant watch for changes in the search popularity marketplace and be particularly sensitive to the dynamics of audience and search user behavior that might impact your site.

In this section we discuss several of these new hybrid search engines, some of which feature cutting-edge algorithms or other advanced sorting capabilities that make them different or interesting.

LookSmart went online in October 1996. Originally an Australian-based subsidiary of *Reader's Digest*, it was bought out by a group of investors in 1997. LookSmart (www.looksmart.com) delivers a set of categorized directory listings presented in a user- and advertiser-friendly format. Recently, LookSmart has focused on providing search infrastructure for vertical portals and ISPs. In March 2000, it inked a deal to provide directory services for go2net.com and its sites, including MetaCrawler and Dogpile.

LookSmart has chosen to fill a niche within the search market. As the industry matures, niche players will continue to develop. SEP professionals will have to stay abreast of these niche players that provide search infrastructure in order to understand the technology powering each type of search on a site.

In 1997, two new search engines, each based on a novel premise, were introduced: **Ask Jeeves** and **GoTo**. Ask Jeeves (www.askjeeves.com), another

innovative search engine from California, launched a beta version in April 1996 and went live on June 1st that year. This engine was developed by David Warthen, a technologist, and Garrett Gruener, a venture capitalist. Ask Jeeves' basic premise is that traditional keyword-based searching tools have not kept pace with the demands of the Web and return thousands of irrelevant sites to searchers.

Ask Jeeves is built on a large knowledge base of pre-searched Web sites designed to select appropriate search results. According to its site, Ask Jeeves uses "sophisticated, natural-language semantic and syntactic processing to understand the meaning of the user's question and match it to a 'question template' in the knowledge base. Ask Jeeves can even link to information contained in databases or accessed by CGI scripts." The site also describes the matching process as follows: "The knowledge base consists of three parts: question templates, smart lists, and answer templates. A question template contains the text of basic and alternative forms of a question. Each question template has an associated answer template that contains links to pages on a site that answers a particular query. Smart lists allow one question template to link to several answers." These templates are particularly attractive to users who are unfamiliar with the workings of Boolean operators and, therefore, unable to find their way into the power features of more traditional search engines. When Ask Jeeves does not find a match in its database, it defaults to Web pages matched from other engines. Ask Jeeves presents an interesting search solution and a challenge for the SEP professional.

GoTo was founded in 1997 by Bill Gross' idealab! and added a new dimension to searches by auctioning off search engine positions. This approach allows

advertisers to attach a value to their search engine placement. Advertisers pay on a per-click basis. The highest bidder earns the top-most position; others are displayed based on their bids. The rates vary from a few pennies for a less popular keyword to several dollars for popular, highly sought-after keywords. Because the market is fluid, an advertiser can be outbid at almost any time by another bidder willing to pay more. GoTo (www.goto.com) uses Inktomi for its non-paid Web site results.

According to a winter 2000 survey of the major Web search engines performed by NPD Group, GoTo ranked higher than 11 major search engines and portals in the key category "Frequency of Finding Information Sought Every Time When Performing a Search." Other search engines and portals participating in the survey included Google, Yahoo!, AltaVista, Lycos, and Excite. Even with auctioned results, users find what they are looking for and like what they find.

In 2000, GoTo expanded its reach. It now provides Web search results for the metasearch services Dogpile, MetaCrawler, and Mamma.com, as well as AltaVista, AOL, and other partners. This is yet another example of the hybridization and cross-fertilization currently prevalent among search engines. For the SEP professional, GoTo offers a means of rapidly achieving search engine visibility at a calculated cost.

On Sept. 22, 1997, CNET, the Computer Network, launched **Snap**. The site was rolled into the NBC Internet Corporation in November 1999. Snap

(www.snap.com) was originally organized into 13 channels: News, Sports, Entertainment, Travel, Business, Living, Money, Health, Computing, Learning, Local, Communities, and Shopping. Editors fed the channels with pertinent information that was updated throughout the day. Each channel included a directory of Web sites powered by Inktomi's technology. Since its launch, Snap has been redesigned to give search a more prominent place with a subsequent growth in search traffic.

In 1999, Snap added the relevancy ranking developed by GlobalBrain to deliver more relevant search results. GlobalBrain invisibly captures the user's preference and develops an understanding of how far down in the search page the typical user must go to find the desired information. This allows the search engine to continuously improve its relevancy. The technology also has the capacity to suggest words to the searcher that it finds linked to each other in searches. Snap's branding has disappeared, but its technology lives on at the NBCi site (www.nbci.com).

Google started as a Stanford University research project and came online in late 1997. In 1998, two Stanford University computer science graduate stu-

dents, Larry Page and Sergey Brin, founded the company, now headquartered in Mountain View, California. Page and Brin, respectively, are its CEO and president. In 1998, Sequoia Capital and

Kleiner Perkins Caufield and Byers, Internet-savvy investors in Yahoo! and Amazon.com, recognized the firm's potential and provided $25 million in equity funding in exchange for 40 percent of the firm. This provided the economic base for the commercialization of Google's innovative technology.

Google (www.google.com) uses a unique technology called PageRank™ to deliver highly relevant search results. Its methodology — based on proximity matching and link popularity algorithms — in part uses link data to assess a site's popularity. It not only considers the sheer volume of links, but it also evaluates them for quality. For example, a link from a Microsoft site is more valuable than a link from a small reseller. PageRank™ is combined with an algorithm that prioritizes the results based on the proximity of search terms. By caching a large number of pages, Google also reduces the probability of searchers receiving a "404 Error Not Found" response, giving them more immediate access to the information.

This search engine was the first to index the United States government's servers and has such confidence in its ability to deliver the right result, it even offers a button called "I'm feeling lucky," which delivers the searcher directly to the first-ranked search result.

Google represents the next generation of search with sophisticated algorithms designed to increase the integrity of the search results. For the SEP professional, these search engines will pose barriers unless they are seeking visibility for content that truly meets the searcher's query.

Northern Light is the product of a development group with expertise in technology and library science. According to its site, www.northernlight.com, its goal is "to index and classify all human knowledge to a unified consistent standard and make it available to everyone in the world in a single integrated search." Although founded in 1995 in Cambridge, Massachusetts, the search service did not come online until 1997.

This search engine features a unique folder structure that allows the user to group documents by topic. Its "special collections" provide users access to many documents that are not found through traditional Web searching. Users may search for the documents for free, but they must then pay a fee to view the document. Northern Light has amassed an extremely large database, and along with its unique structure and special collections, it's become the darling of researchers. As more users find the answers to their Web searches in Northern Light, search engine positioning professionals will want to watch for growing volumes of search referrals from this engine.

Regrettably, Northern Light is the search engine most susceptible to spamming techniques. On any given day, regardless of the number of keyword searches, you may find hundreds of listings for the same Web site that took advantage of this search engine's apparent inability to limit bogus submissions.

AOL Search, MSN Search, and Netscape Search represent search services developed to serve users of services and software. AOL subscribers can

use AOL Search to search AOL's databases and the Web. AOL Search uses a combination of sources for its database, including Inktomi and Open Directory, but it improves its searchers' likelihood of finding the information desired by processing its cache of viewed sites to determine the most popular ones.

MSN Search, launched on Sept. 8, 1998, was designed for users of Microsoft's Internet Explorer and the Microsoft Network. This search service,

like many others serving vertical markets, relies on other search infrastructure providers for its technology and databases. MSN Search uses LookSmart and Inktomi for its technology. Another provider that offers portal services to a broad base of customers is **Netscape Search**, which has evolved as a search portal. Today,

Netscape Search derives its database from several sources including Open Directory and Google.

Open Directory might be best described as a new spin on an old idea. The founders, California programmers Rich Skrenta and Bob Truel, took the concept

of open source code and adapted it to search. Originally called GnuHoo in deference to the GNU project (the volunteer effort to produce a free, Unix-like operating system), and later changed to NewHoo, the directory's development is an ongoing work of thousands of volunteer editors.

Because they needed a framework for the directory, the developers decided to use a list of Usenet groups as an outline for the category structure. Each category is hand-edited, and the development of the database still reflects the various interests of the company's volunteer editors. Some categories have remarkable depth, while others are still somewhat more sparsely filled.

Within just a few months from its start, Open Directory (www.dmoz.com) grew to be the fifth-largest directory in size. It may soon become the largest directory of the Web, surpassing Yahoo!. Netscape purchased it in November

1998. True to its origins, Netscape has continued to maintain free access to the database (http://dmoz.org/license.html) and its essentially open source content.

The ability to obtain high-quality, open source content has led a number of search properties to use the Open Directory in their search databases. Lycos and AOL Search use it extensively, and AltaVista and HotBot feature Open Directory categories in their results pages. Open Directory is another example of a database that provides the infrastructure of search.

Direct Hit, another recent entrant into the search infrastructure, cannot be overlooked in any discussion of the engines and forces that influence the tactics that the SEP professional must employ.

Direct Hit (www.directhit.com) was the 1998 Grand Prize winner of the prestigious Massachusetts Institute of Technology $50,000 Entrepreneurship Competition. Ask Jeeves, Inc., purchased Direct Hit in February 2000 and incorporated the technology into its own product.

Direct Hit's technology is a popularity engine that tracks Web sites actually selected from search results lists. By analyzing the activity generated by searchers, Direct Hit can provide query results with greater relevancy. This creates a challenge for the SEP professional since popularity engines make it difficult for new sites that do not have a following to become more visible in the results.

Direct Hit's site claims "over 63 percent of U.S. searchers have access to the Direct Hit results through our partners such as Lycos, MSN, HotBot, LookSmart, AOL's ICQ, Infoseek Express, Go2Net, InfoSpace, ZDNet, and other partners." Like so many other infrastructure properties, Direct Hit offers its users some customization. Some search partners choose to simply display the first 10 results based on the sites delivered by Direct Hit, while others give searchers the choice of seeing Direct Hit results.

FAST Search was the first search engine to pass the 200 million pages indexed mark. Launched in 1999, FAST (www.alltheweb.com) has rapidly built

one of the largest databases on the Web. FAST, a Norwegian-owned company known originally as All the Web, has developed spidering technology that allows it to spider and index pages very rapidly. The FAST technology can also index audio and video files.

Lycos previously used Inktomi to power its Web results, but it now uses FAST as its infrastructure provider for Lycos Web page searches. By using FAST for results on Lycos and Inktomi for HotBot results, Lycos ensures that its two search properties do not deliver the same results for searches. This allows for better brand differentiation.

The search environment is increasingly becoming a combination of database infrastructure providers: Open Directory, Inktomi, FAST, and a broad range of branded user interfaces. More and more, search engines are sharing the same content providers and just sorting the results a bit differently. Consider that the Open Directory database provides search results to no less than five search engines including Lycos, AOL, HotBot, Google, and Netscape, and you begin to see a problem brewing. How can five different portals all serve the same search matches? Well, technically, they don't. They reserve the right to sort the same database differently and thereby serve different search matches.

Search engine partnerships— who uses whom

	Pay-for-Ranking/ Click-Through Program	Directory	Primary or Secondary Search Results
altavista:	GoTo.com	Looksmart	own database
AOL.COM	GoTo.com	Open Directory	Inktomi
Ask Jeeves	own program	Open Directory	own database
direct hit	own program and GoTo.com	Open Directory	own database plus results from Ask Jeeves
excite.	own program	Looksmart	own database
fast	no program	no directory	own database
Go.com	GoTo.com	no directory	Inktomi
Google	own program	Open Directory	own database
GOTO	own program	no directory	Inktomi
HOTBOT	GoTo.com	Open Directory	Inktomi and "Popular" results powered by Direct Hit
iwon	Open Directory	Looksmart	Inktomi and "Popular" results powered by Direct Hit

Search engine
partnerships—
who uses
whom

looksmart	*SubSite Listing Program*	*own directory*	*Inktomi*
LYCOS	*GoTo.com*	*Open Directory*	*FAST and "Popular" results powered by Direct Hit*
msn	*own program*	*Looksmart*	*Inktomi and "Popular" results powered by Direct Hit*
NBCi	*GoTo.com*	*own directory*	*Inktomi*
Netscape	*GoTo.com*	*Open Directory*	*Google*
Northern Light	*no program*	*no directory*	*own database*
raging	*no program*	*no directory*	*AltaVista*
WEBCRAWLER *"It's that Simple."*	*no program*	*Looksmart*	*Excite*
YAHOO!	*own program*	*own directory*	*Google*

The SEP professional must follow the paths of these infrastructure providers and their users, for a page indexed and ranked on one of the large providers will often ensure results being displayed and rankings achieved in multiple engines. However, there is no reason to believe that a ranking in one search engine will leverage to others using the same provider. To protect their proprietary interests, we can expect search properties to take advantage of any available customization options offered by the infrastructure providers.

The challenge then, is to determine whether and how these "tweaks" provide opportunities for improving a site's visibility. The challenge has shifted from trying to obtain visibility in a search engine employing a specific spidering technology or indexing structure to interpreting the influences of the multiple technologies and data sources employed by search portals.

Now, let's review in detail why a strategic SEP plan is crucial to your site and business.

Chapter 2:

The Case for Search Engine Positioning

here is a pervasive myth among Web site managers that simply submitting a site to hundreds of search engines will increase its traffic. Unfortunately, this is not the case. Submission alone does not guarantee that a Web site will be visible to search engine users. With over two billion pages and 300 million users, the Web is much too large for reliance on random visibility alone to work anymore. Not even the most optimistic Las Vegas bettor would take on such poor odds.

From 1999 to 2000, Web site traffic grew by 300 percent, and Internet commerce is expected to increase through 2002, with world retail sales estimated to approach $60 billion. Business-to-business sales are estimated to surpass $300 billion, according to Cyberatlas. For most Web sites with an economic goal, it's critical they connect with as many customers as possible. There are certainly big dollars at stake, and whether your site is an extension of a bricks-and-mortar business, a pure-play Internet business, or a content resource, you can hardly afford to pass up the opportunities that this huge growth presents.

The Search Engine Value Proposition

Attaining visibility online is an elusive goal, especially through the major search engines. A search for the phrase "small business planning" on AltaVista will yield over five million Web pages as shown in the figure on the following page. A search for "buy a car" on GO.com yields 29 million document matches. Any company or product ranking below the top 30 matches can hardly expect to be found except by the most persistent of searchers. It's obvious that a Web site's random chance for a top 30 ranking is incredibly slim. In some instances, it may even be the proverbial one-in-a-million.

As Web pages continue to proliferate, companies wanting to remain competitive will have to employ even more aggressive search engine optimization and Web site design strategies — especially if they're looking to complement and improve the impact of their traditional advertising and marketing efforts. As e-commerce matures, there will be increasingly less patience with new business models that don't show a clear path to profit, in addition to realistic and cost-effective customer acquisition costs. Search engine optimization may be the most reasonable customer acquisition strategy available for Web-based businesses.

A search for "small business planning" yields more than five million matches in AltaVista.

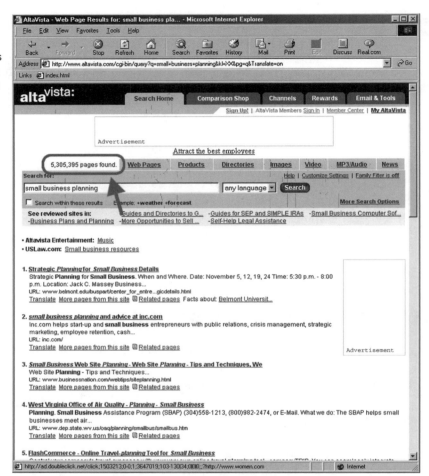

The Numbers Tell the Story

So let's see just how well SEP stacks up against other media, both in results and relative costs for customer acquisition. The first quarter 2000 AdKnowledge, Inc., Online Advertising Report provides some interesting data on banner advertising. The various conversion metrics show that click-throughs and other conversions have hovered below 1 percent, with some variance depending on the time of day and the day of the week. This means you can expect just a single click-through for every 100 banner impressions. For every 1,000 banner impressions, you'll probably get only 10 visitors. Given that banner rates have stabilized at around $33.50 CPM (cost per thousand), with each click-through costing approximately $3.35, this is an expensive proposition — particularly since there's no guarantee that the visitor clicking through has a need for your product or will make a purchase. Your snazzy banner may simply have caught the viewer's attention.

Some have argued that users who see banner ads but don't act on them are at least developing "brand impressions." Well, guess what? Until the brand impressions convert to purchases, they do nothing for your bottom line.

Although 1 percent and 2 percent conversion rates have long been acceptable for direct mail and catalog advertising, neither medium is quite as ephemeral as the Web. Many individuals deposit their direct mail right into the trash, although an equally large number of them will browse a catalog many times before discarding it or placing an order. There is no equivalent lag time on the Web. Individuals don't linger; as soon as they make the next click, they're off your site and heading for another destination. Unless your surfer bookmarks the site or makes a purchase, the probability of return and purchase declines.

Some research has shown that people will return to a site at a later date if they're interested, even if there's nothing to assist their memory. But, according to a Neilsen/NetRatings, Inc., study released in May 2000, the typical user at home visits 10 sites per month and views 664 pages. While at work, users visit 29 sites per month and view 1,387 pages. With so many sites actively competing against each other to obtain a share of customers' attention, the chances that you'll cut through the substantial clutter are slim. If you think these visitors will remember your site, its URL, and content without some assistance, dream on.

The costs and visibility gained through a banner ad campaign simply can't compete against an SEP campaign. Here are three important reasons why search engines are your better bet:

■ **They last longer.** A top search engine ranking will deliver visitors to your site not just for the duration of a banner campaign, but for as long as you maintain the ranking. A single top ranking in a search engine on a single keyword will often translate into hundreds of qualified visitors per month, depending on the search engine and the term's query frequency. Multiple rankings across multiple search engines can yield a steady stream of highly qualified traffic for an extended period of time.

■ **They shorten your sales cycle.** When an individual types a keyword in a search query box, the person has already identified a problem or a needed product and is moving toward a solution. This means he or she is predisposed to your site's offering. Traditional sales models identify four stages in the selling process: attention, interest, desire, and action. Individuals using a search engine have already moved into this sales cycle and may even already be in the desire or action phase. Their query, at the very least, reflects a definite level of interest — the individual is already looking for a source to buy. Why not be there?

■ **They're where people go to find what they need.** Search engines are by far the most important place for finding companies on the Internet. Roughly two-thirds of marketing professionals rate good placement on a search engine as an excellent way to build traffic, according to a 1999 study by ActivMedia. Fully 57 percent of Internet users search the Web every day, making searching the second most popular Internet activity (sending e-mail was the most popular). In other words, being found through the major search engines is simply a necessity for success on the Web.

Since all visitors do not return to a site faithfully, a steady stream of new traffic is essential for the health of the business. Every business must add new customers on a regular basis. However, in cyberspace, business relationships are even more transitory than in real communities where passersby can come upon a business by chance or find a sign or storefront engaging enough to merit visiting. This doesn't happen on the Web. Some Web marketers still cling to the notion that they will build a site and visitors will come. Well, this is not the case.

Online businesses should place the same importance on SEP as a bricks-and-mortar business does on its telephone directory listings, its post office address, and signage. You wouldn't expect customers to find your business if you had an inaccurate directory listing, an erroneous address, and no signage, right? No prudent company could expect to stay in business if it didn't tell anyone where to find it. A poor selection of keywords that do not reflect your business can create significant misconceptions about it and result in the loss of valuable potential customers. (You'll later learn the guidelines for selecting appropriate keywords so that your "online signage" will be effective.)

If you still doubt the value of search engines, consider the following evidence:

Search engines create more awareness about Web sites than all advertising combined including banners, newspapers, television, and radio. (IMT Strategies, a division of the Meta Group, February 2000)

■ Virtually everyone begins his or her Web browsing at one of the major search engines. One out of every 28 page impressions on the Web is a search engine search result page. (*Alexa Insider*, June 1999)

■ Forty-two percent of those who bought from online retail sites arrived via search engines. (NFO Online Retail Monitor, October 1999)

■ Internet users ranked searching as their most important activity, awarding it a 9.1 on a 10-point scale. The next most important activity ranked only 6.3. (Jupiter Research, 1999)

■ Twenty percent of all search queries conducted on AltaVista are product-related. (AltaVista, October 25, 1999)

■ Major search engines attract more distinct visitors than any other Web sites. In fact, 7 out of the 10 most-visited Web sites are search engines. (Media Metrix 2000)

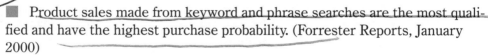

■ Product sales made from keyword and phrase searches are the most qualified and have the highest purchase probability. (Forrester Reports, January 2000)

■ Eighty-five percent of prospective Web customers use one of the search engines to find solutions and vendors, but only the top 30 search results will ever generate serious traffic. (Georgia Institute of Technology Study, 1998)

The Problem is Only Getting Bigger

The Web's growth rate has been phenomenal and exponential, intriguing scientists, mathematicians, and even geographers who yearn to chart its massive and rapid expansion. The number of online Web servers has grown from just 200 less than a decade ago to more than 3.2 million at the end of 1998 — and more are added every day. When William Gibson first coined the term "cyberspace" in his 1982 novel *Neuromancer,* he could only have guessed that cyberspace, like real space, would be ever expanding and endlessly appealing to those who want to travel "where no man has gone before." Today, even with our sophisticated mathematics and computer technology, we are just beginning to chart the Web and develop an understanding of how large it is and what it looks like.

The Web itself can be compared to the New World that 15th-century explorers set out to chart. Current theoretical studies, or for that matter, search engines and their technology, can only chart what they find. So for now, we must rely on search engines to help us find our way.

Several recent theoretical studies reinforce how important it is to be found on a search engine. In essence, they are a call to action for SEP. In a September 1999 article that appeared in *Nature*, authors Albert, Jeong, and Barabasi examined the "diameter" of the Web. They found it to be a huge, almost organic entity growing in a totally uncontrolled fashion. There is no limit to its potential size since anyone can develop a Web site with no limits on the number of pages or links.

According to their study that appeared in the July 8, 1999, issue of *Nature*, Steve Lawrence and C. Lee Giles of the NEC Research Institute estimated the size of the Web at 800 million documents, up from 320 million observed by the same researchers just a year before. In February 2000, a joint study published by Inktomi and the NEC Research Institute estimated that there were one billion indexable pages on the Web, and in June, Google was already touting that its index included over one billion documents. Then, in July 2000, using a complex statistical model of the entire Net, a company called Cyveillance determined that there are some 2.1 billion unique, publicly available pages available on the Internet. Their findings showed that the number is growing to the tune of six million pages a day. Cyber-explorers seem to be reporting new dimensions with the regularity of 16th-century explorers reporting new landmasses. One thing is certain — the Web is growing at an uncontrollable rate.

Among the key findings discussed in Lawrence and Giles' 1999 research was that the search engines were unable to keep pace with indexing the huge and ever-growing Web. They estimated that as of February 1999 the best search engine was able to index just 16 percent of the Web. They also found that the best search tools combined have indexed only 42 percent of the entire Web. These findings sent shock waves through the search industry. This, in essence, threw down the gauntlet for the search engines.

Their research also pointed out to site owners the absolute imperative for taking positive, deliberate actions to get their sites indexed. If large numbers of your Web pages aren't indexed on any search engine, there is little doubt that your site will be invisible. This rapid growth is a call to action for site owners: They cannot take a laissez-faire attitude to their search engine rankings. Site owners will not maintain their position in the search engine rankings unless they are prepared to constantly compete with an ever-expanding universe of sites.

Lawrence and Giles' findings on search engines' inability to index but a portion of the Web set in motion a new race among the engines to rapidly increase their size. As business entities whose very existence hinges on their ability to index the Web, no search engine company wanted to be behind the power curve. No sooner was the study published than the search engines — notably Norwegian company Fast Search & Transfer (FAST) and Excite@Home — issued press releases about their new, improved search technology.

FAST immediately announced that its search engine was able to scan 200 million of the Web's estimated 800 million pages. A full Web crawl by FAST in the early first quarter of 2000 yielded 850 million document pages and a database of 340 million document pages when duplicates and old documents were removed.

In fall 1999, more contenders joined the race to have the largest search engine. Excite@Home announced a beefed-up search engine operation with dozens of new spiders. AltaVista and Northern Light entered the fray with each adding millions of new pages to their indexes. In June 2000, Google announced that its full-text index size had increased to 560 million URLs, making it the largest search engine on the Web. In September 2000, Google expanded its index to 1.06 billion documents, and then in an apparent race with FAST, Google recently announced that it had reached 1,346,966,000 documents. The race for the largest search engine continues. Tune in to Search Engine Watch for continuing race coverage.

Charting the Nebular New World

As impressive as the Web's size is, it's far less important than its topology. Why? Because only by traversing its topology can we map the documents that compose it. The structure of the Web is one of the great mysteries of the Internet Age: How are hundreds of millions of Web sites connected to each other, and how does this impact your Web marketing strategy? Is the Web, in fact, a seamless network of interconnected highways that can lead interested people to your Web site, or is it a frayed web of one-way boulevards and dead ends where prospective customers are likely to become frustrated before ever finding your company?

So, you may be thinking, "Well, who cares about the structure of the Web? Leave that to the academics. I just want traffic!" Well, it's actually very important that you understand how the Web is being charted — your stake as a site owner couldn't be higher. Bear with me for a minute, and I'll explain why.

Bernardo A. Huberman and Lada A. Adamic published a major study of the Web's growth dynamics in the September 9, 1999, issue of *Nature*. They found that the Web follows what is known in physics as a *power law*. A power-law distribution means the Web doesn't follow typical mathematical models associated with random networks. It instead exhibits the physical order seen in galaxies and other similar constructs. There are no known boundaries to its growth, but it does follow a distribution pattern. Their research showed that whereas many sites have just a few pages, very few have hundreds of thousands of pages.

Also in 1999, Notre Dame University physicists Reka Albert, Hawoong Jeong, and Albert-Laszlo Barabasi showed that there **is** a predictable linking construct for the Web. They determined that between two randomly selected sites, there's an average distance of 19 links. If you select any two Web pages, they might link directly with one another, or you might need to make a large number of clicks to reach the other. However, if you performed the same test on thousands of sites, you'd average roughly 19 clicks between every site. They called this "19 Clicks of Separation."

However, a landmark study released in May 2000 suggests the Web is far less connected than was previously thought, leaving many sites to languish in the uncharted waters of cyberspace with little chance of attracting visitors. Conducted by Compaq, AltaVista, and IBM, this study analyzed more than 200 million Web pages and 1.5 billion hyperlinks.

Researchers mapped traffic patterns through the Web and hypothesized a "bow tie" structure for the Web. In this "Bow Tie Theory," the central core, or knot of the bow tie, represents 30 percent of Web pages that are interconnected and easy to find by following Internet links. Another 24 percent represents one side of the bow, or "origination pages" — those pages with links that you can follow into the core but that cannot be accessed through links from the core. Yet another 24 percent (the other side of the bow) consists of "destination pages" that can be accessed from links in the connected core but do not link back to the core. The final 22 percent is completely disconnected from the core.

They found that if you picked two sites where a path existed between them, then you might connect with as many as 16 clicks. However, if you happened to click on a page that has both links into it as well as out of it (a connected site in the core), then the number of clicks between the sites would decrease to just seven.

The bottom line is: For your site to be visible to search engines, you must decrease the distance between it and other documents on the Web. (We'll show you exactly how to do this later.) If your site is not in the central core — and only 30 percent are — it's likely that you don't have a high-traffic site, and it could be difficult for users to find it through links from other sites.

That means you're solely relying on people typing in your URL in the command lines of their browsers — and this only works if your site is well-known and relatively easy to spell. The days of serendipitous surfers and "accidental traffic" stumbling onto your site are over. On this "new" Internet made up of some two billion Web pages, site owners must use every tool available to them to attract visitors. And even then, you face stiff competition. Many site owners consider links simply as a nicety that brings some additional traffic, but this theory proves they can be worth their weight in gold.

The Bow Tie Theory shows the importance of understanding: 1) your contribution to connecting your site to other sites on the Web, and 2) your site's ultimate integration into the high-traffic core.

"So how do I get into this 'core'?" you now ask. The most overlooked and perhaps simplest strategy to tap this central traffic core is by attaining high rankings in major search engines through SEP. As you read this book, you will learn that you should not treat any portion of a comprehensive SEP campaign as unimportant.

Content was once thought to be king on the Internet, but as Web sites proliferate, content will be far less important than strategies to improve the site's ability to attract an audience. The only organic way to generate this site awareness is through improving the site's connections to other sites and by increasing its visibility and positioning in the one place where everyone goes to find answers — the major search engines.

If, as a Web site marketer, you expect to survive and be found, you need to learn how to: 1) place your pages in the high-traffic core, and 2) achieve a high ranking in the major search engines. Otherwise, your sites will be like little islands in the sea: remote, inaccessible, and forgotten. As you hear of new research on the structure and growth of the Web, don't overlook its significance for your site and your SEP programs. This seemingly peripheral information can give you many new clues about how the Web's landscape is changing and how to use it to your advantage.

Chapter 3:

Understanding Search Referrals and Traffic

e'll keep this chapter short and sweet in order to quickly get to the good stuff. But don't skip this chapter — it's important that you understand the basic premise of rankings and how they correlate with traffic and sales. Even if you're a seasoned pro, please read these few pages!

Let's begin by looking at an example. If a user performs a query in AltaVista for "cheese" and your site is not listed, then no matter how many types of cheese you sell, or how great your cheesy recipes are, that user will not and cannot arrive at your site. For a search engine to deliver a visitor to your site, the visitor must first click on a search result for your site. Often, owners of large sites that have been on the Web for a while will discover that they have a very large number of search engine referrals. This is because they actually have rankings (positions in the results pages of search engines) even before they begin optimizing pages. However, many of these "accidental" rankings will most likely be on keywords that are rarely sought by users. This is due to the fact that the most highly queried keywords are also the most competitive. In other words, it's highly unlikely that you would find accidental rankings for "MP3." The difference between "accidental" rankings and SEP is that SEP is the deliberate optimization of search results in the pursuit of traffic.

The whole point of SEP is to increase traffic to a site. But not just traffic — you want qualified users who are seeking content or a product or service that your site can provide. Therefore, it's important to remember what a ranking actually is. Many times SEP professionals will be overjoyed with a top 10 ranking that a site has achieved, and the site owner (rightfully) says, "So what? I still don't have any sales!" A ranking doesn't directly equal traffic, and traffic doesn't directly equal sales.

So, What *is* a "Ranking?"

In the SEP industry, a "ranking" is usually considered to be a top 30 listing in a search engine for a query on a specific keyword related to the site. For example, the following figure shows the top five listings (or rankings) in AltaVista for the query "cheese."

Rankings are the primary target of the SEP professional since they can easily be measured using software such as WebPosition. However, rankings only mean something when they correlate to traffic. The best method to determine your traffic is to conduct detailed log file analyses often. (We'll go into detail on log file analysis later in this book, but for now, just be aware it exists.)

The Harsh Reality: It's Top 30 or Nothing

Log files will tell you how many visitors are coming to your site and from what engines. However, they also give you clues as to what keywords your site has rankings on and in which engine. If you get large amounts of traffic from AltaVista from users seeking "cheese," then you must have a listing in AltaVista for "cheese." To confirm this, you can go to AltaVista and query "cheese." There you might find your site in position 27 (on the third page, because this engine features ten listings per page). If you keep digging, you may find additional pages from your site farther down the list. We only consider a ranking to be a listing

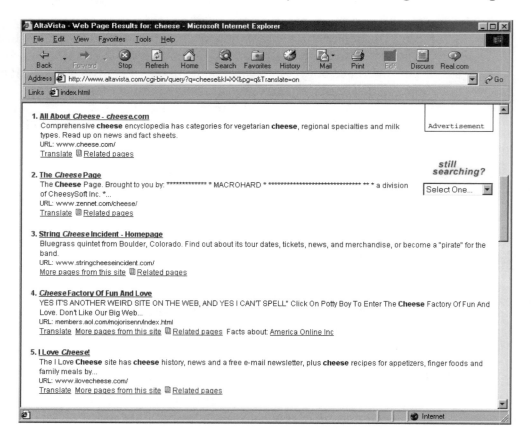

within the top 30, because **studies have shown that most searchers do not keep clicking through past the third page.** In fact, most searchers don't even click-through to the second page. Therefore, a #10 ranking is much more valuable than #27, and #64 is pretty much worthless.

Now, many other search engines do display more than 10 results per page. In fact, GoTo.com displays 40 results on the first page. So in this case, should you be happy if you're within the top 120? No, because most users still don't appear to click below #30, no matter how many listings are on a page.

There are a few different ways to figure out what your current rankings are. One is to do it by hand, the way we did above. Go to each search engine and query every keyword in which you are interested. This is the way early Web marketers checked their rankings — a laborious, time-consuming method. Thankfully, software developers have created many tools that perform these queries for you across all the major search engines using a large universe of keywords. WebPosition Gold is the most broadly used rank-checking software on the market, and there are others as well, which we'll discuss later. However, as we'll stress throughout this book, choosing your keywords well is the single most crucial element of your SEP campaign. Not even the best software on the market will tell you what keywords to target and optimize for. (But the entire next chapter will take you through this process, step by step, so don't worry about it now!)

The Rankings, Traffic, and Sales Equation

If you've chosen your keywords well, you can expect a direct relationship between traffic, search referrals, and rankings. Your results should look something like the table on the following page.

This table shows rankings, referrals from search, and total traffic for an imaginary site. You can see that referrals from search and total traffic appear to be very closely correlated. Usually, unless a firm is actively pursuing SEP, the percentage of referrals from search is fairly static. You can also see that rankings and traffic are loosely correlated. The correlation coefficient between rankings and traffic is not one to one by any means, but it is significant. Why does this correlation exist? Think about it. If you choose keywords that have high query frequencies in the search engines, and you achieve high rankings on those keywords, then users should come to your site.

Rankings and
traffic

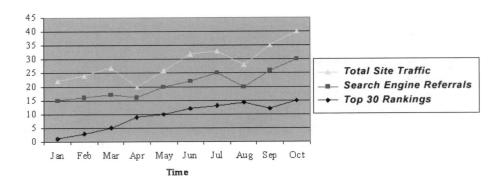

But what about the site owner mentioned before? Why isn't the site making any sales? Most of the time, if a site has high rankings on high query frequency keywords, a problem like this can be traced to the site itself. Perhaps the site is hard to navigate, or maybe the site owner makes users fill out 20 forms before they can even see the product. Very often, SEP professionals find themselves advising site owners to conduct usability studies or take corrective action that is not directly connected to their SEP campaign.

However, even in a case of poor sales, traffic should correlate with rankings. If you find yourself with a large amount of #1 rankings but no traffic, consider it an early warning sign. In fact, just having huge numbers of #1 rankings should be a warning sign. The most highly queried words are typically the most competitive. If you have huge numbers of #1 rankings across all the major search engines, your keyword list probably needs some work. You have not chosen very competitive keywords and should not expect the ranking to yield large amounts of traffic. There is a fine balance between selecting competitive keywords and those on which you can only dream of getting a ranking. This is part of the SEP challenge, and we've dedicated the entire next chapter to it!

Chapter 4:

Choosing the Right Keywords, in the Right Combinations

Given that a search engine query is a query to a database of documents, effective SEP is dependent on accurately defining your keywords. The keywords must ensure that your site will be found when users insert a query, based on those keywords that the searcher uses to find what you are offering. This is an important concept: **You must choose not only keywords that match your site, but also keywords that are used by actual searchers to find sites with content like yours**.

Your keyword selection process should also include a review of the terms that your competitors are targeting. This is particularly important if you are in a specific market segment. You will want your site to appear for the same queries that searchers are frequently using to find goods and services of the type that you offer. As you select your keywords, look and see what sites they pull up in the search engines. Infrequently, a word may seem like a good choice, but when it's applied to searches, it delivers peculiar results. Since keywords are valuable real estate on your site, be very careful in their selection.

One is the Loneliest Keyword Number

You will rarely want to target a single keyword. Why? Given the millions of documents indexed in the Web and the number of possible ways to interpret a single keyword, a single keyword can be more misleading than helpful. For example, suppose you're selling leather date book organizers and you target the word "organizer." There is no way for a searcher to determine if your site has information of interest to someone looking for a "leather organizer" for important papers, a "closet organizer" for a neater home, or a "wedding organizer" to orchestrate that big event. In this case, it's essential that you add a second word to clarify the meaning of "organizer" as it would apply to your site.

The good news is that searchers are increasingly understanding the need to use multiple keywords in their queries. According to a study released by NPD Group on May 9, 2000, multiple keyword searching is the most popular search option. NPD regularly surveys the behavior of search users, and this survey marked the first time that multiple keyword searching had shown a significant rise. This would seem to mean that searchers are becoming more knowledgeable and less tolerant of receiving large numbers of unrelated matches to their searches. As a result they are using more keyword phrases. The authors also postulate that the search engines are doing a better job of educating their users to be more specific in their searches. Results pages now frequently offer searchers suggestions for improving their queries or refining their searches.

We constantly get Web marketers who want to monitor their rankings on keywords that searchers are simply not likely to query! For example, a customer marketing cheap airfares for a travel site suggested we target these keywords:

> cheap
> flights
> cheap flights
> quote
> discounted
> airfare

Now, the word "cheap" by itself does not target any specific audience, but when it's paired with words like "flights" or "airline reservations," it has real meaning. Similarly, "quote" and "discounted" are also too broad, and should be paired with one or two other words in order to gain meaning.

The task is to find which multiple keyword combinations most clearly match your site's intent and yield few enough documents in searches that you will be able to attain rankings. These are your "power combinations."

To determine which of your keywords are power combinations, try conducting searches for your keywords on a variety of engines. Notice how many documents are returned and use this as a basis for determining whether you should target the keyword. Select those that are attainable and use them in your META tags, title, and description.

As you make your selections, you should be careful to identify word combinations that are actually used by searchers. There are several tools that will aid you in the process of determining whether searchers are actually using the terms; these tools are discussed at the end of this chapter.

Let's return to our example now. If you don't achieve a good ranking on "cheap airfares," try an alternative. Be creative and try targeting "inexpensive airfares." It's all about thinking like your customer or clientele. If you get into your customers' shoes, it will be easy for you to find a keyword combination that you can dominate in the search engines. You'll often find there are more people searching for these alternative phrases than were actually searching for the hard-to-get phrase that first came to mind. Carve out your own keyword niche!

Another problem with single word searches is their attainability. Even if a single keyword is what you really want, you may not be able to attain a search engine ranking on it. While it would be nice to be positioned well on a single extremely broad keyword, you might better use your time to pair the keyword with something more specific, as we illustrated above. You still could get lucky and rank well on just "organizer" if it's in your page too, but if not, at least you could rank well on "leather organizer," on which it will be far less difficult to achieve a top 10 or 30 listing. More specific keywords have the added advantage of ensuring that your prospects are more qualified. You don't want to disappoint searchers who visit your site in search of a wedding organizer.

Another example: A search on "software" at almost any search engine will return millions of documents (over 29 million in AltaVista) and often a list of suggestions for refining your search. The sites at the top of the list are there because of an array of factors, some of which are beyond your control, such as the new technology overlay Direct Hit that rates the site's popularity and Google's PageRank algorithm that uses link popularity in its rating. It's highly unlikely that your smaller software company could displace Microsoft or another

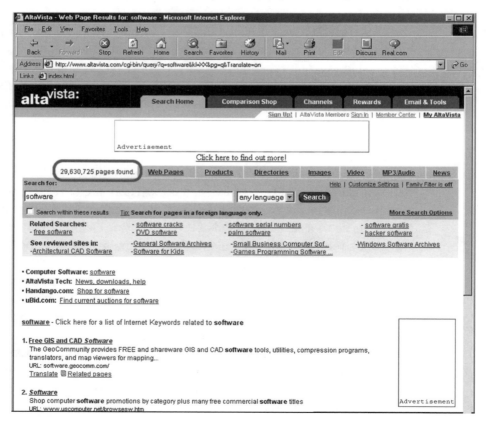

software giant for a first place ranking. Their sites are too popular and have too many links to them to be ousted by a smaller, less well-known software firm. Instead of fighting a losing battle, you should search for a combination term that clearly describes your site and yet returns few enough sites to give you a fighting chance at getting a top ranking.

The bottom line: Don't waste your time fighting for a hard-to-get keyword, unless you're a major player with a powerful brand that dominates your industry. Some keywords will be highly competitive, and you may have to work hard to achieve a top 10 slot. If you find that after all of your hard work, you still can't make it into that top 10, just keep working on your other keywords. There are so many other keywords and combinations where your site can achieve a top 10 ranking that you will find that it's not very difficult at all to develop strong traffic from those rankings.

Identify a niche or pocket of keywords that clearly describe your work and that few others are targeting. Then, go after them! Remember, successful SEP requires persistence and perseverance.

How Vectors Have Changed Keyword Selection

In an attempt to deliver more relevant results faster from an ever-growing Web that results in an ever-larger search database, the major engines have developed and are refining technologies that compress key terms for each page into numbers and then employ "term vectoring" concepts for matching sites with queries. Under this system, a site is classified based on the associations (vectors) of the keywords on the site.

The pages in the site are also assigned vectors. A combination of the vector for the theme (which we'll explain in a minute) and the vector for the page yield the result. When a searcher issues a query, the available pages on the matching sites in the database are compared with the query. Those pages that most clearly match the query are delivered as search results. This is "term vectoring" in a nutshell, representing a significant advance in search technology. The engines are increasingly able to classify sites, just as a directory editor might, yet provide the specificity and drill-down capabilities of spider-based search engines. This means that if the word "apple" is on your site, the search engine's algorithm can determine whether to classify your site as a site featuring Apple computers or fresh fruit.

The concepts and technology that underlie term vectoring used in search engines today are very sophisticated mathematical algorithms that have evolved through a number of years of research by information technologists and data miners. Initial uses of term vectoring developed out of the term-based classifications used by librarians developing controlled vocabularies to assist in the classification and identification of information.

Because each document is given a set of page vector identifiers, it becomes easier to develop filters that identify duplicate pages, i.e., those pages that have the same vectors and match on other criteria. Because each page is given a set of identifiers, the pages can easily be grouped and classified by their term ranges. This enables the search engine to classify the entire site by an overall theme.

Developing Your Keyword Strategy

So what does this mean to you? Well, your challenge is twofold. One, develop a theme for your site and its pages so that it's initially indexed into a classification that accurately describes your site. Two, develop promotional tactics that understand that the search engines have dramatically improved their ability to screen for duplicate or machine-generated, search-and-replace keyword-centric "doorway" pages. Most search engines view these machine-generated pages as spam and penalize sites that use them.

Here are our step-by-step recommendations for how to design your keyword strategy to maximize your qualified search engine referrals.

1. What's your theme?

As you begin brainstorming and selecting keywords, you should determine the "theme" of your site. For example, if your site sells leather organizers, leather attaché cases, and leather planners, you might select "leather cases" or "leather accessories" as your theme and build your keywords around this theme. It's all about your site's content and your understanding of the words that might describe it.

If you want to know if you're on the right track for selecting the correct theme, try this little exercise. First, pretend you don't have to worry about your budget. (Feels good, hmm?) Now that you have all this money, think of the two or three keywords that you might bid for at GoTo.com. These "just right" keywords that describe your site concisely and precisely are your themes. Choosing your theme will likely be increasingly important as more search engines adopt this technology. Currently, AltaVista, Google, Inktomi, Excite, and FAST are believed to be already classifying sites by theme. It won't be long before more engines adopt this methodology, so pay attention to this now.

2. Brainstorm the right keywords

Begin by writing down every imaginable keyword that someone might type into a search engine to find your site. When we ask clients to do this, they usually return a list that is very specific to their products — either what they sell or their industry. Don't fall into this trap. It's important to go beyond these bounds!

If the site described in the earlier "organizer" example was for a wedding planner instead of a leather goods merchant, most individuals would say the best keywords would be:

> weddings
> wedding planners
> wedding planning
> bridal consultant

These keywords, however, hardly touch those that relate to wedding planning. Someone who is planning a wedding is likely to be searching the Web for a broad array of wedding-related products and services, including things not directly related to the actual wedding ceremony. So you'll also want to consider keywords such as these:

bachelor party	disc jockeys
bachelorette party	flower girl
banquet halls	groomsman
best man	honeymoon
boutonnieres	honeymoon vacations
bridal bouquet	limos
bridal decorations	limousines
bridal gowns	ring bearer
bridal registry	toasts
bridal shower	wedding bouquets
bridal veils	wedding cakes
bridesmaid dresses	wedding invitations
caterers	wedding rings

And this is only a partial list of the possible keywords that might apply to a site with a "wedding planning" theme. In developing keyword lists for clients, we typically begin with about 50 keywords, expand the list to hundreds or even thousands, and then narrow the list to those that are most applicable to the site and that we feel are most relevant and where the Web site would satisfy the intent of the query.

3. Develop your title and description

Once the list is developed, you can then develop your site's title and description. (You'll find specific guidance on how to do this in Chapter 6.) It's always best to amplify your title with additional keywords when possible. For example, if you have a wedding planning site, and your current title is, "Bridesmaid's and Best Man's Resource Area," you may want to use, "Bridesmaid's and Best Man's Resource Area — Boutonnieres to Bridal Bouquets" instead. This longer title has more descriptive keyword power.

4. Now, misspell your keywords

Yes, that's right! There's a marketing folktale about how misspelling was actually used for a competitive advantage by telecommunications giants MCI and AT&T. AT&T wanted to counter MCI's highly successful 1-800-COLLECT advertising campaign, so AT&T introduced a collect-calling product of its own: 1-800-OPERATOR.

This ad campaign was short-lived. Can you guess why? Many people were dialing "1-800-OPERATER" by mistake. What's even funnier is that MCI actually owned that number. A sharp-eyed MCI employee noticed an unusually high volume of calls on that MCI number, and the company redirected these calls to 1-800-COLLECT. MCI was snapping up the business until AT&T determined what was happening. Today, it's no surprise that AT&T asks you to dial "1-800-CALL-ATT" — they learned in real time how often people make obvious spelling mistakes. As you develop your keyword list, consider what keywords searchers are most likely to misspell, and be sure to include them. You won't lose points for misspelling here!

A Commonsense Tactic for Misspelled Keywords

We firmly recommend that you consider optimizing your pages for misspelled keywords; however, you should make sure that it would be worth your effort. To save hours of time, do a little testing upfront. First, you should consider using the search frequencies provided by GoTo (http://inventory.goto.com/inventory/Search_Suggestion.jhtml). From a single search box, you can plug in a keyword and see how many times the term was searched on over the last 30 days. (See the figure on the following page.) This handy page will also return related searches that are based on the same keyword. This information can be extremely useful as you develop your keyword list.

A second method for testing the query frequency of your keyword misspellings is to try purchasing banner advertising with some of the search engines based on both the misspelled and correctly spelled keywords. This type of advertising will ensure that your banner ad will be displayed only when somebody searches on your specific target keyword. If you build a relationship with the sales representatives at a search engine, you can ask them how often the misspellings of one of your keywords is searched on as opposed to the correct spelling.

A brief check demonstrates how beneficial these methods are for validating your hunches on misspellings. For example, suppose GoTo shows there were 8,122 searches for "alcohol" during a single 30-day period. Similar checks on two common misspellings showed 197 searches for "alchohol" and 77 for "alcahol" during the same period. Combined, these two terms have less than 3 percent of the referrals of "alcohol." In this case misspellings are rare, but for the promoters of a health site, for example, they're worth targeting because the competition will be much less intense for these misspelled keywords. A top ranking on these keywords would be more easily attainable, and they could expect traffic from those searching on the misspelled words.

Appendix A includes a list of commonly misspelled keywords. Review the list and find any keyword that might pertain to your site. Now, if you don't believe how often some of these words are misspelled, just ask a small group of your friends to spell them, and then try to keep a straight face while they struggle to get them right. Also remember that when searchers type in their queries, 1) they're usually in a rush to get the information and 2) they don't get any notification as to the accuracy of their spelling before completing the search. Try it for yourself. Misspell a query and see how many sites are returned on your favorite search engine.

Good examples of how important misspellings are can be found in the "creative" spellings of names in the news. For example, consider which of these spellings of the name of a famous Russian tennis star is correct (all of these spellings have been spotted in the media):

A. Anna Kurnikova

B. Anna Kournikova

C. Anna Kournikouva

The correct spelling is B. However, if Anna endorsed your products, you would want to make sure most everyone would find your site, so you'd include the misspellings in your keyword list. Your content meets the searcher's mission, so provide as much help with the process as you can.

See how many times the term was searched on over the last 30 days

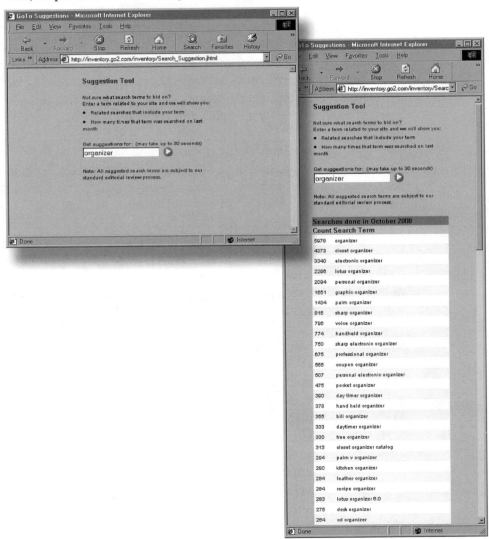

5. Think globally, act locally

Although your site is on the World Wide Web, you must act locally if you provide a good or service with a local or regional appeal. When most people visit a search engine, they are looking for some sort of very broad product or service. For example, someone searching for fresh fruit might search for "apples." However, someone looking for an apple grown in Washington state might search for "Washington apples" or "Washington state apples."

This example reinforces the value of using multiple-word keyword phrases. A naïve searcher who just entered "apple" into the search box would immediately receive thousands of sites with Apple computers and software, certainly not fresh fruit. A search for "apples" or "Washington state apples" on AltaVista immediately delivers sites for the fruit. See the following examples.

The message from this example is clear. Although your site is on the World Wide Web, your shoppers and searchers will often be looking for local goods and services. If you are a Web marketer promoting any product of local or regional

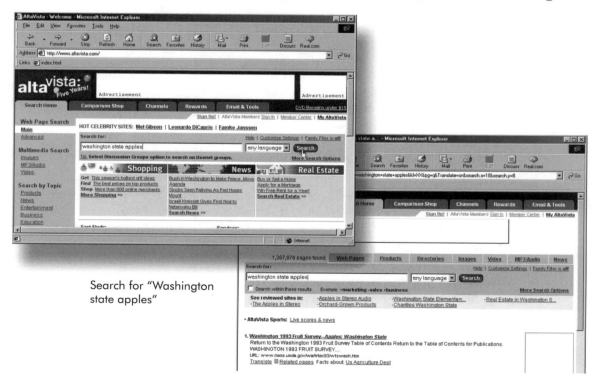

Search for "Washington state apples"

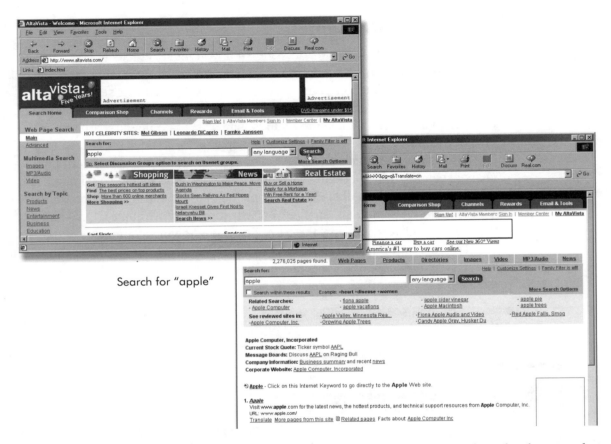

Search for "apple"

significance, it's very important to regionalize your keywords and to be sure that this carries through into your site descriptions and titles.

The need to act locally is particularly important if your site provides a service such as real estate brokering. If the searcher just entered "real estate" into the search box, thousands of sites would result for real estate and services around the world. This would certainly not assist searchers looking for a new home in Omaha, Nebraska. If your site offers real estate services in Omaha, it would be important to include "Omaha real estate" in your keyword list. You might also consider "Nebraska real estate" for those searching with a slightly broader perspective.

6. Make word stemming work for you

When many search engines crawl your site and strip out your text for indexing and display, they parse each word (including keywords) to its roots, removing all prefixes and suffixes. This means that searches for a word will include most variations of that word. For example, unless the searcher specifies an exact search, searches for "transform" would return documents that relate to (business) "transformation," "transformers" (cartoon and game figures), and tools for software and data "transformation."

Frequently, word stemming will work to your advantage. A search for "consultants," will return documents that also contain the words "consulting" and "consult" unless the user chooses to do an exact search.

Theoretically, this means you could reduce the number of keywords in your META tags and on your site's pages because those search engines that practice word stemming will return your site for searches on the other words that stem from them. But (and this is a big But), not all search engines aggressively stem. By using the longer words in your title and description, you cover both the stems and the direct matches.

7. Avoid "stop words"

During their indexing process, most search engines conserve resources by eliminating certain words that have little or no value as search terms; these are called "stop words." They're very common words, such as "a," "the," "and," "of," "that," "it," and "too." (See Appendix B for an extensive list of these.) With all of these commonplace words eliminated, the data-handling algorithms don't have to manipulate such huge volumes of information, thus increasing processing speed.

If your site contains stop words in areas where a spider looks for copy to index, the stop words are ignored. In some cases this can affect how your site is indexed. For instance, suppose you wanted to be indexed as a "systems analyst." There are some search engines that will skip over the word "systems" and read only "analyst." So you would be indexed under "analyst" as opposed to "systems analyst."

The inclusion of stop words in critical locations in your text may also create problems with search engines where prominence of a keyword in the title is crucial for the search engine's ranking scheme. By having the first word in your title be "the," you could damage your ranking.

If a stop word is part of your site name or title, you should either put it in quotes or come up with another name or title that doesn't include the stop word. The use of quotes indicates that the word has a special, "reserved" meaning and should not be overlooked. Since each engine works with its own list of stop words, it pays to do your own testing. Do a search for any keywords with which you are concerned, and take note of which ones it says were ignored on the search page.

Tools for Choosing Keywords

As the SEP industry has developed, so too have the tools available for choosing keywords. The following table gives you information on three tools that you might want to evaluate for possible use in your own campaigns: the GoTo database, Wordtracker, and WordSpot. These tools are broadly used by SEP professionals for choosing keywords, but these are not the only tools. Another tool is Keyword Market Share, which is very similar to WordSpot but also provides a considerable amount of free useful information. Just like WordSpot, Keyword Market Share sends subscribers a weekly e-mail with the top 200 keywords and top 200 search terms. You should know, though, that these e-mails provide more of an interesting window on popular culture than a guide for determining the target keywords for a business, except for those deeply involved with trendy goods (such as MP3 downloads and Pokemon cards) and popular culture (Britney Spears, for example).

The search engines themselves provide windows into their current searches with real-time windows. For example, Yahoo!'s What's Selling Now option lets visitors view what people are buying on Yahoo! Shopping. Mopilot Live Search even shows what queries are being made on wireless devices. Here is a link to a list for these search spy sites:

http://searchenginewatch.com/facts/searches.html

Once the keywords are chosen, you can begin to optimize your site. This process involves placing the keywords on the page in a way that will interact with the search engines to deliver high rankings and traffic for your site.

Feature	GoTo	Wordtracker	WordSpot
URL	http://inventory.goto.com/inventory/Search_Suggestion.jhtml	http://www.wordtracker.com	http://www.wordspot.com/
Address	74 North Pasadena Ave., 3rd Floor, Pasadena, CA 91103	Rivergold Associates Ltd., Wordtracker, 1st Floor, 10 The Broadway, Mill Hill, London NW8 3LL United Kingdom	Beyond Engineering, 1007 US Highway 54 East, La Harpe, Kansas 66751
Phone	(877) 999-4686	none provided	(316) 496-2682
FAX	(626) 685-5601	(011 44) 208-959-1388	(316) 496-2020
Price	Free	Multilevel from $19.95 a week to $197 for annual subscription	Multilevel from $19.95 for a yearly subscription for weekly reports of top 1,000 KW reports to $495 for a single large report
Database	100 million per month	30 million, expanding to 100 million monthly	5-7 million per week, 300 million annually
Features	Includes only information from GoTo Does not differentiate between singular and plurals Searches one phrase at a time Suggests multiple phrases based on same keyword only Gives misspellings	Includes multiple databases Differentiates between singular and plurals Delivers up to 4,000 keywords (price dependent) Suggests up to 300 related words and phrases Has word stemming Gives misspellings Gives number of competing sites Up to 5 projects per account Can save up to 5,000 keywords Can e-mail results	Includes multiple databases Includes related phrases Handles up to 500 keywords at a time Word stemming Offers weekly tracking

NOTE: Still need help? Provide us with a detailed description of your Web site challenge. We'll be pleased to help in any way we can, or will refer you to any number of high-quality search engine optimization specialists whom we know and trust. Feel free to e-mail us at: sales@iprospect.com, or visit our quote request page at: http://www.iprospect.com/book-quote.htm.

Part 2:

Tactics for Search Engine Positioning

Part 2:

Chapter 5:

Factors That Greatly Affect Your Relevancy in Spider-Based Search Engines

I f this book seeks to drive any single point home, let it be that "search engines" as we once knew them no longer exist. The term "search engine" used to be used interchangeably for both human-edited directories like Yahoo!, and strict spider-based search engines like AltaVista. Today, the line between search engine and human-edited directory is blurred. In fact, many search sites that were once considered "search engines" are now actually directories.

For instance, the majority of searches at Lycos now return search matches from the Open Directory index, a human-edited directory service staffed by volunteers, similar to Yahoo!. In fact, most if not all search engines are technically "hybrids," that is, they have several data sources for returning search matches. Some serve the top 10 matches from one source and the rest of the search matches from a database supplied by another partner. For instance, if you perform a search at HotBot, the top 10 matches are supplied by Direct Hit, a popularity-ranking service that measures which sites people visit and how long they stay at those sites after performing a keyword query. The remaining search matches come from either the human-edited Open Directory or Inktomi, a spider-driven search database. Sometimes HotBot even alternates between Direct Hit and Open Directory and eventually includes Inktomi search matches after some number of search matches have been displayed. Overall, "pure" search engines that display search matches derived from only one source are now a rare if not a dying breed. What this means to you is that keyword placement is no longer the holy grail of SEP.

To my knowledge, FAST, Northern Light, and AltaVista's new search service, Raging Search, are the only remaining pure spider-derived, search-database-displaying search engines.

Many other, shall we say, "search services" use their own (or a partner's) spider-derived search database to display what we consider their "primary search results."

For our purposes, if the majority of the search results (greater than 50 percent of the search matches) are derived from a spider-populated search database, we consider it a "search engine."

The only three "pure" search engines

Search services with displayed search results that are primarily from their spider-populated databases

Search engines whose primary search results are still populated by spiders include AltaVista, Excite, HotBot, WebCrawler, iWon, and Google. These search services that display primarily spider-derived content often include significant directory content too, even if they're not placed prominently. Excite, for example, offers a Directory link that displays results from LookSmart.

So what should your strategy be for these types of engines? Here are some guidelines.

1.   Be sure there are no roadblocks to these search engines' spiders that will prevent them from being able to index the contents of your Web pages.

2.   Be sure the viewable content of your Web pages contains your targeted keywords and phrases in the places where these spiders will be looking for them.

3.   Be sure those pages include good metadata, or data that describes data, so that their spiders will score your pages well and have an understanding of what keyword content on your pages they should be weighing more heavily.

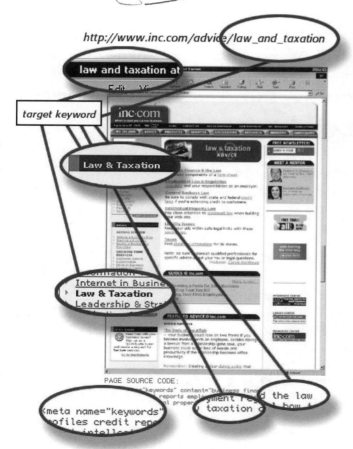

Remember, search engine spiders do only two things: index text and follow links. If you don't have text on the pages, or links to other pages that contain text, the search engine spiders will leave. If you don't have your targeted keywords "amplified" so that they appear to be a significant and important component of the Web page, the search engine will not assign them as much importance as you would like, and your page will not attain rankings on those keywords.

So, to recap, remember in reading this chapter that when we talk about keywords on the page affecting your site's ranking, we're only talking about "search engines" or search services whose indexes are populated by unattended automated search engine "spiders." Search engines face a complex challenge. They have to compile an index of millions of documents (individual Web pages — your Web site may have 10 or 50,000 total documents, depending on its size) and then respond to millions of individuals who construct keyword and phrase queries. The search engines return a list of what they hope to be relevant documents to that searcher. It is important to understand how spiders work and their role in search engine positioning.

How Do Software Spiders Work?

A *software spider* is an unmanned software program operated by a search engine that surfs the Web, visits a Web site, records (saves to its hard drive) all the words on each page, and notes links to other sites. As the spider visits each page, it follows each and every link and will read, index, and store the other pages that the link might lead to. Google, however, sometimes will reference a site without actually visiting the page (Google knows that because several sites link to a page, that page exists). This is a simplistic view of what happens from 60,000 feet above the action. The actual process that converts the site from a Web page to an entry on a results page is a highly sophisticated data warehousing and information retrieval scheme, which will vary from engine to engine. In fact, it is this process of archiving and retrieving documents from a database that is one key point of differentiation for most search engines. The other key point of differentiation lies around the other services offered and partnerships formed by each engine.

Due to the sheer volume and size of the documents indexed, each search engine has developed its own algorithm for which pieces of data are stored and methodologies for compression that allow for rapid searching and more economical storage of huge volumes of data. If you're bursting at the seams to develop an appreciation for the algorithms that drive search engines and directories, we encourage you to do some in-depth reading on information retrieval techniques. You could begin such a search at www.searchenginewatch.com, but unless you have an understanding of higher math and computational physics, you may quickly find yourself happy enough just to have the 60,000-foot view!

By following each Web site's navigation, a search engine's spider can often read and index the entire text of each site it visits into the engine's main database. (For details on the specific spiders crawling the Web and the engines with which they're associated, visit http://www.spiderhunter.com/.) Many engines, such as AltaVista, have begun to limit the depth they will crawl in the site and the number of pages they will index. For any single site, this limit is often about 400 to 500 pages. For owners of very large sites, these limits can present a significant challenge. Apparently, the reason for these limitations is that the Web, with over two billion documents, has become so large that it's simply unfeasible to crawl and index everything. Even the largest search engines, no matter how much and how deeply they crawl, can hardly expect to index but a portion of the Web. Cyveillance (www.cyveillance.com) hypothesizes that the Web is growing by six million documents per day. These spiders have their work cut out for them if they are to look for new documents, let alone revisit previously indexed documents to check for dead links and revised pages. Regardless, search engines that populate their databases using spider technology can grow very large in relatively short periods of time. For example, the FAST database has grown from an academic research project into a formidable search tool at a pace that would yield a speed and acceleration curve befitting a race car.

In developing a submission strategy for spiders, keep in mind that a software spider is like an electronic librarian who cuts out the table of contents of each book in every library in the world, sorts them into a gigantic master index, and then builds an electronic bibliography that stores information on which texts reference other texts. Some software spiders can crawl millions of documents a day! However, the number of pages a spider will index is unpredictable and how long your pages will remain active once they've been indexed is equally unpredictable. Some search engines, such as HotBot, have capped the size of their databases, deleting older content in favor of more recently submitted sites. This enables them to display fresher content and to manage their database more effectively. This means you'll have to submit to this engine more regularly than to some others. Given the variety of algorithms that drive the database development of the search engines, it's a good idea to specifically submit each page in your site that you want to be indexed. Be sure to include those pages that contain important keywords. You should also consider submitting a site map to ensure that the spider will get to the major sections of your site. In addition, include your most important keywords on the top-level pages leading off your site map.

What the spider sees on your site will determine how your site is listed in the search engine's index. Each search engine determines a site's relevancy based on a complex scoring system, or algorithm, which the engines try to keep secret. These algorithms are the core proprietary technology of the search engines. Each system adds or subtracts points based on criteria such as how many times a keyword appeared on the page, where on the page it appeared, how many total words were found, and the ratio of keywords to content. The pages that achieve the most points are returned at the top of the search results, and the rest are buried at the bottom, never to be found.

When searchers type a query into a search engine or directory such as Lycos, Yahoo!, or AltaVista, they are actually performing a database query. To determine which document or Web site to return for a particular keyword search, each search engine must have its own method of indexing, displaying, and ranking the documents (Web sites) in its database. The search engines have borrowed heavily from database development and information retrieval technology. As we've explained, information retrieval relies heavily on mathematical probabilities that determine which document most completely matches the searcher's query. Since there is no way to determine an exact fit, probability is inherent in any of these techniques. Therefore, most search engines use a "probable relevance" scoring method, which means that they will find documents that match your search criteria and give them relevance scores as to how closely they match your request. Documents are then returned to the searcher in order of the relevance score (the highest relevance score first and then so on).

The pursuit of excellence for a search engine is how quickly and completely it can satisfy the searcher's request. This means delivering the sites that will most likely meet the searcher's requirements. SEP is all about making sure that your site is visible to those searchers wanting the specific information that you are able to provide. As search engines try to improve their relevancy algorithms, from time to time they will change their scoring systems and stop rewarding certain techniques that may have previously given you an advantage. It is important to recognize that you must constantly be on your toes looking for these changes. (Again, we recommend you regularly visit www.searchenginewatch.com to keep abreast of new developments.) This book includes those techniques that worked best at the time of publication. It's likely that some of these techniques will no longer be effective if a search engine changes its relevancy scoring system.

Blocking Spiders from Visiting and Indexing Your Site

There are reasons you might not want your Web site to be crawled and indexed by search engines. More likely, there are simply certain pages that you don't want indexed by the major search engines. For instance, maybe you constructed an elaborate direct marketing site that requires the visitor to enter through your main page and then proceed through a highly structured series of links that leads them to a buying decision. The internal pages would only confuse visitors who entered through those pages and they would be less likely to buy a product or service.

Whatever your reason, there is a standard method that you can implement that will keep most of the major search engine spiders from indexing your Web site.

To block the spiders, create a file called robots.txt that includes the following code:

```
user-agent: *
Disallow: /*
```

The first line specifies the agents, browsers, or spiders that should read this file and adhere to the instructions in the following lines of code. The second line stipulates which files or directories the spider or browser should not read or index. The example above uses the "/*" which means the agent should not read or index anything, as the asterisk denotes "everything." The robots.txt file must be placed in the root directory of your Web site. What this means is that if you are hosting your Web site using one of the free services and your domain looks something like http://members.aol.com/Joesmith/home.htm, you cannot use the robots.txt file to keep out the spiders, since you don't have a primary domain name. The primary domain name is aol.com, and America Online will probably not allow you to block all the search engines' spiders from indexing their site and the Web sites of the 11 million other subscribers.

This robots.txt file could look like this if there were specific directories and files that you wish the search engines not to index:

```
user-agent: *
Disallow: /clients/*
Disallow: /products/*
Disallow: /pressrelations/*
Disallow: /surveys/survey.htm
```

In the above example the robots.txt file asks the search engine's spider to omit all pages within the following directories:

```
http://www.yourcompany.com/clients/
http://www.yourcompany.com/products/
http://www.yourcompany.com/pressrelations/
```

And the following specific page:

http://www.yourcompany.com/surveys/survey.htm

If you are one of the millions of people hosting a Web site on America Online's server or one of the other free or subdirectory Web site services and you can't place a robots.txt file in their root directory, you can use a META tag that talks to some of the spiders:

```
<META NAME="ROBOTS" CONTENT="NOINDEX">
```

You will need this META tag on every page in your Web site that you don't want indexed. If your Web site has 30 or 40 pages (or more), this will take a lot of time. This is a good reason to buy a good HTML editor like Luckman's WebEdit or Allaire's HomeSite. These programs allow you to do a global search and replace and add an HTML tag to every Web page that you open in the program. As with all META tags, this META tag goes at the top of your HTML document between the <HEAD> and </HEAD> tags.

The key to improving your Web site's visibility in the different search engines is to understand the basic structure of how they index and retrieve documents. Before you submit your Web site to each search engine, you need to understand the main factors that will affect your ranking.

Key Factors That Affect Your Site's Ranking

You don't need to have an in-depth understanding of HTML to understand the concepts that follow. Instead, we'll review the broader concepts of relevancy and how search engines evaluate a Web page to determine where it should rank for a particular keyword phrase.

The discipline of search engine optimization then, involves changing only those page elements that are scored by the search engine and then determining how your change impacted your Web site's rank in a particular search engine on searches for a specific keyword or phrase.

Search engines are in the business of sorting Web sites in their databases by the keywords contained in a Web site. They can't make any relevancy decisions based on the colors or quantity of your site's graphics — their spiders cannot interpret that information. To a search engine, a graphic, regardless of the words that may be contained in it, is simply: <picture.jpg>. There is no information there on which it can base a relevancy decision.

Which keywords each individual search engine determines your Web site is relevant to and how often those keywords are queried will determine how often your site's description and link are presented to search engine users. How well you organize the important keywords in your Web site to fit each search engine's ranking criteria will determine your Web site's rank, but we're not going to look at these criteria in detail at this point. In our following engine-by-engine chapters, you'll get a literal dissection of each engine's ranking criteria.

Generally, a search engine assigns "points" to Web sites based on some predefined criteria. And, while all search engines measure a keyword's position on your pages, there are a variety of places where you can include your targeted keyword phrases to achieve better rankings.

While the ranking criteria vary among search engines, most grade the placement of keywords and phrases on your Web site based on these factors:

- Keyword prominence
- Keyword frequency
- Keyword weight
- Keyword proximity
- Keyword placement
- Off-the-page criteria (including link popularity, term vectors, and HTML construction)

Keyword Prominence

How early in a Web site do the keywords appear? The very first element in HTML that can contain keywords is the site's Title tag, the tag whose contents are displayed in the title bar at the top of the browser.

But what do most Web designers and companies put in the Title tag? Often it's "Home Page." This is excellent if you are hoping to attain a ranking on searches for the words "home," "page," or "home page." Worse, I've seen some Web designers use the Title tag to say, "Welcome to Company.com."

Or worse yet, "Welcome to Our Site!" Those would be terrific site titles if the company were seeking to achieve a ranking on the words "welcome" or "to." Think about it: If the words "welcome" and "to" are the very first words in the site's Title tag, they must be the most important — or so thinks the search engine.

Your Title Tag is Your New Keyword META Tag

When constructing your Web site's title, do you start with one of your targeted keywords, or is that keyword the fourth or fifth word of the site's title? Truth be told, many search engines no longer weigh the contents of the keyword META tag very heavily. In many ways, the Title tag has replaced the keyword META tag, and some would argue this tag has effectively become the keyword META tag.

"Prominence" means "near the top," not just of the contents of the head statement, but of the viewable page. But prominence is not solely about the site's Title or META tags. Keyword prominence means using your important keywords near the top of the viewable page. That could mean in the headline (the <H1> to <H6> HTML tags that create bold large headline fonts), or in the first few words of the first paragraph on the page (some search engines pay special attention to the first 25 words on a Web page, while others pay attention to character limits of 200 or 1,000), or in the way you organize the page in terms of its HTML construction. Consider the following example:

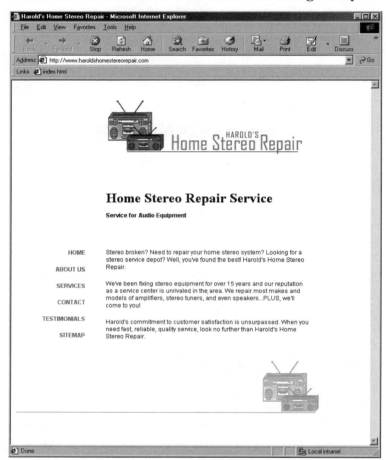

Looks like a typical Web site, right? In fact, on the surface they've done a nice job by including one of the targeted keywords in the headline "Home Stereo Repair," and they've worked several keywords into the first 25 total words of copy on the page. Like many Web sites, they've chosen to include navigational links on the left side of the page. So, on the surface, this page looks ready to submit to the search engines. Not so fast. Here is how the search engine's spider will read this page:

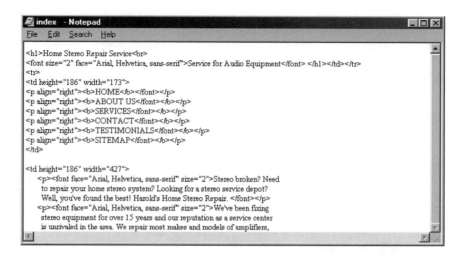

```
index  - Notepad
File  Edit  Search  Help

<h1>Home Stereo Repair Service<br>
<font size="2" face="Arial, Helvetica, sans-serif">Service for Audio Equipment</font> </h1></td></tr>
<tr>
<td height="186" width="173">
<p align="right"><b>HOME</b></font></p>
<p align="right"><b>ABOUT US</font></b></p>
<p align="right"><b>SERVICES</font></b></p>
<p align="right"><b>CONTACT</font></b></p>
<p align="right"><b>TESTIMONIALS</font></b></p>
<p align="right"><b>SITEMAP</font></b></p>
</td>

<td height="186" width="427">
   <p><font face="Arial, Helvetica, sans-serif" size="2">Stereo broken? Need
   to repair your home stereo system? Looking for a stereo service depot?
   Well, you've found the best! Harold's Home Stereo Repair. </font></p>
   <p><font face="Arial, Helvetica, sans-serif" size="2">We've been fixing
   stereo equipment for over 15 years and our reputation as a service center
   is unrivaled in the area. We repair most makes and models of amplifiers,
```

Notice that when the search engine spider views this page it reads all of the keyword-rich site copy below the left-side navigation bar. And, if the Web site contained JavaScript right after the head statement (where most developers place the JavaScript code), the copy would be pushed even further down the page as shown in the following illustration.

```
index  - Notepad
File  Edit  Search  Help

<SCRIPT LANGUAGE="JavaScript"><!--
if (document.images) {
 img2_off = new Image(165,26); img2_off.src = "Home1.gif";
 img2_on = new Image(165,26); img2_on.src = "Home2.gif";
 img3_off = new Image(165,26); img3_off.src = "AboutUs1.gif";
 img3_on = new Image(165,26); img3_on.src = "AboutUs2.gif";
 img4_off = new Image(165,26); img4_off.src = "Services1.gif";
 img4_on = new Image(165,26); img4_on.src = "Services2.gif";
 img5_off = new Image(165,26); img5_off.src = "Contact1.gif";
 img5_on = new Image(165,26); img5_on.src = "Contact2.gif";
 img6_off = new Image(165,26); img6_off.src = "Testimonials1.gif";
 img6_on = new Image(165,26); img6_on.src = "Testimonials2.gif";
 img7_off = new Image(165,26); img7_off.src = "Sitemap1.gif";
 img7_on = new Image(165,26); img7_on.src = "Sitemap2.gif";
 }

 function hiLite(imgDocID,imgObjName) {
     if (document.images) {
         document.images[imgDocID].src = eval(imgObjName + ".src");
     }
 }

 function gotoUrl(url) { location = url; }
 //-->
 </SCRIPT>

 <h1>Home Stereo Repair Service<br>
 <font size="2" face="Arial, Helvetica, sans-serif">Service for Audio Equipment</font> </h1></td></tr>
 <tr>
 <td height="186" width="173">
 <p align="right"><b>HOME</b></font></p>
 <p align="right"><b>ABOUT US</font></b></p>
 <p align="right"><b>SERVICES</font></b></p>
```

When thinking about prominence as it relates to a search engine's ranking algorithm, think about all the ways a search engine could look for keywords "early" in a document, paragraph, sentence, or page in general. Remember, prominence could mean:

- Keywords early in the head statement, including the Title tags or keyword or description META tags
- Keywords early in the headline tags
- Keywords early in the body copy (the first 25 words of the page)
- Keywords early in the second or third paragraphs of copy on the viewable page
- Keyword-rich body copy being presented early in the HTML organization of the Web page

For competitive keyword phrases, SEP professionals will measure keyword prominence in each area of the page. For instance, if they're attempting to gain an advantage over a particular page that currently enjoys a top ranking, they may notice that the competing page contains the targeted keyword as the fourth word of the Title tag, as the third word in the <H1> headline, and as the fourth word in the first paragraph of text on the page. All things being equal (and they seldom are), if you built a Web page where you included the targeted keyword as the second word in the Title tag, the third word of the <H1> headline tag, and the third word of the first paragraph of your page, you might attain a higher ranking than the competing page. That's how the game is played, anyway.

You should also note that a lack of the targeted keyword near the end of the document may scream louder than the keyword being used in all the right places. If your Web page is very long and the targeted keyword is present only in the site title, keyword and description META tags, headline, and first 25 words of copy, but nowhere else in the page, that may set off a red flag with a ranking algorithm.

Do not seek to attain prominence at the expense of all else. When we interviewed executives at Lycos several years ago, they indicated that they liked to see keywords near the end of a document as well. Their thinking is that most long Web pages are constructed like college term papers. You tell people what you're going to tell them, tell it to them, and then tell them what you told them. So, if a document is about a certain topic, it should include that keyword or phrase in the last paragraph of the document as well as the first. Now, no search engine will admit to anything that specific these days, but it certainly could still make a difference.

Keyword Frequency

One way that a search engine determines if a Web page is about a particular keyword or phrase is by looking to see how frequently the keyword or phrase appears on the page; this is called "keyword frequency." It's an important factor, but not your end-all solution. If keyword frequency were the only measure, a page with five occurrences of a keyword or phrase would rank higher than a page with three.

You don't want to go overboard with frequency, because many engines will penalize you for "spamming" or keyword stuffing if you repeat a word too many times. The search engines have reviewed millions of Web pages and have a good idea of how many times a keyword commonly appears in the "average" Web document. They've built statistical models that indicate what a high, low, and average keyword frequency would look like. If your Web page exceeds the number of keyword or phrase repetitions in their model, it may rank poorly.

As a rule, we include the targeted keyword phrase once in the keyword META tag and once or twice in the site's Title tag. As for how many occurrences of a targeted keyword to include on the viewable page, read Chapter 35 on building informational pages and Chapter 10 on site design elements. There's no magic number, but here are some issues to consider:

- How many other Web sites also contain that targeted keyword?
- How competitive is the targeted keyword (e.g., are 50 other companies fighting for rankings on that keyword)?
- How many total words of copy are contained on the particular Web page?
- How is the Web page constructed and in how many important places does the keyword appear? Is the keyword currently being used in the first 25 words of the page or in headlines of any size (e.g., <H1> through <H6> tags)?

As a rule, the keyword placement and a variety of off-the-page issues are more important than keyword frequency in a Web page. Don't obsess over keyword frequency, just understand it and be aware of its implications!

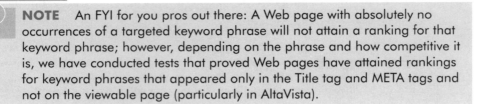

NOTE   An FYI for you pros out there: A Web page with absolutely no occurrences of a targeted keyword phrase will not attain a ranking for that keyword phrase; however, depending on the phrase and how competitive it is, we have conducted tests that proved Web pages have attained rankings for keyword phrases that appeared only in the Title tag and META tags and not on the viewable page (particularly in AltaVista).

Keyword Weight

The number of keywords appearing on a Web page compared with the total number of words appearing on that page is how keyword weight (also called keyword density) is measured. In other words, if your Web page has 100 total words of copy and seven of them are the targeted keyword, your document has a keyword weight for that keyword of 7 percent. Some search engines like higher keyword weight, while others prefer lower keyword weights. But it's important to recognize that keyword weight is a limiting metric, meaning that the search engines measure a document's keyword weight as a way of tempering or limiting keyword frequency. For instance, if a 100-word Web page contains 50 occurrences of a particular keyword, chances are that the Webmaster has "stuffed" many additional instances of that keyword into the document inappropriately. In other words, that document is just trying too hard.

Keyword weight is often measured in different areas of the Web page, e.g., a Title tag with 10 total words and two occurrences of a targeted keyword has a keyword weight of 2 percent. Sometimes when targeting very competitive keyword phrases, an SEP professional seeks to increase the prominence of a keyword in different areas of the Web page, and also the keyword weight in a particular tag. For instance, if a competing Web page that ranks at number 3 for a particular keyword search has 10 total words in its Title tag but only one occurrence of the keyword, a savvy Webmaster might match the total number of words in the title but add a second occurrence of the targeted keyword, thereby exceeding the other page's keyword weight. This way, you could create a page that would be "statistically identical" to a competing Web page, but not a copyright violation or even a copy of the competing page. To the search engine, it just has keywords in the very same positions on the page as the competing page and, therefore, is virtually identical in terms of keyword count (frequency) and weight.

> **TIP**   One technique that often works well is to create smaller Web pages, generally just a paragraph long, which emphasize a particular keyword. By keeping the overall number of words to a minimum, you increase the weight of the keyword you are emphasizing. As a rule, however, the keyword weight measure is used by SEP professionals to ensure they have not built Web pages with too many occurrences of a targeted keyword phrase. For that reason, we typically look at the Web page's overall keyword count as a percentage of the total number of words. In most cases we try not to exceed a keyword weight of 3 to 10 percent.

Generally speaking, keyword weight is a limiting measure that search engines use to ensure that someone is not "stuffing" keywords into their Web page and succeeding in attaining a high ranking for that keyword. It's unusual for an SEP professional to obsess about each little area of a Web page and measure and then tweak the keyword weight in each part of the page. But if you think about it, in the early days of SEP, the search engines were much less sophisticated. Often, a page with 10 occurrences of a keyword would rank higher than a page with five, so why not create a page with 50 or 100 or a thousand occurrences? It grew so ridiculous that search engines began executing this limiting measure that has worked extremely well.

> **TIP**   When designing your site, don't provide detailed product or service information on your home page. Instead, design a page for each product or service and provide a brief description and a link to the home page. This allows you to be more specific with your keywords for each product or service page and increase the weight of the keyword.

Keyword Proximity

The placement of keywords on a Web page in relation to each other, or in some cases in relation to words with similar meanings to the queried keyword, is measured in "keyword proximity." For search engines that grade a keyword match by keyword proximity, the connected phrase "home loans" will outrank a citation that mentions "home mortgage loans" if you are searching only for the phrase "home loans."

Keyword Placement

The search engines believe where and in what HTML your targeted keywords or phrases are placed is a good indicator of what a Web page is about. This is called "keyword placement." Search engines look for clues that might suggest a document's hierarchy and structure, and thereby its content.

If you were designing a search engine's algorithm and you reviewed 500,000 Web pages, you'd probably notice some trends. Most Web documents have headlines or their equivalent bolded copy and introductory text. You may discover that link text is often very descriptive and consistent with the main topic covered in a Web page (instead of just "click here"). Maybe you'd discover that the words used to describe images in the image <ALT> text are often consistent with the contents of the Web page.

 NOTE The contents of the <ALT> tag are displayed when you mouse over a graphic, before the graphic loads, or when you're viewing a Web page with graphics turned off.

Over time, as the Web grows up and Webmasters purchase this guide or others like it, a good number of Webmasters start to cram keywords into certain areas of the Web page that are believed to be important to attaining a good search engine ranking. Over time, keywords found in certain HTML prove to be less reliable at indicating the true content of a Web document. As the person in charge of the search engine's algorithm, you change how much weight you apply to that measure and you seek a different area of the Web page to emphasize. To be fair, changes in algorithms often have less to do with Webmaster abuse than with the way Web page design and content evolve. In the early days of the Web, virtually all Web pages had no backgrounds (just that horrid gray). They contained a centered headline in <H1> style that announced "Joe's Home Page" and then included several hundred words of HTML copy that laid out Joe's life views complete with links to his favorite resources. As Web design evolved, tables came into wider use, and the amount of copy was reduced on Web pages. (One large interactive agency decrees that no Web page should contain more than 250 words of copy.) These are all issues that spiders have had to adjust to.

As a rule, search engines favor Web sites that contain keywords in:

- The Title tag
- The keyword META tag
- The headline tags
- The first 25 words of copy
- Hyperlinks
- Image <ALT> tags
- Text near the end of the document

Generally speaking, the search engines are looking for a theme. In fact, with the growing popularity of "term vector databases," a concept we'll address a bit later, the theme of your Web site is particularly important. If a keyword is included in the keyword META tag, the search engine tests it: Is the keyword also in the Title tag? Is the keyword in a headline tag? Is the keyword in an activated link? If so, that document may, in fact, be about that particular keyword. On some engines, placing keywords in the link text (the text that is underlined on the screen in a browser) can add more relevancy to those words.

In order to attain a good ranking in a search engine, the targeted keyword must be included in more than just one area of the page. It's not enough to include the targeted keyword in just the keyword META tag. A Webmaster must work to build a theme through a Web page by incorporating the targeted keyword into several different areas of the page's HTML and body copy.

And don't think that your Web page starts and stops with its HTML. A Web page is made up of the page and the address. I'm often surprised when Web site designers name their Web pages with numbers. Why not include your targeted keyword phrase in the page filename?

Instead of:

http://www.company.com/88717211.html

why not make it:

http://www.company.com/keyword-phrase.html

Rearranging Keywords to Improve Your Ranking

To know what kinds of keyword placement or other keyword factors can affect a Web site's ranking is to know how to shuffle the elements that make up your Web site so as to outrank any other site on the Web.

Let's play keyword doctor for a minute and consider a few examples. Which of the following hypothetical scenarios would rank higher in a hypothetical search engine for a search on "VanGogh"? (We've omitted or included HTML as necessary to improve the clarity of the illustration.)

Web site #1:

word word, word, word, word, word VanGogh, word, word word, word word, word, word, word, word, word VanGogh, word word, word, word, word, word word word, word, word, word, word word, word, word, word VanGogh word word, word, word, word, word.

Web site #2:

word word, word, word, VanGogh word, word, word, word word, word word, word, word, word, VanGogh word, word, word word, word, word, word, VanGogh word word word, word, word, word, word word, word, word, word word word, word, word, word, word.

Answer: Probably Web site #2, as the occurrences of "VanGogh" are more prominent; they occur earlier or closer to the beginning of document.

Now, consider another more complicated situation, also involving two Web sites that might be returned for a search on "VanGogh":

Web site #3:

<TITLE>VanGogh's life and early work</TITLE>

word word, word, word, word, word VanGogh, word, word word, word word, word, word, word, VanGogh word, word, word word, word, word, word, word word word, word, word, word, word word, word, word, word VanGogh word word, word, word, word, word

Web site #4:

<TITLE>VanGogh</TITLE>

word word, word, word, word, word VanGogh, word, word word, word word, word, word, word, VanGogh

Answer: While there is no definitive answer because each search engine uses a slightly different ranking system, we believe that in theory Web site #4 would win more often. "How can that be?" you might ask. "Web site #3 has four occurrences of 'VanGogh' and the first three have an equal prominence!" Well, it is the keyword **weight** that could help Web site #4 outrank #3.

The point is that while not all situations are as clear as the example presented, most ranking problems can be diagnosed by evaluating the same keyword placement variables. Once you understand how to evaluate the variables, you can build Web pages that achieve top rankings.

Now, simply because you determine how to achieve a high ranking for a particular keyword and then execute it doesn't mean that you'll maintain this rank consistently. Every day, thousands of new Web sites are being built and registered in search engines. Search engines continually refine their search algorithms, and sometimes they effect a fundamental change in methodology in pursuit of more accurate searches for visitors. WebCrawler recently scrapped its entire ranking algorithm and replaced it with Excite's software and search algorithm. Many sites that were ranked well in WebCrawler suddenly needed to redesign their pages to achieve similar rankings under this new system.

Off-the-Page Criteria

Off-the-page criteria consider elements other than those on your Web page for relevance. In the past, search engines only considered the contents of a Web page to determine its relevancy and rank in search results, e.g., how many keywords appear on the page, or how early in the Web page those keywords appear. Off-the-page criteria are often talked about in terms of search engines racing to increase off-the-page measurements in response to spammers. I believe this technology trend has less to do with responding to the illicit few, and more to do with a genuine problem faced by search engines. They need to respond to a landscape where thousands (sometimes millions) of documents can contain a particular keyword phrase, and in some cases, hundreds of those documents can be indistinguishable from one another based on what is on the page. What happens if a search engine encounters 500 Web pages, each with 100 total words and seven occurrences of that keyword in relatively similar locations? Which document should be listed first, second, or third? Search engines must look at alternate relevancy indicators and assess their value in determining a Web page's relevancy to a particular search. In short, the goal is the same: improving relevancy.

Search engines have looked to three primary external indicators of a Web page's relevance for their off-the-page considerations:

- Measuring the quantity, quality, and content/context of links to a Web page
- Measuring searcher behavior after they conduct a query
- Editorial review of Web pages

Few search engines consider all three simultaneously, and more often than not, a search engine places its trust in one criteria in the absence of the others. These off-the-page measurements have the ancillary benefit of thwarting the worst of the search engine spammers, but their primary benefit is more relevant search results. Here are the most common off-the-page factors for you to consider:

Term Vectors

The concept of term vector-based relevancy considers your Web page as well as off-the-page considerations. Relevancy measures that use "term vectors" and link measurement combine two proven methodologies. The use of term vectors, a data mining technology, to determine relevancy has been enhanced with the addition of link popularity schemes. To determine term vectors, each word on a Web page is converted into a number. These vectors can then be readily matched to a database of numeric terms to classify a page. By measuring the inbound and outbound links to and from the page, and then comparing the key-word weight of the page and the weighted value of the links against some standard, the most relevant pages can be identified. For example, if a page is to be found relevant in a search for the phrase "MP3 download," it might need to have a keyword density of 7 percent (or whatever weight is set by the search engine). Then, it would also have to have the most important related documents linking to it and it would have links to the most important Web pages.

This is, hands down, the most provocative topic to enter the discourse of SEP and perhaps the most complicated to explain and understand. We will attempt to make it plain in the following paragraphs — but it will not be easy! Here goes:

What search engines have accomplished by using this technology is rapidly scoring and sorting documents, increasing retrieval efficiency, and improving relevancy by measuring the "importance" and even the contents of all the Web pages that link to a particular Web page. Note the three elements a term vector approach considers:

- The keyword weight, density, or theme of a particular Web page (We'll explain themes in a minute.)
- The keyword weight, density, or theme of the outbound links
- The quantity and quality of the inbound links that point to a Web page

Since each word and phrase in a Web page is converted into a number (the term vector) each is represented by a point in space, if you will, that determines its location or direction. Therefore, related words or words with like meanings will have numerically close numbers. Conversely, if your Web page contains the phrases "tropical fish" and "accounting software," the page will have disparate term vectors. By using this spatially dimensioned model, it's easier to determine the elements that don't fit into a particular space.

Think of this technology like a local street map that you might purchase if you're traveling to a city you've not visited before. If you look up "Boston, Massachusetts" in the index, that location is represented in two-dimensional space by assigning an X and Y axis coordinate to it — let's say it's C:24. When you look across the top of the map for the letter "C" and then drag your finger down the map to the number 24, your finger is pointing to a square on the map where the city of Boston can be found. Other locations that are near Boston will have coordinates that indicate their proximity. Cambridge might be located at C:23 and Brighton at C:25. The locations are related and so they're numbered as being close to one another in space. Now, in reality, my example is not perfect because it's only a two-dimensional representation of a term vector and the term vector database actually uses three dimensions. However, for the purposes of understanding the concept and then understanding how to apply the knowledge to attain higher rankings, it gets the job done.

The search engines that employ term vector database technology also maintain a separate database of the Internet's topography — the interconnections between Web pages. These two databases, the term vector database and the link database, are considered together in determining a Web page's rank.

In order to optimize a Web page to attain a higher ranking under this system, a Web page should focus on or limit a page's topical content to two or three total keyword phrases or themes. A Web page can be penalized if the page contains tangential or unrelated keyword phrases.

As of November 2000, Google, Inktomi, AltaVista, Excite, and FAST are all believed to be using themes in their algorithms. Because Google, Inktomi, and FAST provide results to a number of other engines including AOL Search,

HotBot, Yahoo!, NBCi , and MSN, the results of these engines are also influenced by term vector technology.

What's Your Theme?

The search engines using term vectors now look beyond a single page to determine the theme and relevancy of an entire Web site. Since the search engines crawl the entire site and the inbound and outbound links, the content of the entire site — not just a single page — is taken into consideration in determining its relevancy. The use of term vectors presents the greatest challenge for large sites that have numerous pages on a variety of topics. For example, a site for a very large meat company, www.joesmeats.com, might have separate directories: joesmeats.com/lamb, joesmeats.com/chicken, joesmeats.com/beef, joesmeats.com/pork. Each of these directories creates a problem because the search engine will crawl the entire site and become confused as to whether the site is about lamb, chicken, beef, or pork. Unless each page is rich with meat-centric keywords that clearly suggest that the site is about meat, the site will rank poorly in the search engines. The key is to have common keywords on every page that clearly articulate your theme and play through to your links.

Link and Site Popularity

The number of other Web sites linked to your site is a measure of its "link popularity," sometimes called "site popularity." This ranking measurement is sometimes called a site's "significance" ranking because it's believed that one measure of your site's value is the number of other Web sites that felt your site was sufficiently important to link to. If a lot of other sites link to yours, chances are your site is relatively important, or so a number of other Web site owners thought. It's very similar to the tenets of academic citation: In the same way a large number of thesis papers will cite a particular book as a source on a topic, Web pages that link to others are "citing" them and acknowledging their importance on a particular topic.

The science of using link popularity to determine a Web site's value is borne of search engines seeking external META information (by the way, "META information," or "metadata" is simply data that describes other data) about Web sites. As the Web evolved, search engines discovered that they could place less and less trust in the metadata or META tags found on a given Web page as more and more Webmasters manipulated these tags, stuffing them with tangential keywords to gain an advantage in the search engines.

Many search engines maintain what they call a "connectivity server" or "connectivity graph" or "citation server" that they access to determine how many Web sites link to a particular Web site. These servers maintain information on links between Web sites, how many sites link to a particular site, and how many sites with a lot of links pointing to it link to a particular site. The idea is that a link from the *New York Times*, which has hundreds or even thousands of other sites that link to it, is more important than a link from your local pizza parlor's site that may only have three other sites linking to it. Some search engines call this relationship "authorities and hubs" or "attractors and satellites," but the principles are the same.

It's important to note, however, that search engines that calculate link popularity first consider the page's textual relevancy to a particular keyword phrase. Link popularity is not the predominant deciding factor. For example, Google's algorithm considers many things, and link popularity does weigh heavily in its relevancy calculation. However, like every other search engine (even those that heavily weigh link popularity), Google first must index and analyze the text on a Web page to determine that page's relevancy to a given keyword or phrase query. No page should attain a high ranking on a keyword or phrase that does not appear on the viewable page.

At least 315,990 Web sites link to the IBM Web site (www.ibm.com) in AltaVista's index. Because of these links, IBM would achieve better ranking in certain search engines with all other factors being equal. However, this is only one factor, a complementary strategy, and you can certainly achieve high rankings without being linked from thousands of sites. This is simply another reason why you want to work to gain links from other sites to yours. Sometimes if you agree to link to them, they'll do the same for you. In Web marketing, this is called cross-linking or reciprocal linking, and it's another way to increase traffic to your Web site.

Link popularity, then, measures five primary linking characteristics:

- How many Web pages link to yours
- How many Web pages with many links to them link to yours
- How many Web pages your page links to (links from your site to others)
- The anchor text contained in the links to your Web site
- Keywords or keyword phrases in the text near the activated link to your Web site

Many search engines that consider link popularity also care about the quantity and relevance of links you set to external Web pages. If a document has thousands of links to it, but none to any other documents, it's an island (also easily detectable as a dreaded "doorway page"). Chances are it has little value to a visitor. Studies of the topology of the Web have taught the major search engines that high-quality Web sites typically have some number of links to external resources and some number of links from important sources. The ratio between the two is often considered by search engines. Therefore, a Web site that has only inbound links is an anomaly and will score lower for that component of the search engine's algorithm.

Also, consider that search engines may analyze the anchor text of the link to your Web site for a clue to your site's relevance. If you operate a Web site that provides information about golf courses, when someone posts a link to your Web site, it should say something like, "Click for information about the best golf courses."

Now, the links to your Web site and the textual content of those links is usually outside of your control, but research has determined that the anchor text of these links is a good indicator of the content of the referenced Web site.

High-popularity or high-importance Web sites that establish links to yours carry more weight and will result in higher rankings than links from free-for-all link-list type Web sites. But now, with the introduction of theme-based search engines or search engines that employ term vector database technology, the keyword content of the page that links to your page may play a more important role.

Click-Through Behavior Tracking or "Popularity" Measurements

The behavior of the searcher, the searcher's "vote" if you will, is measured by tracking which (if any) Web site they select after performing a query. This "popularity behavior" idea was hatched by an MIT student in a business plan contest and resulted in a company called Direct Hit (www.directhit.com). There are other systems that seek to leverage user behavior or popularity, but Direct Hit is by far the most recognized.

This relevancy measure is elegant in its simplicity. Where people go, literally which Web sites they visit after performing a specific keyword or phrase query, is evidence of that site's relevance to the queried keyword or phrase. By measuring searchers' behavior after performing a search, "popularity" ranking measurements gain the insight and evaluation power of thousands of searchers.

Direct Hit does require that some number of people conduct searches on a particular keyword or phrase before it has enough click-through data to determine which sites are "popular." Some keywords, or more often, obscure phrases, have not generated sufficient queries to adequately populate Direct Hit's database and so no matches are available. In the case of HotBot, if the top 10 search results are being served by Direct Hit, the Direct Hit logo is present at the bottom of the search results. In some search engines such as MSN, Direct Hit's search matches are not presented in the search results, and instead users must select a link that says, "Get the Top 10 Most Popular Sites for _____." In others, like Lycos, up to four "popular" Web sites as determined by Direct Hit are presented above the main search matches.

The Direct Hit system gathers click-through popularity information from a variety of sources — not just from one search engine. In fact, more than a year ago, I was informed that Direct Hit click-through tracking "instruments" were present at the Lycos search engine before Lycos added Direct Hit popularity matches to its search results. You see, the HotBot search engine, owned by Lycos, was displaying top 10 search matches from Direct Hit but gathering data from several sources. In time, Lycos added Direct Hit results.

Search engines that measure user behavior or click-through behavior typically place a cookie in the searcher's browser and track which Web site they select after performing a search. The searcher is sent to an interim page that they never see before they are automatically redirected to the Web page they selected, allowing the engine to track the selection. The search engine also tracks the length of time the user spent on the selected Web site by noticing if and when that user returns. The search engine will then take notice of additional selections from the same search result set or if that user performs another query.

> **NOTE**   A cookie is a small file, usually a simple text file containing a unique number, that's automatically downloaded from a Web server to a user's Web browser. Information stored in cookies can then be accessed any time the person using that browser returns to the Web site. You've probably downloaded cookies if you've ever returned to a shopping site and it automatically remembered your name, password, and preferences.

If a site is sufficiently popular to attain a top 10 ranking, it will fall in ranking if people stop selecting it. Conversely, if searchers don't find what they're looking for in the top few pages of search results, and dig down deeper (say, past the first three pages of search matches) to select a lower ranked Web site, that site will earn significant relevancy points and begin its rise toward a higher ranking in the Direct Hit sorted results.

It would seem intuitive that to influence your ranking in Direct Hit you could simply perform a particular keyword query multiple times, each time drilling down until you find your Web site's listing and then clicking on it. However, as you might expect, Direct Hit has anticipated these types of subversions and has programmed countermeasures. Direct Hit maintains predictive models of how many people typically drill down to different levels in the search results. If your Web site starts seeing significant "action," and that sudden popularity does not conform to an engine's understanding of how Web sites in that position are typically accessed, your site may be penalized. Plus, if you try doing this by yourself, you'll likely trip a security measure because your browser contains a cookie that Direct Hit will detect, or you will be visiting and searching from the same IP address, which the search engine can also detect.

This is not to say that there is no value in asking friends and family to search for a particular keyword or phrase and then find your Web site and click on it in a search engine that displays Direct Hit results. Sometimes a good Web site needs a "leg up" in the Direct Hit system, and priming the pump a few times will probably not raise too many eyebrows. However, an ongoing strategy designed to trick Direct Hit will likely fail and is not worth the effort. This is especially so when you consider that Direct Hit is gathering click-through behavior from multiple high-traffic search engines. Your few searches and click-throughs may not make a significant difference depending on the popularity of the search term.

Factors That Do Not Affect Your Rank in Search Engines

As we've said all along, search engine spiders are simple creatures. And while they will visit your Web site and capture every element, there are many page elements that they cannot interpret. Therefore, if your targeted keyword phrases are contained in any of these elements, you should consider moving them into other parts of the HTML so that they will have a chance to be read by the search engine's spiders and ultimately returned by the search engines in response to a keyword query. In general, if you cannot highlight it on the page, the search engine cannot read it. Flash is a particular problem, as are most "gee whiz" new Web page technologies. However, the most insidious barriers to attain rankings are often the most obvious.

The following are page elements that will not be read by or considered by the search engines. That is not to say that these page elements can be used with reckless abandon — these are to be considered in a general sense, not specifically. For every rule there is an exception, and exceptions abound.

The Size or Content of Your Graphics

Search engines cannot optically recognize text. If your keywords are contained in a graphic, they will not be read or considered by the search engine. Keywords contained in a graphic are fine for directories whose human editors will read and consider them. Search engine spiders see only the filename of the graphic, not its textual content, if any.

Words That are Graphics

This means an art file (such as a .gif or .jpg) that depicts a word or phrase. While this point is clearly addressed in the previous point, we've included it as a separate item because for some reason, many people don't understand the distinction, and we respond to countless questions about this point. If you have a large headline on your site in some funky font that was created not in HTML but in a graphics program, then it's a graphic. Search engines do not read it as words — they only see the graphic's filename. (The way around this is to name the file using some of your relevant keywords.)

Your Choice of Colors

Some engines will penalize you for hiding words on a page when the text and background have the same or similar colors.

Your Web Site's Overall Layout or Design

This will only matter so far as keyword prominence may be affected if a graphic appears before the body copy on your site. Most Web site marketers support the use of text before graphics as some search engines assign weight to the first 25 words on a page. (See Chapter 10 for how page layout affects ranking.) Frames are problematic, as are nested tables, but page design mostly impacts keyword prominence. When your page design includes Flash and other cutting-edge design elements, it can impact your site's ability to be indexed by search engines. The bottom line: Search engines can only index HTML text and follow hyperlinks between Web pages, and there are only so many places where keywords can be included within a Web site. Where, how often, and how early your keywords are placed will determine your ranking. Remember these variables when you are analyzing other Web sites that have ranked higher than yours. Look at it like a puzzle, not some magic bullet or immeasurable force. Each player has a number of pieces, and the order and distribution of them determines the winner.

A Winning Strategy

The following steps will help you optimize your pages for the highest ranking possible.

1. Check your site's visibility as it stands today

If your Web site has already been submitted to the search engines and directories, you'll want to find out how well you rank right now for keywords and phrases people might use to find you. Install WebPosition Gold from the companion CD and measure your site's rankings on important keywords to establish a baseline.

2. Understand why all your pages are not ranking as well as they could

Study the rankings of the sites above and below you. Look for patterns. Does the site immediately above you have more occurrences of your targeted keyword in the Title tag? Does the site immediately below you have fewer total occurrences or occurrences of the keyword in different elements of the HTML than your site?

Typically, there's no way to make a single page rank well with every search engine for every keyword or phrase someone might use. However, you can work to make at least one page in your Web site rank near the top for each engine or a couple of engines. Ideally, you'll want one of your pages to be well positioned for each of your primary keywords. This may take some thought on how to set up your pages to achieve the desired results.

3. Try to identify and correct problem areas

Are you at least indexed in each spider-driven search engine? Make sure your page design has been optimized for your targeted keywords and phrases, then resubmit. If you submitted recently, make sure you've allowed enough time for the engine to add you to their database. (See our search engine submission chart in Chapter 8 for the engines' index times.)

Are you at least in the top 30 positions for your primary keywords? If not, redesign some of your pages (or create new ones), and resubmit.

4. Keep meticulous records

You may find that your rankings suddenly move up or down dramatically. When this happens, you'll need to understand why. We recommend you keep careful notes on when you submitted or resubmitted your site to each engine and what pages you submitted. You may even wish to create subdirectories with different copies of your Web site at various stages. That way, if you move down in rank after submitting revision B, you can go back and study what made revision A better. This requires some planning to be effective.

5. Continually monitor and adjust your site

This is the key to achieving good rankings. There's no 100 percent effective page design or strategy — especially when you consider that each search engine changes its algorithm frequently. What works this month might not work next month, and then after a month or two, the older technique may begin to work again. Each search engine is different and continually changes and adds new pages to its index. These will affect your positions over time — sometimes very quickly. SEP is an iterative process, not a one-time effort. Be sure to let your submitted pages "settle" before resubmitting. Often it takes time, up to a month or two, for a submitted page to reach its "natural" ranking.

Is This All Really Worth It?

Yes! Even minor changes in page design combined with follow-up work can have significant effects on your traffic. There's also no more cost-effective way to increase traffic to your site. Even better, this traffic is high quality since it's users who are specifically searching for your product or service. If you're indexed on the keywords that properly describe your products or services, you should see your sales noticeably increase.

We're familiar with a company that offered various types of software products. They did some traditional advertising and submitted to the search engines. Web site traffic was slow, and Internet sales accounted for only 7 percent of their business. After following the tips outlined here and resubmitting, the site's traffic tripled over a couple of months! Even more astonishing is that sales via the Internet increased nearly 500 percent (to 34 percent of total company sales) with zero cost in new advertising dollars.

Imitation is the Most Sincere Form of Flattery

If there is one rule that should be referred to as the refrain in SEP, it is this: To achieve a top position in a particular search engine, analyze what other high-ranking Web pages have done.

Search engines change their ranking algorithms from time to time. A page in your Web site that earned a top ranking last week might drop in the rankings a few months later. Then, left untouched, that same page could later climb right back into its old search position, although this is unlikely to happen by chance.

The trick to always being on top is to learn the variables that can be influenced and analyze the contents of the top Web sites to see what they're doing better than you. Literally, click on their listings, visit their site, and select View from the pull-down menu in your browser and then Document Source in Netscape Navigator, or Source in Microsoft Internet Explorer. This allows you to view the actual HTML code that makes up their page.

Ask yourself, "Is a particular keyword more prominent in their Title tag than in mine?" and "Is a particular keyword simply more prominent?" See whether it's repeated more often in their description META tag or in the actual copy that makes up their page than on your own site. Perhaps they're using the keyword in the heading tags, or maybe keywords appear in hyperlinks to other internal pages or some other way that you had not considered or are not using.

How to Avoid Trouble with the Engines

We've included an entire chapter in this book on search engine "spam." More and more, search engines are cracking down on the use of techniques they consider inappropriate for gaining top rankings in their indexes. Search engines have declared a quiet war against SEP practitioners who employ overly aggressive optimization tactics.

Because the search engines are working to penalize the small minority of spammers who inappropriately submit dozens of pages and present off-topic material, legitimate SEP consultants must be careful not to get clipped in one of these stings. Penalties can be draconian and include having your domain name, your IP address, and even pages registered under your domain name registration "handle" banned from a particular search engine. We'll review a full set of guidelines to protect you later on, but here's a quick list:

- Never use keywords in your META tags that do not apply to your site's content.

- Avoid repeating the same keyword dozens of times in a row on your page or in your META tags. List a keyword one to seven times, no more. Any more than that and you're entering the "danger zone."

- Do not create too many informational, doorway, or entry pages. It's good to create multiple doorway pages that each target different sets of keywords or topics related to your site, but do not be excessive! Search engines now watch for multiple submissions that appear the same or very similar. Try a couple of variations, submit them, then wait and see how you rank.

- The easiest way to get into trouble is to have three, four, or more of your pages all appear together in the matches for a single keyword search. One of your competitors will likely report you. This could get you banned from that search engine.

> **TIP** It's important to review your Web site and check your rankings for many keywords that appear in the text that makes up the different pages of your Web site. Often you'll find that your Web site did not rank well for one important keyword, but it may rank very well on some other keyword or phrase found on the page.

■ Avoid submitting too many pages at once. If you have 100 pages you need indexed, first review the rules of the particular search engine to make certain the search engine will index this number. We suggest you play it safe and break up your submissions. Submit half one day and half the next, avoiding any undocumented limits a search engine may have whereby they simply ignore your pages after a certain number of submissions. Also be wary of automated site submission tools that submit too many pages simultaneously.

■ Avoid submitting the same page twice on the same day. Generally, search engines will simply ignore a second submission. You can, however, rename the page and resubmit it, but again, don't abuse the system. Keep page variations to a minimum, follow up, and if you don't rank well for your keywords, redesign the page and submit it again. Consider it doorway page recycling.

Following up by checking your rank for many keywords in 18 or so major search engines sounds like a lot of work. It is. Some people tell us they spend 30 hours a week checking their rank for their important keywords. That's why WebPosition Gold was developed. It automatically checks a Web site's ranking in all of the major search engines for all the targeted keywords. And it does so unattended. If you're serious about working to attain top rankings in the major search engines, you need WebPosition Gold.
A free trial version is included on the CD that comes with this book.   **WebPosition GOLD**™

Chapter 6:

META Tags, Metadata, and Where to Place Keywords

or a long time, the term "META tags" conjured up notions of pure magic. People didn't quite know what they were, but they knew they were an integral part of search engine surfing. I remember a prospective client who attempted to sum up my one-hour presentation like this: "So basically, you're going to jigger with those meta-thingies on all of our Web pages and then the search engines will make us come up in the top spots. Well, we've known about these meta-things for some time, but just haven't really figured out what to do about them or who would be responsible for fixing them."

If you've ever heard Danny Sullivan, the editor of Search Engine Watch (www.searchenginewatch.com), give a speech, you know he has a great sense of humor. He has this META tag spiel that likens people's understanding of META tags to those late-night get-rich-quick infomercials: "All right, I'm going to show you how, by placing tiny bits of text in all of your Web pages, you can cause millions and millions of people to race to your Web site. YES, just by understanding THESE tiny bits of text, THESE hidden pieces of code, you can drive MILLIONS and MILLIONS of visitors to your Web site and earn MILLIONS and MILLIONS of dollars...FROM HOME!"

The point is, META tags are not mysterious. In fact, as far as SEP is concerned, META tags are the oldest and most elementary component of search engine optimization, and many search engines no longer weigh them heavily in determining a Web site's relevance to searches. The actual META tag is merely a place to insert "metadata." Metadata is simply data that describes other data. This is the site designer's opportunity to tell the search engine — or anyone else who cares to sneak a peek at the Web site's source code — what their document is about.

This chapter discusses all potential metadata — not just the actual META tags — including how to construct and use META tags and find the many other places in your site's HTML that search engines look for keywords and phrases. Remember: If search engines had their way, an independent third party would assign all metadata. Search engines have found that much of the self-assigned metadata that is included in Web sites by site owners and designers is unreliable. This means that there are Web site designers out there who think, "Well, I know I'm selling 'car parts,' but more people are searching for 'The Beatles,' so I'll add 'The Beatles' to my keyword META tag so that I'll attract more visitors." Is it any wonder that search engines pay little attention to self-assigned metadata?

As you can see, metadata is really just a way of "amplifying" the keyword content of your page and tilting its relevancy toward one keyword over another. For instance, your page may talk about record albums, CDs, and audio cassettes. If "audio cassettes" is really just an ancillary topic on your Web page, you should avoid amplifying that keyword by placing a copy of it in your META tags. If your Web site does talk about audio cassettes in some depth, you should place it in your metadata and META tags. The bottom line: If amplifying a phrase in your metadata causes your Web site to be returned in searches that do not attract interested parties, don't target that phrase in your metadata.

The classic search engines such as AltaVista and Excite send automated software spiders to capture all of the text that it can read on a Web page.

The Tag of All Tags: The META Tag

META tags are the HTML tags you place in your Web site's head section, which doesn't display in the browser window. META tags allow the developer to communicate certain information to the search engines, other automated services, and other Web developers about their site.

META tags let you tell a search engine's spider:

- The name of your site
- A site description you'd like the search engine to use
- The keywords and keyword phrases under which you'd like your site to be found

META tags give you some limited control over how your site is listed in spider-based search engines. If you don't include them in your document, the spider will likely take the first 25 words on your Web site and use them as the name and description! Perhaps you've seen a Web site listing like this:

[COMPANY] [INFORMATION] [PRODUCTS] [SERVICES] [OVERVIEW]
Hi, and thanks for taking the time to visit our company page. We hope you'll find...
http://www.some-dumb-company.com/ - size 22K - 22 Sept 96

This text is actually the navigation bar that the site developer included at the top of the Web page. The search engine's spider grabbed the first text it found. The result? Nothing about this listing is compelling. You have no idea what the company does or why you should visit the page.

META tags are easy to build. Just follow the format below and replace our title, description, and keywords with your own.

```
<HEAD>
<TITLE>big widgets and small widgets at widget-making-company.com</TITLE>
<META NAME="keywords" CONTENT="big small widgets making company">
<META NAME="description" CONTENT="big widgets and small widgets are
value priced at widget-making-company.com">
<!-- This is a comment tag, you can put keywords here, too, though few search
engines still consider keywords placed in this area of a site's HTML-->
</HEAD>
```

There are really only two META tags that search engines consider when evaluating a Web page: the description META tag and the keyword META tag. There are quite a few other META tags that you could include in your Web page, but all those others really just waste space and unnecessarily increase the file size and loading time of your page. Below is a list of some of the more popular META tags found in HTML:

```
<HEAD>
<META HTTP-EQUIV="Content-Type" CONTENT="text/html; charset=us-ascii">
<META NAME="resource-type" CONTENT="document">
<META NAME="description" CONTENT="This is the description of your
Web site">
<META NAME="keywords" CONTENT="keyword1, keyword2, keyword
phrase1, keyword phrase2">
<META NAME="distribution" CONTENT="Global">
<META NAME="copyright" CONTENT="Copyright 1999-2000 by name of copy-
right holder. All rights reserved, etc.">
<META NAME="author" CONTENT="name of author">
<META NAME="generator" CONTENT="Microsoft FrontPage 5.0">
<META NAME="robots" CONTENT="All">
<META NAME="rating" CONTENT="General">
</HEAD>
```

The only META tags you should use on your Web site are the ones highlighted in boldface above: keyword, description, and robots. There's little point in explaining each one, as none of the others has any impact on your Web site's ability to attain rankings in search engines. If you're dying to know what each META tag is for, visit this link:

http://www.weblecturer.com/lecturenotes/meta.html

A number of site designing software tools, including some versions of FrontPage, will automatically add many of these META tags into your Web pages as you build them. We recommend that if you use one of these tools, you should open your Web page in a text editor such as Notepad or WordPad and delete all but the keyword, description, and robots META tags.

Unfortunately, in addition to adding useless META tags to the head statement of your page, many Web site design tools change the order of the HTML tags in the head statement without the user's knowledge. The order of the HTML tags and even the META tags on your Web site is important because, as discussed in Chapter 5, search engines consider both keyword prominence and keyword placement in their relevancy calculations. In other words, search engines look at how early in the document keywords appear, and they weigh keywords in different types of HTML statements differently. Nearly all the major search engines assign great value to keywords found in the Web site's Title tag, so your Title tag should always be the very first HTML tag in the head statement. If a software tool moves the site's Title tag below the other META tags, the site's ranking can be adversely affected. We first discovered this problem with Microsoft's FrontPage and published a warning about it in the *MarketPosition Newsletter* (www.marketposition.com). Some time later, Microsoft finally got wind of this problem with their browser and began to include their own warning to users of their software at: http://support.microsoft.com/support/kb/articles/q182/6/15.asp.

The moral of the story: Double-check your site's head statement and make sure that the Title tag is ahead of the META tags.

For more info on this topic, visit http://www.accessfp.net/tutorial.htm #How to insert meta tags in FrontPage.

Other Important Tags

Listed below are the most important tags you will need to include in your code.

The Head Tag

Start your META tag section with <HEAD> and end with </HEAD> by adding the forward slash. All of your META tags should be contained within these two tags.

The Title Tag

Although the Title tag is not technically a "META tag," it is hands-down the most important HTML tag on your Web site. The Title tag displays the site's name, which will appear in the top of the browser. All major spider-driven search engines consider keywords found in the site's Title tag in their relevancy calculations — but what is the most common phrase found in the Title tag? You guessed it: "Welcome to Company.com!"

Excellent site title if you seek a high ranking on searches for the keywords "welcome" or "to." (I trust you sense my sarcasm.) Why not place your most important keywords ahead of your company name in the Title tag? How about:

```
<TITLE>keyword1, keyword2 and keyword3 information at
company.com"</TITLE>
```

Between these two Title tags, identify your site, making it sound interesting and worth visiting while trying to get as many of your keywords into it as possible. Always put your Title tag right after the <HEAD> code. Remember: Most search engines will use as their title for your site in the search results the contents of your Title tag exactly as you composed it.

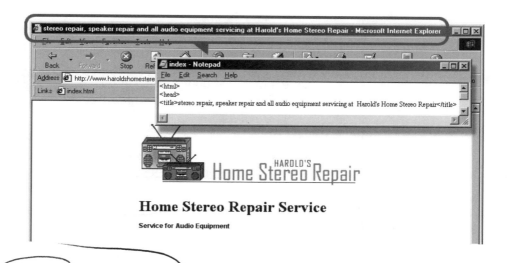

The Description META Tag

Keywords in
description META
tag

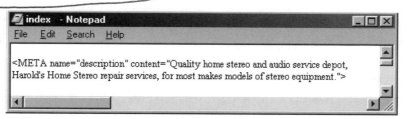

Some search engines allow you to write a description of your Web site that they'll use instead of randomly selecting copy from your pages. Here's how you use this tag:

<META NAME="Description" CONTENT="Description of your site.">

Start your description META tag like the above and follow it with generally not more than 25 tantalizing words describing your site. If you put the same description META tag on every page of your Web site, each page listed with a search engine will lead the searcher to believe that the page is identical to the others. There's value in writing unique description META tags for placement on each page of your Web site.

Some search engines, like Google, don't use the site's description META tag to describe your Web site in their results. Instead, Google uses "snippets," which are sections of text from the viewable page of the Web site that contain the targeted keyword or phrase, so that the searcher can see how the keyword was used on a particular Web page in context. We expect more and more search engines to move toward this method, because it simply provides better information on which a searcher can base a "click or no click" decision.

Even the search engines that do use the contents of the description META tag seldom rely on it for relevancy calculations. For this reason, there is no need to try to jam all of your targeted keywords into a sentence when constructing the description tag. Don't attempt to use the description META tag as an alternate keyword tag; better to think of it as a very short billboard ad. Worry instead about writing a compelling and interesting description of the contents of that particular page of your Web site.

The Keyword META Tag

This tag lets you suggest keywords to the search engines that you'd like your Web site to be returned on. Again, some search engines don't consider keywords included in this tag in their scoring of your Web site, but it's worth including for those that do. Here's how you use it:

```
<META NAME="Keywords" CONTENT="keyword1, keyword2, keyword3, Keyword phrase1, keyword phrase2">
```

There's an ongoing debate over the value of separating the words in your keyword META tag with commas. Most people include them. There is a school of thought, however, that says if you separate your keywords with commas you are forcing the search engine to consider the keywords or phrases individually, whereas leaving out the commas will allow the search engines to mix and match and perhaps find keyword combinations you hadn't considered. Don't lose sleep over this! The keyword META tag becomes less and less important every year as search engines find it to be generally unreliable, so don't worry too much about it. Just in case you're interested, sometimes we leave out the commas and sometimes we include them. Sometimes we just add commas randomly to confuse our competitors, and sometimes we add several commas in a row, in the middle of a list of keywords, just to confound people.

Keywords in META keyword tag (separated by commas)

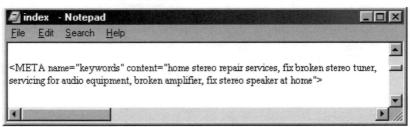

Keywords in
META keyword
tag (no commas)

Here's a more important tactic: Do not repeat keywords more than three times in your keyword META tags. We go so far as to take the following list of keywords:

Bike, mountain bike, road bike, dirt bike trail bike

And build a keyword META tag that looks like this:

<META NAME="Keywords" CONTENT="mountain bike road dirt trail">

The search engines will be able to pair road, dirt, and trail with the word bike, and who knows, maybe someone will search for a "dirt and trail bike," and our page will be returned because we didn't include the commas. Just to be consistent, you could construct this keyword META tag with lots of commas, like so:

<META NAME="Keywords" CONTENT="mountain bike, road, dirt, trail">

Or with just one comma:

<META NAME="Keywords" CONTENT="mountain bike road, dirt trail">

It really doesn't matter much, since these changes will have relatively little impact on your rankings. Remember, search engine algorithms are moving targets. What works one month might not work the next. It's best to have a few different tactics in play so you will notice when one starts working in a particular search engine.

I'm often asked how many keywords should be included in a keyword META tag or what each search engine's limit is for the number of characters they will read in the keyword META tag. If you're interested, we list the known character limits in our engine-by-engine chapters, but I'd urge you not to pay too much attention to such specifics. There's rarely a penalty for including too many keywords in a keyword META tag. More importantly, if your Web page covers so many topics that you need to ask this question, your Web page covers too many topics!

As a rule, if a word or phrase appears on the page, and the page is in fact about that word or phrase, include it in the keyword META tag. This is, after all, a META tag and is supposed to convey metadata or information about the page. However, if the keyword isn't viewable on the page, you probably shouldn't include it in the tag, because this approach is unlikely to attain a ranking.

> **NOTE**   A quick reminder on the directory difference: We've said this before, but it's important to remember: Directories such as Yahoo!, LookSmart, and the Open Directory don't consider any element of a Web site's HTML code when deciding how to list that site in their index. Directory services don't use automated software to index Web sites. Human editors visit your Web page and compare the site title to the description you provide to them (not necessarily identical to the site's Title tag and META description). Then they determine if your Web site is, in fact, consistent with your submission. If not, they edit your submission or reject it.

The Comment Tag

Keywords in
comment tag

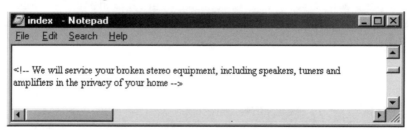

A comment tag is typically used to record comments about your Web site or HTML code that you don't want viewed on the actual page. This tag also can be used to include relevant keyword content when appropriate. Again, some search engines don't use this tag, and some don't even consider keywords included in it for scoring of your Web site. Use it this way:

> <!-- Here are some comments that visitors to your Web site won't be able to see in their browser because the words are included in this non-printing tag -->

Technically, comment tags are not considered part of the META tag family of HTML code, except that for Web site marketing purposes you can include these comments between <HEAD> and </HEAD> where the META tags go.

But you also can include comment tags throughout your Web site to further amplify the keyword content of your page.

> **NOTE**   Just as with the keyword META tag, placing a keyword or phrase in a comment tag that doesn't appear on the viewable page is counterproductive and usually will not result in a ranking for that keyword.

The only major search engine that still, we believe, considers the content of the comment tag is Inktomi. However, Inktomi powers several very important search engines, including results for HotBot, iWon, and many others. (For more details, see Chapter 21 for Inktomi search engine partnerships.)

Other Keyword Placement Opportunities

There are a few other places to include keywords which we discuss below.

Body Copy: Don't Overlook the Obvious

Search engines can do only two things: index text on the page and follow hypertext links. Possibly the most overlooked place on a Web page to include targeted keywords is in the actual viewable body copy of the Web site. You're probably not thinking, "What a revelation! What a unique and groundbreaking idea! Placing keywords in the actual viewable Web page... Eureka!" Well, believe it or not, the obvious is often overlooked. You'd be amazed at how much e-mail I receive from readers of my SEP guides asking me to review Web pages that include targeted keywords only in the META tags or Title tags and not on the viewable page. In fact, you probably shouldn't place keywords in any other area of the Web page if they do not first appear on the viewable page.

I'd like to nail this down so there is no misunderstanding, so I'll repeat: All metadata and META tags should come from the content of the actual Web page. Here's another interesting tidbit: Not all HTML that makes up the viewable page is equal in the eyes of a search engine algorithm. We will discuss the importance of placing keywords in headline tags, hyperlinks, image <ALT> tags, etc., but the viewable body copy is most important. There are several important places in the viewable pages where you should include your targeted keywords, as well as factors to consider when placing them.

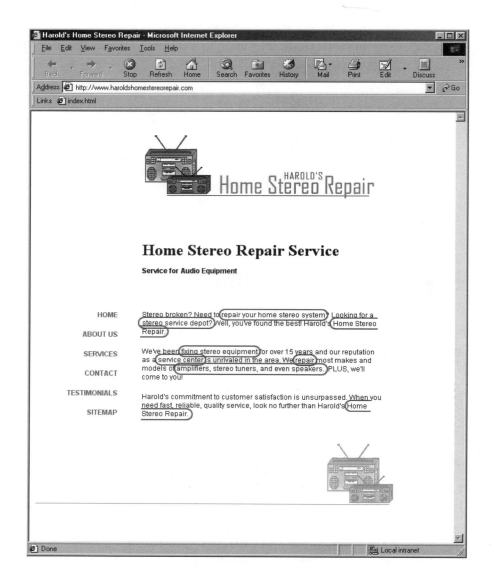

The First 25 Words of Copy on the Page

Search engines often place greater emphasis on keywords found early on a Web page, frequently using the first 25 words of the Web page for the description that appears in search results if you do not include a description META tag.

The Last 25 Words of Copy on the Page

I once interviewed a vice president at Lycos who revealed to me that their algorithm looked for keywords near the end of a Web page. At that time, they believed that all Web pages were constructed like college term papers — in a very hierarchical way. The Lycos search algorithm technicians felt that most Web pages would introduce a subject, talk about it, and then summarize it. Ergo, if a targeted keyword was near the end of a document, it was likely that the document was in fact about that keyword or phrase.

Near Other Related Keywords or Synonyms

Some search engines also consider how near to one another keywords are placed on the viewable page. If someone conducts a search on "foreign car parts," the Web page that includes these keywords consecutively scores higher than the Web page that includes the words "foreign car" in the first 25 words, but the word "parts" in the next paragraph, separated from the first part of the phrase by several dozen words. Some search engines, like Excite and Google, consider synonyms for various keywords included on a page. It may be beneficial when targeting a keyword like "automobile" to include the words "car," "vehicle," and "coupe" on the page near "automobile."

Pay Attention to the Keyword Weight of Your Page

Keyword weight is typically a limiting factor in that search engines use this metric mostly to determine which pages to red-flag as possible spammers. Overly aggressive Web site promoters have been known to repeat a keyword 10, 20, or even 100 times in a Web page in the hope of increasing their ranking on that keyword. For that reason, search engines measure keyword weight to determine when a page has too high a keyword density. By measuring how many occurrences of a keyword millions and millions of Web pages in the general population include when a Web page is, in fact, about a particular keyword, the search engine algorithm writers can determine what the "average" keyword weight should be. The targeted number varies from engine to engine and from month to month. We recommend experimenting with different keywords weights, but use a 5 to 15 percent rule of thumb for any one keyword as your baseline.

Emphasized Keywords in the Body Copy Get Special Attention

Keywords in the body copy that are emphasized, by the use of bold or italic type, for example, are often given increased weight by search engine algorithms. To emphasize a keyword by bolding it, simply place a <B> before the keyword and then a </B> after it. To italicize a keyword, place an <I> before the keyword and then an </I> after the keyword. The <STRONG> and </STRONG> tags seem to have a similar power to emphasize words in the body copy.

The lesson here is that you should make every effort to carefully evaluate the keyword content of your viewable page before you begin populating your META tags and other metadata areas. To overlook the viewable page and focus entirely on the META tags is a recipe for failure.

The <H1> Through <H6> Heading Tags

Headings are the larger print or subtitles on a page. The smaller the number in the heading tag, the larger the font size. For example, <H1> is larger than <H3>. Search engines generally value keywords and text found in heading tags more highly than those found in other text on your pages because text found in headings usually identifies a particular theme or section of content.

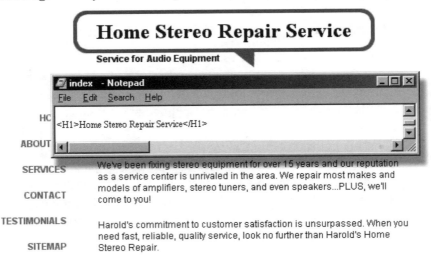

Repeat your most important keywords and phrases in the heading tags just as you do with the Title tag for the page. Here's an example of a page with heading tags:

```
<HTML>
<HEAD>
<TITLE>Widgets and More!</TITLE>
<META name="description" content="Widgets by Jerry's Widget Emporium are
the best widgets money can buy.">
<META name="keywords" content="widgets blue green red Jerry's Widget
Emporium">
</HEAD>

<BODY>
<H1>Widgets Explained:</H1>
Widgets by Jerry's Widget Emporium are the best widgets money can buy.</P>
</BODY>
</HTML>
```

The above example assumes "widget" is the most important keyword, which is why it is used in the heading tag as well as the title and the body. Use multiple heading tags throughout your page if you like, but always try to include the keywords you are seeking to emphasize or amplify. If you're using Microsoft FrontPage or another WYSIWYG editor, it should allow you to select a heading "style" or give you some other way to visually create the equivalent to an HTML heading tag.

It helps to keep the page content focused on a single theme and a limited number of keywords so you don't dilute the effectiveness of the page. Avoid the temptation to write about things unrelated to "widgets" or your primary keywords; this will only serve to broaden the keyword concentration of a particular Web page. It also helps to use your keyword at the beginning of the Title tag, the heading, and first paragraph. When you're having a tough time getting a high ranking for a targeted keyword, having the keyword in the first position rather than as the second or third can make all the difference.

> **TIP**   Notice that we purposely use the plural form of the word "widget" to double our visibility. Always add an s to your targeted keywords or phrases whenever possible. That way you'll likely gain a ranking for both the singular and plural form of the word.

Don't Forget Links

The "widget" example can be improved by taking advantage of another scoring technique favored by some engines. The text within a link is sometimes weighed more heavily than words found in the regular body text. I'm always surprised when I visit a Web page and the designer has included a link on the page that suggests that a user should "click here" for more information on a topic, and the words "click here" are the activated link. This is only a good idea if you seek to attain a ranking on searches for "click" or "here." If you insist on using these words in your link, how about "click for more information on keyword phrase," with the keyword phrase as the activated link?

Here's our revised "widget" example:

```
<HTML>
<HEAD>
<TITLE>Widgets and More!</TITLE>
<META name="description" content="Widgets by Jerry's Widget Emporium are
the best widgets money can buy.">
<META name="keywords" content="widgets blue green red Jerry's Widget
Emporium">
</HEAD>

<BODY>
<H1>Widgets Explained:</H1>
Widgets by Jerry's Widget Emporium are the best widgets money can buy.</P>
To learn about our widgets, choose one of the following:
<A HREF="blue-widgets.htm">Blue Widgets</A>
<A HREF="red-widgets.htm">Red Widgets</A>
<A HREF="green-widgets.htm">Green Widgets</A>
</BODY>
</HTML>
```

The preceding example emphasizes the keyword "widget" as well as other phrases people might search on, such as "blue widget." Most people search on two or more words to narrow the scope of their search, so always include related keywords together whenever possible.

The visible text of the links is where you primarily want to include your keywords. It's also a good idea to create your page names based on your best keywords. That way you score a few more keyword points for the occasional search engine that indexes the page name portion of the link tag as well (as we've done in the example above).

Make sure to annotate links whenever possible. Most search engines, especially Google, consider the text located near the link in considering relevancy.

The <ALT> Tag

The <ALT> tag is an HTML tag used to describe a graphic on your Web page. Often this tag is used simply to describe the graphic a visitor sees when the page finishes loading. Sometimes it's used to describe a photo or graphic that the user never sees. For instance, if the person visiting the site is browsing the Web in the "graphics off" mode, they see the text you place in the <ALT> tag instead of the graphic. People do this when they don't want to be bogged down by slow-loading images.

The <ALT> tag can include targeted keywords. Some search engines will read and assign points to keywords contained in this tag. Again, consult the engine-by-engine chapters in Part 3.

Here's how to use the <ALT> tag:

```
<IMG SRC="manonscooter.gif" ALT ="This is the picture of a man on a scooter">
```

And here's how to use the <ALT> tag to yield a keyword advantage:

```
<IMG SRC="manonscooter.gif" ALT ="keyword1, keyword2, keyword3,
keyword4, keyword5, keyword6">
```

In a recent interview with executives at Google, I asked how they evaluate the content of a Web page that contains only graphical content and no HTML text. Their answer was telling and simple: "Add <ALT> tags to all of the images." AHA! Clearly, in the absence of other metadata or indexable text, Google weights the keywords found in the image <ALT> tag heavily. As a rule, the contents of the image <ALT> tag by itself will not help a Web site gain top rankings in search engines. But when you include accurate metadata — rich with keywords that are consistent with words found in the Title tag, headline tags, body copy, links, etc. — in the image <ALT> tag, you're creating a winning recipe for top rankings.

Keywords in
<ALT> tag

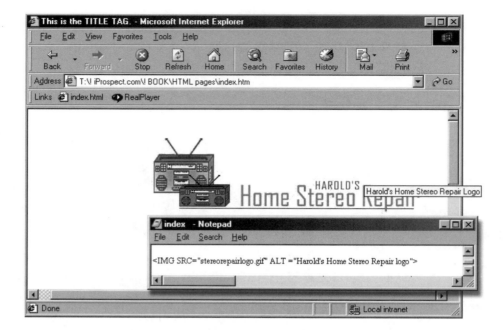

More Options

Following is a list of places where you can include keywords to affect your rank in search engines. The point here is for you to understand the scope of variables you have at your disposal to impact your site's theme — or more importantly, what a site listed ahead of yours in a particular search engine might have done to outrank you. Many of these are described in greater detail in the preceding section.

- Keywords in the Title tag (very important)
- Keywords in the description META tag
- Keywords in the keyword META tag
- Keywords contained in the META author tag
- Keywords in the META http-equiv tag
- Keywords in <H1> or other heading tags (very important)
- Keywords in the link text (very important)
- Keywords in the viewable body copy

- ■ Keywords emphasized in some way in the viewable body copy
- ■ Keywords in the image <ALT> tags
- ■ Keywords in comment tags
- ■ Keywords contained in the top-level domain name
- ■ Keywords in the page filename
- ■ Keywords in the <NOFRAMES> tag of a Web page (if your Web site is "framed")
- ■ Keywords contained in image filenames
- ■ Keywords contained in file link filenames
- ■ Keywords contained in file link filenames to external resources, not just internal links

While these are acceptable places to include keywords, you may be spamdexing, according to some search engines, if the page wouldn't ordinarily contain or need this HTML as part of its design.

Where Not to Place Keywords

The above list of places to insert keywords might be considered "overly aggressive" (to be polite) or just inappropriate, depending on your standards. The test to determine this is to ask yourself whether you would have included the particular HTML element in the design of your Web site if not but for your desire to attain search engine rankings.

Some search engines have identified some of the techniques listed below as violating their policies. I think that most search engines look askance at any HTML you place on your Web page that is intended only to "trick" their algorithm. Search engines have no recourse against people who use unconventional HTML code in designing their Web sites other than adjusting their algorithm to penalize or ignore certain types of HTML code.

However, if you discover that placing one of your targeted keywords in the sixth position in the keyword META tag gains you a significant increase in rankings (it doesn't, by the way), and that this is due to some oversight or peculiarity in a particular search engine's ranking algorithm which even the search engine

may not be aware of, then there is no moral, ethical, or other obligation to avoid this technique.

NOTE: Although there are no state, local, or federal laws governing how you design or code your Web page, the terms *spamming* and *spamdexing* can and have been stretched to include anything that irritates someone at a particular search engine.

Pushing HTML Beyond Its Intended Use

The following represent examples of what I call "pushing HTML." In most cases, the HTML elements either do not or would not include keyword content, or the specific HTML is included on a Web page in spite of the fact that it is not needed or used by the Web page. It is not inappropriate to have an input type HTML statement on a Web page as a part of any number of scripts (the first example below), and it is not inappropriate to include keywords in such a form field. However, in "pushing HTML," some Web marketers include a hidden form field, for example, on pages where it is neither functional nor part of the Web page design. As such, it is just a hidden HTML statement stuffed with keywords. Below is a laundry list of the remaining HTML statements that can, but probably shouldn't, include keywords. While we don't use these techniques, it is helpful for those studying SEP to be aware of how others are coding their HTML for SEP campaigns.

■   Keywords contained in an input type hidden statement (now widely considered spamdexing by search engines).

```
<INPUT TYPE="HIDDEN" NAME="HIDDEN" VALUE="include list of keywords
here"> hidden type tag.
```

■   Keywords included in the head statement, as a homemade HTML tag of sorts.

```
<HEAD keywords="keyword1, keyword2, keywords3">
```

■   Keywords in comment tags that are placed before the begin HTML statement of a Web page, or even after the end HTML statement. Because most search engines have stopped considering keywords found in the comment tag, this technique is unlikely to produce an effect greater than placing keywords in any comment tag.

```
<!-- keyword1, keyword2, keyword3, keyword4, keyword5-->
<HTML>
<HEAD>
<TITLE>Welcome to my home page</TITLE>
etc.
```

■ Keywords improperly included in the <ALT> text of background images. The background of a Web page doesn't ordinarily contain <ALT> text. However, since <ALT> text is generally not weighted very heavily by search engines, including your keywords in the <ALT> tag is unlikely to produce results better than including keywords in any <ALT> tag on the document.

```
<body background="graphic/background.gif" ALT="keyword1, keyword2"
bgcolor="black">
```

■ Keywords improperly included in a font tag.

```
<FONT COLOR="keyword1, keyword2, keyword3"></FONT>
```

■ Keywords included in a style tag (AltaVista and Excite have been known to index text included in the style tag) when a style sheet is not called for or being used. The purpose of the cascading style sheets is to enable a Web designer to stipulate one set of page formatting commands, instead of having to specify each font size, weight, headline color, etc., over and over again. This command is usually placed in the head of the document, and some clever Web marketer discovered that some search engines had neglected to "turn off" this page element in their search engine algorithm. I'm guessing that this was an oversight on the part of the search engines, because the style tag doesn't, or at least shouldn't, ordinarily contain any reliable META information about a Web page. It is only intended to communicate page-formatting information to specific browsers. Therefore, we argue that to use this HTML tag to gain an advantage in search engine ranking is ethically questionable, and likely to be squashed by the search engines.

```
<STYLE>keyword1, keyword2, keyword3</STYLE>
```

Cascading style sheets, or CSS, is a complicated topic and may require more examination for those new to HTML. Follow either of these links for more about HTML style tags or cascading style sheets:

HMTLGoodies cascading style sheet tutorial:
http://htmlgoodies.earthweb.com/tutors/ie_style.html

About.com's cascading style sheet tutorial:
http://html.about.com/compute/html/library/weekly/aa111000a.htm

■ Keywords in a <NOFRAMES> tag, even though the site is not a framed site. Frames are used to split a Web browser's screen in order to display multiple Web pages. You've probably seen a framed Web site before, as they are still pretty common. Typically, the left side of the screen will contain a long list of links. When you select any of them, the right side of the page will refresh and display the new Web page. Most of the major search engines have not been able to follow the links or index more than the first frame that contains the links (usually such search engines index only the left-side navigation text and none of the pages that appear when you select any of those links). Text within a <NOFRAMES> statement or tag is typically presented to someone viewing a framed Web page with an older browser that is non-frames-compliant (it can't read or format the framed content for proper viewing). In these cases, the non-frames-compliant browser is served an alternate Web page that is contained in the <NOFRAMES> statement. Traditionally, this has been the favored workaround for SEP professionals because the search engines would gladly index all of the content of the <NOFRAMES> statement and then follow all of the links, thereby finding and indexing all of the other pages contained in the Web site. However, a <NOFRAMES> statement can be included in any Web page, whether or not it's a framed Web site, and will be invisible to an unknowing visitor to the Web site. Search engines often consider the content of the <NOFRAMES> statement toward a Web page's overall keyword weight, even if the page is not actually a framed Web site. Placing a <NOFRAMES> tag on a Web site that doesn't contain frames is dubious at best and will likely be frowned upon by the search engines. Here is an example of the proper use of the <NOFRAMES> statement:

```
<NOFRAMES>
<HEAD>
<TITLE>Widgets and More!</TITLE>
<META name="description" content="Widgets by Jerry's Widget Emporium are
the best widgets money can buy.">
<META name="keywords" content="widgets blue green red Jerry's Widget
Emporium">
</HEAD>
<BODY>
<H1>keyword1, keyword2, keyword 3, keyword 4</H2>
Keyword-rich body copy, more keyword-rich body copy, lots of <BR>keywords in
```

```
the body copy and even more keyword phrases in the body copy
<A HREF="/folder/filename.htm"></A>
</BODY>
</NOFRAMES>
```

My favorite tutorial on <FRAMES> and <NOFRAMES> was written by Joe Burns, author and editor of the HTMLGoodies.com Web site. Here's a link to it if you'd like to learn more:

http://htmlgoodies.earthweb.com/tutors/frame1.html

We strongly discourage the use of frames. They are problematic for dozens of reasons, not the least of which has to do with poor SEP potential.

HTML Elements That Spiders Ignore

Search engine spiders are not very sophisticated. They like simple and easy-to-parse HTML. Most search engine spider software was written back when virtually all Web sites had gray backgrounds, almost no graphics, and lots of text. Almost all of them had a big, fat, bold heading statement (an <H1> or <H2> tag) in the middle of the page that proclaimed something like "Joe's Web site" or "Donna's Chicken Soup Recipe." Remarkably, search engine spiders still favor Web sites that are just that simple! Web design has left the spider behind. Since humans are bound to use the latest and most complicated technology, whether warranted or not, many Web sites are built without any consideration for how they will fare in search engines. We devote Chapter 10 in its entirety to savvy search engine design — designing Web sites with an eye toward getting them listed in the major engines, that is. But for our purposes here, it's important to take note of HTML elements that slow search engines down or are unreadable.

Keywords in JavaScript

JavaScript is programming code. Even if you've coded a JavaScript to produce a long sentence full of keywords to scroll across your Web page, the search engines likely can't read any of those words. In fact, search engines seem to all but ignore the JavaScript contained in HTML documents.

Years ago, one of the Web pages in my company Web site listed several of our clients' names and links to their Web sites. We enjoyed rankings on searches for virtually every client name in most of the major search engines. One day, a new employee decided to write a JavaScript that created a pull-down menu with all of our clients' names. When someone selected this pull-down menu and scrolled to the client name and selected it, the script would automatically link to that client's Web page. (It was a novel script at that time — now it's commonplace.) But an odd thing happened: In about a month's time, we lost every ranking for searches on any of our clients' company names! The search engines, we discovered, were unable to parse the JavaScript source code and read the company names and links to their Web sites. In essence, they ignored all keyword and link content from the beginning to the end of the JavaScript.

Worse, JavaScript is usually included early in Web pages so that it will load first and take advantage of the "gee-whiz" factor. That pushes your body copy farther down the Web page, decreasing the prominence of the targeted keywords and phrases that naturally occur on your site. A great tutorial on how to fold all of your JavaScript into a file can be found at this Web site:

http://html.tucows.com/programmer/tips/tips-jsFile.html

Netscape posted its own Help document on how to remove the JavaScript code from your Web page and place it in a .js file:

http://help.netscape.com/kb/consumer/19970303-2.html

Keywords Contained in Graphics

Search engine spiders cannot read or recognize the text contained in a graphic image. They can't perform optical character recognition (OCR). All they see is a bunch of picture.jpg or graphic.gif files. If your site is graphic intensive and much of the copy is contained in an image, you have a serious SEP problem. There may be nothing for the search engine to index on your page. If you have no choice but to use graphics, write the copy that is contained in the graphics in the image <ALT> tags. That will help a bit with some search engines, but not all. Excite, for instance, doesn't index or recognize the image <ALT> tag. If at all possible, do what you can to include representative copy on your pages that discusses the same information contained in the graphic. In extreme cases, we've been forced to create informational pages that contain information about topics described only in large graphics.

Additional Keyword Placement Considerations

Many people experiment with their site's HTML in order to produce a better-looking or even higher-ranking HTML page. If you misuse HTML and place your targeted keywords in various tags in an effort to fool the search engines, you will likely be successful for a short while. It is not a wise long-term strategy. And you run the risk of irritating the good folks at the search engines who have total and complete control over their index and can ban your site from their index without even telling you of your violation. In fact, the search engines may make a new rule tomorrow based on some technique you've just invented and implemented, decide that you've offended them or broken this new rule, and ban your site from their index. They are the judge, jury, and executioner. Why "push the envelope" and test their patience?

Building relevant, keyword-rich content where the targeted keywords are contained in the important HTML elements is a good long-term strategy. If you place keywords in the body copy, in the site's Title and META tags, and in activated links, and then work to increase the number of links from external sources to your Web site, you'll attain rankings. I caution my staff against working in a "false economy." You may think you're saving time, but if you apply an overly aggressive tactic and the engines find you out, you'll spend more time undoing the damage, i.e., changing all of the pages you've built that contain the offending HTML code and fixing it, writing apology letters to the search engines, and making calls to them, hoping to learn if your site is banned or not.

Much success can be achieved by working with above-the-board, visible HTML. There may be a slight benefit to reordering your site's META tags or moving the Title tag for a slight benefit in one search engine or another. You can place the description META tag before the Title tag and see what happens in each engine, and from time to time, you'll likely gain a position or two. But tweaking HTML tags that were never intended for metadata so that they can contain your keywords is, in the long run, folly.

You can place your keyword META tag ahead of your description META tag or ahead of your Title tag and watch what happens. In most cases, reordering your HTML tags will provide only a modest incremental advantage in rankings and it will likely be short lived. Search engines change their ranking algorithms frequently, and these "tricks" are not likely to produce a high ranking for any valuable length of time. The search engines will discover them and target users for a penalty or simply disable them. Case in point: In our first book we explained that adding an extra Title tag to a Web page would increase rankings.

```
<HEAD>
<TITLE>keyword1, keyword2, keyword phrase3, company name</TITLE>
<TITLE>keyword1, keyword2, keyword phrase3, company name</TITLE>
</HEAD>
```

The search engines discovered this technique (probably after reading our first book) and changed their algorithm so that the continued use of it had no effect (or possibly even a slight penalty). Those who employed the technique enjoyed several months of high rankings on the most competitive keywords. When the technique stopped working, all of those pages had to be changed. Was it worth it? For some smaller Web sites, yes. For others, no. A lot of time has passed since we published our first SEP guide, and many of the techniques we reported or espoused have fallen out of favor with the search engines. Here today, spam tomorrow. We've done our level best to only espouse the techniques that work and that we feel will remain valuable in the long run.

We encourage Web marketers to invest their time in making sure that their HTML documents contain the targeted keywords in several different places and that the metadata is accurate and complete. Compare your keyword frequency, prominence, and weight with higher-ranking documents. Compare your link popularity with other Web documents and work to improve it. This is all you need to do to increase your rankings in search engines.

How to Create Effective Site Titles and Descriptions

Now that you've discovered all of the many places in your HTML you can include keywords, let's concentrate on the two most important ones: titles and descriptions. These places are not the most important in terms of their ability to improve rankings in the search engines, or in terms of the search engine's algorithm, but are the most important in terms of their ability to compel someone to visit your Web site. That is, after all, the ultimate goal of search engine positioning, isn't it? Not a lot of point in attaining a top ranking in a search engine if you're just going to call your site "Shop Here."

Keep one eye on the prominence and frequency of your keywords in the title and description of your Web site and another eye on the weight of those keywords as a percentage of the total number of words that make up your first page. You'll need to find a third eye to keep on the appeal of the statements you make in your description of the Web site.

The following title and description may get you a high ranking for a keyword search on the word "mortgage."

Mortgage banking, the Mortgage Money Lenders
Mortgage, lenders, money, mortgages, mortgage money, mortgage loans, home equity loans, mortgage money,

What it says, however, is unappealing. Instead, look at another site description that would also rank highly, and see which site you would be more likely to visit:

Mortgage Applications Approved Overnight
Mortgages and mortgage financing techniques that the larger banks just can't offer. Learn the eight important things to include on your application so that your mortgage can be approved in 24 hours, even if you have poor credit.

The listing above has the word "mortgage" as the first word of the title and the first word of the description, and contains the word "mortgage" a total of four times. The difference is that this description is compelling, solves a problem, and offers "eight important things" or pieces of information that could be valuable to consumers visiting the site. It creates curiosity, too: What are those eight things? (For the record, I don't know what they are, I just made it up.)

Direct response companies, those firms that make infomercials and send you all that annoying direct mail, have studied and mastered the art of writing headlines. They learned that headlines are most effective when they accomplish four things:

- Solve a problem
- Solve that problem quickly
- Solve that problem for what appears to be a small or reasonable amount of money
- Make the reader curious to learn more

With that in mind, the following headline is acceptable, but not as effective as it could be:

"I can help you to get out of debt and get a good credit rating — I've done it for others; I can do it for you!"

A better approach is to use a headline that will draw more inquiries:

"Correct your bad credit in under a week for less than $49!"

The second example solves a problem, does so quickly, and shows how much money is involved. People relate to this appeal because it has a fundamental basis. Remember one of the many adages about goal setting: "A goal without a deadline is a wish!" Or, how about what they teach you in business school about proposal writing: "Never offer a plan that doesn't include both time and money."

The direct response model is effective because it addresses these things, especially time and money. As you write your page description and title, think about this. Then ask yourself before you submit them to the search engines:

- Is my title compelling?
- Is it interesting?
- Will it make someone curious to learn more?
- Would I read it and want to visit the site?
- Does it include time and money?
- Does it solve a problem?
- Does it suggest that it solves that problem quickly?
- Does it show a price? (Only emphasize the price if yours is very attractive.)

Be careful! You don't want to offend anyone's intelligence; many direct marketers write headlines that underestimate readers. Read it yourself and make a determination if you would find the title interesting — if you don't, you can be sure that others won't either. This direct response model doesn't apply universally in its purest form. Many Web sites do not sell things directly and are informational in nature or support what ad execs would call image advertising. But do not overlook this fundamental truth:

Being first in the search engines is great, but being first **and** compelling is better! If the description of the site directly below yours is more compelling, you lose.

Writing Killer Page Titles

We begin with what is arguably the most important element of your Web site: the Title tag. All the search engines give keywords in this tag a lot of importance in their ranking systems. Many engines use this Title tag as the title of your site returned in their search results. Don't just work your HTML tag for keyword scoring; make your tag compelling.

Of course, both the title and the description META tag must be compelling, but the Title tag has special relevance, because so many search engines use the title exactly as it appears on your page. Some search engines will use the site description that you give in the META tags, but others will not. For this reason, the title of the site is more important than the site description.

Longer Titles are More Effective, Because More Words Allow You to Build a More Compelling Reason to Visit a Web Site

Because it takes a certain number of words to persuade someone to take action, logic dictates that longer sentences have more opportunity to create that compelling argument. It is difficult to discuss time, money, value, and the problem that the Web site solves in just two or three words. People often scan headlines in brochures and magazines, even when they don't read all the information. Since the title is usually a hyperlink, it is a different color, and it is generally bolded and easier to read than the site's description in the search engine listing. When it's longer, there are more words with which to "hook" a reader. If something catches the reader's eye as they scroll down a list of site titles, they will hopefully read the site description. If you've done your work, they'll be hooked.

People Don't Read Text, They Recognize Words

People don't read individual letters after about the time they turn 12 years old; they recognize words. Educators know that people glance at words and recognize the words by the shapes defined by the tops of the letters. If you don't believe it, take a sentence in any newspaper or book and cover the bottom half of the words. You can still read the words with relative ease. Now, cover the top of a different sentence. You'll find that the words are harder to read because there is not much difference in the shape or line of the bottom of the words. Interesting, but how does this apply here?

Here's how: Since people recognize words because the tops of words vary in height and appearance, then sentences that start with just one capital letter and then use lowercase letters are easier to recognize and get read faster. Every little advantage helps you!

WORDS IN ALL CAPS ARE HARD TO READ. PEOPLE DON'T LIKE TO READ THEM AND DON'T READ THEM AS EASILY. RECOGNIZING THE WORDS IN THE SENTENCES IS TEDIOUS, AND THESE LISTINGS ARE FREQUENTLY OVERLOOKED.

To further illustrate the "tops of words" principle, look at how difficult it is to read this sentence:

SeNtEnCeS ThAT VaRy CaPs AnD LoWErCaSe LeTtErS ArE mAdDEnInG AnD EvEn HarDeR To ReAd.

See what a difference the tops of words can make? For this reason, construct your Title tags and site title submissions with just one capital letter to start the tag, then use lowercase letters for the rest of the site title — maybe even for your company name. This technique is just one more advantage that you can realize over your Web site's competitors in search results.

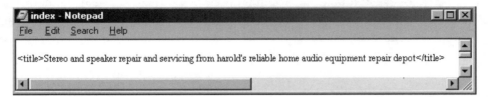

Include Your Phone Number

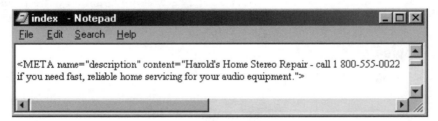

Include your phone number in your site's title and description META tag if you operate a store or other business that people are accustomed to picking up the telephone and calling. I've seen this used to great effect with flower shops. Often I've dialed the phone number without ever visiting the Web site! A true example: When I searched Google last year for "florist Columbus, Ohio," the search results came back with a match just like this in the top 10:

Compari Florist Columbus Ohio, 43215
100 Main Street Columbus, Ohio 43215, (614) 555-5555 — call us today
for fast delivery of flowers and chocolates for that special someone.
http://www.some-smart-florist-in-ohio.com Cached - Similar pages

Guess what? They got my business right away. Why? I could call them instantly without having to even visit the Web page.

This may not be a good technique for all businesses. However, any retail establishment, like a bicycle store, furniture store, or certainly a catalog retailer, would be wise to consider including their telephone number in their META tags so that it comes up right away. How many times have you performed a search for someone like L.L. Bean or Peet's Coffee just because you're looking up their phone number? I do it all the time. If I could find that phone number in the search results, I would be a more satisfied customer.

Some of these companies, especially the e-tailers, would prefer that I place my orders on their Web site or use their customer service e-mail address, instead of calling them. They seek to limit telephone inquiries. If they include their address or telephone number somewhere on their Web site, they will receive a call. If you operate or work for such a company, one tactic is to include your company's telephone number in the META tag of your contact or customer service page only. If people search for "L.L. Bean customer service" or "L.L. Bean 800 number" or maybe "L.L. Bean customer service number," this will hopefully cause your telephone number to be displayed in the search results for those queries exclusively. I recognize that this tactic is not foolproof, and depending on the search engine, how many pages of a particular Web site they have indexed, and how their algorithm is tweaked that month, the page that lists the company telephone number in the Title or description META tag may or may not turn up in a search on "*company name* contact information." When it does, your customers will know that your team took that extra effort to make their lives a little bit easier.

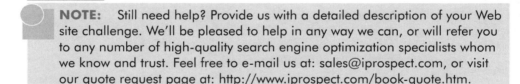

NOTE: Still need help? Provide us with a detailed description of your Web site challenge. We'll be pleased to help in any way we can, or will refer you to any number of high-quality search engine optimization specialists whom we know and trust. Feel free to e-mail us at: sales@iprospect.com, or visit our quote request page at: http://www.iprospect.com/book-quote.htm.

Chapter 7:

Domain Name Selection

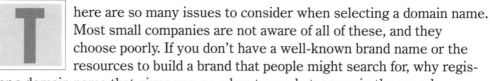

There are so many issues to consider when selecting a domain name. Most small companies are not aware of all of these, and they choose poorly. If you don't have a well-known brand name or the resources to build a brand that people might search for, why register a domain name that gives you no advantage whatsoever in the search engines, where people search for your product or service? The worst offenders are small consultants who operate under three-letter acronym names that mean nothing to most people.

Additionally, you can never own too many domain names. That's a rather bold statement, but think about the implications. If you have just one domain name, and just one Web site, you have limited your ability to attain rankings, to be found in search engines and directories, and to take on your competitors. We know of one company in the flower business that has 40 or maybe 50 different domain names. They show up in search engines on searches for different kinds of flower arrangements (they have sites dedicated to different types of flowers and arrangements), gift baskets, and even localities, e.g., "Columbus Ohio florists," etc.

NOTE This strategy is not about redirecting users, but about building legitimate, bona fide Web sites and placing unique compelling content on each domain name — actual Web sites with actual value.

Developing a Domain Name Strategy

Of the many page elements that can contain your targeted keyword, perhaps the one most often overlooked is the top-level domain name. Some spider-based search engines, however, favor Web sites that contain the targeted keyword in the root domain name. For this reason, we recommend that when you register domain names you keep one eye on your search engine positioning interests.

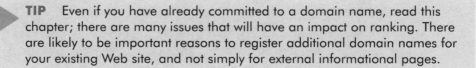

TIP Even if you have already committed to a domain name, read this chapter; there are many issues that will have an impact on ranking. There are likely to be important reasons to register additional domain names for your existing Web site, and not simply for external informational pages.

We include a link to what we have found to be the best deal on domain name registration services on the companion CD. Simply load the CD and click on the BulkRegister.com icon.

Brainstorming for a good domain name can be a time-consuming, if not maddening, exercise. Let's talk about how to pick a domain name, both in general and for the benefit of a search engine positioning program.

Tactic #1: Use Catchy But Relevant Keywords

Unless you have brand awareness, meaning a company or product name so well known that thousands of people are likely to search for you by name, register a domain name that includes keywords describing your product or service.

If you operate a company that offers custom Visual Basic programming services and the company name is "Practical Computer Programming Services Corporation," do not register the name as pcpsc.com — this tells the user nothing about your company and is hard to remember. If your company is named after the founders or partners, perhaps an environmental engineering company named Smith and Jones, LLC, we would advise against registering the domain name smith-and-jones.com (or worse yet, saj.com). Instead, choose something like environmental-engineers.com, or site-remediation.com, or asbestos-removal.com. These domain names contain important keyword phrases and improve your odds of being found in the major search engines.

Tactic #2: Rename Your Company

If you have not yet selected a company name, remember this: Yahoo! lists companies by their names — literally using the company name as the activated link. If the Web is important to your lead generation or sales efforts, nothing will be more important to you than your listing in Yahoo!. If you do not have the marketing budget to "build brand," there is enormous value to picking a company name and domain name that contain targeted keywords for the benefit of your directory listing. If your company has been around for a while and people know the name, think long and hard about whether or not they would care if you renamed your company. A poor company name — one that does not contain keywords — can weigh you down like an anchor in the ocean of search engines. A company name that starts with an alphabetically advantageous letter can also improve directory listings. See Chapter 11 on Yahoo! for more on the ASCII alphabetical hierarchy and some symbols that rank even higher than the letter "A."

Tactic #3: Pick a Name That Doesn't Exist in the English Language

Because we are very well known, people search for our firm by name. Go into just about any engine and conduct a search on our company name, "iProspect." Since the word does not exist in the English language, there are few, if any, documents that compete with ours for ranking. As a result, if you know our company's name, you will find our Web site in just about every search engine.

Our company's original name was ResponseDirect.com, which everyone mistook to be a direct-mail marketing company. We decided to change it for this reason and also because we were competing for rankings with every direct marketing agency and hundreds of thousands of companies whose names contained either the word "direct" or "response" — quite a large playing field, indeed.

We brainstormed company names for months. We wanted something that sounded unequivocally Internet-centric, but our criteria dictated that it had to have an available domain name. At first we liked "equalify.com" but found out the domain name had already been registered by someone. We liked the name because it suggested the highly qualified nature of the traffic that search engines refer. In the end, we abandoned the name because someone pointed out that it also sounded too much like the deadly bacteria *E. coli*. Then one day, I was using my ACT! contact management software and noticed the splash screen, which touted it to be "the world's best prospect management software." The word "prospect" jumped out at me. Because building qualified traffic is, in essence, about driving Internet prospects to a Web site, it just fit. We placed the letter "i" in front of the word prospect so that we'd be in vogue, like the rest of the "e" this and "i" that companies of the time.

We conducted searches in all of the major search engines for the phrase and determined that most had no matching Web sites — literally no search results for that word. We checked with our attorneys, ran a trademark search, registered the domain name (which, remarkably, was still available), and formally changed the company name.

In our industry category, there are some 250 recent entries into the search engine positioning space, all with names like "top ranking first place company," followed by "search positioning ranking placement," and the ever popular "!!! #1 exclamation point search engine ranking first placement co." (Yes, some company actually spelled out the word "exclamation point" in their company name and on their Web site in the hope that Yahoo! would keep the exclamation points at the start of their company name and help them garner a top ranking.) And, as noted in Chapter 11, in the desperate race for the top spots in Yahoo!, our industry segment is filled with company names that look and sound like the curse words in comic strips. I don't recommend you go this far. All of these companies compete for the low end of the market and probably don't have the budget to build a brand or to stand out, since they all seem to offer the same service at similar prices. For this reason, their search engine rankings on the keywords that prospective customers might look for when seeking a vendor matter a great deal to them.

It's hard to tell one from another. For this reason, we opted for a company name that's unique and brand-centric. In your industry category, it may not be so cluttered, so make your decision accordingly.

Tactic #4: Don't Pick an Easily Pluralized Domain Name

Unless you want somebody to steal your traffic, think about domain names that are already plural or that can't be pluralized by the simple addition of an "s." If you register *frame-master.com*, just wait a week. Someone will probably register *frame-masters.com* in hopes of stealing some of your customers. One benefit of registering the plural form of a word is that you'll likely gain the ranking for the singular and plural forms. Let's say you operate a company that rents table linens for banquets, weddings, and other special occasions. People probably don't search for the word "linens" — that's industry vernacular. They probably search for "tablecloths" or "napkins" and combine each with the word "rentals." If the actual company name is "Peterson Linen" there are several domain names you might consider (depending on availability, obviously):

> www.petersonlinen.com
> www.tablecloth.com
> www.tablecloths.com
> www.tablecloth-rental.com
> www.tablecloth-rentals.com
> www.tablecloths-rentals.com
> www.napkin.com
> www.napkins.com
> www.napkin-rental.com
> www.napkin-rentals.com
> www.napkins-rentals.com

Why not register several of the better choices? There is no reason why you can't build several different Web sites to target your different business areas. This tactic will give you additional directory listings if the content is legitimately separate and differentiated, and that will mean more traffic.

We suggest that you rule out any of the domain names above where the word "rental" is presented in the singular form. A crafty competitor can easily outflank you by registering the plural form and piggyback on your marketing efforts. If you register any of the "-rentals.com," plural form, you'll draw searches for both the singular and the plural. Thus, you should consider only those domain names that contain plural versions of the keywords. Just think about how few people would venture out onto the Internet looking for a single "napkin."

While you're at it, register the "www.petersonlinen.com" domain, too. If your company has, or develops, a loyal following, customers may search for you by name for their subsequent rentals; snap up that valuable company name before a competitor gets their hands on it.

Now, there is no reason why your **primary** domain name has to be the domain name for every area of your Web site. If you already have an established site, be sure to register additional domain names for the various content areas. What if you were to divide your Web site into three or four logical business areas — areas of unique content? As visitors traverse your Web site, they may or may not notice that the domain name has changed from one section to another, so long as the look and feel and colors are consistent throughout the site. You reap the benefits of having a keyword in the domain name, the potential of additional listings in search directories like Yahoo!, LookSmart, Open Directory, and NBCi, and, hopefully, some improved relevancy in the spider-based search engines. Your visitors certainly won't mind. Think outside the box.

Truth be told, if it were my company, I'd register all of the domain names above. Registering a domain name is relatively inexpensive, and hosting fees are minimal. Just because you registered 5 or 10 domain names doesn't mean you have to build content on each. Like every company, you will likely decide on one of them to be your "primary" Web presence. The others can be programmed to automatically redirect to that primary Web site so you need not pay hosting fees to maintain them. Regrettably, in today's business climate you have to keep one eye on strategy and another on your defensive posture.

Tactic #5: Make Those Informational Pages Work for You

The informational page serves as a navigational assist to the searcher who might not have located the Web site's content because they were not searching with the same language used in the Web site. Be sure, therefore, to register additional keyword-rich domain names for informational pages.

As we discuss in Chapter 35, an informational page ought to contain valuable, relevant content such that it can stand on its own. Informational pages really become small navigational Web sites. They discuss a particular topic in some detail; perhaps they summarize some content area of the Web site and then link users to that area of the Web site. Often, they discuss a concept or product that is not adequately described in the actual Web site or that is described using the vernacular of the industry rather than that of the general public. There is absolutely no reason why this informational content can't be placed on an external domain name. When choosing a domain name for externally hosted informational pages, there is less of a requirement that the domain name be good or interesting or memorable. What **is** important is that the domain name contains the targeted keyword phrase. If you are working to gain a ranking on the phrase "fractional jet ownership," register the domain name www.fractional-jet-ownership.com. If your company is very well known, i.e., you have an immediately identifiable brand name, you may want to include the company name or brand in the informational page domain registrations, such as www.boeing-fractional-jet-ownership.com.

Don't overlook the importance of naming the files and folders after keywords, too. If you're building an external informational page under the domain name www.tablecloth-rentals.com, make sure that you name the folders and files after the keywords, too. A subpage contained within the tablecloth-rental domain name might be named:

www.tablecloth-rental.com/table-linens/table-cloth-rentals.htm

This strategy is best when used sparingly and worst when overused. External domain names with content-rich informational pages are a valuable and important strategy to supplement a search engine positioning program, but they are not a search engine positioning program in and of themselves. Nothing can take the place of properly optimizing the existing Web site and ensuring that all leverage is realized from your actual Web site.

Is Your Business Missing Out on Long Domain Names?

On December 16, 1999, Register.com announced they would begin accepting domain name registrations up to 67 characters in length vs. the old 22-character limit. While much of the hype promoting the value of this new service is just that, there are compelling reasons to use long names nonetheless. Consider this top-level domain and others like it as illustrations of how **not** to leverage this new freedom:

http://www.ourcompanieshavethebestproductsonthemarketIswear.com

While the preceding example may seem of little value, consider the opportunity for companies whose names are so long that they couldn't be abbreviated effectively under the old 22-character domain name schema. In practical terms, the new longer domain name may hold some real value for companies (including these Fortune 50 examples that follow) whose names lost out to old character restrictions on the Internet. Benefactors include:

www.theprudentialinsurancecompanyofamerica.com (38 characters)

www.internationalbusinessmachines.com (29 characters)

www.statefarminsurancecompanies.com (28 characters)

www.morganstanleydeanwitter.com (23 characters)

Recently, short, memorable domain names have commanded sale prices bordering on the obscene, e.g., "Business.com" selling for $7.5 million in November 1999. "Cybersquatters," sometimes known as domain name speculators, register available domain names with the hope of reselling them for a king's ransom when somebody wants one badly enough. Now that 67-character domain names are available, these parasites are in full-frenzy mode, snapping up the obvious choices.

Ask yourself, is there real value for my company in a longer domain name? If attaining high rankings in major search engines is a goal of your online marketing plan, pay attention. The availability of longer domain names affords an opportunity to educate online marketers about the value of keywords in the top-level domains. Consultants have reported a relevance boost in the following spider-based search engines for Web sites whose domain names include keywords:

- Excite
- AltaVista
- HotBot
- WebCrawler
- Google

Simply put, if your domain name includes keyword phrases, it will tend to rank higher in these engines than Web sites that don't include those keywords. As I mentioned earlier, most search engine users do not scroll past the first three pages of search matches after performing a query. If your Web site is not found in the top 10 to 30 matches, your site may as well be invisible. Any edge you can give yourself will pay dividends.

If your company, Joe Smith Co., Inc., sells indoor/outdoor concert speakers, your Web site might be located at www.JoeSmithCo.com. If you hope to rank well in the search engines when someone queries "Joe Smith Co.," you're on your way. However, if your company name does not have national brand recognition, you'd be well advised to work toward ranking well on targeted keyword phrase queries instead. Under the old domain name length restrictions, the best you could have hoped for was a domain name like www.indooroutdoorconcertsp.com (22 characters before the ".com").

Now, with new longer domain names available, you could register www.indooroutdoorconcertspeakers.com or even www.indoor-outdoor-concert-speakers.com.

We recognize that either of those two domain names would be too long for branding purposes (30 characters in the second example!), and we're not encouraging companies to register such long domain names for their primary company Web sites. But remember, domain names are inexpensive — just $70 for two years and even less at discount registration Web sites like the one listed on the CD included with this book. Hosting a Web site is likewise relatively inexpensive, with some companies charging as little as $25 a month. A top ranking in the major search engines is free. However, just a few top rankings in the major search engines can drive more targeted traffic to your Web site than just about any other online marketing method. The ranking improvement possible through the use of multiple domain names will likely pay for the cost of the additional hosting and registration fees.

The Downside of Long Domain Names

There are several valid reasons for implementing long domain names, including long company names and appropriate keyword and phrase inclusion. However, much of the recent advice toward registering long names comes from Web marketing firms who charge fees based on registering additional domains. Regrettably, there is as much hype as valuable discourse on this topic. Registering very long domain names containing several of your targeted keywords or phrases such as

www.keyword-and-keyword-phrases-and-yet-another-keyword-phrase.com

probably won't help you accomplish your long-term search engine positioning goals. Search engines will likely flag domains that contain more than two dashes or that contain dissimilar keyword phrases. On the other hand, longer domain names that help Web site marketers focus in on a particular product or service that is necessarily composed of more than 22 characters may reap considerable benefits.

New Domain Names

On November 16, 2000, the Internet Corporation for Assigned Names and Numbers (ICANN), the body that coordinates the assignment of the identifiers that must be globally unique for the Internet to function, including Internet domain names, announced that it had approved the creation of the following new top-level domain names:

.aero	for services and companies dealing with air travel
.biz	for businesses and corporations
.coop	for cooperative organizations
.info	for information-based services such as newspapers and libraries
.museum	for museums, archival institutions, and exhibitions
.name	for individuals' and personal Web sites
.pro	for professionals in fields such as law, medicine, or accounting

In theory, this will add some slack back into the overcrowded domain name space. It will enable those previously unable to find a desirable domain name to register one of their favorites with a .biz, .pro, .info, or other extension listed above. In reality, however, it will be a tax on all companies who wish to protect their brand names and intellectual property.

Why? Large manufacturers seeking to protect their many trademarks will be forced to register their coveted brand names in several additional extensions beyond the .com extensions they already own and are probably sitting on to prevent others from misusing them. The only people who will truly benefit are the domain registries that license the registration of these new extensions. They will make millions. The rest of us will simply gain a new expense, a new cost of doing business, an additional overhead expenditure.

Chapter 8:

Submitting Your Site

Submitting to search engines used to be free, easy, and safe. Today it's often fee-based, difficult, and potentially "dangerous." It is difficult because search engines have submission limits. Some are known, others are not. If you submit too many pages from any top-level domain, you may violate a submission limit and your submissions — all of them — will be ignored, or worse yet, flagged as spam. The process can be dangerous to your status, because if you submit too many total Web pages from different domains, even one page per domain, you may be detected and banned by the IP address from where you submitted.

"These Aren't Your Father's Search Engines"

It used to be that every search engine had a submission page (an "Add URL" interface) and all a Webmaster needed to do was to visit each search engine, find the link to the submission page, enter their Web site's URL, and be done with the process. The search engines, however, responding to the many people who abused their submission interface, found it necessary to set undisclosed submission limits, watch the identities of submitters, block many submitters, and even ban Web sites that submitted too frequently or too aggressively.

For this reason, the Golden Rule of submitting today is this: Go slowly, be patient, submit cautiously.

During our interview with one major search engine, our contact indicated that some companies write automated submission scripts and submit so many pages that their submissions are practically a denial of service attack against the submission page. To defend itself, this search engine blocks the IP addresses of such submitters.

Of course, you need to ensure that the search engines index your site, and it is important that as many of the site's pages as possible are indexed. It's a bit like a raffle. The more tickets you buy, the greater your chances of winning. Likewise, the more pages of your Web site that are indexed, the greater your odds of coming up when someone searches on a keyword or phrase relevant to your site.

Submitting, by itself, is not enough: You have to work to ensure that your submitted page attains a top ranking. Pressing the submit button and walking away is not an adequate solution in and of itself. SEP is an iterative process and as such, you will submit your Web site, ensure it was accepted, measure your ranking, tweak and revise your page, and then resubmit it. The four steps below may seem intuitive, but you'd be amazed at how many companies believe that the first step constitutes their complete SEP program:

1. Make your submission. This can be done either by hand or by using a universally accepted submission tool such as WebPosition Gold or PositionPro.com.

2. Receive confirmation of acceptance (add-URL confirmation screen is displayed).

3. Verify your ranking. The submission results in a ranking on one of your targeted keywords or phrases (not a certainty, but a desired outcome).

4. Monitor your status. You should continue to verify that your Web site remains in the search engine.

There are dozens of companies that offer to submit your Web site to "all" of the major search engines for fees ranging from $19.95 to as much as $495 for 12 months' worth of submitting and resubmitting. Most are not worth the fee. Individually hand-submitting your Web site to each search engine, using a professional-grade submission tool such as WebPosition Gold or PositionPro.com, or engaging an SEP services company that hand-submits or uses one of those tools is usually the right choice.

Directory	How and Where to Submit	Max Number of Categories	Max Title Length	Max Description Length	Wait Time for Resubmission
dmoz	"add URL" (top of page)	1 per URL	no limit	25 - 30 words	3 weeks
looksmart	"Submit a Site" (bottom of page) *free submission for non-profit organizations only, Basic Submission: $99, Express Submission: $199	1 per URL	35 characters or less *Title must include company or Web site name	comments only, no limit	n/a
NBCi	"Submit a Site" (bottom of page)	1 per URL	128 characters	255 characters	n/a
YAHOO!	"Suggest a Site" (bottom of page within target category) *$199 submission fee except for non profit companies	2 per site	60 characters *Title must include company or Web site name	25 words, 200 characters	2 weeks

*DMOZ = Open Directory

> ▼ **CAUTION**   Whatever you do, **don't** allow one of these bulk submission companies to touch your Yahoo! submission or any other **directory** submission. Once you submit to Yahoo!, LookSmart, the Open Directory, or NBCi, it is unlikely you will be able to undo that submission. If the submission company doesn't understand your business — if they don't construct the 25-word site description using the right keywords — your Yahoo! listing will be of little value. The cost of having a poor Yahoo! listing can't be underestimated. Read Chapter 11 on Yahoo! and follow the instructions carefully.

Submitting All the Pages That Make Up Your Web Site

Search engines promise that if you supply one page of your Web site they will spider all of the other pages and index your entire Web site. This is rarely the case, and it will probably be necessary to submit all of the pages that make up your site, one by one, to each of the major search engines. We've found that it sometimes takes quite a long time for a search engine's spider to return to complete the task of indexing the pages beyond the one specific page (usually the home page) you submit. Sometimes they never complete the indexing of the whole site.

Be sure to read each search engine's submission guidelines carefully. The search engine submission process is becoming increasingly complicated.

Go ahead and submit all your pages, keeping in mind that each major search engine has submission limits. If your Web site contains 1,000 total indexable pages, it would take 200 days to submit to a search engine that accepts just five pages per day. There are ways around this limit which we will discuss next.

Pushing It to the (Submission) Limit

> *"Anybody who submits more than 50 pages per day from any given URL should have their head examined."*
> — Jim Stob, President, PositionPro.com

There's a lot of talk about submission limits and penalties for exceeding them. However, there are only a few search engines that publicize their submission limits. Inktomi, for example, the search engine that powers HotBot, iWon, and default searches at MSN, AOL, NBCi, Canada.com, and others, has moved to a paid submission model, under which their policy is clear: 1,000 total submissions from any given top-level domain. That's a problem for large corporate Web sites made up of over 25,000 Web pages.

Other Web sites have different limits as shown below.

Submission limits for engines whose primary results are from search engines as opposed to directories

Search Engine	Limit
alta^{vista}	about 5 pages/day
excite	25 pages/week
fast	25 pages/day
Go.com	Unknown, though they may go out of business anyway
Google	5 pages/day
HOTBOT	50 pages/day
Inktomi	1,000 maximum from one domain through pay for inclusion with Inktomi
Northern Light	(less than) 50/day

Directories are very different from search engines when it comes to submitting and have different limits. Typically in a directory, each Web site is allowed one submission, meaning one site title and 25-word site description with two suggested categories proposed.

Spidered Pages

Some search engines appear to favor pages that are spidered by the search engine over those submitted directly. AltaVista, in particular, seems to be giving higher rankings to spidered pages. In order to take advantage of this, submit only one page, which includes links to the rest of your site, to AltaVista. The disadvantage of this strategy is that you may have to wait longer for your site to be spidered; but if you are involved in a competitive keyword area, the wait may well be worth it.

Lead times for listings

Search Engine	Lead Time for Listing	Special Notes
alta**vista**:	1 - 2 days	*pay for inclusion program anticipated*
e**x**cite.	within 2 weeks	*root pages appear faster than subpages*
fast :::	approx. 8 weeks	*pay for inclusion program anticipated*
Google	4 - 6 weeks	*Google will not add your site to their index until there are other Web sites that link to yours*
HOTBOT	*Pages submitted using free "Submit Web Site" interface are penalized and will rank poorly until Inktomi's spider "finds" your page during a future crawl.*	*Avoid this penalty by using paid inclusion program at PositionPro.com.*
Inktomi	*24 hours using pay for inclusion method at PositionPro.com*	
LYC**O**S	3 - 6 weeks	*primary search results provided by Open Directory, secondary search results provided by FAST - Submit at Lycos or alltheweb.com.*
Northern Light	2 - 4 weeks	

Hallway Pages

A hallway page contains little more than links to all of the pages that make up your Web site — sort of a site map of links to whatever pages you want the search engine to find. To avoid exceeding submission limits, you submit the hallway page, and the search engine's spiders follow all the links on the page, thereby indexing all of the pages that make up your Web site. If you have a 1,000-page Web site, you might build a series of hallway pages with links to the rest of your Web site for search engines to follow. Then you would submit only those pages.

Now, remember how we pointed out that pages found by a spider might get ranked higher than submitted pages (e.g., AltaVista)? Here's a plan to use that spider: Instead of submitting pages directly, have the spider visit your submitted hallway page, follow the links on that page, and "find" the page that you have optimized for a higher search engine ranking. The "found page" will realize a slightly higher ranking than it might have were it submitted directly. Not exactly *Eureka!*, but it is a way to play the game.

Spam, Spam, Spam, and More Spam: Submission Traps

Some companies submit the same pages over and over again to a search engine, or submit hundreds of thousands of pages per day. Search engines penalize these spammers in a variety of ways. Limiting the number of submissions per day, week, or month are obvious tactics the search engines can employ, but what other tools might they use to thwart overly aggressive submitters?

Submitter IP Detection

Our contact at MSN told us during a recent interview that some search engines are known to trap the IP address of the offending submitter and ban all submissions from that IP address.

Filtering

Most search engines employ some type of filtering software on their submission input page to detect known spammers, adult Web site submissions, or other questionable input. The adult industry and Webmasters of pornographic Web sites are still believed to be the most egregious spammers by most of the search engines. For this reason, submissions from known adult Web sites receive extra

scrutiny and may be placed in a queue for further review. Submissions from bulk-submission tools or services are often red-flagged and placed in a queue for later review as well. Search engines can detect many Web site submission software products, and treat them with extra scrutiny or ignore them. Remember, submission to search engines ties up search engine resources. They must process your submission and serve the submission page and the resulting "payoff" page or "thank you for submitting" screen. Several search engines have reported to me that they feel the majority of the submissions that come in through their Add-URL page are spam and only a small percentage are actually high-quality Web sites that they wish to include in their index.

URL IP Detection

One search engine we know of ignored submissions of Web sites that submitted too many times in a day. The submission, however, was ignored not by the top-level domain name, but by the Web site's underlying IP address. If your Web site was hosted on a "virtual server" or a hosting server that shared one IP address among several Web sites, and one of the other Web sites that shared that IP address submitted that day, AltaVista displayed a message that went something like "Warning, this page has already been submitted today. Please try again after 24 hours." We discovered this by accident when we registered a domain name containing targeted keywords for an informational page we had built for a client. The very first time we submitted the page, we received that notice. We were shocked, because the domain name had been registered that day, and could not possibly have been submitted previously! When we contacted our hosting provider, they informed us that they had been sharing IP addresses among several sites due to a shortage of available IP addresses from their Internet provider. We explained the problem we encountered and requested that they procure additional IP addresses. Thankfully, they did some arm-twisting and were granted an additional "Class C" license, which meant 254 new IP addresses. When we resubmitted the page with its own IP address, it was accepted.

We don't expect this to be a problem in the future, because it simply won't pay for search engines to discriminate against unrelated Web sites that share the same IP address. The world appears to be running out of IP addresses, and as more and more hosting companies move to a virtual server environment, sharing of IP addresses will become the norm and not the exception.

To Pay or Not to Pay?

A lot of articles have been written about the *monetization* of search: in fact, we discuss it in several chapters in this guide. Inktomi, the search infrastructure company that provides search results to HotBot and iWon and secondary search results at many engines, including MSN and others, was the first major player to introduce a fee-for-submission model. All of the major search engines will likely follow suit. We're big fans of this model because it does three important things:

■ It ensures that your submitted pages are, in fact, spidered and added to the searchable index.

■ It makes the search engine the vendor, who can be held accountable for ensuring that the submissions of their paying customers are added to their searchable index.

■ It places a tollbooth in front of the submission process, which, hopefully, will discourage those companies who build and then submit thousands of bogus pages for the sole purpose of manipulating the search engines. There's nothing like the secure "Enter your credit card number" page of a paid submission to dead-end those automated submission tools built by spammers.

AltaVista is currently reviewing their options for paid submission, as is FAST (alltheweb.com) who told us in a recent interview they intend to roll out a suite of "Webmaster tools" shortly (possibly before the date this book hits the bookstores).

Three major challenges are likely to influence pay-for-inclusion systems and could potentially cause a backlash against the search engines by both Webmasters and search engine users alike. First, size matters. FAST started the arms race by announcing their database had exceeded the size of all of the other major search engines, at some 500 million pages. Several search engines, including Inktomi and Northern Light, entered the fray and announced at various times when they had become the largest player. Google beat them all, claiming 1.3 billion documents, and began displaying their database size on the home page of their Web site. The number is somewhat misleading, as it refers to the number of Web pages "referenced" as opposed to the number of pages their spider had actually visited. Each time one of these search engine companies announces that they have beaten everybody in terms of size, it garners significant press coverage and interest. So, if the search engines are all in pursuit of the largest database, how can they charge Webmasters for submitting sites that they would have to crawl and index in order to keep up, anyway?

The second fly in the ointment of the paid-inclusion model is link popularity. Google and FAST have earned accolades for having the most relevant search results. Both rely heavily on link popularity or the quantity, context, and quality of links to other sites. There is no doubt to anyone in the search engine industry that link popularity has proven to be integral to determining relevance. In order to measure link cardinality, search engines have to spider and visit Web sites and record the links from those pages to other pages. In other words, they need to visit your Web site and as many others as possible to fully calculate the value of not just your site but also those others in their database. So, if measures of external metadata such as link cardinality require that they index other Web sites, how can they charge Webmasters for something they will get to anyway?

Finally, search engine users have the expectation that search engines will do everything in their power to provide them with as many high-quality, relevant Web sites as possible. It is not enough that the search engine provides them with a few high-quality Web sites. What if you were afflicted with a rare disease that had few available treatments and the maker of a new drug had not budgeted for paid submissions and would be unable to free up budget monies until the following fiscal year? As a search engine user, wouldn't you be upset that the search engine you used did not spider that site because they didn't pay up?

The flip side of that is equally troubling. What if you paid to submit all of the pages that made up your Web site at a significant cost, only to find that a competitor's Web site was crawled by the search engine without their paying a fee, simply because another Web site had linked to theirs, effectively placing their Web site in the crawler's way? And make no mistake, this is happening today. If Inktomi removed all Web sites from their index or refused to spider Web sites that did not pay for the privilege, their database would be one-fifth its current size.

So, to some degree, paid submission for inclusion is hypocritical, especially if it is the only submission option, but it is a matter of degree. Depending on the value of its added benefits, paid submission can make good sense. We hope that, in the future, the search engines will increase the value proposition for paid submission beyond merely "You'll get in sooner." As long as search engines add value through their paid submission services, the rank and file won't rise up against them. As long as we are paying for a tangible, measurable advantage, be it speed of submission or assurance that the site stays in the index (not just for the privilege of being added to the database) the model should survive. Keeping free submissions available, though they may take longer (even up to two months), will help insulate search engines against potential negative PR.

NOTE   Paid inclusion does not ensure that your submitted page shows up in search results!

Another major pitfall of paid inclusion is that there is no promise that a submitted page will attain any rankings. While Inktomi does everything possible to make this point crystal clear in their marketing materials, a number of people who pay for submission just don't get it. They complain loudly that after parting with a good bit of money, their Web sites do not show up in the search results. Positioning yourself in the rankings is your responsibility, not the search engines'. You pay to play, but beyond that, it's a wide-open frontier.

The benefit of working with an SEP company is that you can take advantage of their expertise in identifying the pages of a Web site that are most likely to attain a high ranking in each search engine. SEP companies can tell you which pages should be submitted for a fee and which would be a waste of money to submit, thereby saving you untold dollars that otherwise might have been misspent.

As more and more search engines charge fees for submission, thereby increasing overall cost, search engines will need to continue to focus on the value they offer. Less important search engines will find Webmasters saving a few dollars by skipping their submission and that will result in a slate of deepening discounts. Anyone who would pay money to submit to Northern Light or WebCrawler would not be investing their money wisely at this stage, as both search engines refer so little traffic to the average Web site.

Paid inclusion is good for at least one reason: If you pay, you actually get in. Gone are Yahoo's eight-week waiting periods. It's a sad state of affairs that search engines are now charging fees to ensure they won't ignore you. It's akin to tipping the customer service person at a department store so they'll process your return.

The "net-net" of paid inclusion is this: It's a good thing, it's worth doing, but consult a professional before you pay to submit pages that may be unlikely to attain rankings.

Submission Software and Services

Most submission software is garbage, in my opinion. Most paid submission services, especially those that solicit you through bulk e-mail, are garbage. In fact, most of these services consist of guys in their basements who purchased one of those garbage bulk submission products and now wish to charge you the cost of their software tool for the privilege of letting them spam the search engines on your behalf. Submission software was the very first Web marketing product category. The software was relatively easy to write, and quite a few home-based software developers wrote their own submitters. They discovered something that all marketers know: People make buying decisions based on what they perceive to be the greater value proposition. Since the act of submitting to a search engine is difficult to differentiate, they differentiated by submitting to more search engines. However, there are only 20 search engines that matter, and most of the rest exist to collect the e-mail address of the submitter so that they can spam you with multi-level marketing offers. What's a marketer to do? Go hunting for anything that looks or smells like a search engine, broaden the product so that it posts to newsgroups and link building lists, and advertise that your submitter now submits to 200 "search engines, link lists, and directories" while your competitor submits to just 100. The consumer thinks, "they each cost $49 dollars, but this one submits to twice as many search engines — clearly it must be the better value." In fact, the more search engines a submission tool submits to, the more suspicious you should be. Worst of all, some of these software tools attempt to perform directory submissions. Remember: Directory submissions are sacred. Once they're done, they rarely can be undone. If you get it wrong — if you submit quickly without proper planning — your listing will be of low quality, and worse yet, it will refer little traffic.

Industrial Strength Submitting

WebPosition Gold currently submits to fewer than 20 search engines — just the ones that count. And WebPosition Gold is indistinguishable to the search engines from a hand submission. Third, WebPosition Gold is a good citizen in that they limit the number of submissions that can be made using their tool, use pop-up screens to warn users if and when they may be approaching a particular search engine's submission limit, and most important, **never ever** automatically submit to a directory.

Instead, it provides a link to each directory's submission interface and offers help screens and a free guide (our first book) that teaches the user how to properly submit to each directory.

Not just your industrial strength submission tool, WebPosition Gold is also a rank-measurement tool. Usually thought of as a rank-checking tool, it is the finest submission tool on the market today. WebPosition Gold is one of just two submission tools that we use at iProspect.com, and you'll find that every single SEP services company uses WebPosition Gold for either submitting sites, rank checking, or both. The other tool we use is SubmitWolf. We do **not** use SubmitWolf to submit to any of the major search engines that WebPosition Gold covers. Because it is, technically, a bulk submission tool, the major search engines can detect SubmitWolf. This means that you run the risk of having your submissions placed in a bulk submission queue and reviewed or added to a particular search engine at a later date or time. SubmitWolf submits to a large number of search engines and link lists that many customers insist that we cover regardless of the fact that in five years as an SEP service company, we have witnessed little if any traffic from these ancillary search engines. And by the way, if your client or boss is concerned that submissions to these hundreds of search engines have been completed successfully, ask their permission to use their e-mail address in the submissions. Explain to them that this way, they will receive the confirmation e-mails from the different search engines, directories, and link lists. Moments after the submissions are complete, your client or boss will receive hundreds and hundreds of e-mails from these different search engines. They will spend the next two years working to remove themselves from these lists.

One new submission service that is worth mentioning is PositionPro.com, operated by Position Technologies, Inc. We talk about Position Pro in greater detail in Chapter 34 on submission and rank-checking tools. This company has built a Web-based submission service that we've found to be very good — so good, in fact, that iProspect.com was the first SEP services company to enter into a long-term strategic partnership agreement with them. A short time later, we were delighted to learn that Inktomi had Position Technologies as their first paid-submission partner. Today, if you submit to Inktomi using their pay-for-inclusion system, you are using PositionPro's system.

What's unique about Position Pro's submission service? They use a sophisticated spider that actually visits your Web site and captures all of the URLs found there. They bundle these URLs into submissions to each search engine and submit only what each search engine allows, being ever watchful of submission limits. Position Pro offers only a limited rank-checking facility (10 words per engine, I believe) at this time, so you'll still need to use WebPosition Gold if you intend to check your rankings on a large number of keywords in all of the major search engines.

And finally, a few more things I'd like to point out about this Web-based service: While PositionPro.com is currently identified with Inktomi's paid submissions, their Web site offers submissions to all of the major search engines (and links to the directories), they perform regular ongoing submissions monthly, and can re-spider your Web site as it grows, adding your new pages to their submission queue. We wholeheartedly recommend Position Pro for operators of large Web sites, for those of you who are responsible for the submission of several Web sites, and especially if you have a slow Internet connection. While WebPosition Gold offers a powerful submission component that also can be scheduled to perform monthly submissions (through their "scheduler" tool), if you're submitting a large number of URLs and you're connected to the Internet on a dial-up connection, it can take some time to complete its work.

Chapter 9:

Spamdexing and Other Unhealthy Habits

first covered this topic in my original book, *Secrets to Achieving Top 10 Rankings,* in the chapter, "How to Avoid Trouble with the Engines." At that time the search engines had only a few formal policies in place to deal with overly aggressive search engine promoters. As the illicit techniques employed by the most unethical Webmasters were only beginning to come to light, the search engines were responding as quickly as they could to the many transgressions taking place. New ways to cheat your way into top rankings continue to appear every month and continue to be sought by those seeking a "quick fix" regardless of long-term ramifications.

All too often, so-called experts, including analysts and journalists alike, attempt to define our profession by the actions of a wayward few — the "spamdexers" who make us all look bad. I assure you that the persons employing the illicit tactics described in this chapter are the exception and not the rule in our industry. My goal for this chapter is to expose their many illicit practices in the hope of building a community of discourse, a common understanding and language with which we can tar and feather those who would employ such unethical methods.

The goal here is not to sensationalize the inappropriate techniques or the persons who would use them. It is also not the intent to teach the practices either. To the contrary, I'll describe these techniques for what they are and then paint them into the corner where they belong. They are the tools of less professional and certainly less ethical minds, most often wielded by practitioners who can gain rankings no other way. And for what? With a bit of effort, research, and concentration, anyone, and I mean anyone, can gain solid search engine rankings without employing any of these tactics.

To understand what practices constitute "spamdexing" or "spamming" a search engine, you first must learn a few terms. The term *spamdexing* was first proposed by Danny Sullivan in his acclaimed Web site, Search Engine Watch (searchenginewatch.com). The term is a combination of the words *spam* (or *spamming)* and *index*, as in a search engine's index (its database of listed Web sites). Until that point, *spamming* commonly referred to the practice of sending unsolicited e-mail messages to large groups of people who didn't ask to be contacted. Its application to search engine promotion and other irritations borne of the Internet was inevitable.

Spamming a search engine, then, is any practice that devalues the integrity and relevance of a search engine's results.

Spamdexing is to devalue the integrity and relevancy of a search engine's or directory's search results by any number of practices defined as inappropriate or forbidden by the search engines and directories themselves.

So, which search engine optimization practices constitute spamdexing? Well, this question incites a debate that's far from over. The more cynical among Web marketers would argue that spamdexing is any practice that the search engines discover someone using that surprises them, irritates them, offends their sense of fair play in some way, or leads the search engines to believe that the practitioner has gained an "unfair" advantage over someone else.

Working with Search Engines

To better understand this debate, it's worth considering the mindset and attitudes of the search engine operator. Search engines are little more than large repositories of information available to the public for searching. They are much like massive electronic card catalogs containing summaries and reference information about millions of Web sites. It's no surprise that many disciplines of library science apply so well to search engines. In fact, many search engines are staffed by former library science professionals. These are analytical people interested in accurately classifying documents so that they can be retrieved and made sense of by the largest number of users in the general public. According to them, problems arise when Web marketers make changes to their Web sites in the hope of increasing their rankings in the search engines.

 NOTE   It's not that a Web site has been changed, but rather **how** the Web marketer made the change that the search engine operators take issue with.

At the 1998 Infonortics search engine conference in Boston, Massachusetts, I attended a presentation by a prominent search engine designer. After discussing some ranking methodologies, she opined how frustrating it was to build a good sorting and document rating system and then have people make changes to their Web sites in order to take advantage of it! I was shocked by the contempt, disgust, and fury in her voice. She seemed out of touch with the realities of the dynamic marketplace that construct the Internet landscape. I guess that, for her and others in similar positions, document classification systems had always existed in a vacuum without outside interference or dynamic market conditions that cause change. Please note that I don't have any ax to grind with the search engine operators. I present this story simply as an illustration to help Web marketers understand the realities of the environment they will face in their work.

Based on this paradigm, you must recognize that if search engine operators had their way, Web sites would be categorized, classified, and summarized by an independent, impartial, third-party organization staffed by paid library science professionals. The individuals setting policy at the search engines are neither marketing nor advertising professionals — they are specialists in sorting and rating documents. They are not interested in how many visitors they refer to your Web site. They are not interested in whether or not your Web site attains a high ranking for one of your most important keywords. At first glance, it might appear that your interests and theirs are not aligned, but I assure you, they are.

For better or worse, we live in an imperfect world where SEP professionals and search engines must peacefully co-exist. This is not difficult if you recognize the goals and aims of the search engines themselves and do not attempt to impede them.

Understand Your Mission

Whether you're a search engine optimization specialist, SEP agency, or someone working to increase a Web site's ranking in the various search engines, if you understand an engine's fundamental *raison d'etre*, your interests can and should be aligned. The search engines are interested in delivering relevant documents to users of their service. If you do your job properly, are brutally honest with yourself about which keywords and keyword phrase searches your Web site is legitimately relevant to, and optimize your content so that it includes those keywords and phrases in the viewable body copy and META tags of your pages, you are in fact **aiding** the search engines in their mission to supply relevant documents to users.

Your primary responsibility is to ensure that the content of your Web site is properly indexed. In other words, job one is to ensure that the search engines' spiders are able to traverse your site and properly index its content. Job two is to ensure that your content is appropriately labeled so the keywords actually contained in the document (on the viewable page) are "amplified" so that they stand out to the search engine. That way, the document has a chance of attaining a ranking on those keywords. Understand that to accomplish this, you should **not** have to hide keywords or content. Anything intentionally hidden from the search engine fundamentally violates the search engine's reason for being and devalues its index.

More and more, search engines are cracking down on the use of techniques they consider inappropriate for gaining top rankings in their indexes. Though many techniques may constitute spamdexing, some search engines define it more narrowly than others. A simple check of ethics ought to be enough for most people to ensure they're not employing a technique that might be deemed illicit by a major search engine. In some cases, certain techniques or practices could be employed inadvertently or used with the most benign intent but still constitute spamdexing. We have attempted to describe the most illicit and brazen practices as well as those that might be deemed more benign below. It is important to note that techniques once considered spam may not be considered inappropriate today. Likewise, techniques that are widely accepted today could be misused by someone and suddenly be defined as inappropriate at some point in the future by the search engines.

Just Because You *Can* Doesn't Mean You *Should*

You should recognize that just because something **can** be done, doesn't mean it **should** be done. The Internet is a new medium. There is no "Internet police," and few Internet laws exist. While you are unlikely to be arrested for inappropriate and unethical SEP tactics, you may find your site banned and your future submissions ignored by the search engines.

Take, for example, a technique we refer to as "the ol' switcheroo." The fact that you **can** simply visit the top-ranked Web page of a competitor, copy it, and save it to your hard drive doesn't mean you should. While you **can** upload that very Web page to your Web site doesn't mean you should. And that you **can** submit that new page to a search engine while it resides on your domain doesn't mean you should. The fact that you **can**, in some cases, attain or exceed the very same ranking of the page that your competitor once enjoyed, doesn't mean you should employ this tactic. It's unethical, inappropriate, and certainly constitutes spamdexing. If you are caught employing this tactic, your site will undoubtedly be penalized by the search engines. You could also be sued for copyright infringement by the victim.

CAUTION   Don't sacrifice your ethics to achieve your goals. You risk being penalized or banned completely from major search engines.

A search engine's penalties for spamdexing run the gamut. They could drop you from their index until you resubmit, blacklist your site for a certain period of time, or ban you forever from their engine. Worst of all, the search engines rarely, if ever, notify you that they're taking disciplinary action against you. There is literally no way of knowing if you're being penalized or what type of punishment it is. If your site isn't indexed, you have no way of knowing whether it's due to your wrongdoing or a simple technical problem.

Are You Spamdexing? Check These 12 Red Flags

I'm about to give you some very useful information, but I want you to use it wisely. Let me be clear: **Avoid the following spamdexing techniques at all costs.** Though this is not an exhaustive list by any means, it covers the major transgressions that we've witnessed in the past few years.

To avoid risking punishment, review these techniques that are generally considered to be spamdexing by today's major search engines:

1. Promoting keywords not related to your Web site

Perhaps the first and certainly the most common spamdexing technique is to gain a ranking for a keyword that you know is not relevant to your Web site. This is considered spamdexing by all major search engines.

For instance, suppose you sell auto parts, and you're successful in securing a top 10 ranking in Excite for the keyword phrase "Rolling Stones CDs." This would obviously be misleading to anyone who clicked on your listing.

Not only will this technique cause your site to be penalized by the search engines if detected, it will generate little, if any, valuable traffic, as it will all be unqualified traffic. If people are looking to purchase a CD and they arrive at your Web site that sells diesel engine tools, they'll quickly realize they're in the wrong place and leave your site to look for a more relevant one. You've wasted their time, you've wasted your own time in working to gain that ranking, and you've devalued the relevancy and value of that search engine's results. (The users of that engine will likely assume the engine is to blame for their ineffective search results.)

2. Causing search results to show multiple listings for the same content

Back in 1997, or so the story goes, someone who operated a Web site selling water purifiers as part of a home-based, multi-level-marketing business decided to see what kind of rankings could be attained in what was then Infoseek (now known as GO.com). This guy had the bright idea that he could make dozens of copies of his home page and then submit all of them to Infoseek. Suddenly, if someone performed a query for the phrase "water purifier," the first 80 or perhaps even up to 200 search matches were from the same page on his one Web site. Others who had previously enjoyed high rankings for this phrase in Infoseek were alarmed to discover that their rankings had been knocked well below dozens of matches linked to this offender's site.

After Infoseek was alerted to this situation by the offender's competitors, they took swift action. Not only did they remove the offending pages, but they added a feature to their search result pages that virtually every other search engine has since implemented (Northern Light being one exception). Today, if you perform any query in Infoseek, you'll notice that only one page from any domain is displayed in the search results and that a link is included in that listing for "more pages from this domain." This prevents people from simply copying a high-ranking page dozens of times and dominating the search results.

However, there are ways around this protection that some unethical Webmasters exploit. One tactic is to register multiple top-level domains and host identical or similar pages on them. That way, one company can effectively secure several rankings for one keyword search, increasing the likelihood that the searcher will click on a link that ultimately leads to their main Web site. Since domain names and hosting fees have come down in price, this tactic is no longer cost-prohibitive. However, it clearly devalues the integrity and relevancy of a search engine's results.

Sometimes, multiple rankings of a keyword query for the same company are an accidental or relatively innocent byproduct of a successful, rational, and reasonable SEP program. For instance, we've created informational "microsites" for some of our clients that expand on specific content from their main sites. We typically create microsites when we feel the client's main Web site faces technical challenges that would prevent a particular area from attaining a good ranking, when a topic on the site was so focused that it deserved a separate presentation at its own distinct address.

For example, virtually all pharmaceutical companies post main corporate Web sites and also separate sites for each of their individual products. If a product's Web site doesn't adequately address a particular side effect or drug interaction, it makes sense to develop additional content on a separate domain in order to cover the topic in more detail. The content is only valuable and useful to searchers who find it. From time to time, one of these additional Web sites

will unintentionally appear in a particular search engine's search results for the same keyword phrase. But overall, the use of the technique in this way rarely causes more than one or two listings to appear in the search results.

However, if your goal is to intentionally obtain multiple (usually three or four) rankings, and the tactics you employ clearly reveal that intent, you should realize that your efforts do not serve the person using the search engine and such efforts devalue the integrity and relevancy of the search engine's results.

3. Violating unpublished submission limits

Search engines limit the number of pages that can be submitted from any one Web site or top-level domain per day. If you submit your site to them over and over again, they likely will detect your attempts and drop your site from their index. So how can you avoid this? **Do not submit more than one page of your Web site per day to any major search engine.** It's often enough to simply submit your home page to the search engine, and it will spider your entire Web site. However, if you've determined that your site is being underrepresented in a particular search engine, there is nothing wrong with submitting each of the pages that make up your site — just do it slowly.

> ▼ **CAUTION**   Make sure your Web site is hosted on its own unique IP address, or you risk not being able to attain a top ranking.

If your Web site is hosted by a "discount" hosting provider, ask them if your site is assigned its own unique IP address. If they won't accommodate your request, change hosting providers. Your ability to attain and maintain a top search engine ranking may depend on it. Here's why: We've determined that AltaVista is trapping the underlying IP address of the submitted Web site and banning it based on the IP address, not the domain name. (You read it here first, folks!)

Some hosting companies are stingy with IP addresses (they are in short supply). A domain name such as www.yourcompany.com is actually mapped to an IP address such as 102.63.11.123. A domain name server (DNS) translates that IP address into the domain name when a user requests the URL by visiting the site. The problem occurs when a hosting company runs short on unique IP addresses and shares them across multiple domain names. In other words, your Web site and another totally separate site may share the same IP address. We've found some hosting companies using one IP address to serve as many as 200 separate domain names.

4. Using colored text on a same-color background

One drawback of doorway pages, or any other attempt to attain a higher ranking in any major search engine, is the time it takes. Developing 200 to 600 words of compelling, relevant, and interesting copy takes time. Writing is a skill that few people refine once they leave college. However, good writing about diverse topics is a necessary component of a successful SEP effort. Search engines like to see some amount of credible, relevant copy on a page that they index. (There was a time when Lycos reportedly would not index a page that contained fewer than 250 words of copy!)

One way to increase the amount of copy on a Web page without it distracting the visitor (like the "click here to visit my actual site" message that most cheap doorway pages employ) is simply to hide it. One of the most-often used ways of hiding text on a page is to match the color of the text to the color of the background. This way the Webmaster can hide large amounts of text or repeated words in a cloud of white on white. The only way to view this text is to highlight the area where you suspect the hidden text to be located. Most search engines can now detect this practice because the hex codes used to describe background colors and font colors will match or be numerically close. See the illustration on the following page for an example of this.

Some clever Webmasters discovered they could substitute a white-colored .gif file in place of a color hex code and achieve the same effect. While this technique is more difficult to detect, you risk the wrath of the search engines if you're caught. We recommend avoiding it altogether.

5. Page-swapping

This is also known as "the ol' switcheroo." The basic technique is to build a Web page that is likely to attain a high ranking and then, after the original page has been indexed and secured a top spot, swap it out for the page you intend or prefer your visitors to find. Regrettably, this technique is often employed with stolen pages. Unethical Webmasters will copy a page from a high-ranking Web site, change the title and description META tag (the only two tags on the page that are displayed in the search engine's results sets), and then submit the page to the search engines. Once a ranking is attained, they replace the stolen page with one of their own Web pages. The practice of stealing someone else's Web pages is known as "page-jacking."

Hidden
keywords

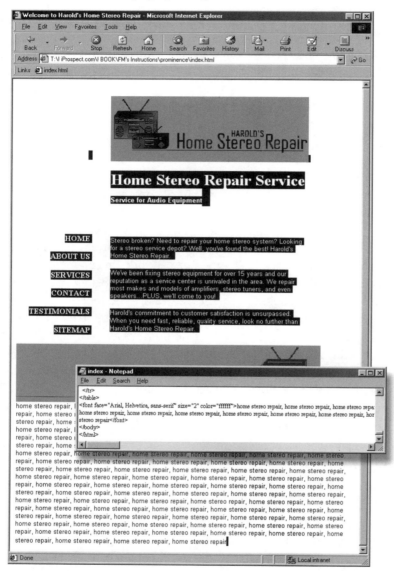

6. Page-jacking

This is the practice of stealing someone else's Web site, uploading it to your domain, and then submitting it to search engines — effectively "stealing" their ranking. This is the most commonly cited justification Webmasters give for employing yet another unethical technique that seeks to combat page-jacking: "cloaking" or "stealth scripting," which we explain below.

7. Cloaking or stealth scripting

The practice of "cloaking" involves writing a server-side script that detects the IP address of the incoming search engine and serves it a Web page that is different from the one displayed to the general public. This tactic is often employed by SEP companies that want the ability to charge on a cost-per-click basis. They hide the indexed Web page behind a stealth script, and when the user clicks on the listing in the search engine, he or she is automatically redirected to a client's site. Because the surfer is redirected from the SEP company's server and originally indexed page to the client's Web page, the SEP company can count the click-throughs and bill the client a fee for each visitor referred to the client's Web site.

People or companies that employ cloaking scripts will often rail against the evils of page-jackers and complain about others stealing their HTML codes to attain a better ranking. But two wrongs don't make a right, and it seldom happens anyway. There are so many off-the-page ranking factors in most search engines today that this is hardly a credible excuse.

8. "Keyword stuffing" (repeating hidden areas of a site)

One way to increase the keyword frequency on a Web site or page is to repeat a targeted keyword somewhere on the viewable page or in some hidden area of the HTML code. On certain sites you may find that when you drag the mouse over an image, the contents of the image <ALT> tag contain a repeated keyword phrase, even though the graphic has nothing to do with that phrase. (The image <ALT> tag displays text before a graphic loads or when you run your mouse over the graphic, or both.)

For example, perhaps you find a Web site that is selling a prescription baldness treatment. On the home page is a photograph of the actual pill. If you move your mouse over the graphic, a little box pops up that repeats the phrase "baldness treatment" seven or eight times. But the graphic is not of a baldness

treatment — the graphic is of a pill. Was this a mistake? No. The site designer "stuffed" a keyword into the image <ALT> tag for this graphic in hopes that the search engine would read it and increase the page's relevance for searches on that phrase. If the site designer had instead included the sentence "photograph of our new baldness treatment, HairGrow" (or whatever they named it), it would not be considered a spam technique.

"Stuffing" keywords into the image <ALT> tag

9. Placing others' trademarked words in a keyword META tag or within other hidden areas of the page

Some unethical Webmasters reason that since their product competes with that of another company, promoting their Web site by using their competitor's trademarked brand name or even the company name itself is a clever way to drive qualified traffic. If you include a keyword in your keyword META tag that is the trademarked property of another company, prepare yourself for a lawsuit if you're caught. Remember, metadata is supposed to describe other data. If you include a word, brand name, or company name in your keyword META tag that is not substantively discussed in the viewable copy of that Web page, you are spamming and violating someone's trademark.

10. Redirecting pages too quickly

One (no longer effective) way to "page swap" is to quickly redirect someone from the page you submit to the search engine to your "target" or destination page. This is accomplished by adding the following line of HTML code to your Web page:

```
<META HTTP-EQUIV="refresh" content="1; URL=http://www.domain
.com/fldr/pg.htm">
```

When the major search engines discovered that companies were using this META tag to redirect visitors who clicked on a search engine listing to a page other than the one that was indexed, they rightly labeled the technique as spam. Currently, most search engines will not penalize a site that uses one of the many forms of page redirection. Instead, they combat the problem by indexing the contents of the destination page and simply ignoring the contents of the page that redirected users to it.

11. Having too many "doorway pages"

A doorway page is a page that is optimized for the purpose of attaining a ranking in a particular search engine for a particular keyword phrase. Some savvy, or should I say sneaky, SEP practitioners figured out that a single doorway page could be duplicated hundreds or even thousands of times. Then, using any simple off-the-shelf HTML editing package, they could perform a search-and-replace action to change just the targeted keywords on the page. They'd end up with thousands of nearly identical pages where the only noticeable difference between the pages would be the keyword found in the headline centered on each page. Obviously, search engine users who stumbled across one of these pages would find little value in them, and because the process of building these pages could be so easily automated, hundreds of thousands of these pages began filling up search engine indexes.

Search engines can and should discriminate against bad pages. Multiple doorway pages that are practically identical and do not contain copy that discusses the targeted keyword phrase for which the page attained a ranking are bad pages. Search engines now watch for pages that appear the same or very similar.

12. Too small text on page

Many spammers will often hide keywords in tiny text at the bottom of a page. Search engines consider this an attempt to hide keywords on the page. Therefore, you should avoid font sizes smaller than the standard size being used on the page. Plain and simple: Avoid tiny text.

Still in Doubt?

The best way to ensure that you don't employ a tactic that could someday be construed as spam is to ask yourself the following three questions:

1. Does employing this technique require me to hide anything from the visitor?

2. Does employing this technique require me to produce generic content that's of little value to the person who visits the page?

3. Would I be perfectly comfortable in calling a major search engine, directing its staff to look at my page being optimized, and asking them for advice on how I could make the page better?

If your answer to the first two questions is "no," and your answer to the third is "yes," you're standing on pretty solid ground.

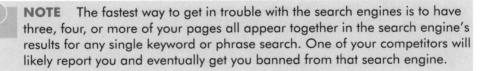

NOTE   The fastest way to get in trouble with the search engines is to have three, four, or more of your pages all appear together in the search engine's results for any single keyword or phrase search. One of your competitors will likely report you and eventually get you banned from that search engine.

Don't sacrifice your ethics to achieve your goals. Tricks like using Princess Diana's name on your Web site simply to bring in traffic are patently offensive. Whether the keyword concerns a sensitive current event or is simply a high-interest keyword, using it in inappropriate and unethical ways is deception by any standard. Most importantly, it won't translate into revenue — only irritated visitors. Even if you make a buck or two, it will be on your conscience. Making money on the Web is not so difficult that you need to resort to such low-brow tactics.

Chapter 10:

Search Engine Positioning Begins with Web Site Design

Search engine visibility begins with your site design. The time to bring in an SEP specialist is during this phase — before decisions are made regarding platform and templates are prepared. Unfortunately, the SEP professional is often brought in too late, after the site is ready for use or when the site owners are perplexed by its lack of traffic from search engines.

We're all familiar with the traditional usability issues that are constantly thrown around: Is it easy to read? Is the branding consistent from section to section? Does the site load so slowly that the user leaves, frustrated by a long wait? A key usability issue for a commerce site might be whether it is easy to make a purchase on the site or the process is confusing. These are issues that impact "stickiness" and overall performance. While they are important to the success of a site, they are not, by themselves, central to its search engine visibility. The impact of site design on visibility goes way beyond these considerations.

It's as simple as this: The secret to increasing search engine visibility is to **focus on interaction with the search engines**. What I mean is that our "customer," for all practical purposes, is a spider or other robot that must find, navigate, and read the site. For this reason, we must look at those usability questions from the perspective of the spider.

Each of the following seven elements can repel spiders in their own unique way:

1. A platform with dynamic content

2. A design dependent on frames

3. The use of design elements such as Flash or multimedia

4. The use of image maps for navigation

5. Password-protected areas

6. The required acceptance of cookies

7. The use of META refresh tags

Now let's explore each of these elements and ways to avoid them.

Dynamic Content: Fix It Now, or Suffer Later

The time to determine the impact of a dynamic platform for content creation on your site's SEP program is **before** you get locked in to the platform and **before** you design the database. If you don't do it now, you will find yourself looking for "workarounds" and other rescues to keep your site from sinking into the quicksand of search engine oblivion.

If your choice of database platform delivers a "?" or some other ASCII character in the Web address, you have a search visibility problem. For example, a spider can't crawl http://www.ourlovelysite.com/cgi-bin/getpage.cgi?name=page or http://www.ourlovelysite.com/default.asp?from=/resources/default.asp.

Search engine spiders are a very old, primitive technology. In recent years, spiders have evolved that crawl the Web faster and can capture more data, but they're still the same basic technology. Today, AltaVista and Google display and index dynamic content pages, but **only when the pages are submitted.**

There are several reasons why spiders don't read dynamic content and leave when they encounter a "?", "=", "!", or other ASCII character in the URL string. These strings are usually the result of an interaction with a script that delivers the content, and the characters represent either escape characters for CGI scripts or database results. (For a complete list of CGI escape characters try: http://www.math.umd.edu/~ant/Test/escape.htm.)

Spiders avoid URLs with these characters because they can lead them into huge recursive traps. The database or CGI script feeds the spider an infinite array of URLs and the same page endlessly. This can bring the server to its knees in a big hurry, as the spider vigorously tries to fetch this unending number of URLs.

URL strings with ASCII characters also are used as unique user identifiers for shopping sites, often indicating the contents of e-commerce shopping carts. I doubt any site would want its shopping carts indexed and displayed on search engine results.

If your platform selection includes ASP, Cold Fusion, or a database option that yields ASCII characters in the URL, you will have to adapt your pages through workarounds.

But take heart: Not all database platforms create pages that are search engine hostile. Among the most notable, Vignette (http://www.vignette.com/) yields search-engine-friendly pages that do not have malformed URLs. All of the URLs end with the .html designation, which search engines can readily read, index, and display.

Workarounds

There are technical solutions for working with dynamic pages which require that the site owner or the Web marketer and the technical team work together knowledgeably. If the technical team insists on using a platform and solution that renders the site invisible, a simple workaround can often yield enough search-friendly pages to generate a substantial volume of needed traffic. So, don't dismiss the notion of workarounds as unnecessary or too much trouble. They are traffic lifelines. Each solution presented below requires a different level of involvement of the technical team, as well as cooperation and, frankly, technical skill.

Available workarounds fall into several categories:

- URL manipulation
- Redirection
- Static republishing of the site
- Selective republishing to create search-friendly real estate

URL Manipulation for ASP and Other Types of Pages

If your site uses Microsoft's Active Server Page (ASP) technology, your pages may end in .asp or .asp?. Most of the major search engines spider the .asp and index its pages, but if your site delivers pages with the .asp? extension, you need to find a way to eliminate that darn question mark. There is software available designed to do just that. XQASP (http://www.xde.net/) is a high-performance NT IIS3+ ISAPI filter written in C++. It is especially intended for database Web sites seeking to increase exposure in search engines by allowing spiders to index the values behind a query string.

If your site runs on the popular Apache Web server software, there is also a rewrite module available that translates URLs with "?" into search-engine-friendly URLs. The rewrite module (mod_rewrite) isn't compiled into the software by default; however, some hosting companies make it available to their users. This module takes a URL that looks like this: http://www.mylovelysite .com/food.html?cat=Zucchini and rewrites it as http://www.mylovelysite.com /Zucchini/index.html. Additional information can be found at http://www.apache .org/docs/mod/mod_rewrite.html.

This solution requires the absolute cooperation of your technical team to install the module and run it correctly. This isn't a trivial task, but the resulting visibility may make it more than worth the effort.

If your site is built using Allaire's Cold Fusion product you will get mal-formed URLs that look something like this: http://www.mylovelysite.com/ page.cfm?ID=132. There are ways you can configure your Cold Fusion pages to provide URLs that look like this: http://www.mylovelysite.com/page.cfm/132. This URL is search engine friendly and loads correctly. For more on how to perform this little miracle of search engine science, see http://forums.allaire .com/DevConf/index.cfm?Message_ID=18401. This is a lengthy thread that pro-vides lots of information on how to create search-engine-friendly pages with Cold Fusion. Yet another solution that requires cooperation between your search engine marketing and technology teams.

Redirection

The use of redirections is also very dependent on the skill and cooperation of those charged with making the site work. This solution requires the writing and installation of *server-side includes* (SSI) to deliver a static URL in place of the dynamic URL created by your database. Because the page is complete when the server sends it, no special action must be taken to make the page itself search engine friendly.

"Client-side include" files that include JavaScript "source=" or Microsoft Internet Explorer's "IFRAME" aren't search engine friendly and will not be indexed. Avoid them.

There are a variety of redirection-based solutions that serve static URLs in place of dynamic pages just to visiting spiders. These require vigilance in that the lookup table of spiders must be expanded and maintained over time. As you select a solution, note that search engines don't seem to have difficulties index-ing content with .shtml file extensions. The problems occur when the page for the SSI includes a cgi-bin path in the extension.

Static Republishing

For many a site, the database that generates dynamic content was designed and developed as a method for speeding development and content creation. The site does not depend on real-time dynamic access to the database for actual content delivery. Some sites that provide content that changes constantly don't even use the database for every access; instead, they use it as a development tool from which a static site of all the potential pages is published on a regular cycle. If you are a content provider, it may behoove you to set a "publishing" schedule for the complete republishing of your dynamic site as a static site.

XBuilder (http://www.xbuilder.net/) is a product that allows site owners to rapidly republish their sites as static HTML pages. This improves site performance speeds and enables rapid site deployment. According to their literature, XBuilder can compile any site on any platform, including sites written in CGI, Perl, Active Server Pages, or any other scripting language. These files can be republished to the Web, to CDs, and to other formats. Along the same line, we have Inceptor's (http://www.inceptor.com) Excedia, a suite of tools that will accomplish the same task. There are advantages to static republishing beyond search engine visibility. A static page will load faster than a database action, bringing the user into faster contact with the information and reducing load on the site's servers.

Depending on how static republishing is deployed, it also requires interaction and cooperation between the technical and Web marketing teams. Its advantages (speed for the site visitor and server load reduction) often outweigh implementation woes.

Selective Republishing

Sometimes there are overarching issues that prevent the implementation of the global solutions mentioned above. These may include a hostile relationship between technical staff and Web marketing, an overwhelmed staff with too little support to consider making any kind of change, or the need for a quick fix while a permanent solution is being evaluated. To increase the number of pages visible to search engines, consider selecting top-level pages of the dynamic site and creating static versions that link to it. Presto! Suddenly you have pages that act as gateways to the site **and** can be submitted and indexed by search engines. Now, it **is** a time-consuming task to determine the pages and then create and maintain exact static replicas. But if a dynamic site is to be found, it must have search-engine-friendly URLs and enough search-engine-visible pages to adequately represent its content. Selective republishing is one option for getting additional real estate in search engines.

The Evils of Frames

Although frames make Web site design and navigation somewhat easier, these little devils wreak havoc on the SEP program. First, many search engines are still not capable of reading the content in the frames. Second, frames increase the file size and number of total words that make up the Web page. This alters the keyword weight on the site.

When a search engine views a framed site, it looks at it just as you might if you were using a very old browser that was not frame enabled. An entry for the framed site www.cheesyfood.com might look like this:

> **3. www.cheesyfood.com.** Cheese's home on the Web
> Welcome to cheese, index, what's melting, what's cool and creamy, cheese recipes, cheese chat.

All that is visible is the framed navigation to the sections of the site. This is not much help for the visitor who wants a fuller description of the site, and the search algorithm does not have much to work with to determine relevancy.

Workarounds

You have several options. The first is the "just say No!" approach. Developing your site without frames, however, severely limits your design options. A second solution is to make sure that search engines can index the site and that the information they receive is of high quality to them. Your first line of defense is having excellent META tags and descriptions. Your second is to use the <NOFRAMES> tag. This lets you create an alternative Web page within the <NOFRAMES> tag so that search engines can use the text. You compose the entire page in HTML laid between the <NOFRAMES> and </NOFRAMES> tags. Make sure that the <NOFRAMES> page is set immediately below the first <FRAMESET> tag so that you present its keyword-rich content as close to the top of the page as possible, like this:

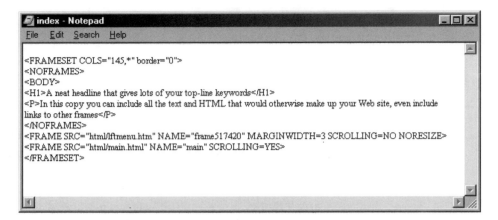

It is an accepted practice to include all the information from the other framed pages on this new separate page contained in the <NOFRAMES> tag. When you design this page, be sure to include the links to other pages in your site, so that the search engine spider can navigate to those pages and index them as well.

Make sure that the <NOFRAMES> tag follows the <FRAMESET> tag. By moving it higher on the page so that it appears in the head section, you make your wording more prominent to the search engines but it becomes incompatible with some browsers.

Because the extra tags used to set up frames dilute the density of the keywords versus other words on the page, you should definitely consider using informational pages. These pages should have no frames at all, but serve as pointers to the main site that uses frames. This represents the best of all possibilities, in that you get the versatility of frames and search-engine-friendly pages.

Graphics and Flash on Entry Pages

A huge graphic on the index page is attractive to those coming to your site, right? Hold on a minute — what about those who don't have fast connections to the Web? That beautiful graphic may also make you invisible to a search engine. Sites that use Macromedia's Flash are often beautiful, animated works, but when it comes to the search engine game, these graphic elements do not enhance the site's visibility. The spiders are blind to the content in that beautiful Flash image.

This problem is particularly significant when the Flash content is on the index page of the site.

Since search engines don't spider graphics, they expect Webmasters to provide alternate (<ALT>) text whenever a graphic includes information. AltaVista is quite clear about this topic (http://doc.altavista.com/adv_search/ast_haw_wellindexed.html).

Workarounds

The workaround for creating search-engine-friendly Flash alternative pages is very similar to that for frames. Your solution is to use a keyword text and phrase-rich entrance page that offsets the copy that is buried in the Flash. Another solution is to create a two-frame frameset where one frame is only one pixel in height. In this mini-frame, you can use the <NOFRAMES> tag (see above for how to code this) to create an area where you can put your content. Still another, less visually pleasing, option is to alternate your use of Flash with static content. Remember: Search engines don't read Flash or text in graphics, and you must include an alternative source.

NOTE   Multimedia files and those that are generated by Java applets can't be indexed either. If your site contains a document in Acrobat, consider providing a text version of the same information, since search engines do not index Acrobat files (the technology is available, but it is not yet offered for public use).

Image Maps for Navigation

Although image maps are visually pleasing, they are not as search-engine-friendly as navigation buttons. All search engines can follow links, but not all can index alternative text in an image map.

Image maps are sometimes quicker to download than an array of buttons, but there is a trade-off in search engine visibility. There is a way of having your cake and eating it too: Just put a set of text links at the bottom of your page, and you can be sure that the search engines can follow your navigation. All search engines can follow text links.

Navigation links . . .

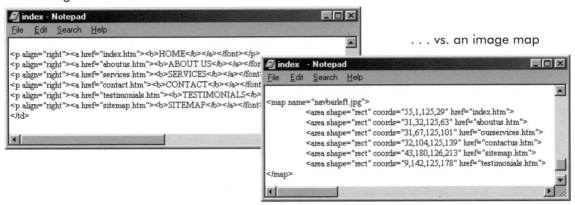

. . . vs. an image map

If you use JavaScript to create your navigation, you should include text links as well, since some search engine spiders don't follow pages that appear to result from a Java applet.

Passwords

If there are areas of your site that are password protected, a spider cannot find content hidden behind these password entrances. Spiders may be excellent at crawling the Web, but they do not pick locks, and they cannot fill out a form to get a password to your site. If you want to have your site visible to spiders, consider having content areas that are open to the anonymous viewer and do not require password entry. Use these pages to develop coverage in search engines and to assist in marketing your valuable password-protected information.

Cookies

Cookies are those small text files that browsers keep on the user's hard disk that allow the site to remember the user's identity and actually may contain a customer or a visitor ID. If your site requires that visitors accept a cookie to enter, you will be creating a search-unfriendly site. No matter how much you try to entice them, spiders are programmed to reject cookies.

As with most technical challenges, there is a way to overcome this barrier. You can use a special "stealth" script that will recognize the search engine's visit and not require a cookie to be served. Note that this is **not** cloaking. You are not trapping the spider's identity to serve it a different page. You are using a similar technology only inasmuch as spider recognition underlies most cloaks. Your intent is different: You want to make your page visible to the spider, not trick or hide from the spider.

META Refreshing

Even if you are not familiar with the META refresh tag, you have undoubtedly encountered it in action. If you have ever been to a site and been automatically redirected to another site within a matter of seconds, you have encountered the META refresh tag. Although this tag is useful for developing slide shows that automatically roll forward or for splash pages that go to the site within seconds, its use can decrease your search engine visibility. The illustration shows how you might code this tag for a five-second delay (content=5).

```
index  - Notepad
File   Edit   Search   Help

<HTML>

<HEAD>
<TITLE>Widgets for Fidgets</TITLE>
<META HTTP-EQUIV="refresh" content="5; URL=http://the URL you redirect to">
</HEAD>
```

Fast redirects, those redirections that occur so quickly that the user has no way of knowing that the redirection has occurred or cannot stop it, are considered by the search engines as an attempt to hide a Web page from the spider and the user. The search engines' rule of thumb here is that taking less than 10 seconds to transition to the actual Web site is spamdexing.

The META refresh tag has been so overused for trickery by adult Web sites and SEP pros looking to redirect traffic to themselves that most search engines view the use of META refresh as spam and have programmed their spiders to avoid or ignore refresh pages.

Clumsy Architecture

If you want your site to be easily navigated by humans and spiders, make sure that your most important content is the most accessible. Don't bury key content deep within multiple directory layers. A search engine might not index important content, since they may not crawl beyond the third, fourth, or fifth level of your directory structure. This admonition comes directly from AltaVista (http://doc.altavista.com/adv_search/ast_haw_wellindexed.html). This means developing a directory structure that supports this goal. It is, therefore, important to analyze your directory structure and avoid developing an architecture that is so steep that the search spiders might not visit your entire site. Fire your biggest guns first!

Broken Links

Just as they prevent a visitor from navigating your site, broken links aren't negotiable by a spider. They can cause your site to lose visibility, because the spider cannot move deeper into the site and does not find all the pages. Broken links can also greatly reduce your link popularity, because you may well lose external links as a result.

Broken links are a major problem when a site is redesigned and relaunched. I have seen sites with strong search engine traction lose large quantities of their valuable rankings by not trapping the 404 errors issued by the server when a page is missing: the result of a broken link. The trap is simply a matter of redirecting the page to the new page that maps to the content on the new site. For example, the site cheesyfood.com might, as a result of a redesign, move a page with a cheesecake recipe from its "recipe" directory (www.cheesyfood.com/recipes/cheesecake.html) into a new directory called "cookbook" (www.cheesyfood.com/cookbook/cheesecake.html). The information is the same, but the location is different. A search engine or a visitor looking for the page at its previous location receives an error message unless the site owners trap their 404s and remap the requests to the new directory.

When you redesign or change the navigation of your site, don't delay putting your 404 trap in place. You can't tell when the spider will come calling. It just might be your luck to have your number-one-ranked page deleted from the index because of the move! Considering how hard it is to get a top ranking, you must be vigilant in redesigning to ensure that all of the pages are mapped from the old design to the new one.

The Bottom Line: Keep It User Friendly

Search engines are content hungry and hard to impress with awesome graphics. Your Web site will be most search engine friendly if its pages are most user friendly.

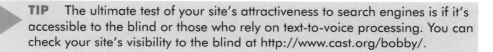

> **TIP** The ultimate test of your site's attractiveness to search engines is if it's accessible to the blind or those who rely on text-to-voice processing. You can check your site's visibility to the blind at http://www.cast.org/bobby/.

If your site includes enough alternative text that a blind person hearing about your site can understand its content, your site is understandable to search engines.

With this in mind, make every effort to ensure that your site is easy to navigate and easy to read. If you design a site that is appealing to the eye and accessible on all types of connections, you will find that it is attractive to search engines.

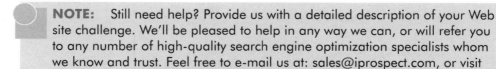

> **NOTE:** Still need help? Provide us with a detailed description of your Web site challenge. We'll be pleased to help in any way we can, or will refer you to any number of high-quality search engine optimization specialists whom we know and trust. Feel free to e-mail us at: sales@iprospect.com, or visit our quote request page at: http://www.iprospect.com/book-quote.htm.

Part 3:
The Engines

f you expect to achieve top rankings on your keywords across multiple search engines, you must develop and maintain a comprehensive understanding of the characteristics and ranking algorithms of the search engines. If you understand how each search engine ranks your pages, then you can adjust your non-ranking pages from a position of knowledge. To assist you in developing your comprehensive search engine knowledge, you will find here an analysis of each of the major search engines.

Just a word of caution! You will do yourself a disservice if you read **only** these engine-by-engine chapters. There is valuable information in other chapters that apply to specific engines. The intent of these chapters is to provide in a single chapter the most significant information you might need to understand a particular engine's relevancy scoring criteria and other related information that might help get your pages indexed and ranked in the engine.

It should be noted that the search engines change their relevancy scoring criteria and their submission requirements from time to time. Although we have made every effort to make this information as up to the minute as possible, the Web is so dynamic that some information may already be out of date. For example, Disney's decision to eliminate GO.com occurred at the same time there was an extensive television advertising campaign underway urging searchers to use GO.com.

The following information is intended to assist you in understanding the information presented on each engine:

1. *Web address:* The URL of the engine.

2. *Type of engine:* Whether the engine is a directory or uses a spider-based algorithm. If the engine combines directory and spider-based elements, it is called a hybrid. *Primary results* indicates primary source for search results. *Secondary results* indicates secondary source for search results.

3. *Partnerships:* This outlines the sources that the search engine uses. For example, if the search engine uses Inktomi as its database provider, or Open Directory as a source for its directory listings, this is indicated here.

4. *Total documents indexed:* The total number of Web sites or other Web documents that the search engine represents as included in its index.

5. *Total page views per month:* Total number of a search engine's pages that are viewed per month. This number does not necessarily suggest the number of people who conducted actual keyword searches. It is an important

number as it gives an indication of how many people are using the search engine and its relative activity. When this information is not available, we have attempted to substitute another metric that offers insight into the search engine or directory's relative value to Web site searchers.

6. *E-mail support:* An e-mail address for communications concerning your ranking in a particular search engine or directory. Don't expect all search engines to reply to your questions, or reply promptly. Many are very busy and appear to make it a policy to ignore most e-mail. At times, you may get a response though, so it's worth trying.

7. *How to confirm listing:* This is how to see if the search engine has a record of your Web site in its database.

8. *Obtain link popularity information:* This is how you can check each engine for the number of other URLs or pages that show links to your Web site. Not all engines support this feature.

9. *Result returns:* Indicates how the search engine returns its results with directory listings preceding Web pages or some other schematic.

10. *Receive higher rankings for link popularity:* Indicates whether the search engine uses some measurement of how many other Web sites are linked to you as part of its relevancy scoring criteria.

11. *Additional off-the-page considerations:* Indicates whether the engine uses human editors or some other means of determining page relevancy other than a search algorithm interacting with the metadata and content of the actual page.

12. *Rankings influenced by after-the-click behavior:* Indicates whether the search engine uses additional technologies such as the Direct Hit popularity engine to supplement its ranking algorithm with information on user behavior.

13. *Recognition and utilization of META tags:* Indicates whether the search engine's page ranking criteria include the information given in the META tags. If the answer is Yes, make sure that you include META tags on all your pages. If the answer is No, you should not expect your META tags to influence your page's ranking.

14. *Consideration of META tags for relevancy:* Indicates whether the META tags figure into the search engine's page ranking criteria.

15. *Importance of Title tag keyword prominence:* Whether the search engine considers the prominence of the keywords in the Title tag in its ranking criteria.

16. *Importance of <ALT> tag:* Whether the search engine considers the <ALT> tag in its ranking criteria.

17. *Importance of multiple occurrences of keywords in Title tag:* Whether the search engine considers the frequency of keywords in the Title tag as part of its relevancy scoring criteria.

18. *Maximum length of Title tag:* How many words or characters this search engine will accept in the Title tag.

19. *Maximum length of keyword META tag:* How many words or characters this search engine will accept in the keyword META tag.

20. *Maximum length of description META tag:* How many words or characters this search engine will accept in the description META tag.

21. *Comment tags considered for relevancy:* Whether the search engine considers the comment tag (<!-->) as part of its relevancy scoring criteria.

22. *Frame support:* Whether the search engine's spiders are capable of traversing pages with frames.

23. *Image map support:* Whether the search engine's spiders are capable of following the navigational information provided in an image map.

24. *Accepts automated submissions:* Whether the engine allows for the submission of pages through a form or requires that a human editor review the site.

25. *Indexes submitted pages only or conducts deep crawls:* Indicates whether you can expect the search engine to find pages of your site that you have not submitted or whether you must submit all of the pages you want indexed.

26. *Instant spidering of submitted page:* Indicates whether the search engine's spider immediately visits your page upon submission or whether there is a delay.

27. *Number of pages that can be submitted per day:* Indicates the number of pages per domain that can be submitted. The precise number of pages each search engine will let you submit each day varies.

28. *Word stemming and plural sensitive:* Indicates how the search engine will handle your keywords. Some engines stem all keywords and consider single and plural forms as the same; others draw a distinction between the various word forms.

29. *Case-sensitive searches:* Whether the search engine notices if keywords have been capitalized or not. In other words, if the engine is case sensitive, a default search for "apple" would yield a different list of sites than a search for "Apple." If the search engine is case sensitive, include capitalized and lowercase versions of important keywords in your META tags.

30. *Alphabetical page listings:* Indicates if the search engine lists pages in its results alphabetically.

31. *Time to index page:* How long it will take you to get added to the search engine. This will vary dramatically.

32. *Spam penalties:* How the search engine responds to pages that it considers spam. Some choose to delete the pages from their index; others will ban all submissions from the URL.

33. *Refuses pages with META refresh:* Indicates whether or not the search engine will index a page with a META refresh tag.

34. *Refuses pages with invisible text:* Indicates whether or not the search engine will index pages that it finds with invisible text and how such pages are treated.

35. *Refuses pages with "tiny text":* Indicates whether or not the search engine will index pages that it finds with "tiny text" designed to stuff keywords.

36. *Remove URL:* The location within the search engine where you can have your URL removed from the index.

Part 3: The Engines

Chapter 11:

Yahoo!

Yahoo! Inc.
3400 Central Expressway
Santa Clara, CA 95051
(408) 731-3300
Fax: (408) 731-3301
User Support: (408) 731-3333

Free updates to this book are available via e-mail newsletter
by visiting: http://www.iprospect.com/book-news.htm.

Yahoo! and the Yahoo! logo are trademarks of Yahoo! Inc.

Facts about This Engine

Yahoo! is both the oldest search service and the most important place for Web marketers to be indexed. Media Metrix indicated that Yahoo! had some 57 million unique visitors a month during October 2000 — that's second only to AOL, and more than twice their closest competitor. Yahoo! is widely perceived by the general public as being the Internet's first search engine (though it is actually a directory) and is still the recognized leader. Get your site listed in Yahoo! first, and do everything else second.

In April 1994, David Filo and Jerry Yang were doctoral candidates in electrical engineering at Stanford University when they began building a link list of their favorite Web sites that would eventually become what we now know as the Yahoo! search engine. It wasn't long before their "hobby" grew to the point where they were having difficulty managing it with their personal resources.

The genesis of the name Yahoo! is interesting — it was actually an acronym for "Yet Another Hierarchical Officious Oracle." The link list originally resided on Yang's student workstation while the search engine technology was located on Filo's computer.

In 1995, Filo and Yang moved Yahoo! over onto the larger servers of Netscape. Today, Yahoo! is a publicly traded company, the original link list now contains some one million Web sites, and the company itself has grown to be the largest search service on the Web. Yahoo! stock is widely considered a bellwether of other Internet companies. Flush with investor money, Yahoo! acquires companies and technology so regularly, and has expanded its service offering so far beyond search, it's sometimes hard to remember that Yahoo! was originally a humble search engine. Today Yahoo! offers free e-mail services, auctions, and myriad non-search related services to its members via its portal.

It's important to keep in mind that Yahoo! is **not** a search engine. Yahoo! is a directory edited by humans. When you submit a site to Yahoo!, you will be submitting only a site title and description that will be reviewed by a genuine human being — not an automated and unattended software spider. Yahoo! employs some 150 professional editors (though the number may have increased since we last spoke with them) who evaluate the site title and description that you submit and actually visit your Web site to have a look at it. They then decide: first, if the site is worthy to be included, and second, how it will be described. Make no mistake, these Yahoo! category editors will pare down your submission at their sole discretion.

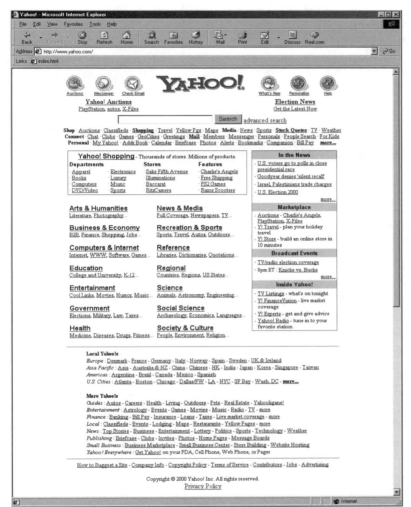

Yahoo! is no longer the largest human-compiled directory of Web sites, since Open Directory — with its 25,000 volunteer editors — overtook it in mid-2000. Though Yahoo! employs in excess of 150 editors and has crossed the one million mark of indexed Web sites, Open Directory has some two million Web sites indexed.

Until June of 2000, Yahoo! supplemented its search results with content from Inktomi, but in July it replaced Inktomi with Google. (Considering that Yahoo! was an investor in Google, this change was no surprise.) All major directory services supplement their relatively limited search databases with content from a major spider-driven search engine. Why is this? Well when you think about it, the worst thing that a search service can do in terms of its users' experience is advise them that their search yielded no matches. However, when you consider that in most directories, a 500-page Web site is described with just a 25-word description, there are many words, product names, brand names, or proper names that will not be included in that description. For that reason, all of the major human-edited directories are supplemented by a larger, more complete search engine and reference to this partner's larger index.

In November 2000, Yahoo! became the second major directory to limit its free submission option. Sites wishing to be listed in the "Shopping and

Services" or "Business to Business" areas of the directory must now use Yahoo's $199 Business Express Program. (A free submission option remains for those submitting to other areas of the Yahoo.com site or to regional commercial areas at Yahoo!'s non-U.S. editions.) This service in no way guarantees the submitter will gain a listing; it only ensures a review and a response within seven days. Yahoo claims it made this change so that it could affordably build out its commercial listings to be as comprehensive as possible.

Yahoo!'s Business Express Program

The program includes:

- Expedited consideration of your commercial web site for inclusion in the Yahoo! directory.
- Guaranteed site review within 7 business days.
- A one-time, non-refundable processing fee of **$199.00** USD.

Submit a site using

Business Express

---

1. **Web address:** www.yahoo.com
2. **Type of engine:** Hybrid. Primary results — Yahoo! directory, Secondary results — Google database.
3. **Partnerships:** Google for search results when no match in Yahoo! directory listings
4. **Total documents indexed:** Approximately one million documents in Yahoo!, and some 1.35 billion documents in Google
5. **Total page views per month:** 12,607,518,000 (Source: Alexa Research, Feb. 2001)
6. **E-mail support:** url-support@yahoo-inc.com
7. **How to confirm listing:** Type www.domain.com into search field.
8. **Obtain link popularity information:** Not applicable. Yahoo! does not consider link popularity in determining ranking.
9. **Result returns:** Top 20 results from Yahoo! index unless there is no match, then it defaults to Google.
10. **Receive higher rankings for link popularity:** Primary results — Not applicable, Secondary results — Yes.
11. **Additional off-the-page considerations:** Yahoo! measures click-through behavior as a component of its algorithm. Human editors will make a determination of your site description. Secondary results are subject to Google's link popularity measures.

12. **Rankings influenced by after-the-click behavior:** Primary results — Yes, Secondary results — No.

13. **Recognition and utilization of META tags:** Primary results — No, Secondary results — Yes.

14. **Consideration of META tags for relevancy:** Primary results — No, Secondary results — No.

15. **Importance of Title tag keyword prominence:** Primary results — No, Secondary results — Yes.

16. **Importance of <ALT> tag:** Primary results — No, Secondary results — Yes.

17. **Importance of multiple occurrences of keywords in Title tag:** Primary results — No, Secondary results — Yes.

18. **Maximum length of Title tag:** Not applicable for primary or secondary results.

19. **Maximum length of keyword META tag:** Not applicable for primary or secondary results.

20. **Maximum length of description META tag:** Not applicable for primary or secondary results.

21. **Comment tags considered for relevancy:** Primary results — No, Secondary results — No.

22. **Frame support:** Primary results — No. Frames impede a site from being submitted to multiple categories since framed sites can't be bookmarked. Secondary results — Yes.

23. **Image map support:** Primary results — No, Secondary results — No.

24. **Accepts automated submissions:** Primary results — No. CAUTION: Yahoo! treats automated submissions as spam and will ban your site. Secondary results — Yes.

25. **Indexes submitted pages only or conducts deep crawls:** Primary results — Not applicable. Yahoo! only indexes the default or home page that is submitted and only with rare exception will accept additional internal pages that are submitted after the home page has been indexed. Secondary results — Yes.

26. **Instant spidering of submitted page:** Primary results — No, Secondary results — No.

27. **Number of pages that can be submitted per day:** Primary results — Not applicable, Secondary results — 10 per day recommended.

28. **Word stemming and plural sensitive:** Primary results — No, Secondary results — No.

29. **Case-sensitive searches:** Primary results — No, Secondary results — No.

30. **Alphabetical page listings:** Primary results — Yes, Secondary results — No.

31. **Time to index page:** Primary results — Free submission: four to eight weeks. Business Express submission: seven days. Secondary results — Takes one to four weeks.

32. **Spam penalties:** Primary results — Yes. Sites deemed to be spamming will not be listed. Spamming includes submitting the same Web site too frequently (e.g., more than once per two-week period) or using automated submission software. Secondary results — No.

33. **Refuses pages with META refresh:** Primary results — Not applicable. However, Yahoo!'s category editors may frown upon a splash page that redirects too quickly. Proceed with caution. Secondary results — No.

34. **Refuses pages with invisible text:** Primary results — Not applicable. However, Yahoo!'s category editors would likely frown upon pages that include hidden text (spam) and deem the Web site unfit for listing. Secondary results — No.

35. **Refuses pages with "tiny text":** Primary results — Not applicable. If the tiny text is intended to "fool" the search engines, Yahoo!'s category editors could deem it sufficient cause to not list the Web site. Secondary results — No.

36. **Remove URL:** Primary results — url-support@yahoo-inc.com. Secondary results — Google will remove links for you.

This information may be out of date by the time of publication. Because search engines frequently change their ranking algorithms and other page scoring variables, we have posted updates and revisions to these chapters on our Web site: http://www.iprospect.com/search-engine-chapters.htm.

Understanding the Results

In most cases, when a user performs a search, Yahoo! displays one of three search result sets depending on the search itself:

■ **Yahoo! Category Matches** If the keyword queried was broad, as in a search for the word "marketing," Yahoo! will display a list of Yahoo! categories for the searcher to pick from. It's important to note that no company can attain a first-page listing for a keyword that yields a full page of Yahoo! categories. Instead, one must hope first that their category is, in fact, displayed in this first set of matches, and then second that the searcher clicks on their listing, which will be organized alphabetically within that category. Yahoo! site titles are almost always the company's actual legal name (regardless of what was submitted). If you target a broad keyword phrase, your Web site will likely be three clicks away from the searcher: Step one, the searcher constructs the query and presses the submit button. Step two, he or she clicks on the Yahoo! category that contains your listing. Step three, the searcher clicks on your listing. (This lengthy process is not ideal, as we'll discuss later.)

■ **Yahoo! Category Matches, Along with Web Sites from Within Those Categories** A more refined keyword phrase search containing two or more words is more likely to bring up relevant categories as well as sites contained within those categories, i.e., sites that contain the targeted keyword in the site title or description. Note that if your Yahoo! positioning strategy is to target a more specific two- or three-word phrase, it's likely that when you attain a ranking, you'll be just two clicks away from the searcher. That's because Yahoo! displays links to some of the actual Web sites contained in each of the categories it lists when a multi-word phrase is queried. If your Web site is one of them, it can be clicked on right away without having to dig through the dozens of other Web sites contained in the category.

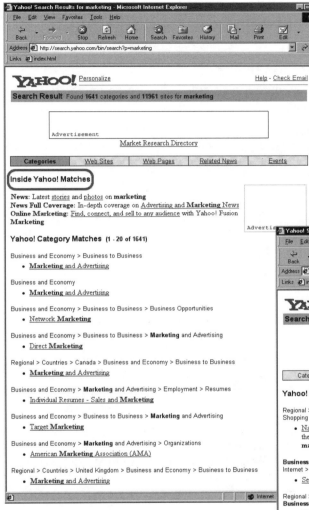

Yahoo! category matches (left) and category matches with Web sites from within those categories (below).

■ **Yahoo! Web Pages**   Yahoo! is forced to default to its search engine partner's database, Google, when a user performs a search for a keyword phrase

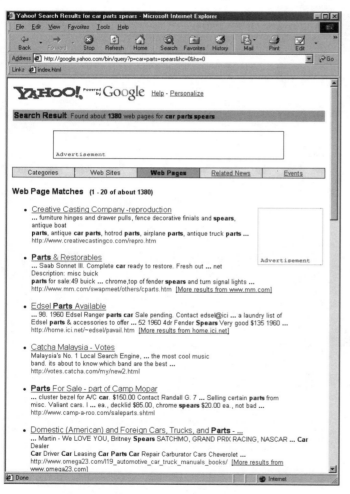

that does not yield a match from Yahoo!'s category descriptions or is not contained in a site title and description from within one of those categories. For example, take a search for "car parts spears," combining "car parts" with Britney Spears' last name for no particular reason. If a particular audience searches for relatively obscure products or services from a particular niche industry or area of inquiry by using obscure keywords, technical language, or a large variety of brand names, it is likely they will often be shown search matches from Yahoo! Web pages that are from the Google index. Depending on your industry, it could be necessary for you to rank well in Google in order for most of your audience to find you in Yahoo!.

Site Elements That Can Cause Problems

Yahoo! will not index Web sites that are incomplete, contain broken links, typos, misspellings, etc., or otherwise do not live up to their standards. A good test is to look at the other sites listed within the category where you feel your site should be listed and make an assessment of the other sites there. If yours is at least as attractive as those and does not contain broken links, incomplete pages, or other errors, you have a good shot at being accepted.

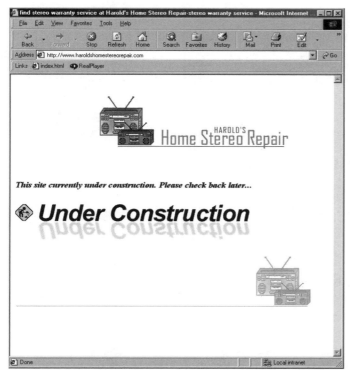

Any "under construction" graphics can be a hindrance to getting listed at Yahoo! since they could indicate to the Yahoo! category editors that the site is incomplete or "not ready for prime time."

We recommend that your site title and description META tags match your Yahoo! submission. We also recommend that the text on the Web page itself supports your Yahoo! submission. For instance, if the description you submitted to Yahoo! includes the phrase "foreign car parts," but your site's home page clearly states, "We Deal in American Car Parts Exclusively!," you'd have been lying to Yahoo! in your submitted description. And the odds of a Yahoo! category editor letting that slip past him or her is 0 percent.

Wherever possible, it helps to have the copy on your home page support your Yahoo! submission. We do not recommend making radical changes to the site copy, headlines, or image <ALT> tags in support of your Yahoo! site title and description; just make sure the two appear consistent or at least not in conflict.

Other site elements that can cause problems are frames. In some instances, it may be appropriate to submit a separate page from your Web site that deals with a unique or specific topic to an additional Yahoo! category. In some cases (though relatively rare), Yahoo! will accept a second submission from a Web site that has already been listed. However, if your site uses frames (and some very expensive Web sites produced by large companies still make this mistake), there is no easy way to link to a particular page other than the home page. That means that any internal page from within your Web site that might have been eligible for an additional listing cannot be considered by a Yahoo! editor. If you cannot set a bookmark to the internal page of your site, Yahoo!'s category editors are unlikely to investigate a workaround for you so the site can be listed. If you needed yet another reason to avoid frames, this is it.

NOTE   There are few good reasons to use the <FRAME> tag, since doing so interferes with spider-based search engines being able to index your Web site. Avoid frames whenever possible.

Recommended Site Optimization Tactics

Even if you're a grizzled SEP veteran, be sure to read this entire section. You're going to learn a few new techniques and strategies, and just a 1 percent advantage can make all the difference with Yahoo!, so read on.

If you read our first book, *Secrets to Achieving Top 10 Rankings,* some of this will be a refresher course. We've retained our original interview with Yahoo! Surfing Manager "Rose," who's been at Yahoo! since day one, because her comments were practical and timeless. ("Rose" is not her real name — we're simply protecting this senior staffer from a potential onslaught of unsolicited phone calls!) She generously provided these interviews back in 1997-98, and we've spoken with her as recently as August 2000. Since that time, we've cultivated numerous other relationships at Yahoo! and we're extremely thankful for each person's assistance and support.

Prepare, Prepare, Prepare

Although you do not "optimize" a Web site for a directory submission, per se, there are steps you should take in preparing your submission to Yahoo!. Typically, most people who submit to Yahoo! simply pick a category or two, write a site title and description, and then submit. Even most "guides" on SEP make a big deal about how important it is to submit to Yahoo! and how critical a good Yahoo! position is to a Web site's success, but then simply instruct the reader on how to properly fill out Yahoo!'s submission forms. This is not a strategic approach. Take six steps back and do some serious planning before you even consider selecting your first Yahoo! category. At this point, you don't even know how to pick a Yahoo! category yet. More importantly, by which criteria should you evaluate the value of a particular Yahoo! category versus another?

Before you pick a single Yahoo! category, before you even **think** about writing a site title and description, you must devise a strategy and you must test, test, and test that plan. If you want to succeed in Yahoo!, you must first determine how you would rank if Yahoo! were to accept your submission exactly as you submitted it to the categories you selected.

 CAUTION   Do not even **think** about submitting to Yahoo! unless you know with close certainty how your Web site will rank beforehand. Otherwise you could be stuck with a poor ranking forever.

Click Through, Click Away

Recently, Yahoo! started tracking click-through behavior as a component of its ranking algorithm. After you have performed a search in Yahoo!, and the results are displayed, you can hold your mouse over the site that you intend to visit and look down in the lower left-hand corner of your browser to see what I mean. If you search for "iProspect" in Yahoo!, iProspect.com is the only site that is returned in the search results. If you drop the mouse over the blue activated link to iProspect.com (Yahoo!'s title for our Web site) and look in the lower left-hand corner of your browser, you'll see the actual link that will be executed should you click on it:

http://srd.yahoo.com/srst/13832989/iprospect.com/1/1/*http://www.iProspect.com/

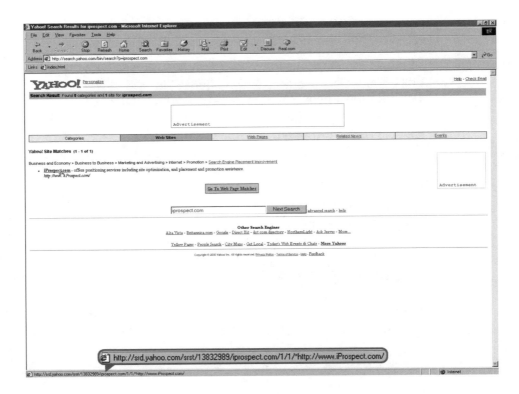

This demonstrates that clicking on this link does not take the user directly to the Web site. It takes him or her to an intermediate page so that Yahoo! can count the click-through, note the keyword that was queried, and log the fact that the user selected that Web site after performing that keyword search. As more people perform the same search and click on the same Web site, that site will rise in ranking for those searches. You can tell that a search engine is not tracking click-through if, when you hold your mouse over the link, it looks just like a standard link to the Web site: http://www.iprospect.com.

Additionally, be aware that Yahoo! is also likely to be tracking "click-away" behavior (though they probably call it by a different name). This means they can tell if users who clicked on a particular link returned to Yahoo! and tried another link (presumably because the first site they selected did not serve their needs), or if they stayed on that site after making their selection and did not return to Yahoo! for a long period of time. Therefore, sites that hold their visitors' interest and satisfy the intent of their queries may fare better than ones that merely do a good job with a compelling site title and description that entices the user to click.

The Keyword Game

This means that the days are gone when you could attain a first-page ranking in Yahoo! by simply ensuring that your site title and description contained that targeted keyword. For many searches, there are sites displayed that do not contain the complete keyword that was queried, but perhaps just a word or two of the phrase and the remaining word is found in the category heading. For example, on searches for "search engine submission" these results were presented on the first page:

Computers and Internet > Internet > World Wide Web > Site Announcement and Promotion > **Search Engine** Placement Improvement

- **Search Engines: Submission** Tips, Help and Use
- Ceremonial Yahoo **Submission** - suggestion for a ceremonial sacrament you can use to help your site get listed on the Yahoo **search** directory.

Note that the second listing for "Ceremonial Yahoo Submission" does not include the word "engine" from our query "search engine submission." That word is apparently keyed to the word in the Yahoo! category heading. (By the way, this page describes a ceremony and chant you can perform in hopes of increasing your odds of getting listed in Yahoo!.)

This is not to say that you should eliminate one of the words that makes up a keyword phrase when preparing your Yahoo! submission, although in some cases, theoretically, you could. In most cases, having all of your targeted keyword phrases next to each other, early in the description's sentence and in the site title, offers you the best chance of having your site pop up in the top listings beneath your category heading.

In the old days (well, just last year), if you submitted a site to Yahoo! and the targeted keyword phrase was in the site title and used as the first words of the site description (and of course, assuming Yahoo! accepted the submission as constructed), you were virtually assured your site would be returned in a top-ranking position for searches on that phrase. But today, a site that does not contain all of the keywords in a given keyword phrase query may pop up before listings that contain all the words if more people are clicking on and visiting their Web site (or if they are performing the query and clicking on their own site over and over — not fair, but it happens).

What You Should Know

Here are some considerations for dealing with this new environment:

■ Site descriptions that are more appealing are more likely to have higher click-through rates, and attain and sustain higher rankings. A long laundry list of keywords is unlikely to be appealing to a searcher and is therefore not likely to cause someone to click-through to your listing.

■ A shorter, more focused keyword-centric site title and description may generate a higher click-through rate and thereby a higher ranking. In studies performed by GoTo.com, it was determined that paid listings containing the targeted keyword phrase in the site title increased the likelihood of click-through to that site dramatically.

■ A Yahoo! listing that does not contain any of the words that make up a targeted keyword phrase will not (at this time) create a ranking for that keyword phrase. We have not observed a ranking in Yahoo! that did not include all of the words in the listing.

■ If you submit to Yahoo! categories that contain few total listings, your site is much more likely to attain a first-page listing if it does not include all of the keywords that make up a targeted phrase (as opposed to competing with 10 to 15 sites containing all of the targeted keywords that make up a particular phrase).

■ The best Web sites that have high-quality content, intuitive design, and information relevant to a particular keyword search are likely to fare well under this new system. Remember, Yahoo! is not just tracking click-through, they're tracking "click-away."

■ In some instances, if you are a well-known company but you do not submit anything to Yahoo!, they will find descriptions of your company and use what they find — we believe they often use the boilerplate information from your press releases. So keep an eye on how you describe yourself in various places, and be sure it's consistent with what you plan to submit to Yahoo!. For example, take a look at the Toys "R" Us press release boilerplate and its current Yahoo! description on the following page — see any similarities?

Chances are, at one point in time, Toys "R" Us' press release boilerplate matched the Yahoo! description more closely, but Toys "R" Us has since grown and added new locations and acquisitions, and now the numbers no longer match up.

Toys "R" Us Press Release Boilerplate:

Toys "R" Us, the world's leading resource for kids, families and fun, currently operates 1,559 stores worldwide: 707 Toys "R" Us stores in the United States; 474 International toy store, including franchise stores; 200 Kids "R" Us children's clothing stores; 138 Babies "R" Us stores; and 39 Imaginarium stores. The company also sells merchandise through its Internet sites at http://www.toysrus.com, http://www.imaginarium.com and http://www.babiesrus.com, and through mail order catalogs.

Yahoo! Site Matches:

Business and Economy > Shopping and Services > **Toys** > Retailers > <u>**Toys R Us**</u>

- <u>**Toys R Us Home Page**</u> - is the world's largest retailer of children's products. As of 1/99, Toys R Us, Inc. operated 1,156 toy stores, 212 Kids R Us children's clothing stores and 113 Babies R Us infant stores.

The fact that Yahoo! considers click-through behavior in determining which sites are displayed makes your advance submission planning that much more important. But even in this new environment, you can make decisions that will impact your rankings before you ever press Yahoo!'s "Suggest a Site" link — and you must, if you want a good ranking with Yahoo!.

Here's the Plan

Remember, in Yahoo! your site title and description are king. There are only 25 possible words, and maybe a few additional words in the site title, from which Yahoo! can formulate its ranking decisions. So take some time to follow this step-by-step plan to formulate your winning submission:

Goal #1: Target the keyword phrases that, when queried, produce first-page ranking opportunities.

It's always better to have your Web site displayed immediately after someone performs a keyword search, as opposed to hoping that the searcher pokes around and clicks through several categories to find you. This means that if you query a keyword or phrase and Yahoo! returns a long list of Yahoo! categories, you should **not** target this keyword phrase or plan your strategy around attaining a ranking on this keyword. For example, nobody attains a first-page ranking on a search for the word "marketing." With Yahoo!, a search for the word "marketing" produces a list of 20 Yahoo! categories — no individual Web sites are displayed on the first page of search results. A better choice would be "small business marketing consulting," or another more targeted phrase that reflects what you offer.

1.   First identify the keywords and phrases you want to target with your Yahoo! submission. Note that this is different from merely determining which keywords you should target for your search engine optimization campaign in general (discussed in Chapter 4). And, even as you prepare a target keyword list for Yahoo!, don't fall in love with any of those choices yet. Even though you may have already devised a 25-word sentence containing your most valuable and important target keywords, slow down — in Yahoo!, not all keywords are created equally. Specifically, querying some single-word keywords yields a long list of category matches, while other two- and three-word phrases produce category matches with sites from within the category listed below them. This is what you want!

     Why? Let's think about this. If the searcher is presented with 20 Yahoo! categories, the odds that he will click on the category where your site is listed is maybe 2 in 20. This assumes that your site gets listed in two Yahoo! categories and that both of those categories are displayed for that particular keyword match. Then, even if he clicks on the category that contains your Web site, if that category contains 30 Web sites, your odds are 1 in 30 that he will click on yours (and remember, some Yahoo! categories contain dozens of sites, giving you much worse odds). For this reason, you want to target keyword phrases that produce categories **and** Web site matches.

2.   Query each of your keywords and keyword phrases one by one in the Yahoo! search field. Review the results. Write down the keywords or keyword phrases that when queried, produce a list of only category matches as opposed to Yahoo! categories with sites from within those categories. Now, remove any keyword from your list that produced a long list of Yahoo! categories.

3.   Make note of which categories correspond to which keyword phrase searches. You'll likely discover that some Yahoo! categories come up for eight out of ten keyword phrase searches while others are returned for just a few. Once you've determined which categories are presented most often, review this list and visit each category. Determine which category would be most relevant for your Web site and where you think Yahoo! would be most likely to include it. Assuming you were performing queries for phrases that were strictly relevant to

your Web site, chances are that several of the categories that were presented are good and appropriate choices. You want to choose the category that is most relevant to your Web site for submission.

▼ **CAUTION**   If the category is not sufficiently relevant or if it's a stretch that your site fits into it, Yahoo! could reject your submission entirely or put you in a different category against your wishes.

One way to test if a category is relevant is by evaluating the other sites listed there. Is your competitor listed in that category? Are sites in similar businesses listed there? These are the types of questions to ask. Now, remember, the classification of a business is not an exact science. It is likely that there are several — sometimes six or seven — categories where your Web site might seem an appropriate fit. Why pick a category that doesn't display as a search match to any of your important queries? You would only do this if none of the categories displayed in response to querying your most important keywords are appropriate — and from time to time that happens.

Once you've decided on your Yahoo! categories, copy them down for later use.

"Submit to Yahoo! manually. Yahoo! is so important that you will want to take the time and do it by hand. Besides, some submission services and tools won't put you in the right category, as Yahoo! categories change constantly.

"You will likely be put in the category with other Web sites or businesses like yours. For instance, though you might really want to be in the 'teachers' category because you sell to teachers, you will end up in the 'textbooks' category if that's what you make."

— *"Rose," Surfing Manager at Yahoo!*

▶ **IMPORTANT**   If your Web site is regional, meaning you're unlikely to do business outside of your local area, Yahoo! may force you into a regional category. For instance, if you operate a local pharmacy, Yahoo! may rightly (based on their taxonomy) consider your submission only for a regional Yahoo! category. However, if you do service the entire United States or beyond (perhaps your local pharmacy sells vitamin supplements throughout the country via mail order), you may have to lobby Yahoo! and explain to them why you deserve a different listing.

Goal #2: Develop a site title and description that contain targeted keyword phrases that will present first-page ranking opportunities and will be accepted by Yahoo!.

Keep in mind that Yahoo! requires your site title to be your company name — unless you've built a Web site for a particular branded product that your company sells. For instance, if Nike introduced a sneaker called "The Terminator" that had its own Web site and URL (as opposed to being a page within the company's corporate site), that site could be titled "The Nike Terminator Basketball Sneaker" and be considered for a separate Yahoo! listing. There is no guarantee that the Yahoo! editors wouldn't reduce that down to "Terminator, The" but they may likely keep the full product name as it was submitted to them. If this is your corporate Web site, stick with just the company name as the site title. If it's a product-specific or service-specific Web site, and that product or service is more well known than your company name, by all means, attempt to use the product or service as the site title.

> *"As a Yahoo! category editor, I will do everything I can to find the legitimate name of the business. We prefer it if you go by the name you gave your business as a site title.*
>
> *"If you're a commercial site, you won't get added [by using a title that describes the site content and not the company name]. Don't use marketing lingo like, 'We're the best.' If I have a choice between a site title like, 'A really good book' or 'The Cambridge Paperback Encyclopedia,' I will spend more time on [the site that submitted] the correct title.*
>
> *"If [using keywords early in your site description] is done appropriately and it really describes the Web site, it will go through. Otherwise we'll change it — but you can try it!"*
> — *"Rose," Surfing Manager at Yahoo!*

Your site title should not exceed 40 characters. Yahoo! ranks sites alphabetically, so try to choose a site title that is alphabetically superior if you can be listed by something other than your company name, e.g., a brand- or product-specific Web site. **Do not** be overt and name your site "A+ techniques to selling paint" or something that obvious — you **will** get caught, and Yahoo! will likely use your actual business name instead. (See the important "Special Tips and Tactics for This Engine" section later in this chapter, which explains the ASCII hierarchy and which letters and symbols rank higher than others.)

Goal #3: "Massage" your site description into a form that will NOT likely be edited by Yahoo!.

One mistake many people make when submitting to Yahoo! is to create a 25-word description that's an obvious attempt to simply cram in as many keywords as possible into a barely credible sentence. This is just begging the Yahoo! category editor to butcher your description and likely remove some of your valuable keyword phrases!

First, take a look at the listings of the sites contained within the Yahoo! category that would be your first choice. You'll notice in some categories that all of the site descriptions begin with the word "offers" or "provides" or "features" or "specializing in" etc., — go with the flow. This means the Yahoo! editor for this category likes this language. Give the editor a site description that sounds like the others in that category — same tone and word choices.

If you don't see your targeted keyword phrase in the description of any of the other companies listed, it may be because the Yahoo! editor for this category doesn't like that phrase or thinks that it's not sufficiently descriptive. Chances are if you use that phrase, it will be edited out of your final description. So for best results, do all that you can to ensure that your submitted description uses similar language to those already included in that section.

CAUTION   If your description sounds clunky, the Yahoo! category editor could carve away your most important keywords in an attempt to make your listing flow better. The more your submission sounds like the ones they already list in that category, the less likely it will be edited.

Also, be very careful about pluralization and separating keywords. We've seen a submission to Yahoo! not attain a ranking on a particular company's most important targeted keyword phrase, "educational toys," because the person who prepared the submission constructed the description using only "toy" — in the singular. (They did have a ranking on searches for "education toy" but fewer people search for it that way — the plural version of the word would have effectively targeted both.) On another occasion, a reader of our previous guide advised us that he thought he could attain a ranking on a keyword phrase, whether or not the words in that phrase were next to each other. As it turned out, due to the volume of sites in that target's categories, only those listings that contained the keywords consecutively attained a first-page ranking.

Are You Functional *and* Attractive?

Think you're ready? Not yet. Make absolutely sure your entire site is fully operational: no broken links, under-construction graphics, or non-working features.
Remember, a person will be visiting your Web site and thoroughly clicking
around. Also, review several (if not all) of the other Web sites in the category
where you will be proposing that your site be listed. Understand that, like it or
not, your site will be compared against the others in the categories where you
seek to be listed. To that extent, beauty is relative.

Now, the Yahoo! directory contains some pretty sorry-looking Web sites —
just like the whole Web itself. Not everyone has a multi-million dollar Web site
to submit to Yahoo!, and that's okay. But let's take the stock trading category, for
example, which contains mostly million-dollar Web sites. If your site was built
by your teenage son using FrontPage and features scanned, crayon-drawn
graphics, you likely won't get listed in this area.

In categories such as multi-level-marketing or dieting self help, you'll find
a multitude of unattractive Web sites. (Search for "diet pills" and you'll see what
I'm talking about.) This is your chance to shine — work to post a truly attractive
and informative site in hopes of getting Yahoo!'s attention.

Off-the-Page Factors That Influence Success

As described previously, Yahoo! now tracks click-through (and click-away)
behavior. Sites that Yahoo! search users actually click on and visit (and stay on)
gain a slight boost in rankings beyond merely keyword placement in the site title
and description. For searches that default to Google results, in Yahoo! called Web
pages, link popularity is considered. For more information on Google's relevancy
requirements, see Chapter 19.

How to Submit a Site to This Engine

First, check to see if you're already listed in Yahoo! by typing your Web site's
complete URL into the search field as follows: http://www.yourcompany.com. If
your Web site is not already listed in Yahoo!, proceed to the Yahoo! category you
selected as your first best choice.

As mentioned earlier, Yahoo! has dropped its free submission policy for the
commercial portion of its directory. If you want to be listed in their "Shopping
and Services" or "Business to Business" areas, you now have to use Yahoo!'s

$199 Business Express Program. (A free submission option remains for those submitting to other areas of the Yahoo.com site or to regional commercial areas at Yahoo's non-U.S. editions.)

That's right — no more free commercial submissions, but you are ensured a review within seven days of your submission. Understand that Yahoo! is making no guarantee that your site will be added to their index, only that they will review it and advise you as to why it was rejected. They also offer you an opportunity to appeal their decision after responding to the issues they've cited.

 CAUTION Do not use automated submission software to submit to Yahoo!. It's much too sensitive a process to put at such risk. Take the time to do it right — yourself.

"Submissions from the submitting software tools and even the submitting services are often gibberish. We much prefer it if you do your submissions manually. That way you can read our rules and do it properly — it makes our job easier."
     — *"Rose," Surfing Manager at Yahoo!*

To begin the submission process, enter into your first-choice category (like you're doing a search). Scroll to the bottom of the page and select the tiny "Suggest a Site" link.

The next screen recommends you read a brief explanation of the submission process, then you're told to "proceed to step one," where you're presented with the Business Express Submission button, which you should select. The next screen describes the Business Express submission process, lists some terms and conditions of use, and prompts you to complete a "qualification form" (shown on the following page). This lets people determine, before paying for the service, whether their site will ultimately be rejected by Yahoo!.

Once you've acknowledged each of the qualifications and indicated your preparedness to proceed to the next step, Yahoo! asks you to "log in" or create an account. Whether you already have a Yahoo! e-mail account or you have never before established one, the forms are the same.

At the bottom of that page, click on the "Suggest a Site" link and proceed to step one. (From time to time, we've found these suggest-a-site links are not working, and they instead take you to a Help page or FAQ about suggesting sites to Yahoo!. Don't worry, try again in a day and it should be working.) You will be asked to enter your site title, which is likely to be your company name (as we discussed above), and your Web site description, which should not exceed 25 words. Next, you will be asked if your Web site is eligible to be included in another Yahoo! category. This is where you should enter your second Yahoo! category selection.

> **IMPORTANT**   Yahoo! will ask if you think it should create a separate category in which to list your Web site. **Don't do it!** As enticing as this might sound, resist the temptation! If Yahoo! grants your wish for a new category, you have no way of knowing whether or not that new Yahoo! category will be displayed for any of your keyword searches. Remember, the key to a great Yahoo! submission is to assess how your site would rank if Yahoo! accepted your submission verbatim. You can know with certainty which Yahoo! categories are displayed and in which order when different keywords are queried, but you will not know if the new category you propose will come up for any of your targeted keyword phrases. So, do not suggest a new category. Leave that pioneering opportunity to someone else. You can always ask to be added to new Yahoo! categories later.

- ☐ **I have read and agree to be bound by the <u>Business Express Terms of Service</u>**.
- ☐ I have verified that my site does not already appear in the Yahoo! Directory and I understand that this is **not** the place to request a <u>change</u> for an existing site. [<u>Section 2.6</u>]
- ☐ My site supports multiple browsers and capabilities. (For example, java only sites will not be listed). [<u>Section 3.1</u>]
- ☐ My site must be in the English language (or have an English language version available). [<u>Section 3.1</u>]
- ☐ I understand that there is **no guarantee** my site will be added to Yahoo! [<u>Section 2.5</u>]
- ☐ I understand that Yahoo! reserves the right to edit and place my site as appropriate. [<u>Section 4.1</u>]
- ☐ I understand that if my site is added, it will be treated as any other site in Yahoo! and will receive no special consideration. [<u>Section 4.1</u>]
- ☐ My site must be up and running 24 hours a day, seven days a week. [<u>Section 3.1</u>]
- ☐ No parts of my site are under construction. All links on the site work. [<u>Section 3.1</u>]
- ☐ My site contains substantively unique content that is not already accessible from the Yahoo! Directory. (For example: a user that submits multiple URLs to the very same content is not submitting substantively unique content.) [<u>Section 3.1</u>]

In seven days, Yahoo! will notify you via e-mail of their decision, but even if they accept your submission, you will not know how they have chosen to describe your site until the listing appears in the directory.

In the event that Yahoo! has elected not to list your site, given you a poor description, or included you in an inaccurate category, you may appeal their decision. If you're advised that it was due to broken links or an incomplete or inadequate Web site, fix it and resubmit. If the rejection was due to some other issue, respond to it as best you can within the 30 days allowed.

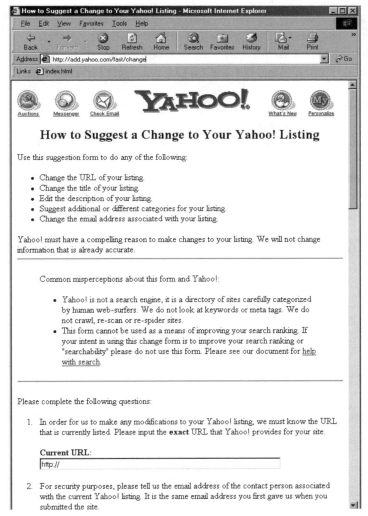

If Yahoo! accepted your submission, hopefully they accepted with few edits and it will attain many of the rankings you had targeted. If it was accepted but was modified to the point that you feel it no longer accurately describes your Web site, you do have recourse. Yahoo! suggests that you use its add/change URL form located here:

http://add.yahoo.com/fast/change

If, after you've completed this form, nothing has happened, contact Yahoo! at the phone numbers listed at the beginning of the chapter to voice your concern. However, we've never observed a change in any site listing after using this form, and have never received a communication from Yahoo! indicating they've taken any action as a result of using this interface.

You will have more success in changing an existing listing if your reason is perceived as something more serious than just for the sake of improving your ranking (which they couldn't care less about). For example, if you've created a new domain name for your site, request that the description be updated, and the new domain name be used as indicated in the change request form you filled out. Other credible reasons you could offer would be a change in your company name (if it has indeed changed), a change in the emphasis of your business, thereby requiring a new description, or a typo that needs to be corrected.

When your Web site is finally added to Yahoo!, celebrate! You've joined an elite fraternity of Web sites that have passed the Yahoo! initiation rite. Your Web site will be listed as "New" for a few days and be listed ahead of the alphabetically sorted listings within that category for a period of time.

We had an interesting experience where a Web site that was newly added to Yahoo! and listed above the category as "new" was not included in search results. Later, when the site was added to the alphabetical listings within the category, that problem corrected itself. That seems to have been a temporary glitch with the Yahoo! system and has not happened since. However, if your site is listed as "new" but does not come up on searches for the exact company name, it could be a victim of that same glitch.

If you don't see your Web site added to Yahoo! within seven days, it's okay. In fact, it's suggested by Yahoo! that you resubmit — once. If after waiting an additional two weeks your site still doesn't show up in Yahoo!, your next step should be to send an e-mail to url-support@yahoo-inc.com, or call Yahoo! at its support line: (408) 731-3333, or the main number: (408) 731-3300. Then follow the voice prompts.

Here's one more submission alternative for Yahoo!. If your site is added to any category under Business and Economy > Shopping and Services or Business and Economy > Business to Business, you also have the option for your site to become a "Sponsored Link." This is a fee-based program which permits commercial sites already listed in Yahoo! to receive priority placement within the categories above. This will place your site above all others. It's especially important for sites that would be placed low in the alphabet to utilize this service. This usually costs between $25 and $300 per month.

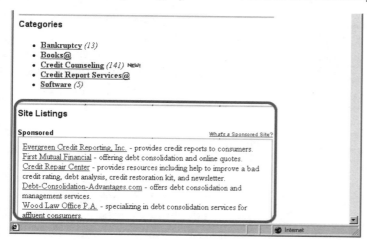

How to Build Informational Pages for this Engine

This topic is not applicable. Yahoo! accepts only submissions for the main Web site.

How to Know If Your Site Has Been Spidered/Listed

Yahoo! spiders all submitted pages to ensure they are online. For this initial spider, your logs will show this trail: add.yahoo.com - [25/Oct/2000:10:21:15-0600] "GET / HTTP/1.0" 200 5640.

After a Yahoo! surfing manager has visited your Web site, the log file will reflect this visitor: http://surfyahoo.com/submissions/990416/102748-19350.html.

Indexing Timetable

A guaranteed seven days for all commercial submissions (which are now $199).

What to Do If Your Rankings Disappear

Resubmit, or send e-mail to url-support@yahoo-inc.com or telephone them at (408) 731-3333. This is a very interesting service. In the past, when you dialed this number you used to reach any of six staffers who would answer specific questions. Now you get an informational voice-mail message only. At the end of the messages, you will hear recorded instructions on how to leave a message concerning any problem you have had getting listed with Yahoo!'s main page. This is a great service for anyone struggling to get a site listed in Yahoo!. Considering that by some accounts Yahoo! adds only one in ten submissions to its index, this number can be valuable in finding out why you are encountering problems, or to get information on how you can get your listing included in Yahoo!'s directory.

Special Tips and Tactics for This Engine

Think Long

Yahoo! indexes characters and word phrases, not just whole words. This means that if you're searching for "travel," you will also find "traveling" and "travels."

Examine your keywords and try to use the longest variation of your important keywords. In our "travel" keyword example, the word "travel" is also present in the words "travels" and "traveling." With Yahoo!, by using the word "traveling" you are assured hits when people search on either "travel" or "traveling." You are, in effect, including two keywords for the price of one!

Got Timely Information?

Some Web sites that contain timely news or information can sometimes get indexed very quickly — if you ask for it! For instance, Yahoo! has a "very specialized movie surfer" who specializes in getting movie sites listed as quickly as necessary for release dates. If you are promoting an event or some product with an expiration date and you must get your site listed quickly, you should consider contacting Yahoo! and seeing if they will help. The staff is very committed to making Yahoo! a terrific product. They will help you if they can.

The @%$#*!! ABCs of the ASCII Hierarchy

A search engine is a database, and databases have rules. Have you ever noticed that when you rename a file to start with an "!" it moves to the top of your file list in Windows? The same holds true for some search engines, certainly Yahoo!, which ranks alphabetically as well as by myriad other criteria.

The ASCII hierarchy dictates which symbol will lead the pack. The highest ranking symbol is actually a space. This invisible symbol ranks highest in the hierarchy of the ASCII alphabet, followed by an exclamation mark, quotes, the pound sign *(#),* and then nearly two dozen other characters before a single letter from the alphabet.

Unfortunately, dozens of SEP professionals have attempted to use this specific technique to their advantage in Yahoo! — most of them in naming their own companies with outlandish ASCII characters.

There are currently some 21 companies in Yahoo!'s "Search Engine Placement Improvement" category who are employing this technique and listing their company with names such as "!Positioning Services," or "#1 Web Marketing Guru." I'm sure we're not far from the day when we'll see a Web site listed in Yahoo! named, "!#@##@!#.com" only to be bested by a newer site named, "!!##!$@#.com," looking like disguised swear words in the Sunday comics.

We recently changed our company name and, like many other companies, had an opportunity to pick a name that started with an alphabetically desirable letter for the benefit of our Yahoo! listing. We came into this world as "Response

Direct" but didn't like it because it sounded like a direct marketing company and not an SEP services company. So did we pick a name that started with *A*? No, and we could have named our company anything — we had a blank slate. We chose "iProspect.com." Not alphabetically advantageous, just memorable.

However, for some companies without large online marketing budgets or without money to adequately brand their products such that people think to search for them by their brand name, an alphabetically desirable name can mean significantly increased traffic from Yahoo!. Frankly, in some Yahoo! categories that contain fewer listings and many company or product names that are less alphabetically desirable, the category is practically begging for a company name that starts with A or even C. The company that has the good sense to take advantage of this will surely enjoy some significant Yahoo! traffic.

The following table is intended to show how machines interpret and sort the alphabet and how to gain an edge. At the risk of finding other fiercely competitive categories filled with company names that begin with ! or #, I preface this table with a cautionary note.

> ▼ **CAUTION**   ATTENTION ALPHABETICAL ADVANTAGE SEEKERS! If you start this arms race (for higher ranking alphabetical characters), where will it end? Do you really want your industry segment to devolve into the mess that is the search engine placement improvement Yahoo! category? How will that reflect on your industry segment? Remember, if you start the arms — or alphabet — race, it will escalate. You've been warned.

Here is your new alphabet; learn it well. For some, it will provide a significant advantage. For others, it will produce a silly company or product name. You decide what's right for your organization.

The ASCII Hierarchy:

1.	(space)	10.	)	19.	<
2.	!	11.	*	20.	=
3.	"	12.	+	21.	>
4.	#	13.	,	22.	?
5.	$	14.	-	23.	@
6.	%	15.	.	24.	A
7.	&	16.	/	25.	B
8.	'	17.	:	26.	C
9.	(	18.	;	27.	D

28.	E	48.	Y	68.	m	
29.	F	49.	Z	69.	n	
30.	G	50.	[	70.	o	
31.	H	51.	\	71.	p	
32.	I	52.	]	72.	q	
33.	J	53.	^	73.	r	
34.	K	54.	_	74.	s	
35.	L	55.	'	75.	t	
36.	M	56.	a	76.	u	
37.	N	57.	b	77.	v	
38.	O	58.	c	78.	w	
39.	P	59.	d	79.	x	
40.	Q	60.	e	80.	y	
41.	R	61.	f	81.	z	
42.	S	62.	g	82.	{	
43.	T	63.	h	83.			
44.	U	64.	i	84.	}	
45.	V	65.	j	85.	~	
46.	W	66.	k			
47.	X	67.	l			

Above are the symbols and letters in their ASCII rank. There are, of course, more characters in the ASCII character set. However, these are the ones you'd be more likely to use and are in ranked order. While we're certain you can read the table above, let us point out several connections that may not be obvious at first.

Capital letters rank higher than non-capitalized letters. "MORTGAGE" will rank higher than its lowercase equivalent, "mortgage." Yahoo! specifically asks you not to use text in all caps in your site description, but you can at least capitalize the first letter.

Where appropriate, replacing letters with certain symbols puts you at the head of a list. It may be inappropriate or blatantly offensive to a search engine's rules to randomly include an exclamation mark ahead of your company name, or worse, doing the phone book trick and adding "AAA" to your site name (especially if that's not what you go by on your Web site). But what if your product or site really is named "@DVANTAGE!" or something similar? You're ahead of any competitor simply named "Advantage."

"So long as the name appears to be used in trade [throughout the Web site] with the ASCII character, we shouldn't have a problem with it."
— *"Rose," Surfing Manager at Yahoo!*

CAUTION   Keep in mind that while using a symbol may improve your ranking within a category, it will also hurt your chances of having people find you based on a keyword search. People are much more likely to search for "sales success" than for "$ales $uccess."

Yahoo! has corrected sites that use overt ASCII hierarchy tricks such as leading with an exclamation point or other non-alpha character. If you do this, you risk a delay in your site being listed, and it will most certainly be corrected by the category editor. If your site is legitimately named something that starts with a symbol, such as "$ales $uccess," when the Yahoo! staff member who visits your site finds that usage throughout, you may be allowed to use this approach and gain an advantage.

When You Should Consider Renaming Your Site

You may consider renaming your site if your company or products are alphabetically challenged. For example, take the case of a sheet music dealer whose core audience is piano players, and its site is named "Sheet Music, Inc." We'd recommend renaming the site "Piano Sheet Music Limited." Not only does the new company name start with P, which is an improved position compared with S, but it also added the important keyword "piano" to the site title.

But if the bricks-and-mortar company is in fact named "Sheet Music, Inc.," is there an ethical problem in naming the online store "Piano Sheet Music Limited?" From a business and branding perspective, not at all. Many bricks-and-mortar companies have online companies or DBAs ("doing business as" names) that are separate, distinct, and different from their storefronts' retail operations. Even MCI operates "unbranded products" such as 1-800-COLLECT.

CAUTION   Do not employ the classic Yellow Pages trick of prefacing your page name with *AAA*. The Yahoo! staff will see right through that and adjust your feeble attempt to spam its directory.

More examples: Some pharmacies legitimately operate online pharmacies selling Propecia or Viagra that operate under a different company name, and some restaurant owners operate Web sites selling only their gourmet coffee beans. The only problem that arises here is if you have only one Web site serving both your physical storefront and your online brand. Then you'd need to make some decisions. There's value in being first, but only you can determine if this would be ethical or appropriate given the type of business or organization you lead. Is having your physical storefront indexed and listed by its known name more important than operating a separate branded Web site? Or do you need two distinct Web presences? It's your call.

For example, if you're named "Zebra Systems" and are well known in the marketplace as such, you're out of luck. Renaming your company or product for the purposes of your Web site means that people who already know your company and are simply trying to find your site (for your business hours, for example) just won't find you. Your best choice is to retain your brand.

Responsiveness and Help Provided

Yahoo! is slow or unresponsive in responding to e-mail inquiries, but if you can get a human on the phone, you can typically get your question answered. In our experience, the Business Express folks have been very responsive.

NOTE: Still need help? Provide us with a detailed description of your Web site challenge. We'll be pleased to help in any way we can, or will refer you to any number of high-quality search engine optimization specialists whom we know and trust. Feel free to e-mail us at: sales@iprospect.com, or visit our quote request page at: http://www.iprospect.com/book-quote.htm.

Chapter 12:

About.com

About.com, Inc.
1440 Broadway
New York, NY 10018
http://about.com
(212) 204-4000
Media Relations: Tabitha Sturm at pr@about-inc.com

Free updates to this book are available via e-mail newsletter
by visiting: http://www.iprospect.com/book-news.htm.

Facts about This Engine

Scott Kurnit and his team originally launched About.com in 1997 as the Mining Company. In 1999, the name was changed to About.com to reflect the site's breadth of content, services, and ease of use. In February 2001, About.com was merged with Primedia, Inc. The About.com network includes 1,500 Luna Network partners, 5,000 experts of Expert Central, 25,000 affiliates of the About.com service, 100,000 affiliates of Vantage Net's freepolls.com, and 1,000,000 sites affiliated with North Sky's properties as well as the Sprinks pay-per-click search engine. The Sprinks results and Luna partners are integrated into the About.com content.

The site is a vortal — a vertical portal — that is divided into 36 channels. Within the channels are over 700 GuideSites™ that cover more than 50,000 subjects with over 1 million links to the best resources. Over 700 human guides maintain these guide sites.

Guides are responsible for filling the listings around their specific topics with the best new content, relevant links, how-to information, and online forums. Guides also have a responsibility to answer any questions posed to them by searchers on their topic. This creates an interactive environment. About.com's guides gather and review pages, links, relevant content from the community, and commercial resources relating to their topic. The intent is to provide the most relevant content with a human touch. About guides live and work in over 20 countries and are selected for their ability to provide the most interesting information for users.

1. **Web address:** http://www.about.com
2. **Type of engine:** Human-edited network of targeted sites
3. **Partnerships:** In February 2001, About.com merged with Primedia, Inc.
4. **Total documents indexed:** Unidentified
5. **Total page views per month:** 449,361,000 (Source: Alexa Research, Feb. 2001)
6. **E-mail support:** Yes! Each guide is responsible for e-mail support for his or her topics. Most e-mail addresses are formatted as follows: topic.guide@about.com.
7. **How to confirm listing:** Type in the full URL.
8. **Obtain link popularity information:** Not applicable

9. **Result returns:** Web results are returned from the About.com topic listings gathered by the guides and the number of results will vary from topic to topic. At the bottom of every page there are paid listings offered by Sprinks.com.

10. **Receive higher rankings for link popularity:** No

11. **Additional off-the-page considerations:** Uses humans to locate, review, and list sites.

12. **Rankings influenced by after-the-click behavior:** No

13. **Recognition and utilization of META tags:** No

14. **Consideration of META tags for relevancy:** No

15. **Importance of Title tag keyword prominence:** No

16. **Importance of <ALT> tag:** No

17. **Importance of multiple occurrences of keywords in Title tag:** No

18. **Maximum length of Title tag:** Not applicable

19. **Maximum length of keyword META tag:** Not applicable

20. **Maximum length of description META tag:** Not applicable

21. **Comment tags considered for relevancy:** No

22. **Frame support:** Not applicable

23. **Image map support:** Not applicable

24. **Accepts automated submissions:** No

25. **Indexes submitted pages only or conducts deep crawls:** No

26. **Instant spidering of submitted page:** No

27. **Number of pages that can be submitted per day:** Not applicable

28. **Word stemming and plural sensitive:** Not applicable

29. **Case-sensitive searches:** Not applicable

30. **Alphabetical page listings:** No

31. **Time to index page:** Not applicable

32. **Spam penalties:** Not applicable

33. **Refuses pages with META refresh:** Not applicable

34. **Refuses pages with invisible text:** Not applicable

35. **Refuses pages with "tiny text":** Not applicable

36. **Remove URL:** Not applicable

This information may be out of date by the time of publication. Because search engines frequently change their ranking algorithms and other page scoring variables, we have posted updates and revisions to these chapters on our Web site: http://www.iprospect.com/search-engine-chapters.htm.

Understanding the Results

Results offered by About.com are all subject to the expertise of the About guides. The guides are paid to maintain the environment of their topic. They scour the Web looking for relevant material to add to their topic. When a searcher selects a channel from the About.com main page, the searcher is offered a topic layer to assist in navigating to sites on the topic of choice. Once a topic is chosen, the searcher is offered a range of additional choices.

The topic level is the realm of the About guide. The guide offers additional topics from which to choose on the left-hand side of the page, a listing of related sites and advertising on the right-hand side of the page, and three groups of listings in the center of the page.

The center grouping is preferred sites, listings, books, news, articles, etc., relating to the search. These are grouped as "In the Spotlight" and "Essentials." The sites are listed according to the guides' preferences. Some sites are listed alphabetically; others are not. The content and sites provided is dependent on the guide and must adhere to About.com's standards. Boxed at the bottom of the page are "Sponsored Links." These are the paid listings offered by Sprinks.com.

Because About.com uses guides to gather and organize relevant information, a listing in Sprinks.com will target the most relevant audience for a keyword phrase. A bidding system at Sprinks.com determines positioning of listings in the "Sponsored Links" groupings. Bidding on keyword phrases in Sprinks can provide good, qualified exposure at a minimal cost. Sprinks uses Inktomi as its default database.

Off-the-Page Factors That Influence Success

The obvious off-the-page factor is that the pages selected for listing in the About.com directory are completely subject to the About.com guide. Only if a site provides good, important, and relevant content will a guide list it. After thoroughly investigating the channels and selecting an appropriate topic, site owners can send an e-mail to the guide requesting their site be reviewed. There are no clear rules governing this practice. The guide for the topic has the final say.

How to Know if Your Site Has Been Spidered/Listed

If you want to know if your site has been added to the About.com family of sites, you will have to periodically type your URL into the search box.

What to Do If Your Rankings Disappear

If your listing disappears, there is a link on the bottom of most pages where you can report a problem or contact the guide for the topic. However, there are no clearly defined rules, and the guide has control over what is listed within the topic.

Special Tips and Tactics for This Engine

The best advice for getting your page considered by an About guide is to provide quality, important, and relevant content.

Responsiveness and Help Provided

Response time will vary from topic to topic and is dependent on the guide. In general, most responses are returned within a reasonable time period, and most responses adequately address the issues queried.

Chapter 13:

AltaVista

AltaVista Company
1070 Arastradero Road
Palo Alto, CA 94304
(650) 320-7700
Fax: (650) 320-7720

alta™vista:

Free updates to this book are available via e-mail newsletter
by visiting: http://www.iprospect.com/book-news.htm.

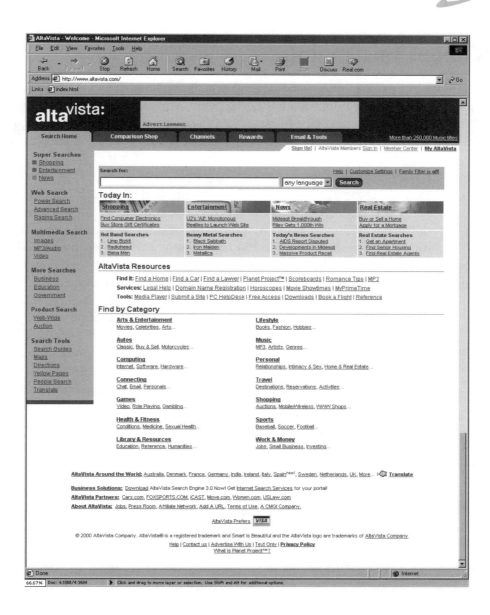

Facts about This Engine

AltaVista was one of the original search engines when started in 1995. It was originally owned by Digital Equipment Corporation and was designed to show off the speed of their products. AltaVista was not originally hosted at www.altavista.com because the company failed to secure that domain. In 1998, Digital Equipment Corporation paid $13 million for the altavista.com domain. Ever since, AltaVista has been a major player in the world of search engines. In 1999, Compaq purchased AltaVista and decided to publicly offer shares in AltaVista. However, when the initial public offering (IPO) was repeatedly delayed, CMGI purchased AltaVista. In conjunction with the recent market activities taking place within the Internet community, another planned IPO was recently postponed in January 2001.

Despite these corporate machinations, AltaVista has evolved from a pure search engine to a hybrid, which combines directory results with traditional search results. These directory results are from LookSmart and Open Directory. AltaVista uses the title and description from LookSmart's directory for a given URL in the AltaVista index. A careful examination of the search results reveals that the results are biased toward the LookSmart title rather than the site description or the actual page content. AltaVista has also created another search engine, Raging Search, which is designed to attract users who desire a simpler search. The Raging Search site is, at least currently, free from advertising and other bandwidth-consuming content or other "clutter" found on major search sites.

Continuing its evolution, AltaVista has become more of an information portal providing news, shopping, entertainment, and financial information. However, in September 2000, AltaVista announced that it would abandon the information portal concept and return to its roots to focus on search. A simple tour through the site reveals that AltaVista continues to offer other search options including comparison shopping, news, and entertainment searching.

1. **Web address:** http://www.altavista.com
2. **Type of engine:** Hybrid. Primary results — AltaVista database, Secondary results — LookSmart directory.
3. **Partnerships:** LookSmart and GoTo. AltaVista is owned by CMGI.
4. **Total documents indexed:** 500 million
5. **Total page views per month:** 1,381,181,000 (Source: Alexa Research, Feb. 2001)

6. **E-mail support:** Forms-based e-mail support is available at http://doc.altavista.com/help/contact/intro_help.html

7. **How to confirm listing:** Enter *host://* + *your URL* into search box.

8. **Obtain link popularity information:** Type in link:yoururl.com.

9. **Result returns:** If you search directly from the AltaVista home page, results are displayed from the AltaVista database. On some searches you may see green listings at the bottom of the page. These are from GoTo. If you click one of the AltaVista directory links and then search, LookSmart results are displayed.

10. **Receive higher rankings for link popularity:** Primary results — Yes, Secondary results — No.

11. **Additional off-the-page considerations:** Primary results — Considers link popularity and presents RealNames results, Secondary results — Uses human editors etc.

12. **Rankings influenced by after-the-click behavior:** Primary results — No, Secondary results — No.

13. **Recognition and utilization of META tags:** Primary results — Yes, Secondary results — No.

14. **Consideration of META tags for relevancy:** Primary results — Yes, Secondary results — No.

15. **Importance of Title tag keyword prominence:** Primary results — Yes, Secondary results — No.

16. **Importance of <ALT> tag:** Primary results — Unconfirmed, Secondary results — Unconfirmed.

17. **Importance of multiple occurrences of keywords in Title tag:** Primary results — Yes, Secondary results — No.

18. **Maximum length of Title tag:** Primary results — No, Secondary results — Not applicable.

19. **Maximum length of keyword META tag:** Primary results — No, Secondary results — Not applicable.

20. **Maximum length of description META tag:** Primary results — No, Secondary results — Not applicable.

21. **Comment tags considered for relevancy:** Primary results — Unconfirmed, Secondary results — Unconfirmed.

22. **Frame support:** Primary results — Yes, Secondary results — Not applicable.

23. **Image map support:** Primary results — Unconfirmed, Secondary results — Not applicable.

24. **Accepts automated submissions:** Primary results — Yes. However, at press time, AltaVista began to incorporate a new method to discourage automated submissions. Secondary results — Not applicable.

25. **Indexes submitted pages only or conducts deep crawls:** Primary results — Indexes submitted pages and crawls one level deep, Secondary results — Not applicable.

26. **Instant spidering of submitted page:** Primary results — No, Secondary results — Not applicable.

27. **Number of pages that can be submitted per day:** Primary results — Five per domain, Secondary results — Not applicable.

28. **Word stemming and plural sensitive:** Primary results — Yes, Secondary results — Yes.

29. **Case-sensitive searches:** Primary results — Yes, Secondary results — No.

30. **Alphabetical page listings:** Primary results — No, Secondary results — Yes, with categories.

31. **Time to index page:** Primary results — Approximately two weeks, Secondary results — Varies depending on submission method chosen.

32. **Spam penalties:** Primary results — Your URL will be banned from the index, Secondary results — Not applicable.

33. **Refuses pages with META refresh:** Primary results — Unconfirmed, Secondary results — Not applicable.

34. **Refuses pages with invisible text:** Primary results — Yes, Secondary results — Not applicable.

35. **Refuses pages with "tiny text":** Primary results — Unconfirmed, Secondary results — Not applicable.

36. **Remove URL:** Primary results — Follow the "Submit a Site" link off the home page. Locate the AltaVista search index heading and click the Submit button. Then follow the directions listed. Secondary results — Not applicable.

This information may be out of date by the time of publication. Because search engines frequently change their ranking algorithms and other page scoring variables, we have posted updates and revisions to these chapters on our Web site: http://www.iprospect.com/search-engine-chapters.htm.

Understanding the Results

AltaVista displays 10 results per page. These are all results from their database. For most searches, AltaVista displays related searches directly below the search box. Editor-reviewed sites are displayed after most searches. These results reflect categories furnished by LookSmart and the Open Directory as well as AltaVista's own categories. In January 2001, AltaVista incorporated GoTo-sponsored links complete with descriptions. These sponsored links appear near the bottom of the search results for AltaVista. AltaVista offers other resources about each search result as well. There are also GoTo listings at the bottom of the page.

LookSmart has become more involved in AltaVista's results and provides directory listings for AltaVista. However, AltaVista now uses the LookSmart title and description where applicable. Also, AltaVista now appears to give a greater weight to LookSmart listings and place them above AltaVista's spidered content.

Given LookSmart's increased presence in AltaVista, it is worth revisiting LookSmart's submissions policies. LookSmart allows submissions of up to five URLs per domain. There is a charge of $199 to review each URL within 48 hours. Should you desire more listings, you may want to consider their new subsite program which will enable you to get many additional category listings if you are willing to pay for any resulting click-throughs on a cost-per-click basis. LookSmart also offers a basic submission for $99, which allows your URL to be reviewed within eight weeks. It is important to remember that you should

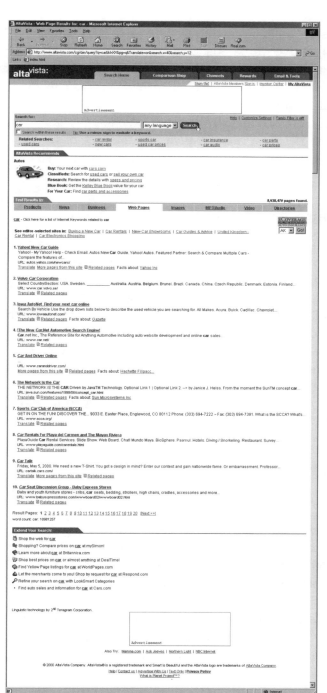

carefully consider the keywords you propose to LookSmart. Although LookSmart editors have the final say, the keywords in the title will go a long way to determining how and where your site is found. Should your LookSmart title not contain quality keywords, your placements in AltaVista (as well as other engines using LookSmart) could be harmed as the title and description from your site's META tags are replaced with those provided by your new LookSmart listing.

The "Translate" option below each link allows you to translate any text into several languages. Simply enter the URL into the Web site field or enter text into the Text box. This feature allows site designers to build and submit their site in one language and allows users to customize the page to meet their language needs.

The "More pages from this site" option provides you a list of other pages from that URL indexed in AltaVista. The "Related pages" option provides you with additional pages that AltaVista believes are related to the ranked page. The related pages are composed of pages that link to the particular site as well as pages that AltaVista's algorithm determines are appropriate. AltaVista sometimes provides a "Facts about" option to show you information about certain companies including the Web sites they have registered.

AltaVista displays the number of pages targeting the queried phrase toward the bottom of the page. This information is useful to individuals considering targeting specific phrases. Words like "book" and "car" return millions of pages. It would be extremely difficult to attain high rankings on these highly competitive words. Also, individuals are constantly competing for high rankings of these words, and therefore, even if you are able to attain a high rank, your listing will probably last only a few hours as individuals aim to "out-do" each other for the top positions.

Below the search results, AltaVista usually displays a section of other resources for individuals whose needs were not satisfied by the page of search results. One such option under this section allows you to check your search on LookSmart categories.

Site Elements That Can Cause Problems

Like all search engines, AltaVista spiders the pages that you submit in order to add them to its database. There are several issues including query strings in your URL, frames, cookies, broken links, user input pages, redirected pages, and graphic-intensive pages that can cause problems with the spidering process.

AltaVista indexes each element of a frame separately. For this reason, if the content of one element of your frame is indexed, the user will only see that part of the frame and not the entire page. It is desirable to avoid frames altogether. However, if you must use frames, either place a <NOFRAMES> tag in your code or create a non-frames version of each page to submit to AltaVista. The <NOFRAMES> tag tells the AltaVista spider to avoid indexing the frame and thereby get around the problem of frames. By submitting the non-frames version of a page you also avoid only displaying part of the page to an AltaVista user.

AltaVista's spidering will affect sites attempting to set cookies. Many sites use cookies to track information about their users. Cookies themselves pose no problems to AltaVista; however, the AltaVista spider will not accept cookies as it crawls your site. Therefore, if a cookie must be accepted before the page loads, the spider will not crawl that page or any pages below it in your site. In short, if you determine that you want to serve cookies, make certain that your pages will load without the cookie being accepted or AltaVista will not be able to fully crawl your site.

Broken links provide two problems to AltaVista. Fundamentally, a broken link prevents the spider from crawling parts of your site and indexing that content. Also, the number of broken links is an indication of how credible the site is. For example, if your site has 20 "indexable" pages, but half of them contain broken links, AltaVista will most likely determine that your site is not a valuable resource and will not thoroughly index it.

Much like the case with cookies, AltaVista's spider does not enter information into forms on your Web site. Therefore, pages that are behind a username and passwords or other input fields will be ignored by the spider.

AltaVista also does not index pages that are simply a redirect to other pages. They view this as a spamming tactic and ignore the page. If you try to submit several redirect pages, AltaVista is likely to detect your activity and may possibly ban your site or IP address — a proposition not relished by the professional Internet marketer.

Graphic-intensive pages also cause problems for AltaVista. Their spider does not index text that is embedded in graphics. Your best bet is to avoid creating and submitting pages that only contain graphics. However, if you have a few pages dominated by graphics, make certain to include an <ALT> tag inside the image describing the image so that AltaVista has some content on your page to index.

Recommended Site Optimization Tactics

The most important element of your site optimization for AltaVista is the Title tag. Your Title tag should contain the most important keyword for the page. Pages that rank well for a particular keyword phrase in AltaVista usually contain that phrase twice in the title.

The description META tag is also read by AltaVista. However, this tag plays only a small factor in determining your ranking. This tag is the text that is displayed underneath each search result. You should create a description for each page you plan on submitting because the first characters on the page are displayed in lieu of the description tag and this text may not entice users to visit your site.

The keyword tag also plays a minor role in determining your position in AltaVista. This list of keywords is not the only area on the page the spider indexes. While it is helpful to have the phrases you are targeting in the keyword META tag, it is essential to have the keywords you are targeting on the viewable page. AltaVista believes that any important keyword will appear in the text. For this reason, AltaVista checks not only the Title tag but also the general text of the page for keywords. If the word only appears in the keyword tag, it will not rank as well. Also, it makes sense that a word deemed important for optimization should be important enough to display on the page.

Off-the-Page Factors That Influence Success

In order to further discourage spamming and other deceitful tricks, AltaVista's algorithm takes link popularity into account. Link popularity is simply a measure of how many other sites on the Web point to your site. To determine a given URL's link popularity, simply type the following string into the search box: "link:yoururl.com." The number of links to the site, however, is only one factor. AltaVista also looks at the quality of these sites to determine if they are reputable sites or simply individual sites, perhaps linking solely to improperly inflate a ranking. For this reason, the quality of the links that point at your site is much more important than the sheer volume.

How to Submit a Site to This Engine

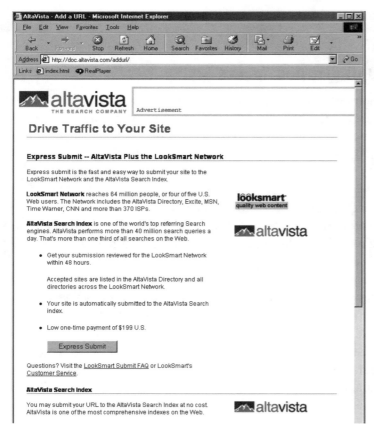

To submit to AltaVista locate the "Submit a Site" link at the bottom of the page and follow the instructions. Make certain to type in your full URL. AltaVista, like many search-engine-related entities, is concerned about spam. For this reason, a submission must be performed with particular care. The safest route is to only submit one page, per domain, per day. However, many people have large sites and wish to speed up the process of submitting to get rankings faster. It is usually acceptable to submit more than one page per day; however, submitting more than five pages per day will most certainly raise concerns and closer scrutiny.

When making changes to your Web site, it is advisable to replace the old pages with new content that has the same filename. This ensures that a user will not come upon your rankings in search engines and click through only to find File Not Found errors. It is also important that your Web site be set up to trap 404 errors.

How to Build Informational Pages for This Engine

AltaVista has taken a strong stance against spam. For this reason, you must be very careful about how informational pages are created, named, and submitted. Your informational pages must look like actual Web pages and contain meaningful content or AltaVista is likely to pick up on your tactics and may take some punitive action.

Informational pages must be optimized properly in order to gain significant rankings in AltaVista. Accordingly, you must focus on writing a powerful title. The title should contain the phrase for which you are optimizing the page twice, and avoid superfluous words. The META description should be written to entice users of AltaVista to visit your site, but should also contain the phrase you are targeting. AltaVista places little importance on the keyword tag and it is recommended that you simply omit this tag where this technique would not otherwise affect submissions to other search sources.

Informational pages should contain at least one <H1> tag. Keep in mind that you can also implement <H2> through <H6> tags containing the phrases you are targeting. In addition to <H1> tags, make certain that the body of your pages contain the phrase to be targeted in more than one location. It is critical to note that excessive use of a phrase or group of phrases on a given page will alert AltaVista to what may be deemed a "spamming" tactic, resulting in punitive actions including being banned. Along these lines, assuring that at least 200 words of viewable content appear on each page will aid in giving the page increased credibility while avoiding the impression of spam.

When selecting the URL for your informational pages, it is helpful to select URLs which contain phrases that you are targeting. The exact effects of keyword-centric URLs in AltaVista are not presently known, however, indications are that this technique aids your pages in achieving better rankings.

Use restraint when submitting any pages to AltaVista, especially informational pages. In order to be absolutely safe, do not submit more than one page per domain, per day. While the one-page-per-day strategy is clearly the most conservative approach to take, submissions of up to five pages, per day, per domain have historically been performed without negative repercussions from AltaVista.

A well-conceived informational page strategy can provide numerous opportunities for increasing your site's visibility in AltaVista. It is best to first start out with a few informational pages targeting your most sought-after phrases and then gradually increase your page count. This approach better assures that submission of informational pages remains under the spam radar at AltaVista, regardless of a lack of spamming intent, and assists the submitter in attaining long-term rankings.

How to Know If Your Site Has Been Spidered/Listed

It is important to track the visit of AltaVista's numerous spiders. Tracking spider visits allows you to approximate when pages should be indexed. You can then check your number of indexed pages to determine which pages were not added and then resubmit them. A list of AltaVista's spiders as well as their IP addresses is provided below.

204.123.9.19	scooter2.av.pa-x.dec.com
204.123.13.65	mercator.pa-x.dec.com
204.123.9.76	add-url.altavista.com
204.152.191.47	scooter.pa.alta-vista.net
204.123.9.123	test-scooter.av.pa-x.dec.com
204.123.9.18	av-dev2.av.pa-x.dec.com
204.123.9.20	scooter.pa-x.dec.com
204.123.9.23	brillo.av.pa-x.dec.com
204.123.9.47	vscooter.av.pa-x.dec.com
204.123.9.95	av-dev3.av.pa-x.dec.com
204.152.191.41	av-dev4.pa.alta-vista.net
204.123.9.53	tarantula.av.pa-x.dec.com
204.152.191.58	brillo.pa.alta-vista.net
204.152.191.57	add-url.pa.alta-vista.net
128.177.243.155	scooter2.sv.alta-vista.net
204.123.13.66	connect2.pa-x.dec.com
204.123.13.36	eec6.pa-x.dec.com
204.123.28.10	crawler0-complaints-to-admin.webresearch.pa-x.dec.com

AltaVista has a straightforward spidering process and it provides some insight into its spidering at the following URL: http://doc.altavista.com/adv_ search/ast_haw_index.html. In brief, AltaVista explains its spidering process as follows:

"The main crawler, named 'Scooter,' sends out thousands of HTTP requests simultaneously like thousands of blind users grabbing text, pulling it back, and throwing it into the indexing machines so that text can be in the index.

Scooter also has 'cousins,' other crawlers that do specialized jobs to help keep the index current, such as checking for 'dead' links — pages that have been moved or deleted and should not be in the index."

(Source: AltaVista information: http://doc.altavista.com/adv_search/ast_haw_index.html)

Indexing Timetable

AltaVista will instantly spider the pages you submit in order to verify that they actually exist. It is pointless to submit pages before they are completed because the spider will not find them. AltaVista typically takes approximately two weeks to index your site and crawl down one level of pages. You should allow at least four weeks before resubmitting your pages. One of the worst things you can do is to continually submit your site. Constant submission and resubmission will raise the attention of the AltaVista staff and such conduct, even with the most "innocent" or proper intentions, may draw repercussions.

In order to monitor your progress in AltaVista, it is essential to utilize an AltaVista feature to check the number of pages on your site which have been indexed by AltaVista. This can be done by typing "host:www.yoururl.com" into the main search box. AltaVista will return the number of indexed pages. However, the number is often exaggerated so it is important to go to the last page of the list and verify the actual number. Your knowledge of the amount of real estate your site possesses in AltaVista is extremely helpful. It is difficult to have significant rankings in AltaVista without having several pages indexed. Once you see your pages indexed, wait about four days for your results to become searchable, then check to see how your pages rank on your desired keyword phrases. By comparing your number of indexed pages to rankings, you can determine how well the site has been optimized. This knowledge will allow you to go back and alter the titles, number of times the word appears on a page, and overall word copy on the page. In addition, after several unsuccessful attempts at achieving substantial numbers of rankings, you may have to revisit the phrases on which you are attempting to gain rankings and determine if they are too competitive and need to be further refined.

What to Do If Your Rankings Disappear

Like any spider-based search engine, AltaVista is continually updating its index of Web pages. Often, your pages will drop in position or fall out of the index altogether. It is important to properly react to a drop in rankings. The initial reaction is to quickly resubmit every page to AltaVista. This massive amount of submissions, however, is considered spamming the index. When you see pages drop in ranking or disappear altogether, it is often because the database is being worked on. In this regard, certain elements of the database may not be available all the time. Consequently, it is important to check back often to see if your site has returned. After a few days without returning, you should begin the process of resubmitting according to the terms and conditions of AltaVista. Make certain to resubmit your most important pages first and allow the spider to add some pages when crawling. If you are unable to get back into AltaVista over the course of a few months, your site may have been banned and you should contact AltaVista to determine your next steps.

Special Tips and Tactics for This Engine

Gaining and sustaining rankings in AltaVista on numerous phrases requires a substantial effort on your part. It is foolish to think that optimizing and submitting one page or a few pages will get the job done. Realistically, you should only target one or two phrases per page. By limiting the number of words you target per page, you will be able to properly optimize your page. It is worth noting again that the Title tag is far and away the most important spot for gaining rankings. Focus on one or two phrases and include them in the Title and description tags. Also, include these words in an <H1> tag and in the body of your page.

When picking the page to optimize for a particular word or phrase, make certain the page contains content that will satisfy the user's query. Choosing relevant pages will allow you to insert the desired phrases in the text of the page more naturally. Also, assuming the page achieves rankings for the targeted word or phrase, users should enter your site through the optimized pages. It is a disservice to both page users and page developers to provide pages of the site that do not provide the information actually sought. For example, the word "car" and phrases containing it are highly searched and, consequently, rankings for the word are highly sought after. Where a company sells "air fresheners," however, and they want to maximize possible search traffic, the organization might very well try to obtain high rankings on the word "car." Statistics would tell the organization that people are looking for "car" an estimated 2,000,000 times per month and air fresheners an estimated 100 times per month. If the air freshener company was able to achieve any ranking on the word "car," people will come to the site only to be disappointed that they have been tricked. Also, people would soon conclude that the organization is a fraud or that it engages in fraudulent conduct and, as a result, the efforts will go unrewarded. In addition, AltaVista is keenly aware of this situation and addresses the problem at http://doc.altavista .com/adv_search/ast_haw_spam.html. As a result, it will be more beneficial for the organization to achieve rankings on relevant phrases because one appropriate visitor is better than 100 visitors duped into visiting the site.

AltaVista strongly opposes spamdexing. The following excerpt has been taken from http://doc.altavista.com/adv_search/ast_haw_spam.html.

> *"Some barriers to being indexed are due to the misbehavior of a handful of Webmasters who have tried to fool search engines into ranking their pages high on lists of matches and including them as matches to queries they aren't appropriate for. This is one kind of behavior that is known as 'spamming.' Spamming degrades the value of the index and is a nuisance for all."*

AltaVista also recommends that you make certain to check with your hosting provider to determine that no one is spamming their database from the same IP address as your site. Your site will be penalized if it shares an IP address with other sites that are spamming. To avoid this problem entirely, insist that your site be given its own IP address. It is recommended that individuals read all information AltaVista provides on spam and other illegal behaviors before attempting to optimize a site for AltaVista.

By implementing a strategy of optimizing your site and setting up informational pages on external domains, you should be able to attain rankings on important keywords. Always keep in mind that your success in any search engine and particularly in AltaVista must be measured over the long haul. Submit conservatively and refrain from spamming the index with thousands of informational pages and you are well on your way to successful placements in AltaVista.

Finally, it is worth noting that pages in AltaVista also tend to rank better with age. New sites need time to build up the link popularity that helps produce successful rankings in AltaVista. Ethical link solicitations and link swap programs can assist the perceived relevancy of the site. As the link numbers increase, rankings may increase as well.

Responsiveness and Help Provided

AltaVista has switched to forms-based e-mail for most e-mail inquiries. As a result of this switch, meaningful responses are hard to come by. We placed several calls to AltaVista and were always transferred into a voice mailbox. Usually, the e-mail help provided is an automatic reply telling you to go to a particular area of the site in order to find what you are seeking. It should not surprise you that the information on the site is often vague and leaves you confused. However, it is also worth noting that AltaVista has an informative section on how it works and determines page rank at http://doc.altavista.com/adv_search/ast_haw_spam.html. This help section provides answers to most of the questions that AltaVista will publicly answer. It is definitely a must read for anyone trying to understand AltaVista and improve their site's rankings.

Chapter 14:

AOL Search

America Online, Inc.
22000 AOL Way
Dulles, VA 20166
http://search.aol.com/feedback.adp
1-888-265-8001

Free updates to this book are available via e-mail newsletter
by visiting: http://www.iprospect.com/book-news.htm.

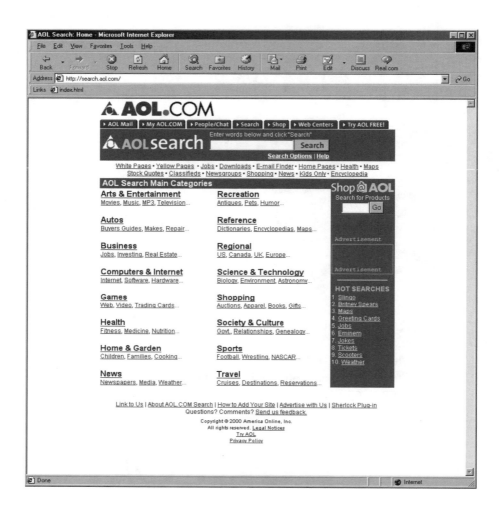

Facts about This Engine

AOL Search is unique among the search engines and directories in that it offers a "two for one" deal. When using AOL Search, you can simultaneously search both AOL and all (or at least most) of the rest of the Internet. Visiting AOL Search from within AOL will allow for similar search queries as well as content provided exclusively by AOL for its users.

If you visit AOL Search from the Internet, you'll have access to a vast number of Web sites as well as what AOL has to offer. However, you will not get the exclusive content that you would have received if you'd visited AOL Search from within AOL.

AOL utilizes the Open Directory Project as the foundation of its search results database. ODP has approximately 2 million Web sites that are collected and organized by more than 20,000 volunteer editors worldwide, with more than 3,000 new sites added daily. AOL joins its Open Directory Project results with thousands of additional sites garnered from AOL and AOL.com.

1. **Web address:** http://search.aol.com

2. **Type of engine:** Hybrid. Primary results — DMOZ (Open Directory), Secondary results — Inktomi.

3. **Partnerships:** Fed by DMOZ (Open Directory Project) as well as Inktomi

4. **Total documents indexed:** 2 million in Open Directory Project; 500 million in Inktomi

5. **Total page views per month:** 1,744,974,000 (Source: Alexa Research, Feb. 2001)

6. **E-mail support:** Must be an AOL member. Enter keyword "net.help" on AOL home page.

7. **How to confirm listing:** If your site is accepted, it will also appear on other sites that use the Open Directory, such as Netscape, Lycos, and HotBot, as well as within AOL Search. Please also see Chapter 29.

8. **Obtain link popularity information:** No

9. **Result returns:** Primary results — DMOZ database, Secondary results — Inktomi. AOL also displays the top three paid listings from GoTo as sponsored links.

10. **Receive higher rankings for link popularity:** Primary results — No, Secondary results — Yes.

11. **Additional off-the-page considerations:** AOL Search is a hierarchical Web directory, organized by subject. All user-submitted Web content is maintained by the Open Directory Project (http://www.dmoz.org). The Open Directory Project is run by a staff of volunteer editors who choose to evaluate and classify Web sites in one or more categories. The editor exercises the option of choosing to add a site, moving sites between categories, and creating new sites. It is important to understand the process and procedures of the Open Directory Project when considering a search engine campaign on AOL.

    Typical off-the-page considerations apply solely to spider-based search engines; the directories, since they are run and monitored by human editors, are powered only by human input and therefore do not use these off-the-page factors.

    AOL is reported to process its cache which tells it which Web sites were frequented by its subscribers. If AOL subscribers visit your Web site, it could cause an improvement in your site's visibility in AOL's search results. For Inktomi results, more weight is given to sites found through deep crawls by Inktomi.

12. **Rankings influenced by after-the-click behavior:** Primary results — Not applicable, Secondary results — No.

13. **Recognition and utilization of META tags:** Primary results — No, Secondary results — Yes.

14. **Consideration of META tags for relevancy:** Primary results — No, Secondary results — Yes.

15. **Importance of Title tag keyword prominence:** Primary results — No, Secondary results — Yes.

16. **Importance of <ALT> tag:** Primary results — No, Secondary results — Yes.

17. **Importance of multiple occurrences of keywords in Title tag:** Primary results — No, Secondary results — Yes.

18. **Maximum length of Title tag:** Primary results — 115 characters, Secondary results — Not applicable.

19. **Maximum length of keyword META tag:** Primary results — Not applicable, Secondary results — No.

20. **Maximum length of description META tag:** Primary results — 1,017 characters, Secondary results — No.

21. **Comment tags considered for relevancy:** Primary results — Not applicable, Secondary results — Yes.

22. **Frame support:** Primary results — Not applicable, Secondary results — Yes.

23. **Image map support:** Primary results — Not applicable, Secondary results — Unconfirmed.

24. **Accepts automated submissions:** Primary results — No, Secondary results — Yes.

25. **Indexes submitted pages only or conducts deep crawls:** Primary results — Submitted pages only, Secondary results — Both.

26. **Instant spidering of submitted page:** Primary results — No, Secondary results — Yes.

27. **Number of pages that can be submitted per day:** See Inktomi and Open Directory chapters.

28. **Word stemming and plural sensitive:** Primary results — Yes, Secondary results — Yes.

29. **Case-sensitive searches:** Primary results — Yes, Secondary results — Yes.

30. **Alphabetical page listings:** Primary results — Yes, Secondary results — No.

31. **Time to index page:** Primary results — At discretion of category editor, Secondary results — 48 hours for paid submissions.

32. **Spam penalties:** Primary results — Removal, Secondary results — Unconfirmed.

33. **Refuses pages with META refresh:** Primary results — Yes, Secondary results — No.

34. **Refuses pages with invisible text:** Primary results — Yes, Secondary results — No.

35. **Refuses pages with "tiny text":** Primary results — Yes, Secondary results — No.

36. **Remove URL:** Primary results — See the Open Directory chapter, Secondary results — See the Inktomi chapter.

This information may be out of date by the time of publication. Because search engines frequently change their ranking algorithms and other page scoring variables, we have posted updates and revisions to these chapters on our Web site: http://www.iprospect.com/search-engine-chapters.htm.

Understanding the Results

You can begin your search by clicking on the "Main Categories" heading beneath the search box. These categories correspond to a set of topics provided by Open Directory. Clicking on one of these categories will bring you to a screen where you may choose again from "Sub-Categories within the main category," "Categories Related To your topic," and "Items in Category." These options allow you to select from a wide variety of smaller, more focused categories that relate to your search.

AOL Search's categories consist of both AOL and Internet sites. The category section is the largest of AOL's set of results and therefore may return thousands of relevant Web sites. If there are no matching categories for your search, AOL will automatically search every page on AOL as well as millions of pages on the Internet. AOL sites are listed together with the categories that contain them. Therefore you can just click on the category link to obtain a list of additional related sites.

If you enter your keyword query into AOL Search's home page search box, the results page will deliver a variety of results including sponsored links (paid listings, provided by GoTo.com), matching sites (provided by Inktomi), matching categories (provided by Open Directory), and in some instances, recommended sites (hand-picked by AOL's editorial staff).

In the results section, next to the "Matching Sites" option, AOL also offers a "Most Popular Sites" link. This section is garnered from a cross-section of the entire Web. AOL then lists its own particular results for your search query. The results are ordered by a "relevance percentage," ranging from 100 percent (for what AOL considers a "perfect match") to 1 percent. Below each individual returned result is a hyperlinked option, "Show me more like this." This option will automatically redirect you to the "Items in Category" section.

Site Elements That Can Cause Problems

The Open Directory will not accept sites that redirect to other pages, contain an excessive amount of affiliate links or other heavily self-promotional content, or are irrelevant to the chosen category. Especially since all AOL submissions will be reviewed by human editors in specialized ODP categories, it is crucial to ascertain that submitted Web sites are completely free of these troublesome characteristics. Please refer to Chapter 29 for further insight into problematic site elements.

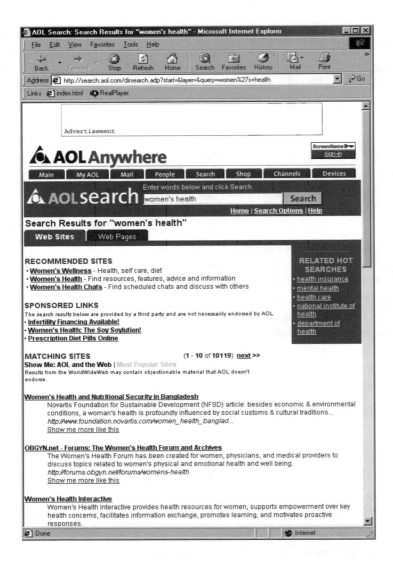

Recommended Site Optimization Tactics

Because AOL Search is primarily fed by the Open Directory, a directory with human editors, it will not respond to site optimization tactics geared toward spider-based search engines. In other words, the wording of META tags, link popularity, keyword density, and other spider-oriented strategy techniques will have no impact upon a directory comprised of human editors who personally review each submitted site.

The best method of optimizing a site for AOL inclusion does not actually involve "optimization" at all. Instead, the most crucial factors to focus on are relevance of the Open Directory Project categories and the content of the description submitted to those categories. Please refer to Chapter 29 for further information.

Off-the-Page Factors That Influence Success

Search engine industry insiders believe that AOL's use of its site cache is an integral part of achieving success within the directory. When determining its ranking results, AOL processes its user cache; therefore, particularly high visitation by AOL subscribers to certain sites can impact the rankings within AOL, giving higher and deeper-reaching positioning to those sites most frequently visited and searched for by AOL subscribers.

How to Submit a Site to This Engine

To submit to AOL Search, go to www.dmoz.org and follow the "Add URL" link on the top right. (The most effective method of submitting for rankings on AOL is to submit directly to the most relevant ODP categories.) See Chapter 29 for more information.

How to Build Informational Pages for This Engine

Not applicable. Since informational pages are geared toward spider-based search engines that "grab" META tags and keywords, and directories lack these qualifying elements, informational pages will not serve as effective rankings vehicles for submissions to AOL.

How to Know If Your Site Has Been Spidered/Listed

AOL does not actually have a spider, although it does use a "pre-fetch" spider that analyzes the contents of the AOL proxy cache. The Open Directory Project does not use spiders. Search for your listing in ODP to determine whether AOL has accepted your submission. Please see Chapter 29 for more information about checking for listings in ODP.

Indexing Timetable

Generally, both AOL and the Open Directory Project agree that if your site has not been listed within one to four weeks, you should consider resubmission. See Chapter 29 for more information.

What to Do If Your Rankings Disappear

If you are suddenly dropped by AOL and/or the Open Directory Project, the usual culprits are descriptions and categories. Typically, you will need to either rewrite your description to better reflect your site's content, choose new categories for submission, or both. See Chapter 29 for more information on recovering from slumping or disappearing rankings.

Special Tips and Tactics for This Engine

In general, when you think "AOL Search," you should also be thinking "ODP" in the same breath. The interconnectedness of these two search mechanisms is important, particularly when strategizing for optimum placement and easier searching.

Key to getting great placement in AOL Search (and, conversely, Open Directory Project) are two principles: writing a strong and accurate description, and choosing the right categories for your site. Choosing your categories should be your first order of business, as category selection will affect how you write your description. Though there is no ascertained limit to the number of categories to which you may submit a site, choose a reasonable number; even the most popular and diverse site risks labeling itself as a spam candidate if submitted to dozens of categories. Take time to surf through the various categories and make special note of those you feel best reflect your site. Remember the prevailing question in search engine positioning: Does your site satisfy the intent of the query? For example, would someone looking through the Collectibles and Miniatures category feel that your site was an appropriate match in that category? Or are you submitting it in that category solely to increase your presence on the Web, regardless of how accurate a fit your site actually is?

Once you have chosen your categories, you should strive to craft descriptions tailored exclusively for your categories and your site. Pay close attention to the descriptions of sites already included in your Open Directory categories — what styles of writing are used? Is there any consistent typical length that you can detect? What kind of information about the sites tends to be included in the descriptions? Detecting patterns in descriptions is very important, because these patterns reflect the preferences of the individual editors in each ODP category. The more you can make your description appeal to the editor of the category you are trying to get your site into, the more likely it is that you'll succeed!

Please also see Chapter 29 of this book for more information on tips and tricks for getting listed.

Responsiveness and Help Provided

AOL is one of the strongest presences on the Internet. It has an amazingly expansive network of users and services, ranging from chatrooms, e-mail, and instant messenger to an exhaustive search database. AOL is also especially notable in that it enjoys one of the most visible brands in the world.

Perhaps this visibility explains AOL's fierce commitment to creating a network of users. Visitors to AOL's main site (http://www.aol.com) will immediately be struck by offers and urges to join AOL and therefore become privy to its bevy of services and options "just for members." This translates directly into the level of help AOL provides: a lot for an AOL member; considerably less for the rest of the world.

It also bears mentioning to point out that AOL does not concentrate the majority of its attention on searches. The AOL Search feature is but one of many smaller backdrops on the shining landscape of e-mail, chat, messaging, and other Internet services. While AOL has an extensive help service and a number of feedback screens accessible to users, search engine positioning is not tops on its list of priorities.

Chapter 15:

Ask Jeeves

Ask Jeeves
5858 Horton Street
Emeryville, CA 94608
http://www.askjeeves.com, http://www.ask.com
(510) 985-7400
Fax: (510) 985-7410, (510) 985-7412

Free updates to this book are available via e-mail newsletter
by visiting: http://www.iprospect.com/book-news.htm.

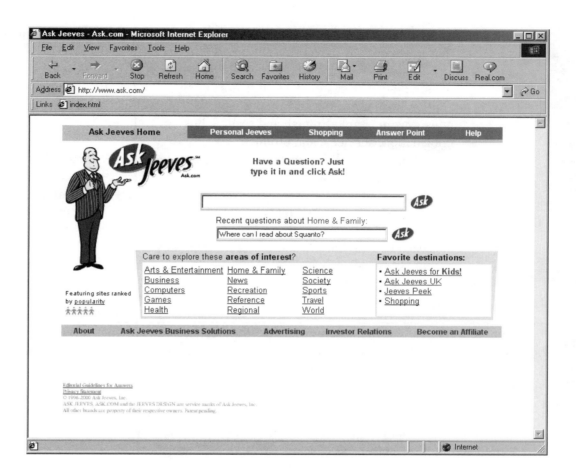

Facts about This Engine

Incorporated in 1996 and based in Emeryville, California, Ask Jeeves is different from the average search engine or directory. Ask Jeeves makes an attempt to expand the capabilities of Internet search services by incorporating natural language searching. Ask Jeeves' objective is to allow people to have a simple, natural way to find online answers to their questions — in effect, it is a "natural language" search tool.

Ask Jeeves doesn't search the Web for keywords or phrases unless it has to. Instead, Jeeves examines the user's query and attempts to match it against a list of relevant questions from its own database. The questions that appear on the results page are related questions that Ask Jeeves found, not the questions that users initially asked.

Instead of searching on single keywords or phrases, Ask Jeeves utilizes a question-answer system so that users simply ask a question and Jeeves, the "butler," will present a variety of results or "answers." Users present their questions in simple English and receive links to Web sites containing relevant information, services, and products.

Ask Jeeves' Web properties include Ask Jeeves at Ask.com, Ask Jeeves for Kids at AJKids.com, and DirectHit.com. Askjeeves.com, launched in April 1997, was the first of its advertiser-supported public Web sites. In March 1998, the company established Ask Jeeves for Kids (www.ajkids.com), a child-friendly adaptation of the original that allows children to also use the simple language approach to searching online. Later on, Ask Jeeves acquired Net Effect and Direct Hit, which provide added live assistance and patented popularity technologies to its capabilities. In March 2000, Ask Jeeves launched its first international joint venture, Ask Jeeves U.K.

1. **Web address:** http://www.askjeeves.com, http://www.ask.com
2. **Type of engine:** Hybrid (uses its own version of the Open Directory and also uses a metacrawler to capture results from several search engines at once)
3. **Partnerships:** Appnet, Direct Hit, Univision Communications Inc., Ticketmaster Online-CitySearch, First Union Bank, Vignette Corporation, PriceRadar Inc., HearMe, CPQ, DELL, BLS, AltaVista
4. **Total documents indexed:** 282 million total questions, 5.5 billion records
5. **Total page views per month:** 188,060,000 (Source: Alexa Research, Feb. 2001)
6. **E-mail support:** jeeves@askjeeves.com
7. **How to confirm listing:** Type in www.yourdomain.com
8. **Obtain link popularity information:** Not applicable
9. **Result returns:** Metasearch results are obtained from the following engines: NBCi, GoTo.com, and Mamma.com. Results are also obtained through the Direct Hit database as Ask Jeeves obtained the company in February 2000.
10. **Receive higher rankings for link popularity:** No
11. **Additional off-the-page considerations:** Uses human editors. See the "Off-the-Page Factors That Influence Success" section later in this chapter.
12. **Rankings influenced by after-the-click behavior:** Yes
13. **Recognition and utilization of META tags:** Not applicable
14. **Consideration of META tags for relevancy:** Not applicable
15. **Importance of Title tag keyword prominence:** Not applicable
16. **Importance of <ALT> tag:** Not applicable

17. **Importance of multiple occurrences of keywords in Title tag:** Not applicable

18. **Maximum length of Title tag:** Not applicable

19. **Maximum length of keyword META tag:** Not applicable

20. **Maximum length of description META tag:** Not applicable

21. **Comment tags considered for relevancy:** Not applicable

22. **Frame support:** Yes

23. **Image map support:** Yes

24. **Accepts automated submissions:** No

25. **Indexes submitted pages only or conducts deep crawls:** Indexes submitted pages only.

26. **Instant spidering of submitted page:** Not applicable

27. **Number of pages that can be submitted per day:** Pages are submitted via e-mail, and they act as "answers" to questions that users pose. There is no section on the Ask Jeeves site that states whether or not there is a limit to the number of pages you can submit in one day. They do allow multiple submissions from the same URL. You can, in fact, suggest an appropriate internal page from your site that will satisfy a user's query. However, for a frame-based site, the URL address may not change, thus limiting your opportunity to gain multiple listings.

28. **Word stemming and plural sensitive:** No

29. **Case-sensitive searches:** No

30. **Alphabetical page listings:** Yes and no. Within the standard Ask Jeeves results section, the foremost set of search results or "questions" are listed by relevance to the user's query. Another set of results within the standard results page, which utilizes the popularity scoring system, ranks sites according to previous user queries, so therefore this section is also not listed in alphabetical order. However, when the user visits the Ask Jeeves home page and clicks directly on one of the directory links at the bottom of the page, under the title "Care to explore these areas of Interest?" he is led to lists of related links in alphabetical order. The returned sites are also listed alphabetically. This format still employs the popularity system; however, because the query is broader (and the user is not searching with a specific keyword or question), there are more results to list. The final sections within the standard search results page, called "related searches," as well as the metacrawler results section, are not listed alphabetically.

31. **Time to index page:** At least six months

32. **Spam penalties:** Not applicable

33. **Refuses pages with META refresh:** Not applicable

34. **Refuses pages with invisible text:** Ask Jeeves does not mention that they will not accept sites containing invisible text. Invisible text is a common spamming technique, never to be encouraged. Furthermore, such techniques provide no value whatsoever with directories. Ask Jeeves looks at content, that is, an editor browses the site as if he or she were the user. What it comes down to is "what you see is what you get." The editor will make a decision based on his interactions with your site. If you deployed such spamming tactics, and an editor observed these techniques, we would imagine that the review would not be favorable.

35. **Refuses pages with "tiny text":** No, however, Ask Jeeves stresses that they prefer sites that are easy to read and follow.

36. **Remove URL:** Users should utilize the same e-mail address they used for submitting (url@askjeeves.com). If you'd like to remove a site from within the Answer Point section because you believe it is incorrect or misleading, you can contact the Answer Point moderator or customer service department by filling out an online form.

This information may be out of date by the time of publication. Because search engines frequently change their ranking algorithms and other page scoring variables, we have posted updates and revisions to these chapters on our Web site: http://www.iprospect.com/search-engine-chapters.htm.

Understanding the Results

Ask Jeeves presents its results differently than the other search engines and directories. Instead of providing hypertext links as matches, it displays samples of how it has interpreted the user's question. Each of these is coupled with an icon that links to the relevant information. Ask Jeeves' results page is separated into various sections. Most searches render four sections of results. However, selected searches may render an additional fifth section (this section is Jeeves' Popularity Scoring System which displays Direct Hit results).

The primary and "regular" set of Ask Jeeves results is called "I have found answers to the following questions." Listed below this title, you'll see a set of five or six questions with red "Ask" icons to the left of each. These "questions" come from the Jeeves' residential editors who attempt to find the best and most relevant answers to a user's inquiry. Once you scan the list and choose which question is most related to your query, click on the "Ask" icon and Jeeves will bring you to a relevant source or Web site.

The popularity results section is only displayed when Direct Hit returns matches from their index of "popular" pages. These popular pages are derived from a process that analyzes click-throughs to determine the most popular pages on the Web. The section is called, and quite appropriately, "People with similar questions have found these sites relevant." These results are coupled with icons that display a row of five people figures. Depending on the popularity and relevance of the site, more figures may be colored orange (for more relevant) or more figures may be colored gray (for less relevant).

The section titled, "You may also wish to try these related searches" lists links to related categories within the Ask Jeeves site.

The Ask Jeeves results page also includes a subset of the links turned up by other major search engines including AltaVista, Excite, GoTo.com, Mamma.com, WebCrawler, and 4Anything Network. This results section is

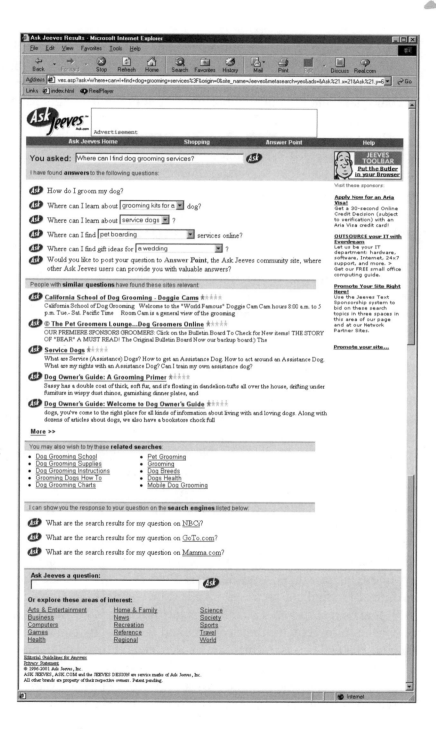

titled, "I can show you the response to your question on the search engines listed below." Like the first set of results, each result is marked with an "Ask" icon. Simply click on the icon next to the match that appears to be most related to your query and the link will take you directly to the results page on a chosen search engine (NBCi, GoTo.com, or Mamma.com).

In addition to the standard results, on the right-hand side of the page you'll find paid links, which list a number of Ask Jeeves' sponsors. These come from the Direct Hit paid text ads system, which has now been renamed the "Jeeves Text Sponsorship Network."

Recommended Site Optimization Tactics

A human editor will not go into your site's source code looking for META tags; he or she will analyze the viewable pages, looking for comprehensive and relevant content as well as ease of navigation and fluidity. For more information, follow the submission guidelines in the "How to Submit a Site to This Engine" section on the following pages.

Off-the-Page Factors That Influence Success

Ask Jeeves has human editors like Yahoo!, but it does not depend on actual submissions to build the Ask Jeeves knowledge base. As an alternative, Ask Jeeves editors come up with ideas for questions on their own, especially for popular topics, and they also watch what people are searching for. Though these editors are a bit more proactive than most directory editors who wait for users to submit sites and then begin the review process thereafter, users can still suggest that a site be linked to a question via e-mail. Simply send a message to url@ask.com.

On the Ask Jeeves home page, there's a list of category links below the search box. These links direct users to the Ask Jeeves directory. Within this directory, sites are ranked in order of their popularity among the searchers. This popularity algorithm is determined by Direct Hit, which uses click-through measurements to find out which sites/pages are the most popular across the Web.

Jeeves incorporates a ranking algorithm that rates Web sites according to how users interact with their content and services. Its combination of ordinary language question answering, human-edited directory, and popularity technology allow users to obtain results from previous searches that were done on similar topics. As users continue to query the Ask Jeeves directory, the value is increased substantially. Jeeves, therefore, becomes a smarter technology and provides more and more relevant information with each interaction. Each time a visitor comes to one of the Ask Jeeves Web sites, information is collected to improve the overall quality of the online experience. This includes product monitoring, product improvement, and targeted advertising.

Although the technique has not been verified, we have found that becoming part of and contributing to special interactive sections that search engines or directories offer sometimes weighs heavily in their decision-making process when reviewing suggested sites. Therefore, if the Ask Jeeves audience is important to you, we propose that you become an Answer Point registered user. Additionally, taking advantage of Ask Jeeves' Answer Point will allow you to better understand Ask Jeeves' methodologies and thus, you may have a better chance of getting your site listed.

The Ask Jeeves Answer Point is a special section where anybody can ask a question and get an answer from another Ask Jeeves user. The service is free of charge for users who are looking for advice from other users in addition to the answers they receive from the standard Ask Jeeves directory. Furthermore, if someone has answered your question, Ask Jeeves will notify you by e-mail so that you do not have to continuously check back.

In addition to having your own questions answered, you can also answer questions posted to the Answer Point by other users. To post questions and answers, you will initially have to register so that Jeeves remembers who you are.

NOTE   You can peruse the questions and answers without being a registered member.

Ask Jeeves' Answer Point also offers the chance to become an "Enthusiast." Enthusiasts volunteer to help manage the questions and answers that are posted by users; they search the Answer Point categories for questions to which they can provide meaningful answers. An individual frequently utilizing the Ask Jeeves Answer Point system may also be invited to become an Enthusiast.

In addition to posting and answering questions with Ask Jeeves' Answer Point system, you can rate answers as well. You'll find a Rating section directly above answers.

Ask Jeeves incorporates a "question subscriptions" method, which allows users to be alerted when a question they've posted has been answered. A user can be immediately notified by e-mail every time an answer has been posted for his question. Or, a user can be notified by e-mail once a day regarding all answers that have been posted (if no answers have been posted, e-mails will not be sent). You may subscribe to another user's question by clicking the Subscribe to this Question button, which is located beneath the question in which you are interested.

How to Submit a Site to This Engine

Ask Jeeves isn't like a traditional service where you can submit pages via a Submit URL button. As an alternative, you can suggest that a site be linked to a question via e-mail. Simply send a message to url@askjeeves.com.

You're likely to have more success with your submission if you find there are no other questions relating to a particular topic. Do some searches, look for gaps, and then suggest an appropriate page from your site to be listed. Be brief and to the point in your e-mail. Explain exactly why your site would provide value to Ask Jeeves users. You can even suggest some appropriate questions in your e-mail; if you make attempts to make things easier for the editors, you may increase your chances of getting your site listed.

Editors prefer sites that load quickly and are user friendly (easy to read and easy to navigate). Sites should be well maintained and have no broken links or areas under construction. Sites should offer thorough and accurate information that answers a user's query as well as additional links or related information within the site. Sites should demonstrate credibility by providing author and source citations as well as accurate and easy to access contact information. Ask Jeeves also prefers free site features that are available without registration.

E-commerce Sites

E-commerce sites can also be submitted via e-mail to url@askjeeves.com. Ask Jeeves looks for quality e-commerce sites that provide secure transactions and disclose policies for customer privacy, returns, and exchanges. The site should also offer a variety of product types and sufficient product information, as well as easily accessible customer service help. As with any site submission, your e-commerce site design should demonstrate credibility and provide user-friendly navigation. The Ask Jeeves site offers regularly updated guidance on submission criteria for e-commerce sites at the following URL: http://www.ask.com/docs/about/policy.html.

Text Sponsorship Network

The Jeeves Text Sponsorship Network, similar to GoTo.com's pay-for-rankings method, offers prominent placement for a fee. Your link appears alongside the search results for every search topic you "sponsor." Your link also appears alongside search results on Web sites that participate in the Jeeves Text Sponsorship Network, including MSN, Bomis.com, SuperCyberSearch, and Direct Hit.

Sponsorships will appear in two areas on the Ask Jeeves site: the Question/Answers pages and the Areas of Interest. Create your sponsorship on the Jeeves Text Sponsorship Network page and bid on relevant keywords. If your keywords match the user-selected keywords that generate a Question/Answers page or Area of Interest and your bid is one of the three top bids, your ad will appear.

Choose search topics that you feel are relevant to your Web site. Once you pick your keywords, decide on a specific amount you'd like to pay to sponsor them. You decide how much each term is worth to you, and you're only charged when your link is shown. You can create as many text sponsorships as you'd like, each with many search topics.

How to Build Informational Pages for this Engine

Do not build informational pages for the Ask Jeeves directory. Submissions are reviewed by actual people, and therefore editors will notice if a Web site is not complete or simply directs users to another site.

Indexing Timetable

Though it hasn't been proven, it is believed Ask Jeeves takes at least six months to accept a site submission. In a small "How do I submit a URL to Ask Jeeves?" section, they acknowledge the fact that a listing may not happen quickly. Because the directory is human-edited, it takes longer for each researcher to visit and review sites than if Ask Jeeves used a machine to evaluate sites like spider-based search engines. Ask Jeeves also states that they do not guarantee to include your Web site in their database at all. Ask Jeeves accepts URLs if they think the site provides a relevant and comprehensive answer to a question posed by a user.

Sometimes Ask Jeeves may accept one submission over another because the preferred site offers more relevant, comprehensive information and the site may also be easier to navigate than the other.

What to Do If Your Rankings Disappear

As the Jeeves Popularity Scoring System is continuously updated, sites will undoubtedly be adjusted within the results section. There is no known way to boost your ranking once your site has been submitted, but you can always send an e-mail to url@askjeeves.com or jeeves@askjeeves.com with questions.

Special Tips and Tactics for This Engine

Changes to your site will not directly impact your rankings. However, considering rankings that are affected by popularity, it would make sense to have a site that is appealing, informative, and functional for users. The more users visit your site, the greater popularity you gain and therefore increase in ranking.

When searching on Ask Jeeves, try putting your query in quotation marks. For instance, if you are searching for "Boston Red Sox," putting it in quotation marks will narrow your search so that only those sites that have the words "Boston Red Sox" together, one after the other, will appear in the search results. As searching the Internet can sometimes become frustrating when, query after query, results are not relevant, this will certainly save time and aggravation.

Chapter 16:

Excite

Excite@Home (At Home Corporation)
450 Broadway
Redwood City, CA 94063
http://www.excite.com/feedback/
(650) 556-5000
Fax: (650) 556-5100
News Bureau: (650) 569-5195

Free updates to this book are available via e-mail newsletter
by visiting: http://www.iprospect.com/book-news.htm.

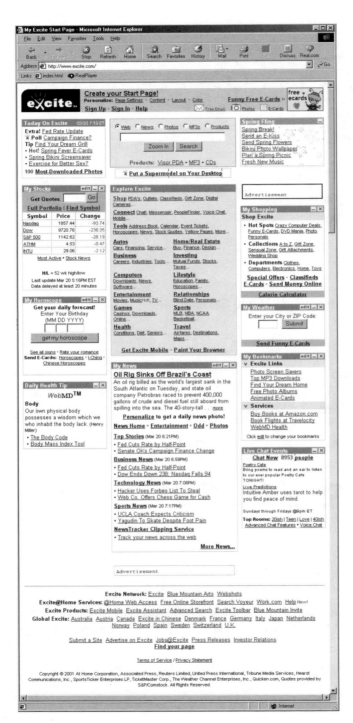

Facts about This Engine

Launched in 1995, Excite is an Internet portal, which offers the user a free customizable home page with information such as news, stock quotes, weather, horoscopes, services, and more, all of which can be personalized on the member Start Page. Relevant searches and services such as chat, Web-based e-mail, and shopping has made Excite popular enough to acquire WebCrawler and Magellan.

A partnership with LookSmart, creating "Excite Plus," has added searches organized by categories, and a recent merger with the @Home Corporation will take the Excite products and services on to the broadband platform.

1. **Web address:** http://www.excite.com
2. **Type of engine:** Hybrid. Primary results — Excite's database, Secondary results — LookSmart.
3. **Partnerships:** LookSmart and its partners by extension
4. **Total documents indexed:** 250 million as of January 2001
5. **Total page views per month:** 2,049,581,000 (Source: Alexa Research, Feb. 2001)
6. **E-mail support:** http://www.excite.com/feedback/
7. **How to confirm listing:** Type in the full URL.
8. **Obtain link popularity information:** Not applicable
9. **Result returns:** Web results are returned from Excite exclusively, but category searches are from LookSmart.
10. **Receive higher rankings for link popularity:** Primary results — Yes, Secondary results — No.
11. **Additional off-the-page considerations:** Primary results — Unconfirmed, Secondary results — Uses human editors for directory results.
12. **Rankings influenced by after-the-click behavior:** Primary results — No, Secondary results — No.
13. **Recognition and utilization of META tags:** Primary results — Yes, Excite recently began using the description META tag. Secondary results — No.
14. **Consideration of META tags for relevancy:** Primary results — Yes, Secondary results — Not applicable.
15. **Importance of Title tag keyword prominence:** Primary results — No. Excite claims not to recognize any META tags other than the description tag. However, when searches were conducted, the first place results contained some or all keywords searched in the Title tag. If no description is provided, a page summary will be created by Excite and presented in place of the description. Secondary results — Not applicable.
16. **Importance of <ALT> tag:** Primary results — No, Secondary results — Yes.
17. **Importance of multiple occurrences of keywords in Title tag:** Primary results — No, Secondary results — No.
18. **Maximum length of Title tag:** Primary results — Not applicable, Secondary results — Not applicable.

19. **Maximum length of keyword META tag:** Primary results — Not applicable, Secondary results — Not applicable.

20. **Maximum length of description META tag:** Primary results — Not applicable, Secondary results — Not applicable.

21. **Comment tags considered for relevancy:** Primary results — No, Secondary results — Not applicable.

22. **Frame support:** Primary results — No, Secondary results — Not applicable.

23. **Image map support:** Primary results — No, Secondary results — Not applicable.

24. **Accepts automated submissions:** Primary results — No, Secondary results — Not applicable.

25. **Indexes submitted pages only or conducts deep crawls:** Primary results — Indexes submitted pages, Secondary results — Not applicable.

26. **Instant spidering of submitted page:** Primary results — No, Secondary results — Not applicable.

27. **Number of pages that can be submitted per day:** Primary results — No published limit, Secondary results — Not applicable.

28. **Word stemming and plural sensitive:** Primary results — Yes, Secondary results — Yes.

29. **Case-sensitive searches:** Primary results — No, Secondary results — No.

30. **Alphabetical page listings:** Primary results — No, Secondary results — Yes, with categories.

31. **Time to index page:** Primary results — 4-6 weeks, Secondary results — Varies depending on submission method chosen.

32. **Spam penalties:** Primary results — Excite penalizes you for each instance of spam, most likely repetition of keywords; Excite claims that each "penalty" makes it more difficult for your page to rank on that phrase. Secondary results — Not applicable.

33. **Refuses pages with META refresh:** Primary results — Unconfirmed, Secondary results — Not applicable.

34. **Refuses pages with invisible text:** Primary results — Unconfirmed, Secondary results — Not applicable.

35. **Refuses pages with "tiny text":** Primary results — Unconfirmed, Secondary results — Not applicable.

36. **Remove URL:** Primary results — you can either add a robots.txt file telling Excite's spider not to crawl your site or remove the old pages from your server and resubmit the empty URLs. Both methods will cause your pages to drop out during the spider's next visit. Secondary results — Not applicable.

This information may be out of date by the time of publication. Because search engines frequently change their ranking algorithms and other page scoring variables, we have posted updates and revisions to these chapters on our Web site: http://www.iprospect.com/search-engine-chapters.htm.

Understanding the Results

Excite offers the searcher plenty of options for viewing results. A search for "fresh sausage" in Excite is demonstrated in the following graphic. First, Excite lists the number of matches returned which in this case is 367,140. Directly below this, the user is presented with the option of viewing results from The Web or Web Directory. Results from The Web are automatically displayed and come from Excite's database. Web Directory results are category matches served from LookSmart.

The Web results are displayed in increments of ten. The default display shows the title, URL, directory category (where applicable), and description. However, there are also options to "Show Titles Only" and "View by URL."

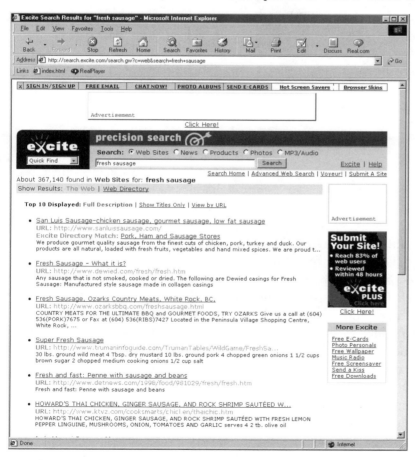

These options present less information on the original matches according to the user's choice. For example, "Show Titles Only" still displays the same ten matches but omits the description. "View by URL" displays the top 30 matches on one page but also lists relevant subpages indexed for those sites.

Web Directory listings display the top 20 category matches and their selected site listings. Click on the category link to view a list of all sites within that category.

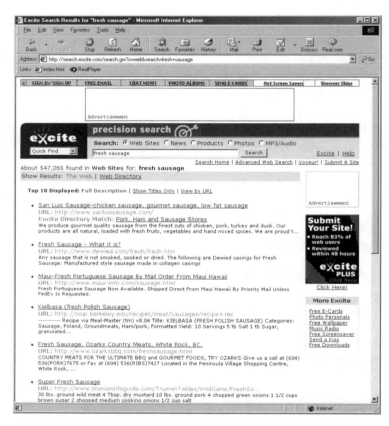

The next group of options from which the searcher can choose are topic related: Web Sites, News, Products, Photos, MP3/Audio, and Video. Each of these options presents the searcher with listings for the desired search term and the results are focused within the topic selected by the searcher. Along these lines, for example, entering the search term "Photography" under the News option would deliver a listing of news articles relating to photography, and the Products option would produce a listing of products for sale relating to photography. Each of the results under these search options can be further manipulated to display the results in a number of ways to customize the listings to suit the searcher's taste.

Additionally, Precision Search offers the following options: "Search Home," "Help," "Advanced Web Search," "Voyeur!," and "Submit A Site." "Search Home" will lead the searcher to Excite's channel search pages, allowing the searcher to select a topic of interest and conduct a search through the topic-oriented channel. Topics or channels range from "Celebrity Info" to "News Tracker" or "Weather Forecasts." On the left-hand side of the Search Home page Excite offers links to what it considers the "most interesting searches of the week" which are selected by Excite's editors.

Searchers wishing to conduct more defined searches may want to use the Advanced Search option. This option allows the searcher to manipulate some of the conditions for up to four desired search terms, conditions such as Must Have, Good to Have, and Must Not Have. The searcher can also control the number of results returned, the inclusion or exclusion of titles and descriptions, the language in which the results are returned, and finally what geographical region is searched; however, the use of quotes and Boolean search terms is not recognized here. Searching for "black, white, photography, exhibits" in Advanced Search returned results matching the specific intent of the search, where the same search term entered in the Precision Search page returned results on a much broader base of "photography."

Finally, there is the "Voyeur!" option, which is a fun option. A disclaimer is first presented to the searcher regarding the uncontrolled environment of "Real-Time Searches." Opening Search Voyeur! will allow the searcher to view a list of actual searches currently being conducted on Excite. The list is randomly selected and updated every thirty seconds. If you find a search which interests you, just click on the link and you will be served the same results as the original searcher.

Site Elements That Can Cause Problems

Excite's spiders run into difficulties with several elements of Web sites. These include: frames, query strings, broken links, secure pages, 404 errors, and page redirects. All the aforementioned cause problems with Excite's spiders crawling and indexing pages.

Frames seem to be the biggest indexing issue with Excite. Excite's spiders cannot index the content in frames. Therefore, your frames site will remain invisible to Excite until you add a <NOFRAMES> tag to your source code. The <NOFRAMES> tag can be placed anywhere in your source code and will provide the spider with content to index. Excite provides guidance on this issue at http://www.excite.com/info/getting_listed/find_your_site/ and via automated help at http://www.excite.com/info/ by typing "frames" into the search box and selecting "Website Not Getting Indexed." Another option for frames would be to utilize a robots.txt file. For instance, <META NAME= "ROBOTS" CONTENT= "NOINDEX"> can be placed in the META tag of the pages that contain frames; however, adding the "robots.txt" file will restrict Excite's spider from indexing that particular page and will defeat the purpose of optimizing your site for Excite. The optimum solution would be to avoid frames altogether.

Secure pages, query strings, broken links, 404 errors, and page redirects are not indexable and therefore hinder your ability to gain site visibility. All elements that have been touched upon already in this book but it is sufficient to say that broken links and 404 errors also diminish the reputation of your site and go against Excite's desire to provide content to users. It is necessary to trap 404 errors in order to avoid losing valuable real estate in Excite should the page be temporarily down. However, avoid simply redirecting the user to another page; this tactic is very questionable because it promises the engine and user one thing and delivers them to another page or site.

Recommended Site Optimization Tactics

Excite looks for content on the actual viewable page. This means that a keyword META tag, <ALT> tag, and any comment tags in your source code do little to help your optimization and may, in fact, hurt you by showing up as spam. Excite claims to reduce your chances for rankings on a keyword every time you repeat the word. Therefore, make sure that the page you are optimizing for a particular keyword actually talks about that word and doesn't simply use the word in META tags. The Title and description tags are important for determining your placement. If you do not provide a description in your META tags, Excite will scan your page and create one on your behalf. This poses two problems: Excite's description may not contain any of the keywords you are trying to attain rankings on, and the description will point out the discrepancies between what you are targeting with META tags and what the page actually talks about. For example, if you have a page about dog food, the content of the page should be about dog food and not pet food, which would certainly encompass dog food, but also could include cat food, bird food, rabbit food, fish food, and many other types of "pet foods." The desired listing under "dog food" would be unlikely if the summary of the page pertains to "pet food."

Although Excite claims not to consider other META tags, such as the Title or keyword tags, for its relevancy rating, it does appear to place pages which have the search term in the Title tag in more prominent positions. Several searches conducted on various topics such as wine, knee socks, chocolates, and recipes returned results where the first place listing went to pages that had the search term in the title and description. Pages placing second and third also contained the search term as the first keyword in the keyword META tag. Additionally, it appears that Excite may rank a page higher if there is a link on the page that contains a keyword. Using the keyword in an <H1> tag also helps draw attention to it. However, there is never any substitute for having meaningful content on your pages.

Off-the-Page Factors That Influence Success

Two off-the-page factors that influence how well a page is ranking include link popularity and the editor's review. Recently, Excite appears to have joined the trend of not only considering link popularity of a site, but also considering the strength of those links. This link quality concept considers the strength of a link from a well-known source to be a more valuable endorsement as a link than hundreds of links from lesser known sources.

This is not to say that the hundreds of links from lesser known sources will not add value to the link popularity factor, but one link from a well-known source will carry equal or greater value.

Excite has partnered with LookSmart, and now directory listings for Excite are provided by LookSmart. Be sure to read Chapter 23 to determine how to proceed with the actual submissions. However, your success or lack thereof in LookSmart will certainly affect your placements in Excite.

How to Build Informational Pages for this Engine

Building informational pages for Excite is a good way to increase the number of pages that get indexed. These informational pages should have a separate domain registered from them as Excite is only likely to index approximately 25 pages of the default or index.htm page. Also, a separate domain will allow you to place keywords in the URL. Excite gives higher rankings to pages that contain the keyword in the URL. For example, the domain name www.auto-parts.com will help you attain a ranking on the phrase "auto parts." Excite makes it known that it prefers not to index pages that are low in content, so make your informational pages content-rich and relevant. Also make a page with only a few keywords in mind and place the keywords in your Title tag, description, and <H1> tags. Concentrate on creating a good META description, which includes the targeted keyword near the beginning of the description. Remember that Excite will display the META description as the site's description. The content of the page should also include the targeted keyword, however it should not be repeated too frequently or without context as this would be considered spamming. Finally, don't use frames, as Excite's spiders will not enter them.

How to Know if Your Site Has Been Spidered/Listed

Checking Excite approximately two to three weeks after initial submission of a site by typing in the URL of the site will provide the confirmation needed to know if the site has been added to the Excite database. Confirmation of spider visits can be obtained from the site's logs by looking for the Excite spiders listed below:

Spider IP	Spider DNS Name	Search Engine	Spider User Agent
198.3.103.66	piccolo.excite.com	Excite	ArchitextSpider
198.3.103.97	maturana.excite.com	Excite	ArchitextSpider
198.3.103.50	gentong.excite.com	Excite	
198.3.103.35	bongos.excite.com	Excite	
198.3.103.56		Excite	
198.3.103.57	kazoo.excite.com	Excite	ArchitextSpider
198.3.103.58	kettle.excite.com	Excite	ArchitextSpider
198.3.103.59	mandolin.excite.com	Excite	ArchitextSpider
198.3.103.65	piano.excite.com	Excite	ArchitextSpider
198.3.103.68	ride.excite.com	Excite	
198.3.103.69	sabian.excite.com	Excite	
198.3.103.70	sax.excite.com	Excite	ArchitextSpider
198.3.103.72	snare.excite.com	Excite	
198.3.103.81	viola.excite.com	Excite	ArchitextSpider
198.3.103.84	ziljian.excite.com	Excite	
198.3.103.93	lukacs.excite.com	Excite	
204.62.245.167	crawl2.atext.com	Excite	
204.62.245.187	ichiban.atext.com	Excite	
204.62.245.32	crimpshrine.atext.com	Excite	
198.3.103.108	camus.excite.com	Excite	
199.172.148.105	bunsen.excite.com	Excite	libwww-perl/5.33
198.3.103.24	voltaire.excite.com	Excite	ArchitextSpider

(Source: http://www.spiderhunter.com/spiderlist)

This is not a complete list and Excite may have made changes to it.

Indexing Timetable

Submitting directly to Excite does not guarantee that your site will be added to the database. Indexing times are usually between four and six weeks. However, Excite has recently taken six months to index sites. Submitting to Excite through one of LookSmart's paid programs will guarantee that your site will be reviewed by a LookSmart editor but does not guarantee inclusion. Submissions accepted into LookSmart are usually added to Excite and other LookSmart partners within a short time.

What to Do If Your Rankings Disappear

There are many reasons why rankings can disappear or be dropped by Excite. On a database refresh, the Excite spider starts at the home page and follows links until approximately 25 randomly selected pages are indexed, and the remaining pages may be dropped. Some control over which pages get indexed can be achieved by adding the robots.txt file (previously mentioned) to less important pages, which would exclude those pages from indexing. For more specific information about the pros and cons of utilizing the robots.txt file, see Chapter 5. Diligent resubmission every two weeks is the best insurance against pages disappearing in Excite.

Special Tips and Tactics for This Engine

Excite is a keyword-focused engine, so concentrating on good and relevant content is necessary to a successful listing. Definitely use the paid submission for the initial submission of your site to Excite, as the free indexing could take three or more weeks before your site is listed. Additionally, keeping up a resubmission schedule to ensure that pages don't disappear is time well spent.

Excite offers an informative help section at http://www.excite.com/info/. This section will introduce you to the workings of Excite and provide useful information to help you get well listed in Excite.

The best recommendation for success in Excite comes from the engine itself. At http://www.excite.com/info/getting_listed/improve_your_ranking/, Excite offers the following scenario: "you want users searching for 'Hawaiian bed and breakfasts' to find your site among the first 20 sites retrieved." The solution provided is to "relegate unrelated topics to subsidiary pages. If you're advertising your Hawaiian bed and breakfast, don't use the home page to emphasize price, the way the ocean looks from a bedroom window, or your famous pineapple rum concoction. Instead, emphasize bed, breakfast, Hawaii, and vacation." This advice is oversimplified as other factors such as link popularity, domain name, and where the listing came from can have an impact. However, in Excite's view there is nothing better you can do than provide real content that will solve searchers' problems.

Excite now appears to limit the number of indexed pages to 25 per domain. You must make certain to choose content-rich pages that will provide value to Excite. Also, remember that submitting additional pages will not provide you with much additional value.

Responsiveness and Help Provided

Excite's responsiveness and help provided were mediocre at best. Its Help screens provide very general answers to a variety of topics. There also seems to be some conflicting information from what appears to be pages for older versions of Excite when a relevancy percentage was displayed next to each result. Excite is surveying its Help services with a "yes" or "no" request box, asking the searcher to rate if the answer provided satisfied the intent of the query. Excite also has a feedback box where the searcher can type in a question to get a response. An automated response is immediately dispatched to the searcher's e-mail, which promises that a detailed response will follow.

The response was not fast and the information it provided was the same information from the results in the Help search box on the site.

Chapter 17:

FAST

Fast Search & Transfer Inc. (FAST USA)
1700 West Park Drive
Westborough, MA 01581
sales@fast.no
(508) 616-2400
Fax: (508) 616-2410

Free updates to this book are available via e-mail newsletter
by visiting: http://www.iprospect.com/book-news.htm.

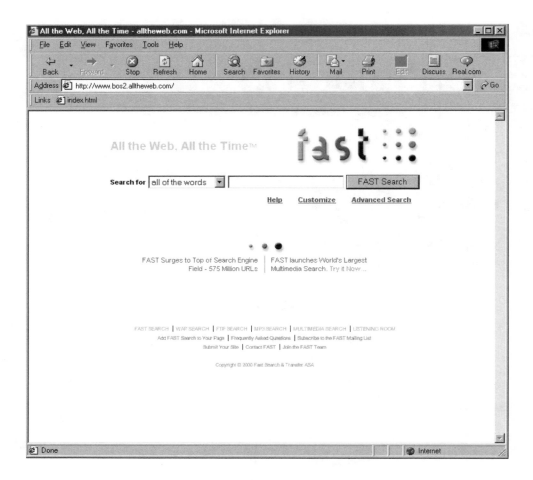

Facts about This Engine

The search engine known as FAST, or "All the Web," began as a joint venture between Dell Computers and a Norwegian company called Fast Search & Transfer. The trademark name of this joint venture is All the Web, All the Time™. alltheweb.com was created simply to showcase FAST's Internet search technology. The company offers two types of services: search engine technology and image/video transfer.

FAST provides search technology for both Lycos and LookSmart, although there are differences. Lycos is actually using the same data as alltheweb.com as well as FAST's algorithms and search technology.

1. **Web address:** www.alltheweb.com
2. **Type of engine:** Pure spider
3. **Partnerships:** FAST has a number of partnerships around the world, but the most important for anyone interested in U.S.-based search engines are Lycos and LookSmart.
4. **Total documents indexed:** Approximately 500 million individual documents
5. **Total page views per month:** 111,464,000 (Source: Alexa Research, Feb. 2001)
6. **E-mail support:** http://www.ussc.alltheweb.com/feedback.php3
7. **How to confirm listing:** Search for your URL.
8. **Obtain link popularity information:** Select the "Advanced Search" link. Set the first Word Filter to "Should Include," type the domain you want in the text box, and set the drop-down box to "in the link to URL." Then hit the FAST Search button.
9. **Result returns:** All results are provided from the FAST database.
10. **Receive higher rankings for link popularity:** Yes
11. **Additional off-the-page considerations:** No
12. **Rankings influenced by after-the-click behavior:** No
13. **Recognition and utilization of META tags:** Yes
14. **Consideration of META tags for relevancy:** alltheweb.com appears to index every word on the page, including the META tags.
15. **Importance of Title tag keyword prominence:** If the keywords do not agree with the content of the page, it is likely that there will be little to no relevance impact.
16. **Importance of <ALT> tag:** Limited
17. **Importance of multiple occurrences of keywords in Title tag:** Minimal
18. **Maximum length of Title tag:** Unconfirmed
19. **Maximum length of keyword META tag:** Unconfirmed
20. **Maximum length of description META tag:** Unconfirmed
21. **Comment tags considered for relevancy:** No

22. **Frame support:** Claims to
23. **Image map support:** Claims to
24. **Accepts automated submissions:** Yes
25. **Indexes submitted pages only or conducts deep crawls:** Conducts deep crawls
26. **Instant spidering of submitted page:** No
27. **Number of pages that can be submitted per day:** No published limit
28. **Word stemming and plural sensitive:** Yes
29. **Case-sensitive searches:** No
30. **Alphabetical page listings:** No
31. **Time to index page:** Some sources claim 4-8 weeks
32. **Spam penalties:** FAST does not disclose its penalties for spamming
33. **Refuses pages with META refresh:** Unconfirmed
34. **Refuses pages with invisible text:** Unconfirmed
35. **Refuses pages with "tiny text":** Unconfirmed
36. **Remove URL:** None, however, FAST will honor robot exclusion tags.

This information may be out of date by the time of publication. Because search engines frequently change their ranking algorithms and other page scoring variables, we have posted updates and revisions to these chapters on our Web site: http://www.iprospect.com/search-engine-chapters.htm.

Understanding the Results

alltheweb.com is fairly straightforward as search engines go. The first thing you see on the page is the number of documents found along with the search time. One of FAST's goals is to reduce the search time as much as possible and their search times are incredible. When a search for "cheeseburger" was performed, alltheweb.com found 63,209 documents in 0.3666 seconds. This is incredible when you consider that FAST claims to be searching its entire index of over 500 million pages! You then see a list of 10 results. These results show the site's Title tag as a hyperlink to the site, some text from the site, and the URL of the indexed pages. The text appears to be the first 256 characters of visible text from the page. This does not appear to affect the site's ranking. One of the odd things about alltheweb.com is that it doesn't support the description META tag like most search engines.

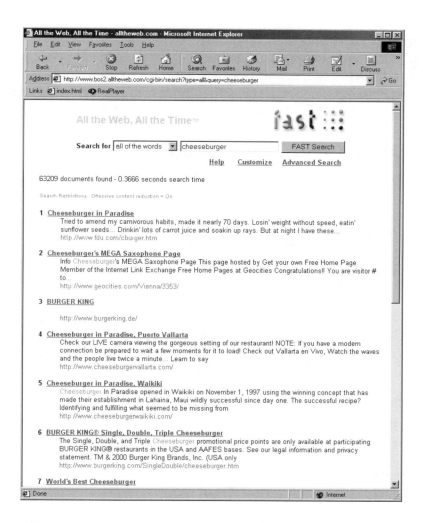

Site Elements That Can Cause Problems

While alltheweb.com seems to accept any URL, even those with query strings, URLs with query strings do not appear to get indexed.

Recommended Site Optimization Tactics

The most important factor when optimizing for alltheweb.com appears to be the Title tag. While alltheweb.com spiders the entire page, the title appears to give the most "weight" to your page. The results of any search on alltheweb.com for any keyword or phrase show the query in the META title. The next target for optimization would appear to be the first 256 characters of **visible** text on the page. While it is not definitive that alltheweb.com uses these characters to determine relevance or ranking, the simple fact that they show these characters instead of the META description does indicate importance.

Off-the-Page Factors That Influence Success

FAST considers link popularity in their relevance algorithms. However, on-the-page factors that influence rankings are equally important.

How to Submit a Site to This Engine

Go to www.alltheweb.com and click on the Submit Your Site link. The e-mail field appears to be optional.

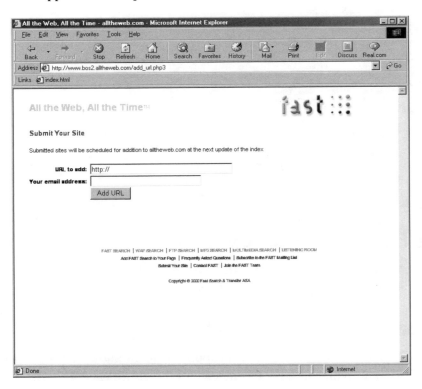

How to Build Informational Pages for this Engine

As stated above, the Title tag appears to be the most important thing when constructing informational pages. It is also worth noting that adding lots of keyword-laden content seems beneficial. This is not to say that inserting, for example, "keyword, keyword, keyword" on your page is the answer. Rather, try putting actual content on your page. Placing links to other sites relevant to your keywords in the viewable text of your page should also help.

How to Know If Your Site Has Been Spidered/Listed

The FAST spider is clearly marked as "FAST-WebCrawler" either version 2.1 or 2.2 (both appeared to be active as of this writing). Concerns about this spider can be addressed to crawler@fast.no and FAST has posted an FAQ at http://www.fast.no/fast.php3?d=support_faqs&c=crawler&h=3, which includes instructions on how to block the spider from your site or page.

Indexing Timetable

Non-FAST sources claim four to eight weeks.

What to Do If Your Rankings Disappear

Resubmit your pages.

Special Tips and Tactics for This Engine

This engine does not need myriad special tips. FAST clearly wants to index as much of the Web as possible.

Responsiveness and Help Provided

The FAST Web site, http://www.fast.no, has a lot of interesting and useful information. They are very proud of their technology and want the world to know what they can do. However, they will only reveal so much.

Chapter 18:

GO.com

Infoseek Corporation and GO Network
1399 Moffett Park Drive
Sunnyvale, CA 94089-1134
comments@help.go.com or http://comments.go.com/comments.html
(408) 543-6000
Fax: (408) 734-9355

Free updates to this book are available via e-mail newsletter
by visiting: http://www.iprospect.com/book-news.htm.

GO.com is a trademark of Disney Enterprises, Inc.

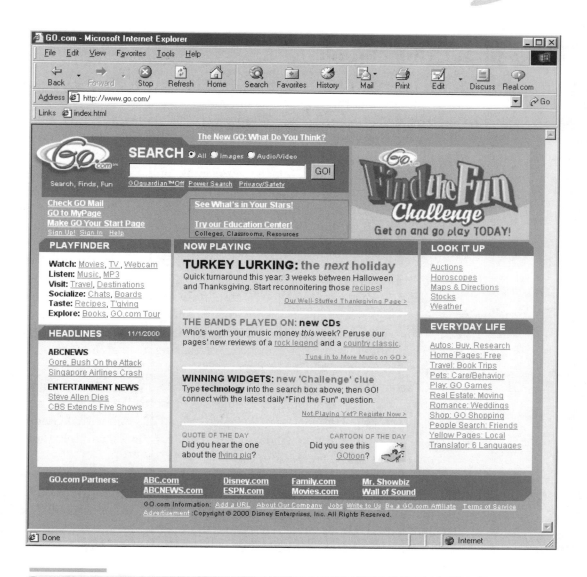

NOTE: Just prior to press time, Disney removed the GO.com database and began serving GoTo paid listings. This chapter was written prior to this change and thus reflects the old rules for this engine. We have kept this information in the book as it is rumored that GO.com will sometime in the future return to its previous format.

Facts about This Engine

In December 2000, Disney announced that they were closing GO.com. At press time, the future of this engine was unclear.

Founded by Steve Kirsch in 1994, Infoseek Corporation first went live in 1995 as the "first one-step information retrieval service." A spider-based search engine, Infoseek quickly gained in popularity and became one of the top search engines of the mid-1990s. Helped by its simple interface, user-friendliness, and the quality of the results it returns for simple searches, Infoseek has been an ideal match for the novice Internet user.

In November 1998, Disney shareholders approved a deal for Disney to take a 43 percent stake in Infoseek, securing the partnership that helped form the GO Network and renaming Infoseek as GO.com. As a partner in the GO Network, GO.com is a portal site and has expanded its features to include personalization with its My Page feature, free e-mail, and expanded news and sports coverage through the Disney-owned sites ABCNEWS.com and ESPN.com, respectively. As the search engine for the GO Network, GO.com's search capabilities were also enhanced, increasing its search index by 50 percent and the speed at which results are returned by 30 percent.

GO.com also became a hybrid search engine, taking a page from the Open Directory school of thought that "Humans do it better" and including a human-edited directory portion on their Web site called GO Guides. GO Guide results are used to complement its spider-based results, rating separately those sites that appeal to the GO Guide editors.

In March 2001, Walt Disney Internet Group, the parent company of GO.com, added a new look and focus for the search engine. After this facelift, GO.com focused on leisure and lifestyle topics. GO.com also included features like auctions, celebrity commentary, and more ad space.

---

1. **Web address:** http://www.go.com
2. **Type of engine:** Hybrid (spider-based search engine with "GO Guides" content to complement)
3. **Partnerships:** ABC.com, ABCNEWS.com, ESPN.com, Disney.com, Family.com, and MrShowbiz.
4. **Total documents indexed:** 50 million as of June 6, 2000
5. **Total page views per month:** Estimated 1,021,350,000 (Source: Alexa Research, Jan. 2001)
6. **E-mail support:** comments@help.go.com or http://comments.go.com/comments.html
7. **How to confirm listing:** url:http://www.yoursite.com
8. **Obtain link popularity information:** link:http://www.yoursite.com

9. **Result returns:** Provides a link to GO Guide results under Web directory topics. "Web search results" are from spider-based search engine.

10. **Receive higher rankings for link popularity:** Yes

11. **Additional off-the-page considerations:** Higher rankings can be gained for those sites with favorable GO Guide review. GO.com also takes into consideration link popularity.

12. **Rankings influenced by after-the-click behavior:** No

13. **Recognition and utilization of META tags:** Yes

14. **Consideration of META tags for relevancy:** Yes. Considers Title tag for relevancy.

15. **Importance of Title tag keyword prominence:** Yes

16. **Importance of <ALT> tag:** Yes, supports <ALT> tag.

17. **Importance of multiple occurrences of keywords in Title tag:** Yes, however, rankings will decrease if the same word is repeated more than once in the Title tag.

18. **Maximum length of Title tag:** 70 to 75 characters

19. **Maximum length of keyword META tag:** 1,024 characters

20. **Maximum length of description META tag:** 246 characters

21. **Comment tags considered for relevancy:** No

22. **Frame support:** No. If the site you submit uses frames, be sure to include a <NOFRAMES> element in the <FRAMESET>. This element should fully describe the entire Web site. GO.com will index this text in the <NOFRAMES> tag, if the site is accepted. Be sure to include description and keyword META tags in the <FRAMESET>.

23. **Image map support:** Yes

24. **Accepts automated submissions:** Yes

25. **Indexes submitted pages only or conducts deep crawls:** "Shallow" crawl. Will index only those pages that are submitted. To submit sites with more than 50 URLs, send an e-mail to www-request@infoseek.com, listing the pages and including "http://."

26. **Instant spidering of submitted page:** Yes

27. **Number of pages that can be submitted per day:** GO.com will accept a maximum of 50 pages per day through the Submit Your Site link. Remember to begin each entry with "http://."

28. **Word stemming and plural sensitive:** Yes, different results are returned when the word is queried in plural and singular forms. For example, you will find querying the word "CAR" delivers different results than "CARS," and "Car" delivers different results than "Cars." However, when querying a word in all lowercase, the same results are presented (e.g., the results for "car" are the same as the results for "cars").

29. **Case-sensitive searches:** Yes, results vary from "CAR" to "car."

30. **Alphabetical page listings:** No. GO.com returns results sorted by relevance.

31. **Time to index page:** 4 to 6 weeks

32. **Spam penalties:** Violation of the spam policy can result in removal or exclusion from the index. Persistent spammers will have their ISPs notified and face possible legal action.

33. **Refuses pages with META refresh:** Yes

34. **Refuses pages with invisible text:** Yes

35.   **Refuses pages with "tiny text":** Unconfirmed

36.   **Remove URL:** dead-links@corp.go.com

This information may be out of date by the time of publication. Because search engines frequently change their ranking algorithms and other page scoring variables, we have posted updates and revisions to these chapters on our Web site: http://www.iprospect.com/search-engine-chapters.htm.

Understanding the Results

Depending upon the phrase that has been queried, GO.com will present up to three parts to their Search results: "GO Directory," "Proven Picks" (those listing rated by GO Guides), and "Web Search Results." At the heart of these results are the "Web Search Results," a list of sites ranked by relevancy and presented ten per page, which are created directly from GO.com's spider-based search engine. GO.com displays the number of matches in its database as well as a number of options including "Hide summaries," which lists only links to Web sites and display 20 results per page; "Sort by date," which displays results according to those most recently submitted; and "Ungroup results," which displays only one result from the particular site that is ranking.

"Proven Picks," another portion of the GO.com results, lists those categories from the GO Guides that are relevant to the search query. When the user clicks on one of these category topics, he or she is directed to the GO Guide editors' picks. These results are sorted in rank order, with three stars equaling the highest rating, and are displayed alphabetically. Subcategories may also be displayed if the category is very broad.

The third portion of GO.com's search results is "Try a related search." These suggestions are displayed at the top of the page near the search box and are only displayed on broad queries to help narrow the search and deliver more qualified results. Clicking on one of these suggestions is in effect like performing a new query on the selection and will deliver a whole new list of results.

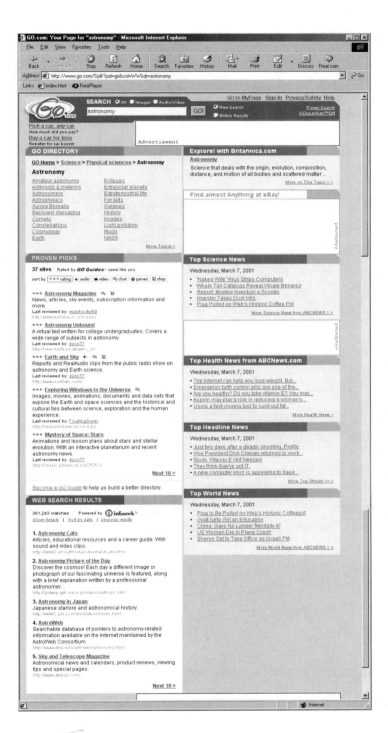

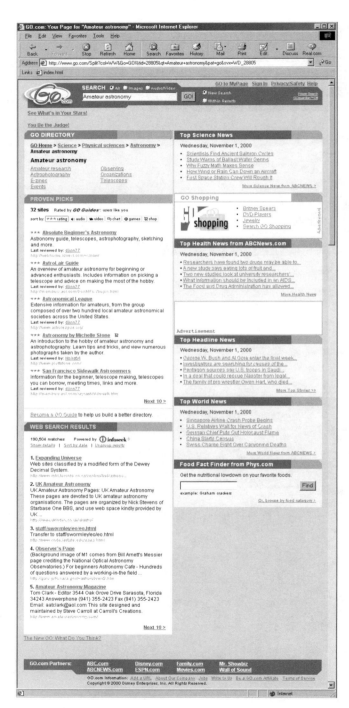

Results displayed when clicking on "Amateur astronomy" from the results presented in the previous illustration

Site Elements That Can Cause Problems

When submitting a site to GO.com's spider-based search engine, there are many site elements you should avoid because they can cause problems and diminish your rankings. Such elements include using frames, using cookies, decreasing keyword weight by including large amounts of code, and employing techniques that set off GO.com's many spam filters.

Like many search engines, the GO.com search engine spider is unable to index text within frames. Therefore, any META tags or keywords included in a frame will not be crawled and your site's relevancy will be decreased. If your site uses frames, include a <NOFRAMES> tag in the <FRAMESET> that fully describes the entire Web site.

Pages that serve a cookie in order to load also pose a problem for your rankings. This is due to the fact that the GO.com spider will not accept cookies as it crawls the page, making it impossible for GO.com to index your site. Therefore, it is imperative to ensure that your pages will load without a cookie being accepted.

Because GO.com relies partly on the information and links included within the body of the Web page, pushing that copy farther down the page in favor of large amounts of code such as JavaScript can also diminish rankings.

GO.com also has numerous spam filters which check the Web site when it is submitted. Among those engines checking for repeatedly using the same keyword within tags or text, the GO.com spider is able to reject those pages that have the same color text as the page's background color. This, however, can pose a problem for those sites that use tables. For example, GO.com will reject a page with a white background and white text, even if the white text is only included within a table with a black background.

Submitting a site to GO Guides is just like submitting to other human-edited directories such as Yahoo! or Open Directory. You must make sure your site is of high quality, both in appearance and content.

Recommended Site Optimization Tactics

The most important part of a Web site submitted to GO.com by far is the Title tag. GO.com has indicated that the Title tag is eight times more important than the rest of the body text within the page. Therefore, to ensure a better ranking on a particular keyword, make sure that it is included in the Title tag. The title should be highly descriptive and it is also helpful if the targeted keyword is at the beginning of the tag, as the spider will only crawl through the first 70 to 75 characters within the tag.

The next most important item that GO.com looks for is the keyword META tag. The keyword tag should contain comma-separated phrases. It is also important to use synonyms, as GO.com will consider variations and synonyms when it delivers results.

Therefore, to place highly within GO.com's results, you should optimize your site in the following manner:

- Use keywords in the title.
- Use keywords at the beginning of pages.
- Use keywords in META tags.
- Use synonyms in the keyword tag.

It is important to remember, however, that you should not repeat the same words within the META tags over and over again. GO.com's policy regarding this practice is as follows:

"Don't try to increase your site's relevancy by repeating the same keyword over and over again. GO.com severely penalizes Web sites that attempt to subvert the index in this way. This abuse may lower the ranking of your site in Search Results pages or cause it to be removed from the GO.com index altogether."

Off-the-Page Factors That Influence Success

Along with the importance of META tags, GO.com's ranking algorithm also takes link popularity into account to determine the relevancy of a particular site. While it is important to have many sites linking to your site, it is more important to ensure that at least a few of those links are of high quality. To determine which sites that link to your site are listed in GO.com, type link:http://www .yoursite.com within the search box.

Additionally, another important factor that can influence the success of your site is whether you are listed within the GO Guides human-edited portion of GO.com and the rating that the GO Guides editors give your site. The better the rating, the better the ranking.

How to Submit a Site to This Engine

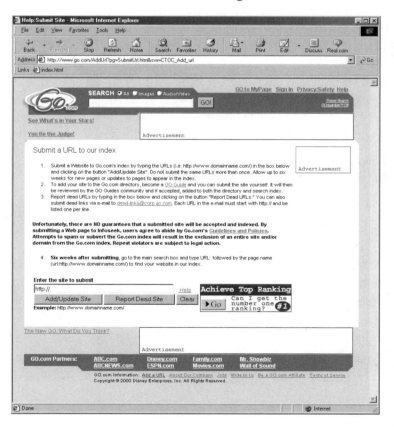

To submit your URL to the GO.com spider-based search engine, find the "Add a URL" link and follow the instructions.

Because the GO.com spider only "shallow" crawls the sites, no other URLs from your site will get indexed beyond those submitted. To index more of your site, you must submit the rest of those URLs using the same method. Make sure that while doing this you do not submit a URL that has already been submitted or you will be seen as spamming the index and may get banned altogether.

If you need to submit more than 50 URLs from your site, you may submit an e-mail to www-request@infoseek.com.

Remember to submit each URL, one per line, within the e-mail and include "http://www."

For example, your e-mail should be in this notation:

http://www.yoursite.com
http://www.yoursite.com/page1.html
http://www.yoursite.com/page50.html

To submit your site to the GO Guides directory, you must first find the category in which you believe your site belongs. To do this you should first search for those keywords that match your site's content. After choosing the appropriate category from the "Web directory topics," you can submit an e-mail to url_review@infoseek.com with the following information:

- The category you wish to submit to
- The URL of your site
- The title
- The description

You also have the option of becoming a GO Guide editor yourself and then submitting your own site. To become a GO Guide editor go to http://guides.go.com/ and sign up. According to GO.com, your submission will be reviewed by the GO Guides, and if accepted, added to both the directory and search index.

How to Build Informational Pages for this Engine

GO.com places great emphasis on the META tags within your site. Therefore, just as a regular site should incorporate META tags, so too should your informational pages. In fact, GO.com has provided specific ideas of how to incorporate those tags within your site.

GO.com recommends that you create a descriptive page title that lets people know what the page is about. You should include specific keywords within the title that are within the site and central to the page you are optimizing.

GO.com also recommends that you include the description META tag. GO.com utilizes the description tag to display the summary description for your page in the search results. Be aware that if you do not supply a tag, GO.com will create one based on the page's text. This automatically generated description is often created from the first few lines of text of your page and does not usually rank as well as a page with a description specifically created for it. The description tag should also not include any formatting (for example, any heading tags).

The keyword META tag should also be implemented within your informational page. It is imperative that within the keyword tag you incorporate synonyms of those keywords that fit your informational page to increase the chances that your site will show up in a search for a topic related to your site. The words and phrases within the keyword META tag should be separated by commas.

It is important to remember that while creating your META tags, you should not repeat the same keyword over and over again. GO.com penalizes Web sites that do this. This type of abuse may lower your site's ranking or could even cause it to be removed.

How to Know If Your Site Has Been Spidered/Listed

GO.com's spiders and their IP addresses are provided in the following list. This information will be included in your site's log files after the spider has visited.

204.162.96.92	wilbur-bbn.infoseek.com
205.226.203.56	cde2cb38.infoseek.com
198.5.208.100	c605d064.infoseek.com
198.5.210.181	c605d2b5.infoseek.com
198.5.210.189	c605d2bd.infoseek.com
204.162.96.124	cca2607c.infoseek.com
204.162.96.3	bud-bbn.infoseek.com
204.162.96.66	cole-bbn.infoseek.com
204.162.96.73	blue-bbn.infoseek.com
204.162.97.17	cca26111.infoseek.com
204.162.97.1	cca26101.infoseek.com
204.162.97.231	cca261e7.infoseek.com
204.162.98.38	cca26226.infoseek.com
204.162.98.11	cca2620b.infoseek.com
205.226.201.30	cde2c91e.infoseek.com
205.226.203.35	cde2cb23.infoseek.com
205.226.204.238	cde2ccee.infoseek.com
210.236.233.155	155.128/25.233.236.210.in-addr.arpa
204.162.96.2	corp-bbn.infoseek.com
204.162.96.76	cca2604c.infoseek.com

To find out if your site has been listed, go to the main GO.com page, enter url:http://www.yoursite.com, then click Search. If the site has been added to the index, you will see its title and description on the Search Results page.

Indexing Timetable

After you have submitted your site to GO.com, it will take approximately four to six weeks to be listed. In the past, however, there have been blackout periods affecting the time in which a site will be listed. During these times, the only thing that you can do is wait until the spider is back online.

Also, at times, the submission URL box will disappear from the site. When this occurs, you must submit all of the URLs via e-mail to www-request @infoseek.com.

What to Do If Your Rankings Disappear

Like any spider-based search engine, GO.com is continually updating its index of Web sites. Often, your pages will drop in position or fall out of the index altogether. It is important to properly react to a drop in rankings. The initial reaction is to quickly resubmit all of your ranking pages to GO.com. This massive amount of submission is considered spamming the index. When you see pages drop, it is often because the database is being worked on. Certain elements of the database may not be available all the time, so it is important to check back often to see if your site has returned. After a few days have passed and your rankings have not returned, you should begin the process of resubmitting according to the terms and conditions of GO.com. If your rankings still do not reappear over the course of a few months, your site may have been banned and you should contact GO.com to determine your next steps.

Special Tips and Tactics for This Engine

In an effort to improve upon its branding and consumer awareness, GO.com has decided to move away from the general interest search engine arena to become a more focused niche search engine. GO.com will leverage Disney's core capabilities of all things entertainment and incorporate those sites that fall under Walt Disney Interactive Group's umbrella (ABC.com, ABCNEWS.com, Disney.com, MrShowbiz.com, and ESPN.com) to deliver content more tightly focused on leisure and lifestyle. According to CNET, this transition is likely to occur over the course of the next few months and will be "an evolution, not a revolution."

During this process, GO.com will not dump its current content altogether but rather prioritize the content to fall in line with their entertainment-based message. It does appear, however, that GO.com will utilize its GO Guide information in a more prominent manner and will probably display the GO Guide results before the spider-based results.

Those leisure and lifestyle sites better suited for the revamped GO.com will probably reap the benefits from this transition through higher rankings. If your site, however, does not have an entertainment focus, it is important that you are at least listed within the GO Guide. It is best, therefore, to actually become a GO Guide yourself to submit your site. Other GO Guides within your category will review your submission, so you must ensure that the description you have created accurately reflects the content within your site and that the content and design of your site is exceptional. Elements such as audio, video, chat, and shopping capabilities can also increase your rating within the GO Guide database and in return increase your ranking.

Responsiveness and Help Provided

GO.com offers three levels of help: information contained on the site, e-mail support, and phone support. The GO.com site is helpful in and of itself, providing a Help section which includes a list of commonly asked questions and answers regarding the processes and procedures for submitting a site, as well as a list of helpful tips to improve your site's relevancy and ultimately gain a higher ranking in GO.com. This, as well as more information about GO.com, can be found at http://www.go.com/Help/help.html.

You can also e-mail GO.com at comments@help.go.com for questions regarding your site's submission. There is also a submission-based e-mail at http://comments.go.com/comments.html from which you can choose an area to submit a comment or question. We have placed several queries to GO.com using the "Other" selection and have had some success. A human technical support expert has answered our questions within 48 hours of the e-mail submission. However, the help provided can be vague in nature and leave you more confused than before.

If e-mail does not work, GO.com also provides phone support at (408) 543-6000. Again, we have been successful in contacting a person and have spoken with a customer support representative. Our experience has been favorable and the help has been friendly.

Chapter 19:

Google

Google
2400 Bayshore Parkway
Mountain View, CA 94043
search-quality@google.com
(650) 330-0100
Fax: (650) 618-1499

Google[SM]

Free updates to this book are available via e-mail newsletter
by visiting: http://www.iprospect.com/book-news.htm.

The Google logo is a trademark of Google, Inc.

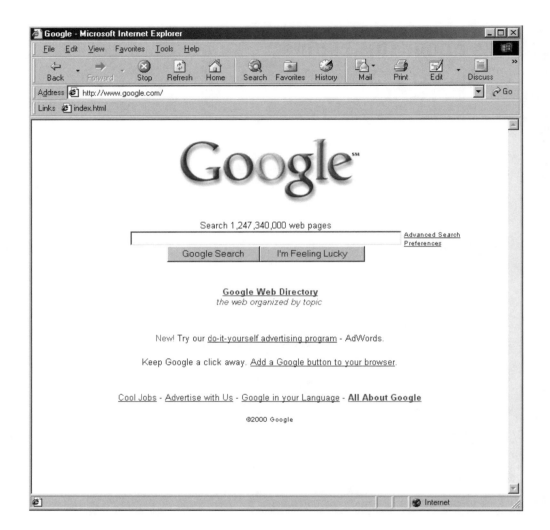

Facts about This Engine

Google is one of the most popular search engine destinations on the Web. Two Stanford doctoral students, Larry Page and Sergey Brin, founded Google in 1998. They coined the name "Google" based on "googol," a mathematical unit equal to 10 to the power of 100.

Google is a hybrid search engine, which means that it contains results from both a search function as well as from the Open Directory. Google is growing quickly, and its prominence was established when Yahoo! announced it had selected Google to replace Inktomi in powering Yahoo!'s non-directory results beginning in June 2000. Google is also presently powering parts of the search results at Netscape Search. Companies seek Google's services because of its exceptionally accurate search technology that mainly involves the analysis of link structure.

In addition to its high level of accuracy, an even greater incentive to use Google is its speed in finding and displaying results. Google is remarkably fast, and usually completes the task of finding results in less than one second. The page itself is also extremely quick in loading, since Google does not show many advertisements that take a long time to appear on the screen.

1. **Web address:** http://www.google.com
2. **Type of engine:** Hybrid. Primary results — Google database, Secondary results — Open Directory.
3. **Partnerships:** Google uses the Open Directory to return its Web directory results. Yahoo! and Netscape have selected Google to power their search results.
4. **Total documents indexed:** 1,347,000,000 Web pages
5. **Total page views per month:** 2,301,230,000 (Source: Alexa Research, Feb. 2001)
6. **E-mail support:** Google provides a list of e-mail addresses at http://www.google.com/contact/index.html.
7. **How to confirm listing:** http://yoururl.com
8. **Obtain link popularity information:** link:yoururl.com
9. **Result returns:** Primary results — Google returns 10 results per page from its own extensive database. However, the user can customize the amount of results displayed per page by clicking Advanced Search on the main page. Secondary results from the Open Directory are displayed by user choice from either the main page or from the top of search results pages.
10. **Receive higher rankings for link popularity:** Primary results — Yes. Google considers link popularity very important when ranking a Web page. Secondary results — Not applicable.

11. **Additional off-the-page considerations:** Primary results — Yes. Google measures both the number of links pointing to your site and the credibility of those sites to determine rankings. Secondary results — Open Directory is a human-compiled directory, therefore sites are subject to editorial review.

12. **Rankings influenced by after-the-click behavior:** Primary results — No, Secondary results — Not applicable.

13. **Recognition and utilization of META tags:** Primary results — Yes, Secondary results — Not applicable.

14. **Consideration of META tags for relevancy:** Primary results — No, Secondary results — Not applicable.

15. **Importance of Title tag keyword prominence:** Primary results — Google does not calculate Title tag keyword prominence, but rather focuses on the keywords in the body text. The keywords at the top of a page are just as important as the keywords on the bottom of a page, so make sure the whole page is interesting and relevant. Secondary results — Not applicable.

16. **Importance of <ALT> tag:** Primary results — No, Secondary results — Not applicable.

17. **Importance of multiple occurrences of keywords in Title tag:** Primary results — Yes, Secondary results — No.

18. **Maximum length of Title tag:** Primary results — Not applicable, Secondary results — Subject to Open Directory editorial guidelines.

19. **Maximum length of keyword META tag:** Not applicable to primary or secondary results.

20. **Maximum length of description META tag:** Primary results — Not applicable, Secondary results — Subject to Open Directory editorial guidelines.

21. **Comment tags considered for relevancy:** Primary results — No, Secondary results — No.

22. **Frame support:** Primary results — Yes, Secondary results — Not applicable.

23. **Image map support:** Primary results — No, Secondary results — Not applicable.

24. **Accepts automated submissions:** Primary results — Yes, Secondary results — No.

25. **Indexes submitted pages only or conducts deep crawls:** Primary results — Google will conduct deep crawls, therefore, it is not necessary to submit individual pages as long as you have submitted your main page. Secondary results — Not applicable.

26. **Instant spidering of submitted page:** Primary results — No, Secondary results — Not applicable.

27. **Number of pages that can be submitted per day:** Primary results — 10 per day recommended limit. Secondary results — Unlimited, however, acceptance is subject to editorial discretion.

28. **Word stemming and plural sensitive:** Primary results — No, Secondary results — Yes.

29. **Case-sensitive searches:** Primary results — No, Secondary results — No.

30. **Alphabetical page listings:** Primary results — No, Secondary results — Yes, if the user chooses to browse through the categories instead of searching.

31. **Time to index page:** Primary results — Takes one to four weeks, Secondary results — Takes four to six weeks.

32. **Spam penalties:** Primary results — No, Secondary results — Banishment.

33. **Refuses pages with META refresh:** Primary results — No, Secondary results — Not applicable.

34. **Refuses pages with invisible text:** Primary results — No, Secondary results — Not applicable.

35.   **Refuses pages with "tiny text":** Primary results — No. Secondary results — Not applicable.
36.   **Remove URL:** Primary results — Google will remove links for you. Secondary results — No.

This information may be out of date by the time of publication. Because search engines frequently change their ranking algorithms and other page scoring variables, we have posted updates and revisions to these chapters on our Web site: http://www.iprospect.com/search-engine-chapters.htm.

Understanding the Results

Google has a very clean interface. The search engine wants to remain a pure search engine, unlike many others that have chosen to include a lot of miscellaneous information on their Web sites such as news and weather. The advertisements on Google's site are kept to a minimum and the information is displayed in an easy-to-read fashion. This, again, keeps the loading time of the page to a minimum.

Google displays 10 results per page by default. The total number of pages found relevant to your search topic is listed at the top of the page under the search box, as is the amount of time it took for the search to occur. Google does not allow more than two pages per site to appear in the results. If more than one page per site does appear in the results, the secondary pages will be indented, underneath the primary site. The search engine contains an option of clicking "I'm feeling lucky." This option simply selects the Web site that has captured the top-ranking position for that search. This option is intended as a way to quickly find what you want. Imagine how great it would be to have that button point to your site!

Once the search engine has displayed the search results, you can either select the cached version or the regular version of the Web site. The cached version of the Web site is simply a copy of the Web site that Google saved onto its server when it indexed the page. The cached version of the Web site will load very quickly. The drawback of viewing the cached version is that it may not be the current version of the Web site if it was indexed a while ago. However, if the server that the Web page is running on temporarily fails, users can always visit the cached version of the Web site. If you do not want your Web site to be available through Google's cache you can disable this feature. (Please read the "Special Tips and Tactics for this Engine" section for more information.) Google also allows you to find pages similar to one of the pages that was listed under the search results. This function merely provides a list of pages that contain a link to the primary Web site as well as pages that Google found relevant to the topic. You can also access this option by typing "related:www.url.com" (without the quotes) into the search field.

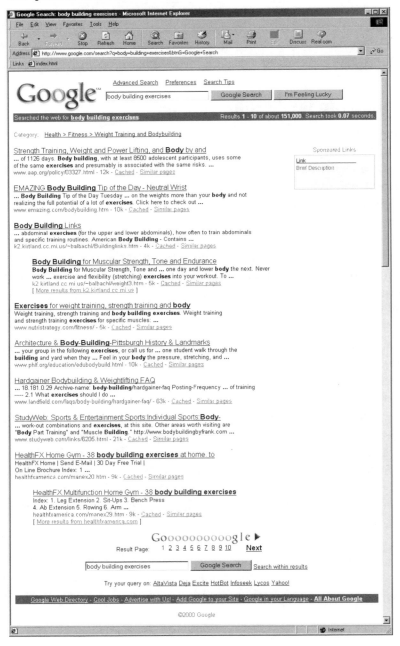

Site Elements That Can Cause Problems

The most important factor that would cause a problem in Google would be to have no other sites within the Google index that link to your site. Link popularity is very important in Google's ranking system, and to not have any relevant links would return a very poor ranking for your Web site.

Redirects are not a problem here. Instead of penalizing sites that have redirects, Google follows the links and indexes the pages it finds. Given that Google automatically spiders all parts of your site, a broken link will restrict the spider from doing so. As a result, it is important to make sure you have no broken links. Since Google performs deep crawls, image maps would pose a problem here. Search engine spiders do not have the luxury of clicking a link from your image map; they cannot index any pages that are linked to your site by an image map. If you do have an image map, you may want to consider including text-based hyperlinks to those pages as well. If you like, you can include them on the bottom of your page. This will provide the spider a pathway for finding those pages.

On many search engines, frames could present a problem when your Web site is indexed. With Google, frames do not present any problems, and therefore you do not need to use the <NOFRAMES> tag with this search engine.

Recommended Site Optimization Tactics

Google is very concerned with the number of Web sites that are linked to your site. The search engine considers a link from one page to another as a vote for that Web site. Google's ranking are determined not only by the actual number of links, but also by the quality of the Web site that has placed the link. The concept behind this is that important Web sites will not link to another Web site unless they find that site worthy of a link. The importance of a Web site is calculated by the link popularity of that Web site. A link from a personal Web site would not be as important as a link from a well-known and popular Web site. One way in which Google calculates the relevancy of the links is by making use of the text within the hyperlinks. If the text within the hyperlink is appropriate when compared to the page it is pointing to, then the link is considered relevant. If the hyperlink text is unrelated to the site at which it is directed, this is considered an irrelevant link that is poor in quality.

A concept that is important to Google's ranking algorithm is using a central theme throughout the site. When determining a theme, a search engine looks to see if text included in the title, META tags, and links is consistent throughout the site. You should include information relevant to your Web site and include common topics all the way through the site. Do not include keywords or other information irrelevant to the rest of your site in hopes of gaining a higher search ranking.

Off-the-Page Factors That Influence Success

Google places great importance on link popularity. Google considers what other sites think of your site (by way of link) and what other sites believe your site to be relevant to, as important. They place importance on this perspective rather than what you believe your site to be about and relevant to.

How to Submit a Site to This Engine

To submit a Web site to Google, go to http://www.google.com and click on the "All About Google" link, then follow the "Submit Your Site" link. It is not necessary to submit each page individually, as Google automatically spiders each individual page from the main site. The maximum number of pages you are allowed to submit per day is unlimited, but 10 pages per day is recommended. The time it takes to get listed is dependent on when the pages are submitted as well as the queue order, but the average time is around one to four weeks. Google also indexes from the Open Directory Project. If you are listed well with Open Directory, you will have a good chance of being listed well with Google. On the other hand, if you are not listed in Open Directory and you want to rank well with Google, it is highly recommended that you submit your site to Open Directory.

When submitting a Web site, you are allowed to send comments, which Google states are used only for their information and do not affect how your Web site is indexed or used by Google.

How to Build Informational Pages for this Engine

Google picks up your page description from the text within the page, and that way search results are based upon the actual content of the page.

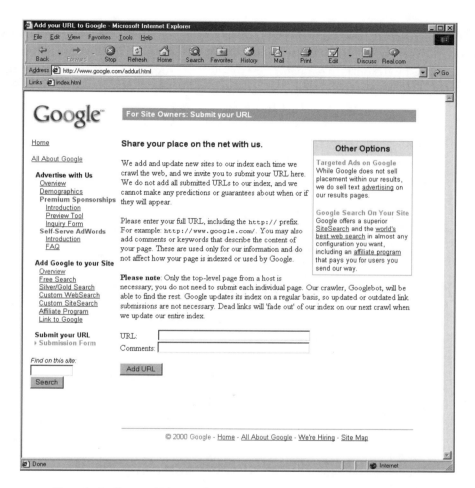

Google believes it is the information contained on a page that the user is looking for rather than lavish words that the Web designer placed in a description tag in hopes of matching search terms. Google produces relevant results that match the search terms by examining the words on a site, where the words sit on the page, and how important the text is by comparing font sizes. The text contained in bold tags, heading tags, or large font sizes are used as important keywords in the calculation.

Google disregards the description META tag and the keyword tag, but thinks the Title tag is important. The text within the Title tag is a representation of what is inside the site. The Title tag is best when it includes 75 characters of keywords. If there is no Title tag on a Web site, Google will only display the page URL. If you find that your site is listed only with a URL and no

Title tag, this could be a result of the search engine finding and indexing your Web site on its own, without you physically submitting your site.

To optimize a page for Google, it is highly recommended to include keywords within headings and use bold type and large font sizes. For best results, make sure that these keywords are located within close proximity, as Google calculates the distance between keywords. The keywords near the bottom of the page are just as important as the keywords at the top of the page. Google also favors keywords located in, and close to, hyperlinks. Google performs part of its ranking calculations upon the keywords that are contained in the URL. Once again, it must be noted that Google relies heavily on link popularity in determining ranking. Despite your best efforts to create a highly optimized informational page, if this page has no link popularity, there is a good chance it will not achieve a high position.

How to Know If Your Site Has Been Spidered/Listed

Knowing when a spider is visiting your site and which pages it is visiting can be valuable. A list of Google's spiders, as well as their IP addresses, are listed below:

209.185.253.175	crawler.googlebot.com
209.185.108.147	a10.google.com
209.185.108.155	a18.google.com
209.185.108.140	a3.google.com
209.185.108.141	a4.google.com
209.185.108.143	a6.google.com
209.185.108.145	a8.google.com
209.185.108.148	a11.google.com
209.185.108.150	a13.google.com
209.185.108.152	a15.google.com
209.185.108.154	a17.google.com
209.185.108.157	c3.google.com
209.185.108.159	a19.google.com
209.185.108.161	c4.google.com
209.185.108.164	a23.google.com
209.185.108.165	a24.google.com
207.88.29.130	dsl.google.com
209.185.108.139	a2.google.com
209.185.108.162	a21.google.com
209.185.108.136	switch.google.com
209.185.108.138	a1.google.com
209.185.108.142	a5.google.com
209.185.108.144	a7.google.com
209.185.108.146	a9.google.com

209.185.108.149	a12.google.com
209.185.108.151	a14.google.com
209.185.108.153	a16.google.com
209.185.108.156	c2.google.com
209.185.108.158	c1.google.com
209.185.108.160	crawler.googlebot.com
209.185.108.134	ns.google.com
209.185.108.163	a22.google.com
209.185.108.135	ns2.google.com
64.208.33.33	crawl1.googlebot.com
64.209.181.52	crawler1.googlebot.com
64.209.181.53	crawler2.googlebot.com

Indexing Timetable

Googlebot normally crawls at least once per month. If you use the robots.txt file to stop Googlebot from crawling parts of your page, it is important to know that Google only downloads the robots.txt file once a day in order to save bandwidth. As a result, it may take Google a while to learn of any changes made to this file, and to implement any changes into the displayed results.

Google does not index each submitted page. If your Web site has not been indexed it is probably due to insufficient relevant Web sites linking to your site.

What to Do If Your Rankings Disappear

The Google spider is very active and over one million new Web pages are being submitted per day. It is not uncommon for you to drop down in the rankings or disappear entirely with this competition. You should always check the number of links that are directed to your competitors' sites and compare that to the amount of votes to your site. You can find the number of sites linked to your site by typing "link:yoururl.com" into the search box, without the quotes. If you want to increase your positioning, you may need to have more links of importance pointing to your site, since the number one search criteria that Google uses is link popularity.

If your Web sites have lost substantial ground in their positions, you should make sure that your content reflects the search terms that you would like to display your site. Confirm that your site contains all of the search terms within close proximity of each other and that they are right through the whole document, particularly in all of the headings and links.

Google is not overly concerned with spam, as they believe their algorithm can filter any spam out of search results. Rumor has it that if your site does get banned (regardless of why), it is up to the individual Google engineer who banned the site to consider your appeal to lift the ban.

Special Tips and Tactics for This Engine

As mentioned earlier, this search engine stores copies of your Web site on its own server. The Web page on this server can be outdated and you may not want your audience to visit an older version of your Web site. To stop Google from displaying the cached version of your Web site you can insert the <NOARCHIVE> META tag. This change will take effect the next time the Google spider crawls the page that contains the META tag. If you want immediate removal of the cached version of your Web site you must contact Google. The <NOARCHIVE> tag must be inserted into the head of your HTML document. The syntax for the tag is: <META NAME="ROBOTS" CONTENT= "NOARCHIVE">. If you want to allow search engines other than Google to cache your Web site, then insert this tag in the head of your document:

<META NAME="GOOGLEBOT" CONTENT="NOARCHIVE">.

Google recently purchased Deja.com and spiders and indexes the contents of this vast newsgroup. Being mentioned in a newsgroup posting that includes your URL is a great way to improve your link popularity score for Google.

Responsiveness and Help Provided

Google provides a very informative FAQ that includes information on anything from how to perform better searches to how to prevent Google from indexing a page. You can access the FAQ by going to http://www.google.com/help/faq.html. If your questions are not answered in this section, you can always contact Google by e-mail. Google provides a list of e-mail addresses for different divisions. You can find the e-mail addresses at http://www.google.com/contact/index.html.

Chapter 20:

HotBot

HotBot
Lycos SF, Inc.
660 3rd Street, 4th Floor
San Francisco, CA 94107
(415) 276-8400
Fax: (415) 276-8499

Free updates to this book are available via e-mail newsletter
by visiting: http://www.iprospect.com/book-news.htm.

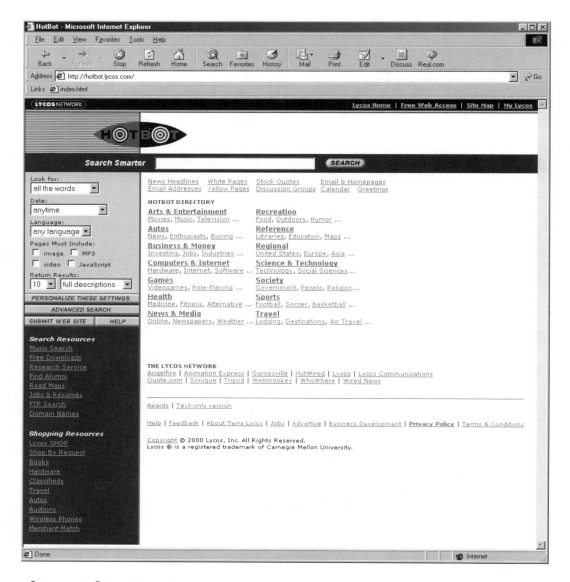

Facts about This Engine

In 1996, Wired Digital launched HotBot.com, considered to be one of the "major" Web portals currently operating. HotBot has won awards from top computer and personal finance publications and has enjoyed significant traffic growth in the past couple of years. In 1998, Lycos acquired Wired Digital, which includes HotBot, and in early 2000, the engine became a hybrid, incorporating Open Directory results. HotBot.com is a division of the Terra Lycos Network.

Currently, HotBot incorporates directory listings from the Open Directory project and Web search results from Inktomi as well as Direct Hit and paid listings from GoTo.com.

1. **Web address:** http://hotbot.lycos.com/

2. **Type of engine:** Hybrid. Primary results — Direct Hit popularity database, Secondary results — Open Directory, Tertiary results — Inktomi database.

3. **Partnerships:** Terra Lycos, Inktomi, Open Directory, Direct Hit, and GoTo.com

4. **Total documents indexed:** 500 million

5. **Total page views per month:** 88,730,000 (Source: Alexa Research, Feb. 2001)

6. **E-mail support:** support@lycos-inc.com

7. **How to confirm listing:** Select "Submit Web Site" on the left navigation bar about halfway down the page. On this page, select the link "See if your site is already indexed." Enter your domain in the form field and click on "Find a Web Site." All of the pages within your domain that are in the HotBot index will be listed.

8. **Obtain link popularity information:** linkdomain:yourdomain.com

9. **Result returns:** The top listings are from Direct Hit and directory listings are from Open Directory. Inktomi results are displayed if nothing else is found.

10. **Receive higher rankings for link popularity:** Primary results — No. Secondary results — No, Tertiary results — Unknown.

11. **Additional off-the-page considerations:** Primary results — Yes. Direct Hit is a popularity engine that measures the number of times a site is visited. Secondary results — Open Directory is a human-compiled directory and sites are subject to editorial review. Tertiary results from Inktomi are not subject to additional off-the-page factors.

12. **Rankings influenced by after-the-click behavior:** Primary results — Yes, through the Direct Hit popularity engine, Secondary results — Not applicable, Tertiary results — Not applicable.

13. **Recognition and utilization of META tags:** Primary results — Yes, Secondary results — No, Tertiary results — Yes.

14. **Consideration of META tags for relevancy:** Primary results — Unknown, Secondary results — No, Tertiary results — Yes.

15. **Importance of Title tag keyword prominence:** Primary results — Unknown, Secondary results — Yes, Tertiary results — Yes.

16. **Importance of <ALT> tag:** Primary results — No, Secondary results — Not applicable, Tertiary results — Unknown.

17. **Importance of multiple occurrences of keywords in Title tag:** Primary results — No, Secondary results — Yes, Tertiary results — Yes.

18. **Maximum length of Title tag:** Primary results — Not applicable, Secondary results — 80 characters for keywords, Tertiary results — Unknown.

19. **Maximum length of keyword META tag:** Primary results — Not applicable, Secondary results — 75 characters, Tertiary results — Unknown.

20. **Maximum length of description META tag:** Primary results — Not applicable, Secondary results — 150 characters, Tertiary results — Unknown.

21. **Comment tags considered for relevancy:** Primary results — Yes, Secondary results — Yes, Tertiary results — No.

22. **Frame support:** Primary results — Not applicable, Secondary results — Not applicable, Tertiary results — Yes.

23. **Image map support:** Primary results — No, Secondary results — Not applicable, Tertiary results — Unconfirmed.

24. **Accepts automated submissions:** Primary results — Not applicable, Secondary results — No, Tertiary results — Yes.

25. **Indexes submitted pages only or conducts deep crawls:** Primary results — Not applicable, Secondary results — Not applicable, Tertiary results — Crawls, but it is recommended to submit all pages.

26. **Instant spidering of submitted page:** Primary results — Not applicable, Secondary results — Not applicable, Tertiary results — Yes.

27. **Number of pages that can be submitted per day:** Primary results — Not applicable, Secondary results — Unlimited, however, acceptance is subject to editorial discretion, Tertiary results — 50 per day through "free inclusion," unlimited (up to 1,000 per domain) through pay-for-inclusion method.

28. **Word stemming and plural sensitive:** Primary results — No, Secondary results — Yes. This is an optional feature that is found in HotBot's Advanced Search page. Tertiary results — No.

29. **Case-sensitive searches:** Primary results — No, Secondary results — Yes, Tertiary results — No.

30. **Alphabetical page listings:** Primary results — No, Secondary results — No, Tertiary results — No.

31. **Time to index page:** Primary results — Not applicable, Secondary results — 4-6 weeks, Tertiary results — Approximately three weeks to 60 days for free submissions and 48 hours for paid submissions.

32. **Spam penalties:** Primary results — No, Secondary results — Significantly downgrades a page's ranking, Tertiary results — No.

33. **Refuses pages with META refresh:** Primary results — Not applicable, Secondary results — Yes, Tertiary results — No.

34. **Refuses pages with invisible text:** Primary results — Not applicable, Secondary results — Yes, Tertiary results — No.

35. **Refuses pages with "tiny text":** Primary results — Not applicable, Secondary results — Yes, Tertiary results — No.

36. **Remove URL:** Primary results — Not applicable, Secondary results — Insert a robots.txt file and submit the URL via the "Submit Web Site" link on the home page. HotBot does not automatically remove URLs. HotBot refreshes its database every 60 days, so when it detects a dormant URL or robots.txt file, it will then remove the page from the database. Tertiary results — Inktomi automatically re-spiders all indexed pages and will automatically remove URLs that no longer exist.

This information may be out of date by the time of publication. Because search engines frequently change their ranking algorithms and other page scoring variables, we have posted updates and revisions to these chapters on our Web site: http://www.iprospect.com/search-engine-chapters.htm.

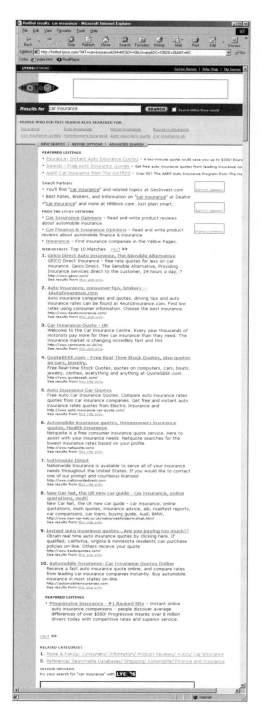

Understanding the Results

HotBot provides many unique features to its users including "People Who Did This Search Also Searched For." This section appears at the top of the page, directly beneath your search term, and "Related Searches" provides a list of more specific or general search terms determined by your query. When you select one of the keyword/phrases, a new Top 10 results page will appear.

Within the search results, the first three listings, called "Featured Listings," are paid GoTo listings.

The "Search Partners" section provides additional Web site resources to fulfill your query. DoubleClick powers this section. Wired News, Webmonkey, and CareerBuilder.com are examples of some of HotBot's search partners.

"Related Categories" for the most common searches appear next on the results page. On certain queries the categories are shown at the bottom of the page below the top 10 results. The HotBot Directory gets its information from the Open Directory and is maintained by Open Directory editors.

"Web Results Top 10 Matches" appear next and are often powered by Direct Hit. Direct Hit determines its results by popularity, so a new site ranking in the top 10 would be highly unlikely. For a new site to be in the top 10 it must first be in Inktomi's results and have sufficient user popularity. Direct Hit calculates how popular the site is by how many times it has been clicked on and how long the searcher remains on the site. In certain instances, where a query does not result in a top 10 match by Direct Hit, Inktomi will serve these results.

Direct Hit continuously tracks click-through information by recording keywords and Web sites. For example, a person searching for the *New York Times* would bring an embedded link that would look like this:

```
http://hotbot.lycos.com/dirctor.asp?target=http://www.nyt.com/
&id=1&userid=5QxgNKzgodQJ&query=MT=nyt.com&rsource=INK
```

target=	Tells the engine which site you selected.
id=	Where on the page you found this site.
userid=	This is the searcher's ID used when he revisits the engine.
query=	What words the searcher typed in to get these results.

When you click on this link, Direct Hit knows that a searcher chose this site; it knows where the site was ranked on the results page and what search term brought them to it. Direct Hit then takes this information and uses an estimated percentage of clicks to determine the ranking of this particular site. If the site exceeds the estimated percentage, its ranking would climb. If it does not meet this percentage, its rankings may fall. You may have a number one ranking, but if the percentage of clicks drops to less than a typical number one ranking, your site may drop to a number two ranking or even slip out of the top 10. Similarly, you might think a site that ranks in the number 35 position would be viewed less; however, if searchers do not find what they are looking for in the top 10 results they may delve deeper to find a site that answers their query. The more clicks a site receives the greater the chance of it moving to a top 10 position.

The next pages of results, "Web Results ##### matches," are served by Inktomi's database. The number signs represent the number of pages that have been found by Inktomi to match the search query. For more information, please refer to Chapter 21.

The "Search within these results" feature is found on the HotBot result page to the right of the search box. This feature is designed to help the searcher break down the results to target their particular query. For example, if you query "boats" you will get a wide array of Web site results all relating to the word "boats." However, clicking on "Search within these results" and typing in "stingray" will ask HotBot to sort through the results of "boats" and display only Web sites from within this list that match the query "stingray."

If you are not satisfied with the results from your first query you can click on "New Search," which will bring you back to HotBot's home page where you can start your search over again.

The Revise Options feature enables you to alter your original query. Clicking on "Revise Options" will return you to the HotBot home page. On the left of the page you will see a small box that contains options for changing the format of your results. You can customize the result page to display 25, 50, or even 100 matches per page. You can also click on "Personalize These Settings" to find more options to adjust the results page.

Advanced Search is similar to the "Revise Search" option and includes enhanced settings to narrow your search and return the most relevant results for the query entered.

Site Elements That Can Cause Problems

NOTE: HotBot is powered by the Inktomi database. Therefore, when we refer to "HotBot's spider" you can infer that we are talking about Inktomi's spider since, technically, HotBot does not operate its own spider.

A possibly problematic element of a Web site is its link popularity. HotBot takes into consideration the number of links from other Web sites that point to the domain you are submitting. It performs this as a spam check to check the validity of the site you are submitting. A legitimate site would have other sites linking to it; less credible sites are usually standalone and direct users outwards.

Recommended Site Optimization Tactics

To optimize your site for HotBot, base your site optimization on keyword weight and placement. HotBot ranks pages higher for having keyword phrases in the Title tag over text in the body. HotBot also ranks pages that have keywords in META tags higher than those that have keywords in the body, but they do not rank as high as having keywords in the Title tag.

Off-the-Page Factors That Influence Success

Link popularity is an off-the-page consideration. With more and more Web sites emerging on the Web and being submitted, search engines need to find alternative criteria with which to measure a site's worth. A mature site that has great content will tend to have many other sites pointing to it. This is known as link popularity. Having high link popularity adds to the credibility of a site. A brand new site that has been launched with a new URL may experience difficulty in acquiring real estate in the search engines because of low link popularity. As time progresses and other sites begin to link to the Web site, these new sites will begin to see more pages within the HotBot index.

How to Submit a Site to This Engine

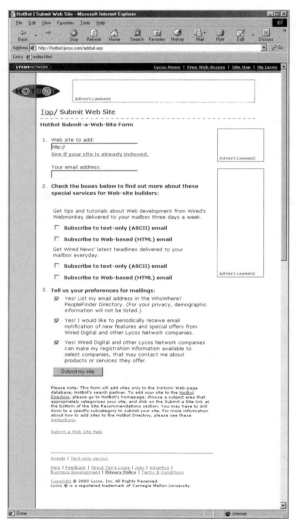

To submit to this engine, first click on the Submit Web Site button located on HotBot's home page to the left of the HotBot directory. This link will take you to the HotBot Submit-a-Web-Site Form. Also located on this page is the "See if your site is already indexed" link, and at the bottom of the page is information on how to submit to the HotBot Directory.

This submitting form will first ask you for the URL of the Web site that you would like to submit. You do not need to add "http://," as this is already provided for you. You are required to provide your e-mail address.

HotBot gives you the option of receiving e-mail newsletters from Wired News and other affiliates of HotBot. You also have the option to list your e-mail address in the WhoWhere? PeopleFinder Directory. The final step to submitting your site to HotBot is to click on the Submit My Site button. A page will display showing the URL you submitted, the e-mail address used, and a message saying that your site will be added into HotBot's index (Inktomi database) within the next 60 days. Below this statement are the FAQs from HotBot's help section. At the bottom of this page you will find the option to submit another site to HotBot's index.

NOTE: Inktomi, the search partner of HotBot, actually penalizes Web sites that submit through the HotBot Add URL interface — but only slightly. And, that penalty will be removed if the Inktomi spider finds your Web site at a later date by following a link from another Web site. The safest way to submit to HotBot (or any Inktomi-powered Web site such as iWon.com or MSN) is to use the paid submission program at PositionPro.com. Submissions make through this paid submission partner will not be penalized and will guarantee that your Web site is added to Inktomi's database.

How to Build Informational Pages for this Engine

HotBot is very clear about what it looks for on a Web site when considering where to index the page. Some of the most basic factors affecting query result ranking when building informational pages include:

■ Word frequency in document: The more often a query word occurs in the document, the higher the rank. The obscurity of the word also has an impact. Common words like "the" contribute less to the rank than rare and discriminating words such as "tiki."

■ Search words in Title tag: Pages that use your search terms in the Title tag will be ranked significantly higher than documents that contain the search term in the text only.

■ Search words in keyword META tag: Pages that use your search terms in the keyword META tag will be weighted more highly than terms appearing in the text, but less highly than terms appearing in the title.

■ Document length: When the search words appear frequently in a document with little text, the page will be ranked higher than when the search terms appear the same amount of times in a longer document.

In short, when constructing a page to target HotBot, keep the document length short and provide information about the search term you are attempting to rank on. There must be a common theme throughout the page, from the title to the META tags to the visible text.

How to Know If Your Site Has Been Spidered/Listed

To know if your site has been listed by HotBot, look through the referrer information of your server log files and trace to find if any of the Inktomi spiders have been to your site:

Spider IP	Spider DNS Name	Spider IP	Spider DNS Name
216.35.116.92	si3002.inktomi.com	216.35.103.81	si4002.inktomi.com
216.35.103.69	j108.inktomi.com	216.35.103.80	si4001.inktomi.com
209.185.141.226	y400.inktomi.com	216.35.116.108	wm3023.inktomi.com
216.35.103.54	j4014.inktomisearch.com	216.35.116.109	wm3024.inktomi.com
209.185.141.185	j6000.inktomi.com	216.35.103.61	j100.inktomi.com
216.32.237.18	j4008.inktomisearch.com	216.35.103.45	j4005.inktomisearch.com
216.32.237.23	j4013.inktomisearch.com	216.35.103.79	si4000.inktomi.com
209.185.122.111	b204.inktomi.com	216.35.103.60	j4020.inktomisearch.com
209.185.143.85	j5005.inktomisearch.com	216.35.103.59	j4019.inktomisearch.com
209.185.143.98	q2002.inktomisearch.com	216.35.103.58	j4018.inktomisearch.com
209.185.143.97	q2001.inktomisearch.com	216.35.103.53	j4013.inktomisearch.com
216.32.237.29	j4019.inktomisearch.com	216.35.103.52	j4012.inktomisearch.com
216.32.237.7	j5006.inktomisearch.com	216.35.103.51	j4011.inktomisearch.com
216.32.237.11	j4001.inktomisearch.com	216.35.103.57	j4017.inktomisearch.com
216.32.237.12	j4002.inktomisearch.com	216.35.103.56	j4016.inktomisearch.com
216.32.237.13	j4003.inktomisearch.com	216.35.103.50	j4010.inktomisearch.com
216.32.237.14	j4004.inktomisearch.com	216.35.103.55	j4015.inktomisearch.com
216.32.237.16	j4006.inktomisearch.com	216.35.103.49	j4009.inktomisearch.com
216.32.237.17	j4007.inktomisearch.com	216.35.103.48	j4008.inktomisearch.com
216.32.237.19	j4009.inktomisearch.com	216.35.103.47	j4007.inktomisearch.com
216.32.237.20	j4010.inktomisearch.com	216.35.103.46	j4006.inktomisearch.com
216.32.237.21	j4011.inktomisearch.com	216.35.103.44	j4004.inktomisearch.com
216.32.237.22	j4012.inktomisearch.com	216.35.103.43	j4003.inktomisearch.com
216.32.237.24	j4014.inktomisearch.com	216.35.103.41	j4001.inktomisearch.com
216.32.237.25	j4015.inktomisearch.com	216.35.103.40	j4000.inktomisearch.com
216.32.237.27	j4017.inktomisearch.com	216.35.103.63	j102.inktomi.com
216.32.237.28	j4018.inktomisearch.com	216.35.103.64	j103.inktomi.com
209.1.12.68	i2001.inktomi.com	216.35.103.65	j104.inktomi.com
209.185.141.209	y700.inktomi.com	216.35.103.66	j105.inktomi.com
209.185.141.211	y702.inktomi.com	216.35.103.67	j106.inktomi.com
209.185.141.236	j100.inktomi.com	216.35.103.68	j107.inktomi.com
209.185.143.43	y1501.inktomi.com	216.35.103.70	j109.inktomi.com
209.185.143.58		216.35.103.71	j110.inktomi.com
209.185.143.80	j5000.inktomisearch.com	216.35.103.72	j111.inktomi.com
209.185.143.84	j5004.inktomisearch.com	216.35.103.74	j4021.inktomisearch.com
209.185.143.87	j5007.inktomisearch.com	216.35.103.75	j4022.inktomisearch.com
209.185.143.89	j5009.inktomisearch.com	216.35.103.76	j4023.inktomisearch.com
209.185.143.96	q2000.inktomisearch.com	216.35.103.77	j4024.inktomisearch.com
209.185.143.81	j5001.inktomisearch.com	216.35.103.78	j4025.inktomisearch.com
216.35.116.93	si3003.inktomi.com	216.35.116.42	j3002.inktomi.com

Spider IP	Spider DNS Name	Spider IP	Spider DNS Name
216.35.103.42	j4002.inktomisearch.com	216.35.116.91	si3001.inktomi.com
209.185.143.40	x1500.inktomi.com	202.212.5.30	goo212.goo.ne.jp
209.185.143.41	x1501.inktomi.com	216.35.116.90	si3000.inktomi.com
209.185.143.42	y1500.inktomi.com	216.35.116.41	j3001.inktomi.com
209.185.143.44	x1600.inktomi.com	216.35.116.78	lz3018.inktomi.com
209.185.143.45	x1601.inktomi.com	209.67.206.133	si520.inktomi.com
209.185.143.46	y1600.inktomi.com	209.131.48.100	brimstone-u2.inktomi.com
209.185.143.47	boobook.idp.inktomi.com	216.35.118.231	b301.inktomi.com
209.185.143.48	boobook.idp.inktomi.com	216.35.116.44	j3004.inktomi.com
209.185.143.49	kestrel.idp.inktomi.com	216.35.116.106	wm3021.inktomi.com
209.185.143.50	kestrel.idp.inktomi.com	216.35.116.105	wm3020.inktomi.com
209.185.143.51	vulture.idp.inktomi.com	216.35.116.43	j3003.inktomi.com
209.185.143.52	vulture.idp.inktomi.com	216.35.116.45	j3005.inktomi.com
209.185.143.53	vulture.idp.inktomi.com	216.35.116.48	j3008.inktomi.com
209.185.143.54		216.35.116.49	j3009.inktomi.com
209.185.143.55		216.35.116.50	j3010.inktomi.com
209.185.143.56		216.35.116.52	j3012.inktomi.com
209.185.143.57		216.35.116.53	j3013.inktomi.com
209.185.143.59	sc3-dhcp-1.inktomi.com	216.35.116.54	j3014.inktomi.com
209.185.143.60	sc3-dhcp-2.inktomi.com	216.35.116.55	j3015.inktomi.com
209.185.143.82	j5002.inktomisearch.com	216.35.116.56	j3016.inktomi.com
209.185.143.83	j5003.inktomisearch.com	216.35.116.57	j3017.inktomi.com
209.185.143.86	j5006.inktomisearch.com	216.35.116.58	j3018.inktomi.com
209.185.143.88	j5008.inktomisearch.com	216.35.116.59	j3019.inktomi.com
209.185.143.90	j5010.inktomisearch.com	216.35.116.82	wm3002.inktomi.com
209.185.143.91	j5011.inktomisearch.com	216.35.116.83	wm3003.inktomi.com
209.185.143.92	j5012.inktomisearch.com	216.35.116.88	wm3008.inktomi.com
209.185.143.93	j5013.inktomisearch.com	216.35.116.99	q5100.inktomi.com
216.35.103.62	j101.inktomi.com	216.35.116.47	j3007.inktomi.com
216.35.103.73	j5006.inktomi.com		

Indexing Timetable

HotBot uses Inktomi's spiders and index. Refer to the Inktomi chapter for the indexing timetable.

Submitting to HotBot via Inktomi's paid submission partner Position Technologies will ensure your site is added to Inktomi's database in 48 hours.

What to Do If Your Rankings Disappear

In search engine forums it is suggested that you resubmit your site every two weeks because it is believed this is when HotBot does a small "spring cleaning" of their index. There are mixed feelings about doing this; some have seen excellent results while others have seen little if any changes in their rankings. For more information, see Chapter 21.

Special Tips and Tactics for This Engine

HotBot is beginning to try and filter out those people who are trying to fill their databases with irrelevant content. Considering that HotBot derives its main results from the Inktomi database, how you get into the Inktomi database adds credibility to your submission. Rumors are that if you submit via HotBot's submission page, the submission is put through more rigorous filters to detect spammers. The rumors go so far as to say that any page submitted via HotBot has less credibility and therefore ranks lower than if it were submitted to Inktomi from other avenues.

Responsiveness and Help Provided

Located on each page of HotBot is a link to the HotBot Help page. HotBot Help provides a Frequently Asked Questions section specifically for Webmasters, along with FAQ sections for Getting Started, Basic Search, Advanced Search, Results Page, and Directory. The Submit a Web Site & Webmaster's FAQ provides information on indexing, such as how long it takes for HotBot to index a site and how to check that your site has been indexed. This section also briefly discusses how HotBot ranks Web pages with links to tutorials on how to structure META tags. This is provided by one of HotBot's affiliates, Webmonkey. There is a link to HotBot's customer support on the bottom of each FAQ page and also on HotBot's home page located beneath the HotBot directory titled Feedback. From the customer support section, you can choose a specific topic from a pull-down menu on which to get support. HotBot sends back an automatic e-mail response to your query, which gives you general information on the topic. If the information provided is not sufficient, you may reply to the e-mail with further questions and this will be routed to a live customer support agent at HotBot. The automatic response came back within 15 minutes, while the response from Customer Support took anywhere from 30 minutes to 24 hours.

Chapter 21:

Inktomi

Inktomi Corporation
4100 East 3rd Avenue
Foster City, CA 94404
info@inktomi.com
(650) 653-2800
Fax: (650) 653-2801

Free updates to this book are available via e-mail newsletter
by visiting: http://www.iprospect.com/book-news.htm.

Inktomi and the Inktomi logo are trademarks of Inktomi Corporation.

Facts about This Engine

Founded in February 1996, Inktomi is unusual in that its primary function is not as a search engine. Inktomi is best known for its capabilities as a "back-end" database provider. Inktomi is an unbranded search engine that is "private labeled" by search engine sites wishing to outsource their technology. Each site that licenses the Inktomi database will utilize different options to vary how search results are served from the database. Inktomi powers several major search engines, including AOL, iWon, MSN, HotBot, LookSmart, and NBCi.

Inktomi is a powerful force in global search technology, as its patented technology has been utilized to power some of the world's largest Internet search engines. Inktomi's search utilities also have the ability to customize searches either regionally or globally, to conduct retrieval searches for large text archives, and to lend online search support for publisher archives. Inktomi's search application is optimized to handle the combination of massive data and large user bases, and appeals to clients because it eliminates the need for expensive "supercomputers."

Inktomi also offers diversified search engine services, including a directory engine and a shopping engine. Inktomi Directory Engine 1.0 is the Web's first scalable, automated solution for the creation and maintenance of Web directories. The Directory Engine automatically categorizes Web content from across the Internet, making it readily available to end users through user-friendly, private-label directories that plug easily into individual Web sites. Inktomi's Shopping Engine software enables users to compare merchandise on a variety of factors and standards. Inktomi plans to integrate its scalable technology and search engine with the Shopping Engine software to provide Web sites with a "sophisticated private-label shopping product, thereby combining the industry's most comprehensive and scalable search capabilities with an advanced shopping application."

Inktomi received some negative press in June 2000, when Yahoo! announced that it would be switching from Inktomi to the newer, yet fast-rising Google engine for its site match results. Nevertheless, Inktomi continues to reign as one of the most powerful suppliers of information to the major search engines.

1. **Web address:** http://www.inktomi.com

2. **Type of engine:** Inktomi is a back-end database, providing spider-based search results to major search engines.

3. **Partnerships:** Inktomi powers parts of the following search sites: HotBot, NBCi, MSN, GoTo, LookSmart, Anzwers (Australia), Goo (Japan), Canada.com, and Radar UOL (Brazil). It maintains additional business alliances with Ameritech, Excite@Home, BellSouth, British Telecom, Cisco, DIGEX, Digital Island, Compaq, Geocities, Intel Corp., Microsoft Corp., Nippon Telegraph and Telephone (NTT), Real Networks, Silicon Graphics, Sun Microsystems, Inc., Telenor, Nextel, Wired Ventures, Inc., and more.

4. **Total documents indexed:** Approximately 500 million

5. **Total page views per month:** Not applicable. Inktomi does not act as a search engine; rather, it powers other search engines.

6. **E-mail support:** http://inktomi.emarkethost.net/mk/get/info_contact

7. **How to confirm listing:** See specific engines to confirm listings in each. For example, to check an Inktomi-powered listing in HotBot, go to http://hotbot.lycos.com/help/checkurl.asp.

8. **Obtain link popularity information:** This varies according to the rules of the specific Inktomi-fed engine in question.

9. **Result returns:** The result returns will vary depending on the partner being used.

10. **Receive higher rankings for link popularity:** Yes

11. **Additional off-the-page considerations:** Inktomi places more weight on documents it finds on its own and via its paid submission service, found at PositionPro.com.

12. **Rankings influenced by after-the-click behavior:** Not applicable, but some partner engines do have additional relationships that measure and process after-the-click behavior.

13. **Recognition and utilization of META tags:** Yes

14. **Consideration of META tags for relevancy:** Yes

15. **Importance of Title tag keyword prominence:** Yes

16. **Importance of <ALT> tag:** No

17. **Importance of multiple occurrences of keywords in Title tag:** Yes

18. **Maximum length of Title tag:** Varies according to partner engine.

19. **Maximum length of keyword META tag:** Varies according to partner engine.

20. **Maximum length of description META tag:** Varies according to partner engine.

21. **Comment tags considered for relevancy:** No

22. **Frame support:** Yes

23. **Image map support:** Unconfirmed

24. **Accepts automated submissions:** Yes, through Position Technologies.

25. **Indexes submitted pages only or conducts deep crawls:** Crawls, but it is recommended to submit all pages.

26. **Instant spidering of submitted page:** Yes

27. **Number of pages that can be submitted per day:** The submission limit per day is 50 pages via the "free" method. "Paid" inclusion has no daily limit, but has a cap of 1,000 pages from one domain.

28. **Word stemming and plural sensitive:** Varies according to partner engine.

29. **Case-sensitive searches:** Varies according to partner engine.

30. **Alphabetical page listings:** Varies according to partner engine.

31. **Time to index page:** Approximately three weeks to 60 days for free submissions and 48 hours for paid submissions.

32. **Spam penalties:** Varies according to partner engine.

33. **Refuses pages with META refresh:** No

34. **Refuses pages with invisible text:** No

35. **Refuses pages with "tiny text":** No

36. **Remove URL:** Inktomi re-spiders all indexed pages and will automatically remove URLs that no longer exist.

This information may be out of date by the time of publication. Because search engines frequently change their ranking algorithms and other page scoring variables, we have posted updates and revisions to these chapters on our Web site: http://www.iprospect.com/search-engine-chapters.htm.

Understanding the Results

In order to judge results from submissions processed through Inktomi, it is necessary to examine the results in specific partner engines. Although Inktomi feeds the data that the engines use to create and rank their results, the actual manner in which results are calculated and displayed is at the discretion of the individual engines.

Site Elements That Can Cause Problems

See chapters on specific Inktomi partner engines to determine which elements cause problems and how they can be avoided.

Recommended Site Optimization Tactics

Since Inktomi itself is not an "engine" in the traditional sense, it is theoretically impossible to optimize individual sites so that they will become accessible through Inktomi's database. If you wish to achieve results in MSN, for example, you should optimize your site according to the suggestions tailored to MSN (see Chapter 25 for details).

Off-the-Page Factors That Influence Success

To achieve success in visibility you must first be accepted into a search engine's index. That's where off-the-page factors come in. Although nothing is done to target Inktomi itself because it's not a search engine, Inktomi holds the key to achieving results in its partners' results. It is better to be found by Inktomi's spiders than to submit directly to Inktomi via its free submission process. Take note of the way to submit to this engine, because that is the key to the first part of success. Other factors that will determine success may vary depending on the partner that is being targeted. Refer to those chapters directly.

How to Submit a Site to This Engine

In November 2000, Inktomi introduced a new pay-for-submission service, whereby someone could submit pages of their site through one of Inktomi's partners, such as Position Technologies (www.positiontech.com), for a fee. As of this writing, the fees were the following:

Pages	Price per Page
First page	$30
Any other page from the same domain	$15

The main features you receive for this annual fee are:

- Indexing into the "IFD" database every 48 hours.

- Acceptance of dynamic content/pages (i.e., pages with query strings).

- Re-indexing of the pages every 48 hours, thus allowing people to make changes to the page and see the results quicker.

- URLs are added to the main database that is shared with all of Inktomi's search partners.

- Unlimited substitution of a URL during the subscription period. Substitute URLs must be from the same domain.

NOTE   While this service provides many great features, paying for inclusion in Inktomi does not guarantee ranking position. You still need to create solid content and optimize each submitted page to attain rankings.

 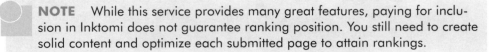

After Inktomi spiders the submitted pages, they will appear in the search partner's results within 48 hours. Note that the URLs submitted via this service will initially be indexed in the "IFD" database and not the "Long Term Database" until Inktomi has a full index, which happens every 30 days. The Long Term Database is populated through deep crawls by the Inktomi spider. This spider will crawl the web and index relevant content that is located. Thus, you may be in the Long Term Database without ever having submitted to Inktomi.

While Inktomi hasn't removed the free "Add URL" submission service, there are clear signs that pages submitted via this service are being penalized. If you submit a new page to Inktomi, this page will be ranked lower until the Inktomi spider finds it via links from other sites. Once the spider locates the page, this penalty will be removed. Inktomi's reasoning is that any page with existing links to it is more "popular" than a new page that is submitted. If your page is already indexed in the Long Term Database and you resubmit it, the page will be penalized until the spider finds it again. Pages submitted via the paid service will not receive this penalty.

How to Build Informational Pages for this Engine

Reference the corresponding partner chapters in this book to determine the right informational page building techniques for your site in order to meet your ranking goals.

How to Know If Your Site Has Been Spidered/Listed

Although it is impossible to determine how well and where you have been listed simply by examining Inktomi itself (you would need to search for your site in the various Inktomi partner engines in order to determine the success of your listing efforts), it is possible to detect the presence of Inktomi's spiders. Although Inktomi's primary spider goes by the memorable name of "Slurp," its spiders can appear in a number of forms and names. Check your log files for signs of any of the following Inktomi spiders having traveled through your site:

Spider IP	Spider DNS Name	Spider IP	Spider DNS Name
216.35.116.92	si3002.inktomi.com	216.35.103.81	si4002.inktomi.com
216.35.103.69	j108.inktomi.com	216.35.103.80	si4001.inktomi.com
209.185.141.226	y400.inktomi.com	216.35.116.108	wm3023.inktomi.com
216.35.103.54	j4014.inktomisearch.com	216.35.116.109	wm3024.inktomi.com
209.185.141.185	j6000.inktomi.com	216.35.103.61	j100.inktomi.com
216.32.237.18	j4008.inktomisearch.com	216.35.103.45	j4005.inktomisearch.com
216.32.237.23	j4013.inktomisearch.com	216.35.103.79	si4000.inktomi.com
209.185.122.111	b204.inktomi.com	216.35.103.60	j4020.inktomisearch.com
209.185.143.85	j5005.inktomisearch.com	216.35.103.59	j4019.inktomisearch.com
209.185.143.98	q2002.inktomisearch.com	216.35.103.58	j4018.inktomisearch.com
209.185.143.97	q2001.inktomisearch.com	216.35.103.53	j4013.inktomisearch.com
216.32.237.29	j4019.inktomisearch.com	216.35.103.52	j4012.inktomisearch.com
216.32.237.7	j5006.inktomisearch.com	216.35.103.51	j4011.inktomisearch.com
216.32.237.11	j4001.inktomisearch.com	216.35.103.57	j4017.inktomisearch.com
216.32.237.12	j4002.inktomisearch.com	216.35.103.56	j4016.inktomisearch.com
216.32.237.13	j4003.inktomisearch.com	216.35.103.50	j4010.inktomisearch.com
216.32.237.14	j4004.inktomisearch.com	216.35.103.55	j4015.inktomisearch.com
216.32.237.16	j4006.inktomisearch.com	216.35.103.49	j4009.inktomisearch.com
216.32.237.17	j4007.inktomisearch.com	216.35.103.48	j4008.inktomisearch.com
216.32.237.19	j4009.inktomisearch.com	216.35.103.47	j4007.inktomisearch.com
216.32.237.20	j4010.inktomisearch.com	216.35.103.46	j4006.inktomisearch.com
216.32.237.21	j4011.inktomisearch.com	216.35.103.44	j4004.inktomisearch.com
216.32.237.22	j4012.inktomisearch.com	216.35.103.43	j4003.inktomisearch.com
216.32.237.24	j4014.inktomisearch.com	216.35.103.41	j4001.inktomisearch.com
216.32.237.25	j4015.inktomisearch.com	216.35.103.40	j4000.inktomisearch.com
216.32.237.27	j4017.inktomisearch.com	216.35.103.63	j102.inktomi.com
216.32.237.28	j4018.inktomisearch.com	216.35.103.64	j103.inktomi.com
209.1.12.68	i2001.inktomi.com	216.35.103.65	j104.inktomi.com
209.185.141.209	y700.inktomi.com	216.35.103.66	j105.inktomi.com
209.185.141.211	y702.inktomi.com	216.35.103.67	j106.inktomi.com
209.185.141.236	j100.inktomi.com	216.35.103.68	j107.inktomi.com
209.185.143.43	y1501.inktomi.com	216.35.103.70	j109.inktomi.com
209.185.143.58		216.35.103.71	j110.inktomi.com
209.185.143.80	j5000.inktomisearch.com	216.35.103.72	j111.inktomi.com
209.185.143.84	j5004.inktomisearch.com	216.35.103.74	j4021.inktomisearch.com
209.185.143.87	j5007.inktomisearch.com	216.35.103.75	j4022.inktomisearch.com
209.185.143.89	j5009.inktomisearch.com	216.35.103.76	j4023.inktomisearch.com
209.185.143.96	q2000.inktomisearch.com	216.35.103.77	j4024.inktomisearch.com
209.185.143.81	j5001.inktomisearch.com	216.35.103.78	j4025.inktomisearch.com
216.35.116.93	si3003.inktomi.com	216.35.116.42	j3002.inktomi.com
216.35.103.42	j4002.inktomisearch.com	216.35.116.91	si3001.inktomi.com
209.185.143.40	x1500.inktomi.com	202.212.5.30	goo212.goo.ne.jp
209.185.143.41	x1501.inktomi.com	216.35.116.90	si3000.inktomi.com
209.185.143.42	y1500.inktomi.com	216.35.116.41	j3001.inktomi.com
209.185.143.44	x1600.inktomi.com	216.35.116.78	lz3018.inktomi.com
209.185.143.45	x1601.inktomi.com	209.67.206.133	si520.inktomi.com
209.185.143.46	y1600.inktomi.com	209.131.48.100	brimstone-u2.inktomi.com

Spider IP	Spider DNS Name	Spider IP	Spider DNS Name
209.185.143.47	boobook.idp.inktomi.com	216.35.118.231	b301.inktomi.com
209.185.143.48	boobook.idp.inktomi.com	216.35.116.44	j3004.inktomi.com
209.185.143.49	kestrel.idp.inktomi.com	216.35.116.106	wm3021.inktomi.com
209.185.143.50	kestrel.idp.inktomi.com	216.35.116.105	wm3020.inktomi.com
209.185.143.51	vulture.idp.inktomi.com	216.35.116.43	j3003.inktomi.com
209.185.143.52	vulture.idp.inktomi.com	216.35.116.45	j3005.inktomi.com
209.185.143.53	vulture.idp.inktomi.com	216.35.116.48	j3008.inktomi.com
209.185.143.54		216.35.116.49	j3009.inktomi.com
209.185.143.55		216.35.116.50	j3010.inktomi.com
209.185.143.56		216.35.116.52	j3012.inktomi.com
209.185.143.57		216.35.116.53	j3013.inktomi.com
209.185.143.59	sc3-dhcp-1.inktomi.com	216.35.116.54	j3014.inktomi.com
209.185.143.60	sc3-dhcp-2.inktomi.com	216.35.116.55	j3015.inktomi.com
209.185.143.82	j5002.inktomisearch.com	216.35.116.56	j3016.inktomi.com
209.185.143.83	j5003.inktomisearch.com	216.35.116.57	j3017.inktomi.com
209.185.143.86	j5006.inktomisearch.com	216.35.116.58	j3018.inktomi.com
209.185.143.88	j5008.inktomisearch.com	216.35.116.59	j3019.inktomi.com
209.185.143.90	j5010.inktomisearch.com	216.35.116.82	wm3002.inktomi.com
209.185.143.91	j5011.inktomisearch.com	216.35.116.83	wm3003.inktomi.com
209.185.143.92	j5012.inktomisearch.com	216.35.116.88	wm3008.inktomi.com
209.185.143.93	j5013.inktomisearch.com	216.35.116.99	q5100.inktomi.com
216.35.103.62	j101.inktomi.com	216.35.116.47	j3007.inktomi.com
216.35.103.73	j5006.inktomi.com		

Indexing Timetable

Indexing via the paid submission program located at www.positionpro.com takes 48 hours. Indexing via the free "Add Url" link on one of the partner sites can take up to two weeks.

What to Do If Your Rankings Disappear

In the event that your rankings suddenly vanish on any or all of the Inktomi-powered partner engines, you should first examine your site and its elements to make certain that you have not violated any of the terms of agreement outlined in each search engine's respective guidelines and regulations. For example, have you violated the acceptable submissions policy (exceeding the allowable number of submissions, submitting pages with irrelevant content and/or META tags, using "cloaking" or other stealth tactics)? Have you inadvertently changed the structure or content of your page, so that the META tags are no longer visible or easily accessible to visiting spiders? Are there dead links or has content been removed?

If none of these scenarios appear to be the reason, it may simply be that one or more of Inktomi's partner engines have cleared out its index. While the pay-for-inclusion service will guarantee that you are in the Inktomi database for one year, submitting via the free service does not make that guarantee. In fact, if you submit via the free service and your page is not visited, you will be removed from the index. The time frame on this is not clear though. See specific partner engine chapters for more information on proper submitting and resubmitting tactics.

Special Tips and Tactics for This Engine

The key to success in Inktomi is clear (albeit not easy!): Achieve success in each of its partner engines. By learning the style, preferences, and rules of the Inktomi partner engines, and customizing your content and submissions to satisfy these preferences, you will enjoy a successful search engine positioning campaign in the Inktomi-powered engines.

Responsiveness and Help Provided

Inktomi is not, first and foremost, a search engine. Inktomi is the "back end" for other search engines; it finds and scores Web pages, but in the end, the heart of ranking success or failure comes from the individual engines to which Inktomi supplies its index. See the chapters on Inktomi's partner engines to learn about the responsiveness and assistance each provides to the search engine positioning industry.

Chapter 22:

iWon

iWon, Inc.
1 Bridge Street, Suite 42
Irvington, NY 10533
(914) 591-2000
Fax: (914) 591-0205

Free updates to this book are available via e-mail newsletter
by visiting: http://www.iprospect.com/book-news.htm.

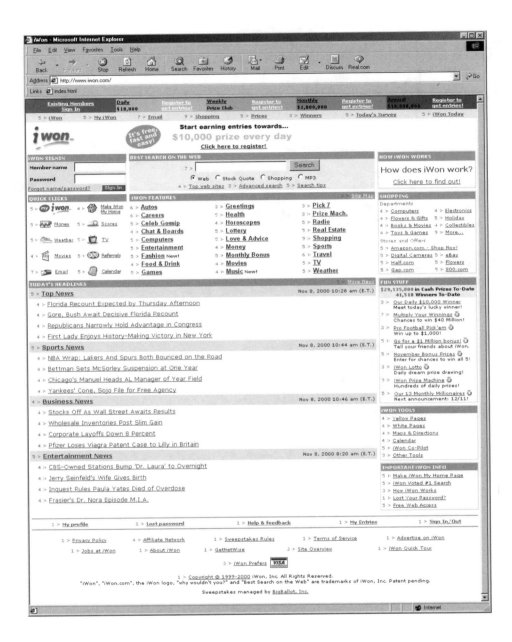

Facts about This Engine

iWon.com was launched in October 1999. This site has been ranked #1 in advanced search on the Internet and also ranked #1 in user satisfaction (Source: NPD Search and Portal Tracking Study). iWon gives away $10,000 every day to people who are simply using the site for searches, shopping, checking the latest news and weather, and other Internet activities such as checking e-mail. Users earn points by clicking virtually anywhere. iWon also ranks in the top three for Stickiest Site on the Web. "Sticky sites" are judged on three criteria:

1. Visits per person
2. Pages viewed per person
3. Time spent per person

1. **Web address:** www.iwon.com
2. **Type of engine:** Hybrid. Primary results — LookSmart, Secondary results — Inktomi, Tertiary results — Direct Hit. Also displays paid GoTo listings.
3. **Partnerships:** Many Web companies including Inktomi, LookSmart, GoTo, Direct Hit, Associated Press, CBS, Reuters, TheStreet.com, Travelocity, and WeatherNews Inc.
4. **Total documents indexed:** 500 million through Inktomi
5. **Total page views per month:** 722,707,000 (Source: Alexa Research, Feb. 2001)
6. **E-mail support:** iWon.com uses form-based e-mail support. There is a selection of forms that can be used for different circumstances.
7. **How to confirm listing:** domain:site-domain
8. **Obtain link popularity information:** Not applicable
9. **Result returns:** Search results are placed in numerous spots all over the page. The top four paid listings from GoTo are generally displayed first. The top four or five LookSmart listings are generally displayed in a box to the right of that. Below the LookSmart results there is usually another box with the top 10 results returned by Direct Hit. Inktomi results begin below the GoTo results.
10. **Receive higher rankings for link popularity:** Primary results — Not applicable, Secondary results — Yes, Tertiary results — Yes.
11. **Additional off-the-page considerations:** Primary results — Yes, category editors, Secondary results — No, Tertiary results — Yes, user click behavior.
12. **Rankings influenced by after-the-click behavior:** Primary results — No, Secondary results — No, Tertiary results — Yes.
13. **Recognition and utilization of META tags:** Primary results — No, Secondary results — Yes, Tertiary results — Yes.
14. **Consideration of META tags for relevancy:** Primary results — No, Secondary results — Yes, Tertiary results — Unknown.

15. **Importance of Title tag keyword prominence:** Primary results — No, Secondary results — Yes, Tertiary results — Unknown.

16. **Importance of <ALT> tag:** Primary results — No, Secondary results — No, Tertiary results — No.

17. **Importance of multiple occurrences of keywords in Title tag:** Primary results — No, Secondary results — Yes, Tertiary results — No.

18. **Maximum length of Title tag**: 120 characters

19. **Maximum length of keyword META tag:** Unconfirmed

20. **Maximum length of description META tag:** 250 characters

21. **Comment tags considered for relevancy:** No

22. **Frame support:** Yes, Inktomi has a new spider that supports frames.

23. **Image map support:** Unconfirmed

24. **Accepts automated submissions:** Yes, for Inktomi results.

25. **Indexes submitted pages only or conducts deep crawls:** See Inktomi chapter.

26. **Instant spidering of submitted page:** See Inktomi chapter.

27. **Number of pages that can be submitted per day:** See Inktomi chapter.

28. **Word stemming and plural sensitive:** Yes

29. **Case-sensitive searches:** Yes, with Inktomi results.

30. **Alphabetical page listings:** No

31. **Time to index page:** See Inktomi chapter.

32. **Spam penalties:** Unconfirmed

33. **Refuses pages with META refresh:** No

34. **Refuses pages with invisible text:** No

35. **Refuses pages with "tiny text":** No

36. **Remove URL:** Not applicable

This information may be out of date by the time of publication. Because search engines frequently change their ranking algorithms and other page scoring variables, we have posted updates and revisions to these chapters on our Web site: http://www.iprospect.com/search-engine-chapters.htm.

Understanding the Results

iWon's search results page is busy to say the least. The results are extracted from six different sources. The results that you will be presented with depend on the query conducted.

The results from the different sources are labeled differently by iWon. The first set of results is labeled "Inside iWON" and are powered by FACT CITY. The second set of results is labeled "Partner Search Results" and is powered by GoTo.com. These are sites within GoTo.com that are bidding within the top

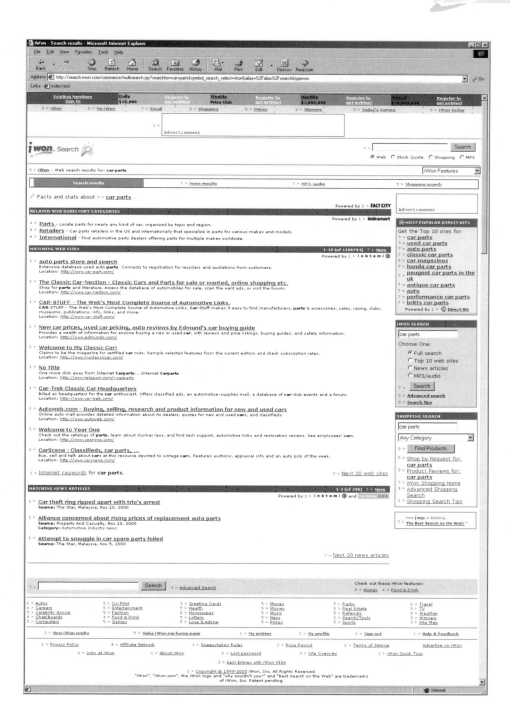

seven results for the term queried. The third set of results is labeled "Web Sites" and is powered by Inktomi. The fourth set of results is labeled "News Articles" and is powered by Inktomi and Moreover. These four sets of results are within the main body of the page.

The fifth set of results is labeled "Directory Categories" and is powered by LookSmart. The sixth set of results is labeled "Most Popular Direct Hits" and is powered by DirectHit. The fifth and sixth set of results are both presented on the right side of the page.

iWon provides the user with the flexibility of retrieving more results from within the "Partner Search Results," "Web Sites," or "News Articles" sections — click on the "More" link from the specific results section. The iWon Web site also provides information based on the query from Amazon and a few shopping channels.

Recommended Site Optimization Tactics

Refer to Chapter 21.

Off-the-Page Factors That Influence Success

Refer to Chapter 21.

How to Submit a Site to This Engine

There is no direct link to the "Submit a Site" section of iWon. You must first choose "Site Overview" found at the bottom of the iWon home page. Scrolling down this page will bring you to the "Submit a Site" link. Clicking on this link will bring you to the submission page where you can submit to LookSmart, Direct Hit, and RealNames. Coming soon is a feature that allows you to submit your site to iWon's main search engine, which is powered by Inktomi. Submitting your site through HotBot used to be the best way to assure that you were found by the Inktomi crawler and submitted to its database. However, a recent research indicates that submitting your site through HotBot's free add URL system may, in fact, give your site a ranking penalty. Michael Palmer, chief technical officer of Inktomi's search services division, said, "The free add URL [system] is very much a magnet for spam and low-quality pages, so we do intentionally give those pages a lower ranking."

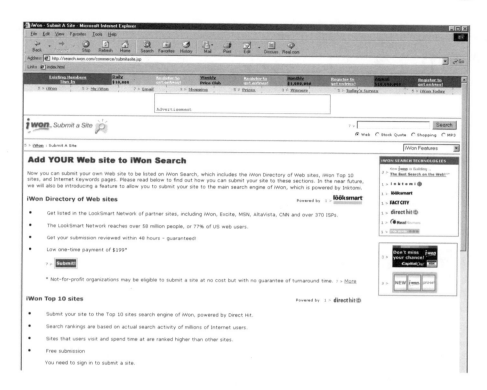

How to Build Informational Pages for this Engine

Refer to Chapter 21.

Indexing Timetable

Refer to Chapter 21.

What to Do If Your Rankings Disappear

You can contact Member Services by clicking on the "About iWon" link found at the bottom of the iWon home page. Then scroll down to the "Click here to access iWon Help" link. On this page you will find a link to "Contact Member Services" for assistance which will bring you to yet another page where you identify your problem. This page will bring you to a form where you can address your question to the iWon member service staff.

Chapter 23:

LookSmart

LookSmart, Ltd.
625 Second Street
San Francisco, CA 94107
(415) 348-7000
Fax: (415) 348-7050

looksmart

Free updates to this book are available via e-mail newsletter
by visiting: http://www.iprospect.com/book-news.htm.

Facts about This Engine

LookSmart began in October 1996 with a small staff and 145,000 sites in their database. Today, LookSmart has approximately 2 million Web sites in their directory and over 64 million unique visitors a month, which is almost 83 percent of Internet users in the United States. LookSmart offers a distinct express listing service, which allows you to be listed in the LookSmart directory for a fee.

Until recently, LookSmart only allowed one category submission per site into their directory. They have, however, added a new product called "Subsite Listings." This is a small deviation from their Express and Basic Submit products. "Subsite Listings" offer multiple listings deeper in the LookSmart directory. They have a team of editors that browse and crawl your site and find as many distinct and diverse content areas as possible which they then go back and match with their categories. There does not seem to be a limit on how many listings you can get via this particular method; it seems to all come down to dollars. LookSmart has recently added a link called "Subsite Listing Program," which can be found on the Submit Multiple URLs to LookSmart page. The link will take you to a form where you provide some basic information about your company and a representative will get back to you. LookSmart's network of partners gives them an added advantage in that they have the greatest reach on the Web. They state that they have an 83 percent reach, which is greater than their biggest rival, Yahoo!, which has a 65 percent reach. LookSmart also includes AOL and Lycos in their comparison, which have 64 percent and 43 percent reach respectively.

1. **Web address:** www.looksmart.com
2. **Type of engine:** Directory
3. **Partnerships:** MSN, AltaVista, Excite@Home, Time Warner, Sony, British Telecommunications, US West, NetZero, and 370 ISPs
4. **Total documents indexed:** More than 70,000 subject categories and approximately 2 million Web sites
5. **Total page views per month:** 231,178,000 (Source: Alexa Research, Feb. 2001)
6. **E-mail support:** http://www.looksmart.com/aboutus/contact/inquiry.html
7. **How to confirm listing:** Search on the Web site's URL.
8. **Obtain link popularity information:** Not applicable
9. **Result returns:** The main results are from the LookSmart directory. If no results are found, the user is asked whether they wish to search Inktomi.

10. **Receive higher rankings for link popularity:** Not applicable, directories do not spider sites.

11. **Additional off-the-page considerations:** LookSmart editors must review submissions.

12. **Rankings influenced by after-the-click behavior:** No

13. **Recognition and utilization of META tags:** Not applicable

14. **Consideration of META tags for relevancy:** Not applicable

15. **Importance of Title tag keyword prominence:** Not applicable

16. **Importance of <ALT> tag:** Not applicable

17. **Importance of multiple occurrences of keywords in Title tag:** Not applicable

18. **Maximum length of Title tag:** Not applicable

19. **Maximum length of keyword META tag:** Not applicable

20. **Maximum length of description META tag:** Not applicable

21. **Comment tags considered for relevancy:** Not applicable

22. **Frame support:** Not applicable

23. **Image map support:** Not applicable

24. **Accepts automated submissions:** No

25. **Indexes submitted pages only or conducts deep crawls:** Submitted pages only

26. **Instant spidering of submitted page:** Not applicable

27. **Number of pages that can be submitted per day:** Depends on submission type

28. **Word stemming and plural sensitive:** Yes

29. **Case-sensitive searches:** No

30. **Alphabetical page listings:** With categories, yes

31. **Time to index page:** Via Express Submit, reviewed within 48 hours and added within a few days after that. Via Basic Submit, reviewed within 8 weeks and added within a few days after that. Via the Subsite Listing Program, this will vary from days to weeks, depending on the scope of the submissions.

32. **Spam penalties:** Not applicable

33. **Refuses pages with META refresh:** Not applicable

34. **Refuses pages with invisible text:** Not applicable

35. **Refuses pages with "tiny text":** Not applicable

36. **Remove URL:** Not applicable

This information may be out of date by the time of publication. Because search engines frequently change their ranking algorithms and other page scoring variables, we have posted updates and revisions to these chapters on our Web site: http://www.iprospect.com/search-engine-chapters.htm.

Understanding the Results

Because it is a directory, LookSmart's editors review all submissions and accept or decline submissions personally. This helps them maintain a quality database. This allows LookSmart to rely heavily only on their own database to deliver results. Only in cases where the query does not find any matches within the LookSmart database will it return results from the Inktomi database.

Let's first assume that a query has a match within the LookSmart database. When you actually conduct a query in the LookSmart directory, you are presented with a page that has three different result sections.

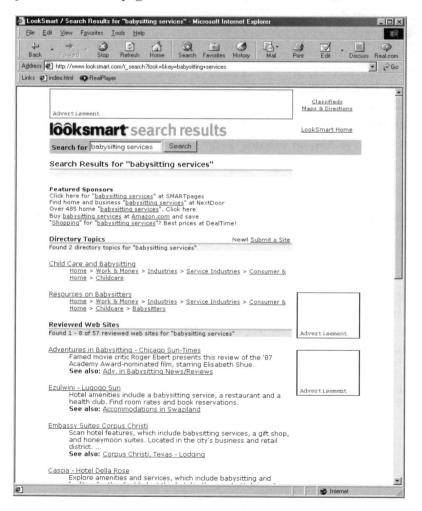

The first section is a "Featured Sponsors" section, which is included at both the top and bottom of the page. The "Featured Sponsors" section is an area where sites are paying for brief listings based on particular keywords.

The second section is "Directory Topics." This area contains category listings within the LookSmart database that are relevant to what is queried. In some cases, the category matches that are returned are a high-level category, which requires the user to drill down further into subcategories before they have a list of sites from which to choose. Depending on the queried keyword and the results returned, you may have a category match that is deep enough and refined enough that site listings are presented when you click on a category match. The number of results returned in this section varies depending on the keyword queried; some may return one result and others may return nine.

The third section is "Reviewed Web Sites." This is the most valuable area to a site owner or representative because it means a user is only one click away from visiting a site. LookSmart will return five results within this section on the first page. Clicking the "Next 10" link will present you with 10 additional results and so forth.

Should a LookSmart user query the database for a keyword for which LookSmart does not find a match, the user will be presented with a page similar to the one described above. However, on this type of search there are only two sections: "Featured Sponsors" and "Web Sites."

The "Featured Sponsors" section is identical to that described above. The "Web Sites" section contains 12 result matches extracted from the Inktomi database. Inktomi is the default database used by LookSmart in the event that a query does not match any content within the LookSmart database.

Site Elements That Can Cause Problems

For a site to be eligible for review by a LookSmart editor, the site must meet the following minimum requirements:

- The site must be in English.
- The site must target the U.S. audience.
- The site must contain original content that is not duplicated or mirrored from another site.
- The site cannot contain any sexually explicit content.
- The site cannot contain any graphic violence.

- The site cannot contain any materials or content that may be construed as a violation of someone's rights.

- The site cannot contain material that promotes or encourages illegal activities.

- If the site deals with pharmaceutical products, it must meet and adhere to all FDA regulations.

- The site must contain content that is both qualitative and quantifiable.

- The site must be operational 24 hours a day, 7 days a week.

- The site must be fully functional at the time of submission and not contain areas that are still under development.

- The site must respond to user requests in a sufficient time frame.

- Submissions made with the intent to gain additional listings even though they are already contained in the database are not allowed.

Recommended Site Optimization Tactics

You should ensure that the site is simple to navigate, so that editors reviewing the site can easily identify its goal and benefits. The value of the content should stand out easily. The LookSmart editors will be trying to identify which category on their site is most relevant to the content of the site. The simpler you make the editor's role, the better your chances of having the editor understand and accept your submission.

Off-the-Page Factors That Influence Success

LookSmart is a true directory that relies solely on the site title and description listed in its database to rank results. The more keyword-centric the title and description are, the greater the chance of ranking on such queries. These titles and descriptions are not derived from the metadata on the site, but instead from the submission made to LookSmart. The LookSmart editors reserve the right to modify, change, and/or discard any part or all of the submission. There is a distinction between the title and description. The site title content holds more value in ranking than the site description, even though it can be constructed with a maximum of 55 characters. Keeping this in mind, pay particular attention to the content of the title.

How to Submit a Site to This Engine

To submit to LookSmart, go to www.looksmart.com and click on the "Submit a Site" link.

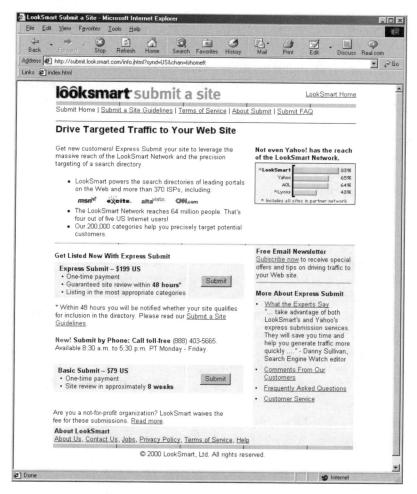

You will notice there are four forms of submission: Express Submit One URL, Submit Multiple URLs, Basic Submit, and Subsite Listings Program (within the Submit Multiple URLs options).

Express Submit One URL is a submission process that guarantees a LookSmart editor will review a site submission within 48 hours of the submission, not including weekends or holidays. It is important to note that

LookSmart's guarantee is only for review, not inclusion into their database. To meet this timeframe, LookSmart will send an e-mail notification regarding your submission progress. A LookSmart editor will then match the submission with the most appropriate categories. Express Submit is available at a one-time cost of $199 U.S.

The Submit Multiple URLs option is identical to that of the Express Submit One URL, although you can submit up to five unique URLs. Currently the process involves filling in the information of the submission and payment details, one time per URL. LookSmart is currently working on enhancing this process to allow multiple submissions at once with one payment.

The Basic Submit process also requires a one-time payment, but for only $99. This option entitles a site submission review within approximately eight weeks. On the LookSmart site, there is no mention of a guarantee or multiple listings via this method.

LookSmart also offers nonprofit organizations an alternative method of submission. What this really refers to is the Basic Submit process with a waiver of the fee.

The fourth method of submission, the Subsite Listings Program, is a form to be filled in which requires minimal information about you and your company and how many URLs you propose to list with the LookSmart directory. There seems to be no limit, but in fact, there is an option of 500+ URLs. Once LookSmart receives this request for information, a representative will contact you to discuss feasibility and cost.

Regardless of the method selected for submission, LookSmart will take several days to include the site in their database should the submission be accepted. Once the inclusion has taken effect, this listing will migrate across the LookSmart network within several weeks. This network includes prominent sites such as MSN, Excite@Home, AltaVista, Time Warner, Sony, British Telecommunications, US West, and NetZero, in addition to more than 300 ISPs. LookSmart will allow up to five submissions, each of a different URL. A different URL is classified as a subdomain or subfolder associated with the same domain name. For example: www.yoursite.com, www.boston.yoursite.com, www.newyork.yoursite.com, or www.yoursite.com, www.yoursite.com/boston, www.yoursite.com/newyork. It is still the decision of the editor whether a single submission warrants a single or multiple category listing. The limitation is merely on the number of different URLs submitted to LookSmart.

Once you have selected the submission method and clicked the appropriate area, you need to fill in some basic Web site information. You are required to fill in a Web address (URL), site title, comments, e-mail address, and phone, and you must indicate one of two agreement options. Keep in mind that the site title is very important in the way LookSmart ranks listings, so pay particular attention to what you include in this title. The comments section is where you want to identify the category you wish to be listed in along with any compelling and persuasive reasons you would like to convey to the editor. Once you have completed this information, click the Next button. The same page will reload if you have not filled in all the required fields. When you have passed this page, the next form is Payment Information. Simply fill in the payment details and click the Pay button. After authorization has been granted, you will be presented with an order number for the transaction. This order number is to be used in conjunction with correspondence regarding this particular submission.

To use the Subsite Listings Program, you need to provide the following information in order to have a representative respond to you for an agreement: name, e-mail, phone, company name, URL, number of pages, sample URLs, and how you found out about the Subsite Listings Program.

How to Know If Your Site Has Been Spidered/Listed

LookSmart is a directory, so no actual spider will come and crawl the submitted site. However, as confirmation of an Express Submit submission, LookSmart will send an e-mail notification regarding your submission progress. Upon submission acceptance, you need to search for your site after a few days to check its inclusion in the LookSmart database. To check that a submission has actually been included in the database, search for the complete domain of the site submitted.

Indexing Timetable

Depending on the submission method selected, the lead time for indexing varies. Via the Express Submit method, a guarantee of 48 hours for review and e-mail notification of progress is given. If acceptance is granted after the review, a few days are required for the site to be added to the LookSmart database. For the Basic Submit method, allow approximately eight weeks for review and then several days for inclusion into the LookSmart database for a successful submission. Through the Subsite Listings Program, the time required will vary depending on the number of URLs that are being added. However, the editors try to do these type of requests rather quickly, within a week or so.

What to Do If Your Rankings Disappear

A successful submission to LookSmart, which leads to an inclusion in their database, will remain in the LookSmart database (and therefore the LookSmart network) for as long as it complies with the editorial guidelines.

Special Tips and Tactics for This Engine

It is more challenging to appeal to a directory such as LookSmart as opposed to a spider-based search engine like AltaVista. The fact that a human editor will actually visit and review the site being submitted places a greater importance on delivering valuable content to both users and the editor. Directory editors try to maintain the credibility and quality of the content in their databases; therefore, they analyze a site in many ways. This varies from testing the functionality of the site all the way to the importance and quality of content on the site. In particular, LookSmart openly claims that they prefer sites that are "high quality, reliable, up-to-date, accurate, easy to use, fast, interactive, unique in content, interesting, visually appealing, and useful to consumers." In essence, what these characteristics add up to is an appealing, resourceful, and valuable site.

Chapter 24:

Lycos

Lycos, Inc.
400-2 Totten Pond Road
Waltham, MA 02451
(781) 370-2700

Free updates to this book are available via e-mail newsletter
by visiting: http://www.iprospect.com/book-news.htm.

Lycos is a registered trademark of Carnegie Mellon University.

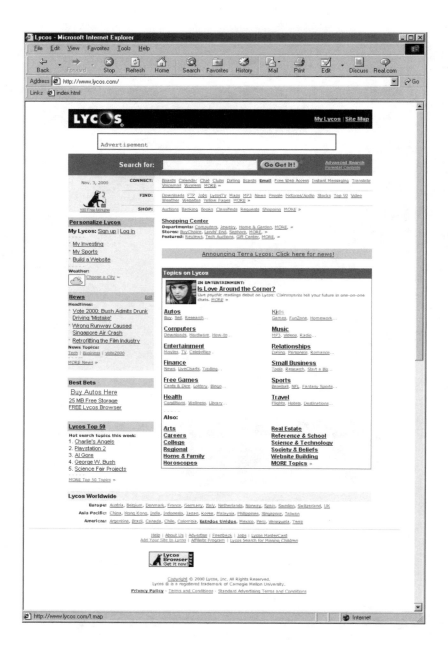

Facts about This Engine

When Lycos was founded in June 1995, the world of search engines was still in its infancy. The technology behind Lycos was developed at Carnegie Mellon University with the aim of helping users locate information on the Internet. In April 1996, Lycos became a publicly traded company. In April 1998, Lycos acquired WiseWire Corporation which built Lycos' editor-reviewed section of sites. This ranking system was designed to highlight credible sites. The technology made Lycos the first true hybrid. In November 1998, Lycos launched the "Go Get It" advertising campaign. In May 2000, Lycos was acquired by Terra Networks. In June 2000, Lycos reached a partnership with FAST Search & Transfer whereby FAST would provide results for Lycos. The two companies have embarked upon a mission to index one billion documents by the end of 2001.

1. **Web address:** http://www.lycos.com

2. **Type of engine:** Hybrid, Primary results — Open Directory, Secondary results — FAST.

3. **Partnerships:** Tripod, Angelfire, WhoWhere, MailCity, HotBot, and Quote.com

4. **Total documents indexed:** Lycos presents search results from a variety of sources including its own editors, GoTo.com, Direct Hit, Open Directory, and FAST. Collectively, Lycos has more than 350 million pages to draw from for search results.

5. **Total page views per month:** 937,397,000 (Source: Alexa Research, Feb. 2001)

6. **E-mail support:** Forms-based e-mail at http://home.lycos.com/feedback/

7. **How to confirm listing:** Type +h:www.domainname.com u:www.domainname.com in the field on the Advanced Search page. This will display any of your Web pages that are currently indexed.

8. **Obtain link popularity information:** Primary results — Not applicable, Secondary results — Select the "Advanced Search" link. Set the first Word Filter to "Should Include," type the domain you want in the text box, and set the drop-down box to "in the link to URL." Then hit the FAST search button.

9. **Result returns:** Lycos search results are derived from three different database sources. Search results displayed when searchers select "Popular" are powered by Lycos' own editors or Direct Hit. Search results labeled "Web Sites" are derived from two different sources: Open Directory and FAST.

10. **Receive higher rankings for link popularity:** Primary results — Not applicable, Secondary results — Yes.

11. **Additional off-the-page considerations:** Primary results — The Open Directory is made up by scores of volunteer editors; over 29,000 as of September 2000. These editors have full control over their categories, including the site title and description. Secondary results — No.

12. **Rankings influenced by after-the-click behavior:** Primary results — No, Secondary results — No.

13. **Recognition and utilization of META tags:** Primary results — Not applicable, Secondary results — Yes.

14. **Consideration of META tags for relevancy:** Primary results — Not applicable, Secondary results — alltheweb.com appears to index every word on the page, including META tags.

15. **Importance of Title tag keyword prominence:** Primary results — Not applicable, Secondary results — If the keywords do not agree with the content of the page, it is likely that there will be little to no relevance impact.

16. **Importance of <ALT> tag:** Primary results — Not applicable, Secondary results — Limited.

17. **Importance of multiple occurrences of keywords in Title tag:** Primary results — No, Secondary results — Minimal.

18. **Maximum length of Title tag:** Primary results — While Open Directory does not use actual META tags, when you submit a site you may suggest a title. The title you suggest will be edited, especially if it is long. Open Directory guidelines state that the title should only be the official name of the site, without keywords; however, this rule is not strictly enforced. Secondary results — Unconfirmed.

19. **Maximum length of keyword META tag:** Primary results — Not applicable, Secondary results — Unconfirmed.

20. **Maximum length of description META tag:** Primary results — As with the Title tag, you may suggest a short, 25-to-30 word description. It will be edited. Secondary results — Unconfirmed.

21. **Comment tags considered for relevancy:** Primary results — No, Secondary results — No.

22. **Frame support:** Primary results — Not applicable, Secondary results — Claims to.

23. **Image map support:** Primary results — Not applicable, Secondary results — Claims to.

24. **Accepts automated submissions:** Primary results — No, Secondary results — Yes.

25. **Indexes submitted pages only or conducts deep crawls:** Primary results — Not applicable, Secondary results — Conducts deep crawls.

26. **Instant spidering of submitted page:** Primary results — Not applicable, Secondary results — No.

27. **Number of pages that can be submitted per day:** Primary results — Appears to be unlimited if submitting different sites to different categories. However, many of the editors are picky about allowing sites into their categories. Secondary results — No published limit.

28. **Word stemming and plural sensitive:** Primary results — Yes, Secondary results — Yes.

29. **Case-sensitive searches:** Primary results — No, Secondary results — No.

30. **Alphabetical page listings:** Primary results — If you browse through the categories instead of using the search features, the page listings are alphabetical. Secondary results — No.

31. **Time to index page:** Primary results — 4-6 weeks, Secondary results — Some claim 4-8 weeks.

32. **Spam penalties:** Primary results — Banishment, Secondary results — FAST does not disclose its penalties for spamming.

33. **Refuses pages with META refresh:** Primary results — Not applicable, Secondary results — Unconfirmed.

34. **Refuses pages with invisible text:** Primary results — Not applicable, Secondary results — Unconfirmed.

35. **Refuses pages with "tiny text":** Primary results — Not applicable, Secondary results — Unconfirmed.

36. **Remove URL:** Primary results — No, Secondary results — No, but FAST honors robot exclusion tags.

This information may be out of date by the time of publication. Because search engines frequently change their ranking algorithms and other page scoring variables, we have posted updates and revisions to these chapters on our Web site: http://www.iprospect.com/search-engine-chapters.htm.

Understanding the Results

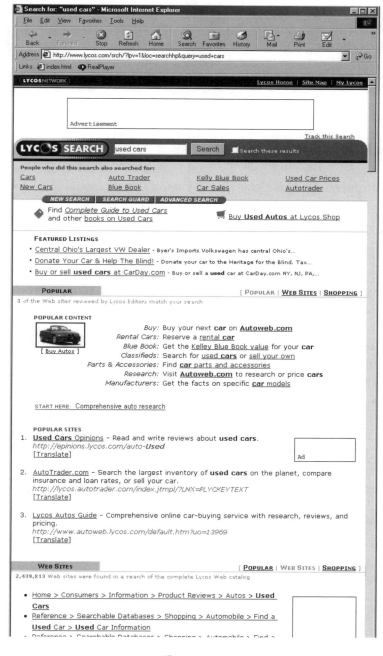

Lycos derives its search results from several sources and presents them to users differently depending on the query. Lycos uses its own editors, GoTo.com, Direct Hit, Open Directory, and FAST to power its search results. The source of the search results returned depends on the search term being queried. Not all keyword queries will produce search matches from each database.

A query on the search term "used cars" will return search results from all of Lycos' search sources.

The first search results displayed are paid listings from GoTo.com. Lycos labels these "Featured Listings" which is misleading. The rankings should more properly be labeled "sponsored listings." These "Featured Listings" are displayed in several areas on the search results page: the first three "featured sites" near the top of the page and then the "featured site" displayed between rankings four and five in the search results.

The second set of search results is labeled "Popular." Two types of results are found in this section and are labeled "Web sites reviewed by Lycos Editors match your search" or "Web site was selected based on user selection traffic." The Lycos editor matches are sites that Lycos human editors deemed valuable based on their own editorial selection process. "Popular" search results based on "user selection traffic" are powered by Direct Hit's database. Results from Direct Hit are ranked according to the popularity of a listing, meaning how many searchers selected the site after performing a specific keyword or phrase query and how long they remained on that Web site before returning to Lycos and constructing another query.

The third set of search results is labeled "Web Sites" and contain search matches from several different sources including the Open Directory, GoTo.com, and FAST.

Any indented bulleted listings labeled "Featured Listings" are always sponsored listings derived from GoTo.com's pay-for-placement search engine.

Site Elements That Can Cause Problems

Problematic site design issues are a concern primarily for the spider-driven search results powered by FAST or "Popular" search matches powered by Direct Hit. As with any spider-driven search engine, frames, query strings, broken links, pages hosted on secure servers, and fast redirects all cause problems.

Lycos' complexity means that issues such as query strings, user input pages, broken links, and redirects often present a challenge to all or part of Lycos' results. Elements that cause problems for the FAST results may not influence the Open Directory results. An analysis of each of the potential problems is analyzed for both types of results.

Query strings are URLs that contain punctuation such as question marks. Query strings are usually the result of a software program and are often associated with shopping carts on e-commerce sites. FAST and Direct Hit do not index pages that contain query strings. For this reason you must select pages of your site that do not contain query strings to optimize and submit to FAST and Direct Hit. However, query strings in the URL present no problems for Open Directory since the Open Directory does not use a spider.

Broken links cause two problems with the search engine part of the Lycos hybrid search engine. First, they stop FAST and Direct Hit from crawling and indexing your entire site. Second, they decrease the overall credibility of your site, thereby giving FAST and Direct Hit less incentive to index your pages. Also, broken links will discourage a human editor from adding your site. The editor will realize that your site is not of the caliber they desire for the Open

Directory and will most likely not accept your site until the problems have been corrected.

Pages behind a search box, login screen, or any other type of input required area will not be spidered. It is acceptable to have pages on your site behind a login page.

Redirects are also problematic for search engines in general. FAST and Direct Hit will not index pages that simply redirect to another page. You should submit the destination URL and not the redirect. Since a human editor looks at all Open Directory submissions, you should not submit redirected pages. The editors may believe that you are attempting to trick them and will most likely reject your site.

Recommended Site Optimization Tactics

Again, you must treat Open Directory and FAST/Direct Hit as separate entities when planning your optimization program. The Open Directory requires no formal site optimization. However, you should be very selective in the keyword phrases that you target in your descriptions. You need to strike a balance between words that accurately describe your site and words that will achieve rankings. For example, your site sells meat products online. You have determined that "meat products" is a phrase that you would like to be found under. You determine that you have a good chance of attaining rankings on "meat products" in the Open Directory. You should include "meat products" in the submitted description of your site. However, people often construct a description such as "Mymeatsite offers meat products, steaks, chicken, duck, pork products, sausage, and other meat products." An Open Directory editor will see right through your description and realize that you have simply stuffed your description full of keywords. Your site will either be rejected or your description will be completely stripped down and might possibly not even include your best phrase "meat products." Make certain that you pick a few phrases and construct your description around them. As always, remember that an editor can change your description for any reason.

When targeting secondary search results in FAST, remember that phrases in the Title tag and on the viewable page are important. It is ideal to place the desired phrase in the Title tag as well as the description and keyword META tags. Also, place the targeted phrase near the top of the viewable page. It is important to have a fair amount of text, say around 200 words, on the page. FAST will discredit pages without text on them. It is not clear how much weight

FAST places on the <ALT> tag. However, a well-constructed tag containing the phrase you are targeting and providing information about the graphic should not hurt rankings.

Off-the-Page Factors That Influence Success

As discussed previously, Lycos first displays results it has deemed popular. These sites have been reviewed by Lycos editors or come directly from Direct Hit. They are given this special designation because Lycos believes they are good resources for users. Also, this prevents spammers from getting the highest rankings.

Lycos uses Direct Hit technology to determine placements in the popular section if the section results say "based on user selection traffic." Again, this means that site rankings are largely influenced by users. Therefore, your Title and description META tags are essential as they will either entice users to visit your site or send them down the list to another site.

The Open Directory can be influenced by off-the-page considerations. A well-known brand name will carry weight with Open Directory editors who will be eager to add the site to their category. Also, the site's overall quality will impact its ability to get listed by the Open Directory.

FAST claims to examine hyperlinks. However, it is unclear whether they count the number of links in a manner similar to AltaVista or Google or if they give more weight to keywords that are contained in hyperlinks.

How to Submit a Site to This Engine

There are four ways to submit to Lycos. First, you can submit all non-query string pages to Lycos by going to www.lycos.com and clicking on "Add Your Site to Lycos." Your page will be spidered, and you will be immediately told of any errors. You can also submit to FAST by going to the main page at FAST (www.alltheweb.com) and clicking on the "Submit Your Site" link. Third, visit http://www.directhit.com/util/addurl.html to submit your site to the Direct Hit database. Finally, you can submit your site to a category in the Open Directory. Be sure to pick a relevant category and construct your description using a few of your more important keywords. Editors will not add your site to irrelevant categories.

Lycos and FAST both have high page submission limits. Both limit you to 50 pages per day. Lycos does not appear to crawl your site beyond the pages submitted. FAST does crawl your site and index pages appropriately. Direct Hit's submission limit is unknown at this time.

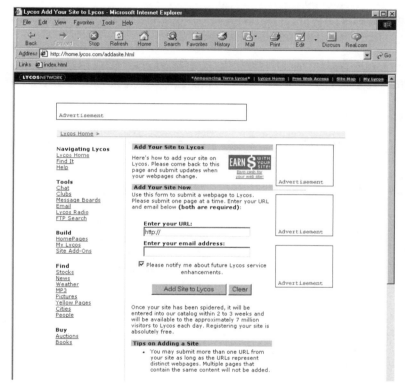

Submitting a site to Lycos

How to Build Informational Pages for this Engine

Informational pages can be built to help your Lycos rankings. You can submit informational pages directly to Lycos. However, popularity weighting may limit the success of these pages. It is a good idea to target your informational pages for FAST.

Remember to place the targeted phrase in the Title tag as well as in the first 256 characters of the viewable text. It is best to omit the description META tag since FAST ignores it. Instead, FAST simply grabs the first 256 characters of viewable text and uses that for the description. It is crucial to have the keyword phrases you are targeting in this first block of text.

How to Know If Your Site Has Been Spidered/Listed

It is important to know when a search engine spider visits your site. This information will help you determine if your work has paid off. Also, you can begin to estimate when additional indexing will occur and set timetables for when you should expect results. A list of Lycos spiders is below. Please see Chapter 17 for information regarding FAST's spiders.

207.77.90.185	lycosidae.lycos.com
208.146.26.19	mail2.lycos.com
209.67.228.21	bos-fe4-1.bos.lycos.com
209.67.229.139	bos-spider2.bos.lycos.com
206.79.171.18	sjc-fe2-2.sjc.lycos.com
206.79.171.19	sjc-fe3-1.sjc.lycos.com
206.79.171.20	sjc-fe3-2.sjc.lycos.com
206.79.171.21	sjc-fe4-1.sjc.lycos.com
206.79.171.22	sjc-fe4-2.sjc.lycos.com
206.79.171.23	sjc-fe5-1.sjc.lycos.com
206.79.171.24	sjc-fe5-2.sjc.lycos.com
206.79.171.25	sjc-accipiter1f.sjc.lycos.com
206.79.171.81	sjc-fe8-1.sjc.lycos.com
207.77.90.187	lycosidae.lycos.com
207.77.90.186	lycosidae.lycos.com
207.77.90.14	icreport.lycos.com
207.77.90.20	a2z.lycos.com
207.77.90.183	lycosidae.lycos.com
207.77.90.136	www-jp.lycos.com
208.146.26.233	zebra.eng.pgh.lycos.com
209.67.228.109	bos-fe8-1.bos.lycos.com
209.67.228.15	bos-fe1-1.bos.lycos.com
209.67.228.174	bos-fe11-1.bos.lycos.com
209.67.228.17	bos-fe2-1.bos.lycos.com
209.67.228.178	bos-fe12-1.bos.lycos.com
209.67.228.19	bos-fe3-1.bos.lycos.com
209.67.228.23	bos-fe5-1.bos.lycos.com
209.67.228.42	bos-fe6-1.bos.lycos.com
209.67.229.100	bos-spider9b.bos.lycos.com
209.67.229.101	bos-spider10b.bos.lycos.com
209.67.229.102	bos-spider11b.bos.lycos.com
209.67.229.140	bos-spider3.bos.lycos.com
209.67.229.141	bos-spider4.bos.lycos.com
209.67.229.138	bos-spider1.bos.lycos.com
209.67.229.142	bos-spider5.bos.lycos.com

209.67.229.143	bos-spider6.bos.lycos.com
166.48.225.254	lycosinc.NorthRoyalton.cw.net
209.67.229.62	bos-catalog4.bos.lycos.com
209.67.229.85	bos-catalog2.bos.lycos.com
209.67.229.144	bos-spider7.bos.lycos.com
206.79.171.156	sjc-fe7-1.sjc.lycos.com
206.79.171.157	sjc-fe13-1.sjc.lycos.com
206.79.171.16	sjc-fe1-2.sjc.lycos.com
206.79.171.17	sjc-fe2-1.sjc.lycos.com
206.79.171.67	sjc-fe6-1.sjc.lycos.com
206.79.171.85	sjc-fe9-1.sjc.lycos.com
206.79.171.89	sjc-fe10-1.sjc.lycos.com
206.79.171.93	sjc-fe11-1.sjc.lycos.com
206.79.171.97	sjc-fe12-1.sjc.lycos.com
209.67.228.106	bos-fe7-1.bos.lycos.com
209.67.228.154	bos-fe1-4.bos.lycos.com
209.67.228.156	bos-fe3-4.bos.lycos.com
209.67.228.159	bos-fe6-4.bos.lycos.com
209.67.228.166	bos-fe9-1.bos.lycos.com
209.67.228.170	bos-fe10-1.bos.lycos.com
209.67.228.182	bos-fe13-1.bos.lycos.com
209.67.228.107	bos-fe7-2.bos.lycos.com
209.67.229.137	bos-catalog1.bos.lycos.com

Indexing Timetable

Different timetables exist for each component of Lycos. FAST takes approximately four to eight weeks to index your site. However, FAST has one of the few spiders that will deep crawl your site and add pages that you do not submit. This makes it much easier to submit your site because FAST will do most of the work for you.

Lycos still offers a Submit page on its site. At this time, it seems to be running around six to eight weeks to index a site.

Your submission to the Open Directory will be added at the discretion of the editor assigned to your category. Some editors are quick to review sites. It is realistic to expect to see your site added in four to six weeks. Submissions to Direct Hit will take four to six weeks to index.

What to Do If Your Rankings Disappear

Lycos results are stable compared to many of the other search engines. The popular listings and Open Directory categories change infrequently. Results influenced by Direct Hit rise and fall a few slots due to the number of click-throughs but are unlikely to rise and fall radically. FAST is constantly adding documents in its attempt to index the entire Web. As a result, the number of pages competing for rankings (especially on the most coveted phrases) is constantly growing. However, your rankings are unlikely to vanish suddenly. With the competition continuing to pour in, it is important to monitor your results and make changes to your titles and viewable text to stay ahead of your competition.

Special Tips and Tactics for This Engine

Again, we need to discuss Open Directory, FAST, and Direct Hit search results separately. The Open Directory requires you to determine a category which is served when your phrase is targeted. Then you need to make certain your site is relevant for that category. Next, construct your description around those few keyword phrases but avoid simply stuffing your description full of keywords.

FAST requires that you place the targeted phrase in the title and at least once in the viewable text. It is ideal to place the keyword phrase near the top and again at the bottom of the page. However, avoid overuse of the phrase, as that is considered spam and may hurt your rankings.

No special tactics will directly affect listings from Direct Hit. The main point to note is the more useful and usable your site is, the more users will visit it. The more users that visit your site from the search results, the higher you will rank. So make sure you submit attractive and functional pages to Direct Hit.

Responsiveness and Help Provided

Lycos offers a link to a Help page from its index page. This Help page covers numerous topics concerning adding a site, excluding your site, the Open Directory, feedback, and contacting Lycos. We received adequate help via telephone but could not get specific questions answered. We also utilized the forms-based e-mail and received a quick reply. However, the help provided was an automated response and did not directly address our question. Overall, the help provides no meaningful solutions to any specific problems or questions.

Chapter 25:

MSN

Microsoft Corporation
One Microsoft Way
Redmond, WA 98052
webmaster@msn.com
(425) 882-8080

Free updates to this book are available via e-mail newsletter
by visiting: http://www.iprospect.com/book-news.htm.

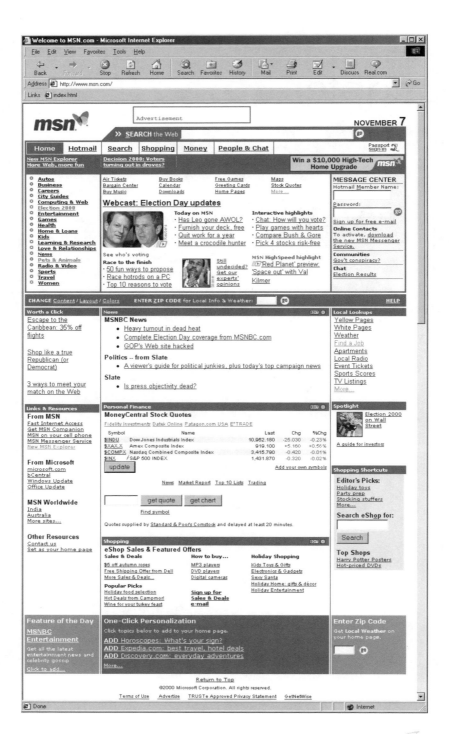

Facts about This Engine

MSN Search was previously based solely on Inktomi's results. MSN now pulls its results from numerous sources and applies its own algorithm. In the past, this search engine did not make any distinctions between the directory results and search engine results. MSN felt that it did not need to make any separation between the two. However, its results are now separated nicely on the page, which makes it very easy to understand the search results.

The MSN search engine can be found with ease. The default Internet Explorer home page links to the MSN main page. In Internet Explorer, the user can simply click the Search button from the browser to search MSN. The fact that Microsoft owns MSN improves the search engine's publicity, and evidence that MSN is well recognized can be found in the fact that MSN.com has more page views per month than Yahoo.com.

1. **Web address:** http://www.msn.com
2. **Type of engine:** Hybrid, Primary results — LookSmart, Secondary results — Inktomi.
3. **Partnerships:** MSN Search uses LookSmart for the directory searching, while it uses Inktomi for the main search results. RealNames and Direct Hit also have a smaller presence on this site.
4. **Total documents indexed:** Not applicable
5. **Total page views per month:** 16,231,725,000 (Source: Alexa Research, Feb. 2001)
6. **E-mail support:** There is no e-mail support directly off of the MSN Search Web site; however, you can find MSN contact information from Microsoft's site.
7. **How to confirm listing:** Not available
8. **Obtain link popularity information:** Primary results — To find the Web site containing links to a particular site, click on "More Options" from the MSN Search page. In the Find field, select the option "Links to URL." Make sure you include the "http://" as well as the "/" at the end of the address. Secondary results — Unknown.
9. **Result returns:** MSN displays a maximum of four results from the Web Directory and 15 results from the Internet results per page.
10. **Receive higher rankings for link popularity:** Primary results — No, Secondary results — Yes.
11. **Additional off-the-page considerations:** Primary results — MSN edits the top 10 rankings to make sure quality sites make it to the top. Secondary results — Inktomi places more weight on documents it finds on its own and via its paid submission service, found at PositionPro.com.
12. **Rankings influenced by after-the-click behavior:** Primary results — Yes, Secondary results — Not applicable.
13. **Recognition and utilization of META tags:** Primary results — No, Secondary results — Yes.
14. **Consideration of META tags for relevancy:** Primary results — No, Secondary results — Yes.
15. **Importance of Title tag keyword prominence:** Primary results — No, Secondary results — Yes.

16. **Importance of <ALT> tag:** Primary results — No, Secondary results — Yes.

17. **Importance of multiple occurrences of keywords in Title tag:** Primary results — Not applicable, Secondary results — Yes.

18. **Maximum length of Title tag:** Primary results — 110 characters, Secondary results — Unknown.

19. **Maximum length of keyword META tag:** Primary results — Unconfirmed, Secondary results — Unknown.

20. **Maximum length of description META tag:** Primary results — 250 characters, Secondary results — Unknown.

21. **Comment tags considered for relevancy:** Primary results — No, Secondary results — No.

22. **Frame support:** Primary results — Yes, Secondary results — Yes.

23. **Image map support:** Unconfirmed for primary and secondary results.

24. **Accepts automated submissions:** Primary results — No, Secondary results — Yes, through Position Technologies.

25. **Indexes submitted pages only or conducts deep crawls:** Primary results — Indexes submitted pages, Secondary results — Crawls, but it is recommended to submit all pages.

26. **Instant spidering of submitted page:** Primary results — Not applicable, Secondary results — Yes.

27. **Number of pages that can be submitted per day:** Primary results — Not applicable, Secondary results — The submission limit per day is 50 via the "free" method. "Paid" inclusion has no daily limit, but has a cap of 1,000 pages from one domain.

28. **Word stemming and plural sensitive:** Primary results — No, Secondary results — No.

29. **Case-sensitive searches:** Primary results — Yes, Secondary results — Yes.

30. **Alphabetical page listings:** Primary results — No, Secondary results — No.

31. **Time to index page:** Primary results — Not applicable, Secondary results — Approximately three weeks to 60 days for free submissions and 48 hours for paid submissions.

32. **Spam penalties:** Primary results — No, Secondary results — No.

33. **Refuses pages with META refresh:** Primary results — No, Secondary results — No.

34. **Refuses pages with invisible text:** Primary results — No, Secondary results — No.

35. **Refuses pages with "tiny text":** Primary results — No, Secondary results — No.

36. **Remove URL:** Primary results — Not applicable, Secondary results — Inktomi re-spiders all indexed pages and will automatically remove URLs that no longer exist.

This information may be out of date by the time of publication. Because search engines frequently change their ranking algorithms and other page scoring variables, we have posted updates and revisions to these chapters on our Web site: http://www.iprospect.com/search-engine-chapters.htm.

Understanding the Results

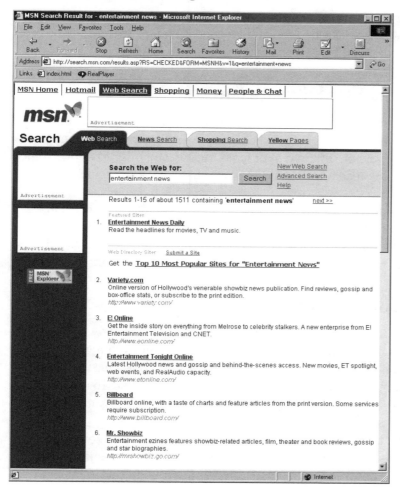

MSN displays a section titled "Featured Sites" below the search box when a search is performed. This section includes official company and product Web sites, which are provided by RealNames, and the most popular sites, provided by Direct Hit. This section also contains sites from MSN and MSN sponsors, some of which MSN is compensated for. There is a second section titled "Web Directory Sites" that displays results from the Web directory. MSN depends on LookSmart to provide these results. Directly below "Web Directory Sites" is a link to Direct Hit results that displays the 10 most popular sites related to your query. Finally, there is a third section, which includes results from the World Wide Web. Inktomi and LookSmart provide the Internet search results.

Site Elements That Can Cause Problems

In light of the fact that MSN relies on other engines' databases for their results, you should read the chapters on the specific search engines used by MSN for further information including Chapter 23 on LookSmart and Chapter 21 on Inktomi.

Recommended Site Optimization Tactics

MSN pulls a majority of its results from LookSmart. As a result, it is important to submit your site to LookSmart and achieve good rankings. It is also beneficial to rank well in Inktomi and Direct Hit.

Off-the-Page Factors That Influence Success

MSN uses the information provided by after-the-click behavior. For example, when an end user performs a search and clicks on a particular link, the link that has been clicked on gets an improvement in its ranking. In order to entice someone to click on the link leading to your site, you must have a compelling description and title.

MSN also adjusts the top 10 search results for particular keywords, in order to make sure that only quality Web sites make it to the top. If you do not want MSN to adjust your site to a lower ranking, you should create a site that is of good quality and which MSN would consider valuable and useful.

How to Submit a Site to This Engine

On the MSN Search page, there is an Add URL link. This page allows you to submit your site to the LookSmart directory. It is important to remember that there is a cost involved when submitting your site to the LookSmart directory. MSN does, however, offer a non-business submission at no cost. To qualify, your Web site must represent a non-profit organization, community organization, government agency, or a personal Web site.

The Add URL form only allow the submission of a site to be reviewed for placement in the LookSmart directory. However, MSN is currently using Inktomi and Direct Hit for its Internet search results. It is therefore important to submit your site to each of these search engines if you want to rank well in MSN. Please see the chapters for these particular search engines for further information on their submission and optimization procedures.

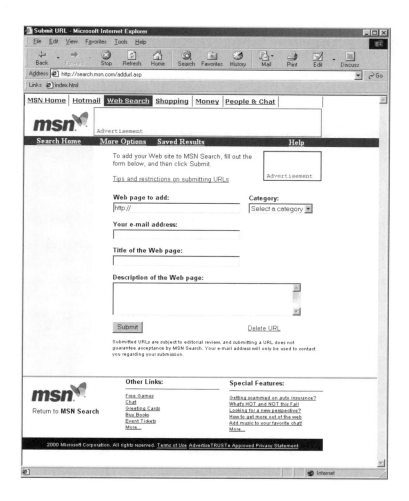

How to Build Informational Pages for this Engine

Because MSN's primary search results are powered by the LookSmart directory, informational pages are not recommended for this engine.

How to Know If Your Site Has Been Spidered/Listed

MSN does not do any crawling of its own. At the same time, it is possible to see if spiders from other search engines that MSN depends on are visiting your site. Specific chapters on these search engines contain a list of those spiders.

What to Do If Your Rankings Disappear

Please read the chapters on the search engines that provide MSN with search results for information.

Special Tips and Tactics for This Engine

Carefully submit your site to LookSmart and Inktomi via their paid inclusion programs.

Responsiveness and Help Provided

MSN Search provides help for search engine users on its Web site, although they do not provide much information for search engine professionals. Another problem with MSN is that there is no contact e-mail address on the search Web site. To find a contact you must visit Microsoft's main site and surf through the site to find an appropriate e-mail address, which can be extremely time consuming.

Chapter 26:

NBCi

NBC Internet, Inc.
The NBCi Building
225 Bush Street
San Francisco, CA 94104
support@nbci.com
(415) 375-5000
Fax: (415) 989-1365

Free updates to this book are available via e-mail newsletter
by visiting: http://www.iprospect.com/book-news.htm.

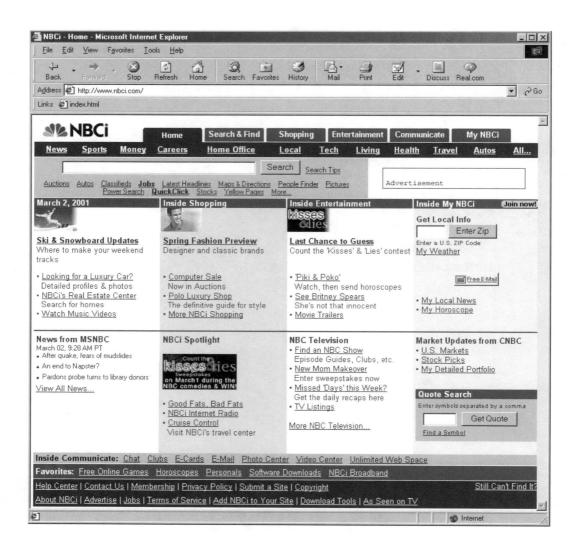

Facts about This Engine

The search engine formerly known as Snap.com has been integrated into NBCi.com and no longer exists as a separate entity. This appears to be an attempt by NBCi to leverage the NBC brand by integrating their various Internet properties. NBC Internet, Inc. (NBCi), was created in November 1999 through the combination of Snap, XOOM.com, NBC.com, NBC Interactive Neighborhood, AccessHollywood.com, VideoSeeker, and a 10 percent equity stake in CNBC.com. NBC Internet trades publicly under the ticker symbol NBCI on the NASDAQ. NBC, a subsidiary of General Electric (NYSE: GE), holds a 39.3 percent ownership stake in NBCi. NBCi is headquartered in San Francisco and has offices in New York City, Los Angeles, and Chicago.

In June 2000, NBCi announced that all of its online properties, including Snap.com, would be combined into NBCi.com in the fall of 2000. In September 2000, NBCi Beta was unveiled and all the other URLs became redirects to this site. As far as search features, NBCi.com appears to be exactly the same as the old Snap.com site. The content of the old NBCi.com site, which was optimized for broadband users, seems to have been moved to http://speed.nbci.com.

NBCi.com is a unique type of directory. Unlike most directories, NBCi.com allows members (i.e., anyone who registers a username and password) to submit sites directly into their "LiveDirectory." A human editor does not review these sites at this point. It is only when sites receive a certain level of traffic that they are reviewed by NBCi.com staff. NBCi.com does offer a $99 Web site promotion service. This guarantees review for promotion to the editor-reviewed or "Top Sites" listings. Sites submitted using the Web site promotion service receive professionally written site descriptions and "enhanced keywording."

1. **Web address:** www.nbci.com
2. **Type of engine:** Hybrid. Primary results — LiveDirectory, Secondary results — Inktomi.
3. **Partnerships:** GlobalBrain, Inktomi
4. **Total documents indexed:** Inktomi has 500 million. NBCi does not reveal that information.
5. **Total page views per month:** 781,107,000 (Source: Alexa Research, Feb. 2001)
6. **E-mail support:** support@nbci.com
7. **How to confirm listing:** E-mail confirmation within 24 hours of submission.
8. **Obtain link popularity information:** Primary results — Unconfirmed, Secondary results — Unknown.

9.   **Result returns:** Returns editor-reviewed sites first, then LiveDirectory sites. Inktomi results will display if the other two categories do not have results. There does not appear to be any limit on the number of editor-reviewed sites that are returned. A recent search for "car parts" resulted in 109 pages of editor-reviewed sites!

10. **Receive higher rankings for link popularity:** Primary results — Not applicable, Secondary results — Yes.

11. **Additional off-the-page considerations:** Primary results — Uses human editors to check popularity. Secondary results — Inktomi places more weight on documents it finds on its own and via its paid submission service, found at PositionPro.com.

12. **Rankings influenced by after-the-click behavior:** Primary results — Yes, staff editors review popular sites in NBCi's LiveDirectory. These editors may then add the site to the editor-reviewed results. Secondary results — Not applicable.

13. **Recognition and utilization of META tags:** Primary results — Description tags definitely influence rankings, but Title tags appear less important. Secondary results — Yes.

14. **Consideration of META tags for relevancy:** Primary results — The META tags impact the placement of the site quite a bit. The description tags appear to be used to help determine a site's relevancy to a specific keyword. Secondary results — Yes.

15. **Importance of Title tag keyword prominence:** Primary results — The two-tier directory structure seems to minimize the impact of META tags. Secondary results — Yes.

16. **Importance of <ALT> tag:** Primary results — No, Secondary results — Yes.

17. **Importance of multiple occurrences of keywords in Title tag:** Primary results — Limited importance, Secondary results — Yes.

18. **Maximum length of Title tag:** Primary results — Title tag must be 128 characters or less. Secondary results — Unknown.

19. **Maximum length of keyword META tag:** Primary results — Only allows five keywords, Secondary results — Unknown.

20. **Maximum length of description META tag:** Primary results — 255 characters max, Secondary results — Unknown.

21. **Comment tags considered for relevancy:** Primary results — No, Secondary results — No.

22. **Frame support:** Primary results — Yes, Secondary results — Yes.

23. **Image map support:** Primary results — Yes, Secondary results — Unconfirmed.

24. **Accepts automated submissions:** Primary results — No, Secondary results — Yes, through Position Technologies.

25. **Indexes submitted pages only or conducts deep crawls:** Primary results — Not applicable, Secondary results — Crawls, but it is recommended to submit all pages.

26. **Instant spidering of submitted page:** Primary results — No, Secondary results — Yes.

27. **Number of pages that can be submitted per day:** Primary results — One, Secondary results — The submission limit per day is 50 via the "free" method. "Paid" inclusion has no daily limit, but has a cap of 1,000 pages from one domain.

28. **Word stemming and plural sensitive:** Primary results — Yes, Secondary results — No.

29. **Case-sensitive searches:** Primary results — No, Secondary results — No.

30. **Alphabetical page listings:** Primary results — No, sites in both the editor-reviewed area and LiveDirectory are listed by popularity. Secondary results — No.

31. **Time to index page:** Primary results — About 25-48 hours, Secondary results — Approximately three weeks to 60 days for free submissions and 48 hours for paid submissions.

32. **Spam penalties:** Primary results — NBCi.com's Terms of Service contain the following:

     "It is a condition of your use of the Service that you do not:...(xiv) submit to the LiveDirectory multiple Web sites with different URLs that redirect a user to one Web page, (xv) submit to Live Directory more than one URL for a single category, or (xvi) update LiveDirectory listings with intent to distort or misrepresent them, including but not limited to changing titles of the entries, descriptions of the entries, URLs, or keywords."

     Any violation of these rules could result in banishment from NBCi.com The full Terms of Service are available at http://www.nbci.com/LMOID/resource/0,566,home - 764,00.html?st.sn.ft.0.term. Secondary results — No.

33. **Refuses pages with META refresh:** Primary results — No, Secondary results — No.

34. **Refuses pages with invisible text:** Primary results — No, Secondary results — No.

35. **Refuses pages with "tiny text":** Primary results — No, Secondary results — No.

36. **Remove URL:** Primary results — No for NBCi. Secondary results — Inktomi re-spiders all indexed pages and will automatically remove URLs that no longer exist.

This information may be out of date by the time of publication. Because search engines frequently change their ranking algorithms and other page scoring variables, we have posted updates and revisions to these chapters on our Web site: http://www.iprospect.com/search-engine-chapters.htm.

Understanding the Results

The first part of the results are the "Top Sites" which are described as the most popular sites reviewed by NBCi editors. The next set of results are from Snap's LiveDirectory. It appears that the term "LiveDirectory" is being phased out by NBCi. At the time of writing, LiveDirectory results are being called "Member-Submitted Sites." These are described as the most popular sites submitted by members to NBCi LiveDirectory. According to NBCi.com, sites are promoted from the LiveDirectory to the editor-reviewed area once they have achieved a certain popularity score (or paid $99). Another set of results is labeled as "Additional Sites" and are Inktomi results. "Search MarketPlace" searches NBCi's sponsored links.

Site Elements That Can Cause Problems

As this site is primarily a directory, any site can be submitted.

Recommended Site Optimization Tactics

Optimizing for NBCi.com can be quite frustrating since there are limits on what you can do. The only thing that you can influence is the description of your site, and even that is subject to editorial review. The best strategy is to host areas with different content on different subdomains, or even separate domains, and submit each of these content areas to different categories. Once your site has been accepted to the LiveDirectory, you can update your listing to use your META tags as the title and description. The most important thing to consider when optimizing for NBCi.com is that the most popular sites are listed first, both within the editor-reviewed and member-submitted sections. Therefore, you should make your title and description as appealing as possible to the end user. It seems the only way to get more clicks is to get more clicks!

Off-the-Page Factors That Influence Success

NBCi.com claims to rank sites in order of popularity for both the editor-reviewed and member-submitted sections. The description appears to affect the site's relevance to a topic, but not its ranking on the results page.

How to Submit a Site to This Engine

Before you can submit a site to NBCi.com's LiveDirectory, you must first sign up. Once you've created a username and password, you can begin submitting. The entry to the submissions area is found by clicking on the "Submit a Site" link on the home page.

How to Build Informational Pages for this Engine

There are a few reasons why it is not wise to build informational or doorway pages for NBCi.com. The first reason is that sites must be reviewed by human editors in order to get into the top rankings. The second is that NBCi.com makes extensive use of cookies and user names; therefore it is quite possible that if they find one of your informational pages, they will ban all sites you've submitted. Lastly, while NBCi.com's Terms of Service do not specifically say "no doorway pages," they do say not to submit pages hosted on multiple domains that redirect the user to the same site.

How to Know If Your Site Has Been Spidered/Listed

The My Sites feature will show you the sites you've submitted.

Indexing Timetable

NBCi.com claims to index sites within 24 hours.

What to Do If Your Rankings Disappear

It is extremely unlikely that any rankings you have in NBCi.com would disappear overnight, since they are a directory and are not actively refreshing their index. However, in the event your rankings disappear, check out the My Sites feature and submit more pages.

Special Tips and Tactics for This Engine

NBCi.com has one of the best features I've ever heard of on any search engine. Once you've created a user name and a password and submitted a site, you have access to something called "My Sites." My Sites lists all the sites you've submitted. It allows you to change your title and description, even so far as using your META tags for the title and description. This is the only directory that gives you this kind of control over your listing.

Responsiveness and Help Provided

NBCi.com has been incredibly non-responsive. The only reply we've received was from a manager for user interface design, documentation, and support. She replied to our e-mail with "I don't have this information." Their customer service may have improved. We hope it has.

Chapter 27:

Netscape Search

Netscape Communications Corporation
501 E. Middlefield Road
Mountain View, CA 94043-4042
http://help.netscape.com/emailsupport.html
(650) 254-1900
Fax: (650) 528-4124

Free updates to this book are available via e-mail newsletter
by visiting: http://www.iprospect.com/book-news.htm.

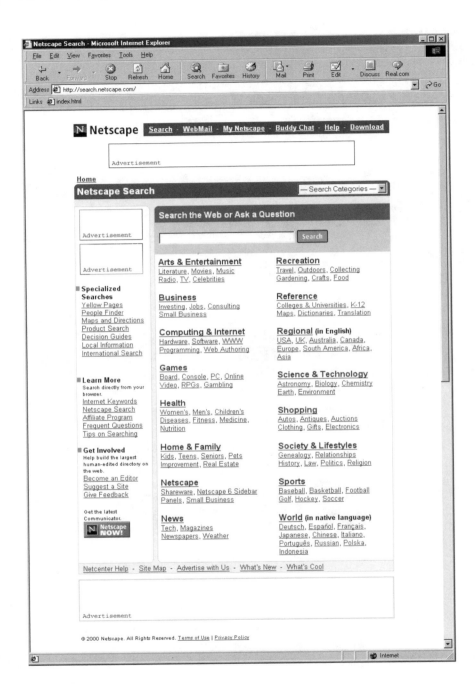

Facts about This Engine

Silicon Graphics founder Jim Clark and NCSA Mosaic creator Marc Andreessen founded Netscape Communications Corporation in April 1994. Within six months, the company released its first Netscape Navigator Web browser, freely available to Internet users to download over the Internet, from Netscape.com.

As the default page for millions of Netscape users, Netscape.com has become one of the most heavily trafficked sites on the Web. According to Netscape.com, it serves nearly five million users and receives more than 120 million hits each day. Not only has the site continued to serve as a location to download the latest Web browser and other Netscape software products, it has grown to encompass a multitude of information and service functions, becoming a portal site. As such, Netscape.com now offers e-mail, shopping, news, and search capabilities.

Netscape.com offers a unique way to search the Internet with a drop-down menu of partnered search engines, including AltaVista, Ask Jeeves, Google, Excite, HotBot, Lycos, LookSmart, and GoTo.com. After choosing which search engine you would like to use and typing your request, Netscape.com directs the search to that engine and presents those results.

Netscape Search, which can be found at http://search.netscape.com/, however, is the actual search engine for the Netscape.com site. Netscape Search delivers results from Google and the Open Directory, which like Netscape is also owned by AOL, Inc. Therefore, you cannot directly submit to Netscape Search. Your rankings in Netscape Search are a direct result of those you have achieved in either Open Directory, which delivers primary results, or Google, which delivers secondary results. GoTo.com was integrated into the Netscape Search results in September 2000. The results provided by GoTo.com do not replace any content from Google or the Open Directory, but provide additional listings for only some queried results. GoTo.com results are listed under "Partner Search Results."

1. **Web address:** http://www.netscape.com/ (Netscape's address), http://search.netscape.com/ (address for Netscape Search)

2. **Type of engine:** Hybrid. Primary results — Open Directory, Secondary results — Google.

3. **Partnerships:** Sun Microsystems, Open Directory, AltaVista, Ask Jeeves, Excite, GoTo, HotBot, LookSmart, Lycos, and Google. Netscape Search also delivers a list of partner search results, listing retail sites if appropriate.

4. **Total documents indexed:** Because Netscape delivers results from Open Directory and Google, it does not index any documents. Please refer to the Open Directory and Google chapters for this information.

5. **Total page views per month:** 510,441,000 (Source: Alexa Research, Feb. 2001)

6. **E-mail support:** http://help.netscape.com/emailsupport.html

7. **How to confirm listing:** Because Netscape delivers results from Open Directory, Google, and GoTo you are unable to confirm your site's listing directly through Netscape. Please refer to those chapters for this information.

8. **Obtain link popularity information:** Primary results — Unconfirmed, Secondary results — Yes, http://yoururl.com.

9. **Result returns:** Netscape Search uses Open Directory for its primary result returns. If, however, Open Directory does not contain information on the queried topic, Netscape Search will provide results from Google. Recently, GoTo.com has been integrated within the Netscape Search results and is used to provide complementary information.

10. **Receive higher rankings for link popularity:** Primary results — Not applicable, Secondary results — Yes.

11. **Additional off-the-page considerations:** Primary results — The Open Directory is made up by scores of volunteer editors. As of September 2000, there were over 29,000 editors. These editors have full control over their categories, including the site title and description. Secondary results — Yes, link popularity. Both the number of links pointing to your site and how credible those sites are play a big part in ranking determination.

12. **Rankings influenced by after-the-click behavior:** Primary results — No, Secondary results — No.

13. **Recognition and utilization of META tags:** Primary results — Not applicable, Secondary results — No.

14. **Consideration of META tags for relevancy:** Primary results — Not applicable, Secondary results — No.

15. **Importance of Title tag keyword prominence:** Primary results — Not applicable, Secondary results — Google does not calculate Title tag keyword prominence, but rather focuses on the keywords in the body text. The keywords at the top of the page are just as important as the keywords on the bottom of a page, so make sure the whole page is interesting and relevant.

16. **Importance of <ALT> tag:** Primary results — Not applicable, Secondary results — Yes.

17. **Importance of multiple occurrences of keywords in Title tag:** Primary results — No, Secondary results — Yes.

18. **Maximum length of Title tag:** Primary results — While Open Directory does not use actual META tags, when you submit a site you may suggest a title. The title you suggest will be edited, especially if it is long. Open Directory guidelines state that the title should only be the official name of the site, without keywords; however, this rule is not strictly enforced. Secondary results — Not applicable.

19. **Maximum length of keyword META tag:** Primary results — No relevance, Secondary results — Not applicable.

20. **Maximum length of description META tag:** Primary results — As with the Title tag, you may suggest a description. This description should be short, between 25 and 30 words. It will be edited. Secondary results — Not applicable.

21. **Comment tags considered for relevancy:** Primary results — No, Secondary results — No.

22. **Frame support:** Primary results — Not applicable, Secondary results — Yes.

23. **Image map support:** Primary results — Not applicable, Secondary results — No. Google cannot follow image map links.

24. **Accepts automated submissions:** Primary results — No, Secondary results — Yes.

25. **Indexes submitted pages only or conducts deep crawls:** Primary results — Not applicable, Secondary results — Google will conduct deep crawls; therefore it is not necessary to submit individual pages as long as you have submitted your main page.

26. **Instant spidering of submitted page:** Primary results — Not applicable, Secondary results — When submitting a site to Google, your URL is added to the list of sites to be spidered. There are no guarantees of your site being added to the index.

27. **Number of pages that can be submitted per day:** Primary results — Appears to be unlimited as long as you are submitting different sites to different categories. However, many of the editors are very picky about allowing sites into their categories, so be prepared for a lot of rejections. Secondary results — There is no maximum limit, however, the recommended number is one per day.

28. **Word stemming and plural sensitive:** Primary results — Yes, Secondary results — No.

29. **Case-sensitive searches:** Primary results — No, Secondary results — No.

30. **Alphabetical page listings:** Primary results — If you browse through the categories instead of using the search features, the page listings are alphabetical. Secondary results — No.

31. **Time to index page:** Primary results — 4-6 weeks, Secondary results — 1-4 weeks.

32. **Spam penalties:** Primary results — Banishment, Secondary results — Though Google seems to be quite lenient on spamming, spam techniques do not tend to help in achieving high rankings. Google ranks pages mainly by link popularity and body text, causing legitimate Web pages to rank higher.

33. **Refuses pages with META refresh:** Primary results — Not applicable, Secondary results — No.

34. **Refuses pages with invisible text:** Primary results — Not applicable, Secondary results — No.

35. **Refuses pages with "tiny text":** Primary results — Not applicable, Secondary results — No.

36. **Remove URL:** Primary results — No, Secondary results — It is not necessary to remove dead links. Google will find these on its own. Also, updated submissions are not necessary.

This information may be out of date by the time of publication. Because search engines frequently change their ranking algorithms and other page scoring variables, we have posted updates and revisions to these chapters on our Web site: http://www.iprospect.com/search-engine-chapters.htm.

Understanding the Results

The Netscape Search results page includes elements from many different sources as seen in the illustration on the following page, which shows results for the phrase "presidential candidates."

The "Partner Search Results" section provides those listings from GoTo.com. In this case, the first two listings have been returned. As part of

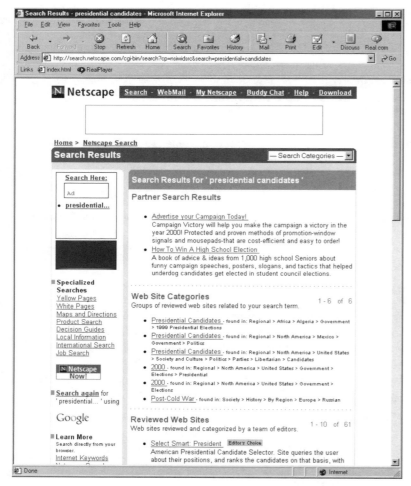

their agreement with AOL, GoTo.com is unable to provide very many of Netscape Search's results since it is a "pay-for-performance" engine. GoTo.com provides only "premium listings" for certain queries.

The "Netscape Pages" section was a recent addition. Its content is provided by various commerce partners. The number of available pages varies based on the search.

The "Web Site Categories" section appears if Open Directory lists categories when a phrase is queried. In this case, four categories, which are an exact match of those listed in Open Directory, appear for this query.

The "Reviewed Web Sites" section, usually the main portion of Netscape Search's returned results, lists those same sites reviewed by the Open Directory editors.

Included among these results is an "Editor's Choice," which may also be returned in Open Directory.

Also, if a visitor is unhappy with the results that have been returned, he or she can click on the link to Google on the left or AltaVista, Ask Jeeves, Excite, HotBot, LookSmart, or Lycos on the bottom and query the same phrase in one of these engines. Netscape Search provides its users with a great deal of choice.

Site Elements That Can Cause Problems

Site elements that can cause problems include query strings, frames, and redirecting pages. Please read the Open Directory and Google chapters to learn how these factors can influence your page's success.

Recommended Site Optimization Tactics

Please follow those site optimization tactics presented in the Open Directory and Google chapters.

Off-the-Page Factors That Influence Success

Off-the-page factors include link popularity, after-the-click behavior, and use of human editors. Please read the Open Directory and Google chapters to learn how these factors can influence your page's success.

How to Submit a Site to This Engine

Please follow those guidelines presented in the Open Directory and Google chapters for this information.

How to Build Informational Pages for this Engine

Informational pages for Netscape Search should be built according to those guidelines presented in the Open Directory and Google chapters.

How to Know If Your Site Has Been Spidered/Listed

Netscape Search does not directly spider pages. Please follow information provided in the Google chapter, as Open Directory is a human-edited directory.

Indexing Timetable

Please follow information outlined in the Open Directory and Google chapters to learn when your site should be indexed.

What to Do If Your Rankings Disappear

If your rankings disappear from Netscape Search, you should resubmit your site following the submission guidelines for Open Directory, Google, and GoTo.

Responsiveness and Help Provided

Because Netscape Search uses other search engines for its results, it is best to address any questions regarding search results to those search engines directly.

Chapter 28:

Northern Light

Northern Light Technology, Inc.
One Athenaeum Street
Cambridge, MA 02142
cs@NorthernLight.com
(617) 621-5100
Fax: (617) 621-3459

Free updates to this book are available via e-mail newsletter
by visiting: http://www.iprospect.com/book-news.htm.

Northern Light is a trademark of Northern Light Technology, Inc.

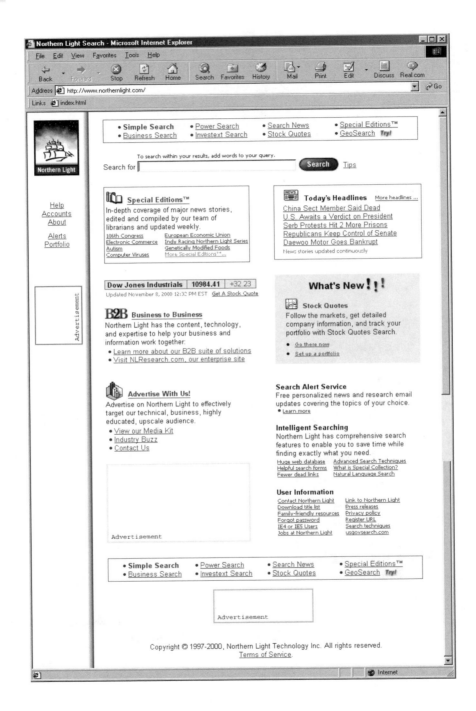

Facts about This Engine

Northern Light is a relatively new engine as it launched its one-page search service in August 1997. Because of this "late" release date, Northern Light may have hindered its ability to gain market share against better-known search engines and directories such as Yahoo! and AltaVista, two of the early bloomers. However, since then, Northern Light has been recognized as having one of the largest Web indexes of all the search engines. In addition, it provides an alternative service to its traditional search engine capabilities: access to over 1,800 publications including books, newspapers, magazines, full-text journals, and many more reference sources through its Special Collection™ online business library, making the engine popular among research professionals.

In order to continue the flow of useful information and prevent overload, Northern Light has devised a system that presents the returned results in a unique and organized fashion. This has been achieved by the development of the patented Custom Search Folders™ technology, which organizes those results based on subject matter, document type, document, source, and language in an effort to help narrow a user's search. For example, if a user types in the query "skiing in vermont," Northern Light returns such suggestions and/or alternatives as "camping & hiking," "ski resorts," "commercial sites," "cross-country skiing," and so on.

For the general results returned by the user query, Northern Light's rankings are sorted by relevance. The engine, however, does not take into consideration META tags, comment tags, or <ALT> tags when determining the relevancy of a page. Rather, Northern Light's spider, "Gulliver," indexes all visible text on a page, including frames and image maps, and then determines the relevancy, according to NorthernLight.com, by the presence and number of occurrences of query terms within the document.

1. **Web address:** http://www.northernlight.com/

2. **Type of engine:** Pure spider-based search engine

3. **Partnerships:** Broadwing, Compaq

4. **Total documents indexed:** 316,466,850 as of February 2001 (Source: NorthernLight.com)

5. **Total page views per month:** 76,331,000 (Source: Alexa Research, Feb. 2001)

6. **E-mail support:** cs@NorthernLight.com

7. **How to confirm listing:** url:http://www.yoursite.com

8. **Obtain link popularity information:** link:http://www.yoursite.com

9. **Result returns:** Northern Light ranks its results by relevance. Concurrently, Northern Light's patented Custom Search Folders™ organize the same documents based on subject matter, document type, source, and language. A Northern Light visitor can also choose to search for a document in the Special Editions™ listings. This area can be accessed from the bar at the top of the page.

10. **Receive higher rankings for link popularity:** Yes

11. **Additional off-the-page considerations:** Presents results in lists as well as folders.

12. **Rankings influenced by after-the-click behavior:** No

13. **Recognition and utilization of META tags:** The Northern Light crawler does "make note" of META tags; however, the keywords contained therein have not been proven to have any impact on positioning within the results, nor do META tags control the site descriptions on the results page.

14. **Consideration of META tags for relevancy:** No

15. **Importance of Title tag keyword prominence:** Yes

16. **Importance of <ALT> tag:** Northern Light does not support <ALT> tags.

17. **Importance of multiple occurrences of keywords in Title tag:** None

18. **Maximum length of Title tag:** 80 characters

19. **Maximum length of keyword META tag:** Unconfirmed

20. **Maximum length of description META tag:** 200 characters

21. **Comment tags considered for relevancy:** No

22. **Frame support:** Yes

23. **Image map support:** Yes

24. **Accepts automated submissions:** Yes

25. **Indexes submitted pages only or conducts deep crawls:** The Northern Light spider indexes all visible text on the page and will follow and index all of the links found on the page.

26. **Instant spidering of submitted page:** Yes

27. **Number of pages that can be submitted per day:** No more than 5 pages should be submitted per day.

28. **Word stemming and plural sensitive:** No

29. **Case-sensitive searches:** Yes

30. **Alphabetical page listings:** No

31. **Time to index page:** 2-6 weeks

32. **Spam penalties:** To date, Northern Light has posted no information about their spam policy. Unfortunately, due to the nature of its ranking algorithm (basing a site's relevance on the number of occurrences of query terms within the document) Northern Light has had to deal with spam.

33. **Refuses pages with META refresh:** Unconfirmed

34. **Refuses pages with invisible text:** No

35. **Refuses pages with "tiny text":** Unconfirmed

36. **Remove URL:** Send a request using the form at http://www.northernlight.com/docs/gen_help_comments.html

This information may be out of date by the time of publication. Because search engines frequently change their ranking algorithms and other page scoring variables, we have posted updates and revisions to these chapters on our Web site: http://www.iprospect.com/search-engine-chapters.htm.

Understanding the Results

Northern Light presents its results in two parts, a list of sites sorted by relevancy and those same sites categorized and organized into folders via Northern Light's patented Custom Search Folders™ technology. At the heart of these results is the main list of sites, which are sorted according to Northern Light's relevancy algorithm, ranking those pages with more occurrences of the queried search term or phrase higher within the search results. These sites are listed 10

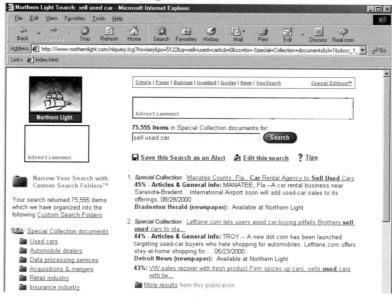

Company information
Sales & marketing
Loans
Antiques & collectibles
Sport utility vehicles (SUVs)
all others...

US Patent 5,924,090

Home   Help   Accounts
About   Alerts   Portfolio

3. *Special Collection* Avis, Navidec to **sell used** cars online
   44% - Articles & General info: Navidec and Avis Europe formed a joint venture to launch an online used car buying service in Europe 03/13/2000
   Automotive News Europe - United Kingdom (magazine): Available at Northern Light
   More results from this publication

4. *Special Collection* BESTOFFER.COM OFFERS 'FREE FOR ALL' PREVIEW OF PAINLESS WAY TO BUY AND **SELL USED**...
   44% - Press releases: SAN FRANCISCO, Dec 14, 1999 /PRNewswire via COMTEX/ -- Consumers can say goodbye to the headaches and hassles of buying and selling used cars today with ... 12/14/1999
   PR Newswire: Available at Northern Light
   44%: BESTOFFER.COM ASSEMBLES MARKETING TEAM TO LAUNCH BETTER WAY TO BUY AND **SELL USED** ...
   More results from this publication

5. *Special Collection* Avis teams with Net company to **sell used** cars
   44% - Articles & General info: Avis Europe PLC and Navidec Inc to jointly launch online used-car buying service in the UK in 2000 and then expand into other European ... 03/06/2000
   Automotive News (magazine): Available at Northern Light
   43%: Seattle Internet company sells **used** cars sight unseen
   More results from this publication

6. *Special Collection* Used-car dealer sells via the Web IMotors.com uses Internet to find, **sell used** c...
   44% - Articles & General info: Elk Grove, Calif. -IMotors.com has turned two parking lots plus the large industrial warehouse in between into a used-car assembly line for the ... 03/04/2000
   Des Moines Register (newspaper): Available at Northern Light
   More results from this publication

7. *Special Collection* Avis Europe plc Announcement of Joint Venture to **Sell Used** Cars Over the Interne...
   44% - Press releases: BRACKNELL, Berkshire, Feb 24, 2000 (BUSINESS WIRE) -- Avis Europe plc, the leading car rental company in Europe, Africa, the Middle East and Asia, today announced ... 02/24/2000
   Business Wire (newswire): Available at Northern Light
   40%: CarDay Inc. Signs Strategic Agreement With carOrder.com; CarDay Exchange Service ...
   More results from this publication

8. *Special Collection* ****Ford Wants Court's Help To **Sell Used** Cars Online
   43% - Articles & General info: Ford Motor Co. [NYSE:F] is turning to a federal court for the green light to market used cars to Texans over the Web. 12/07/1999
   Newsbytes (newswire): Available at Northern Light

9. *Special Collection* AUTOBYTEL JAPAN FINDS 3 PARTNERS TO **SELL USED** CARS
   42% - Articles & General info: Story Filed: Friday, August 26, 1999 11:51 PM EST TOKYO, Aug 27, 1999 (Asia Pulse via COMTEX) -- Autobytel Japan announced Thursday that it will ... 08/26/1999
   Asia Pulse (newswire): Available at Northern Light
   More results from this publication

10. *Special Collection* Dealership can't **sell used** cars on lot, but another business use may be fine
    42% - Articles & General info: An Overland Park car dealership on Metcalf Avenue was incorrectly identified in Shawnee Mission Star stories on Sept. 10 and Wednsday. The dealership, which had ... 10/08/1997
    Kansas City Star (newspaper): Available at Northern Light
    More results from this publication

[Next Page]

[sell used car] (Search)   Tips
                                 Edit this search

Simple | Power | Business | Investext | Quotes | News | GeoSearch   Special Editions™

per page. To view additional results from the same query, click on the Next Page button at the bottom of the page. This will deliver another list of relevant sites.

Concurrently, Northern Light delivers those same results categorized via its Custom Search Folders™ technology, which organizes the results based on subject matter, document type, document source, and language. A section of the search folder includes matches that appear to include Northern Light's Special Collection documents.

When one of the Special Collection documents is selected, the visitor is presented with bibliographic information including the site's title, a summary of the article, the document's source, and the price of the article, which can range from $1 to $4. An example is provided below.

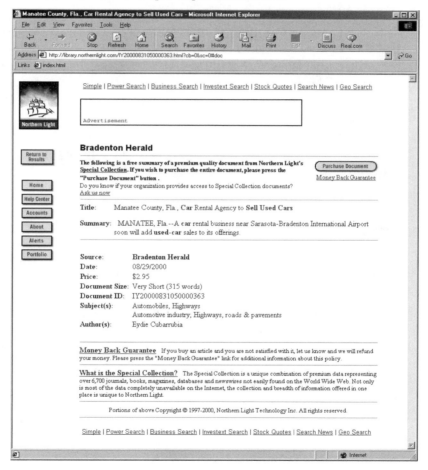

Site Elements That Can Cause Problems

When submitting a site to Northern Light, there are a number of elements you should avoid because they can cause problems and diminish your rankings. Such items include query strings, cookies, and broken links.

Like many search engines, Northern Light cannot index pages that contain query strings. If a page is submitted that contains a query string, you will receive an error message that states the following: "Sorry, we only process text or HTML pages, we look for extensions of: .html .htm .shtml .stm .asp .phtml .cfm .php3 .php .jsp .jhtml .asc .text .txt."

Since Northern Light excludes pages with query strings, you must ensure that this method for tracking visitors on your site is kept to a minimum.

Pages that require that the visitor accept a cookie in order to load also pose a problem. This is due to the fact that the Northern Light spider will not accept cookies as it crawls the page, making it impossible to index your site. Therefore, it is imperative that your pages load without cookies.

Broken links can also create problems. Acting as a dead end, they prevent Northern Light's spider from crawling and indexing all pages on your site. Consequently, your site will not reach its full ranking potential if you have broken links.

Recommended Site Optimization Tactics

Northern Light has a very interesting relevancy algorithm. Northern Light does not take into consideration your keyword META tag, description META tag, <ALT> tag, or comment tag to determine your site's relevance. Instead, Northern Light focuses on your site's Title tag and the first 250 words of viewable copy. The engine utilizes copy from both of these areas to create the Web site's description that appears in the search results. Because of this, it is important to ensure that your title and first words of visible text do not say the same thing, thereby eliminating redundancy. Therefore, when optimizing your site for Northern Light, pay particular attention to the development of the Title tag and opening copy on the page.

Off-the-Page Factors That Influence Success

Along with the importance of the Title tag and visible text on the page, Northern Light's ranking algorithm also takes link popularity into account to determine the relevancy of a particular site. While it is important to have many sites linking to your site, it is more important to ensure that at least a few of those links are of high quality. To determine which sites link to your site within the Northern Light search engine, type "link:http://www.yoursite.com" in the search box.

How to Submit a Site to This Engine

To submit your URL to Northern Light, go to the "Register URL" link contained in the user information section of the home page.

You must submit your URL and include your name and e-mail address. If accepted, within six weeks your site will be spidered, indexed, and added to the Northern Light database.

Northern Light's spider, "Gulliver," deep crawls your Web site and the engine has made it a point that it is unnecessary to submit more than one page from your Web site because Gulliver follows the links throughout your site and indexes each page. Internal pages, however, can be submitted to Northern Light if they are added in small numbers; no more than five pages of any site should be submitted on any given day. Northern Light's spider also crawls the Web on a continuous basis in search of new information to add to its index and to update existing pages. If, however, you have recently updated the content of your site, it is best to resubmit that page.

How to Build Informational Pages for this Engine

Northern Light places a great deal of emphasis on the Title tag and the actual copy within your site. Therefore, just as a regular site should incorporate certain elements to achieve higher rankings, so too should your informational pages.

When your site is listed in Northern Light, your Title tag will be used in the returned results as the link to your page. The description will automatically be created from a combination of your Title tag and the first 250 characters of visible text on your page. With this unique combination of elements, which is used to create and develop your relevancy, it is important to integrate pertinent information in these two areas and, ideally, focus on three or four main keywords in your title and opening copy. The purpose of targeting three or four keywords is that when Northern Light automatically generates the description, the information will not be redundant but will contain those targeted keywords that relate directly to your page, thereby attracting the most qualified traffic.

Creating a page with at least 200 words of copy with good syntax and a natural language flow is also imperative to increase the credibility of the site. You should also remember to include those three to four focused keywords throughout the copy as well.

How to Know If Your Site Has Been Spidered/Listed

Northern Light's list of spiders and their IP addresses are provided below. This information will be included in your site's log files after the spider has visited. Northern Light's spider will follow all links on your Web site and index them (before you submit, make sure you check for broken links as they act as a dead end). According to Northern Light, the spiders fetch a maximum of one page per minute, thus keeping the impact on your site to a minimum.

208.219.77.29	marvin.northernlight.com
208.219.77.19	scooby.northernlight.com
208.219.77.9	taz.northernlight.com
216.34.109.190	sherman.waltham.northernlight.com
216.34.109.191	natasha.waltham.northernlight.com
216.34.109.192	dudley.waltham.northernlight.com

Indexing Timetable

Getting listed in Northern Light typically takes two to four weeks. Recently, however, a message appeared on the Northern Light Web site stating, "Our average turnaround time for submitted sites to appear in our index is about six weeks." In our experience, six weeks has been the longest it has taken for a Web site to be indexed with Northern Light.

What to Do If Your Rankings Disappear

Like any spider-based search engine, Northern Light is continually updating its index of sites. Often, your pages will drop in position or fall out of the index altogether. It is important to properly react to a drop in rankings. The initial reaction is usually to quickly resubmit all of your ranking pages. However, this massive amount of submissions is considered spamming the index. When you see pages drop, it is often because the database is being modified in some way. Certain elements of the database may not be available all the time, so it is important to check back often to see if your site has returned. After a few days have passed and your rankings have not returned, you should begin the process of resubmitting according to the terms and conditions of Northern Light. If your rankings still do not reappear over the course of a few weeks, you may need to readjust your Title tag and/or the copy on your site.

Special Tips and Tactics for This Engine

Creating a descriptive Title tag and working to achieve a balance between the copy on your site and the keywords that you are focusing on are the most important items to pay attention to when optimizing your site for Northern Light. If you follow those guidelines, you should be able to achieve a good representation of your site within Northern Light's results.

While you should include your targeted keywords throughout your Web site's copy, make sure you do not overdo it. Northern Light has not posted specific information regarding their submission guidelines; however, we believe they're able to detect spam. Furthermore, it is safest not to spam any engine, thereby eliminating any chances of having your site rejected or banned.

Responsiveness and Help Provided

Northern Light's site offers many useful FAQ pages to help its users not only complete successful searches but also create and develop a Web site to rank well.

Specific questions can be e-mailed to cs@NorthernLight.com. The responses that we received for our questions were a bit vague and we recommend calling Northern Light's Customer Service number at (617) 621-5100 as an alternative. We were successful in contacting and speaking with a customer service representative and found his answers to be helpful.

Chapter 29:

Open Directory

Netscape Communications Corporation
501 E. Middlefield Road
Mountain View, CA 94043-4042
info@netscape.com
(650) 254-1900
Fax: (650) 528-4124

Free updates to this book are available via e-mail newsletter
by visiting: http://www.iprospect.com/book-news.htm.

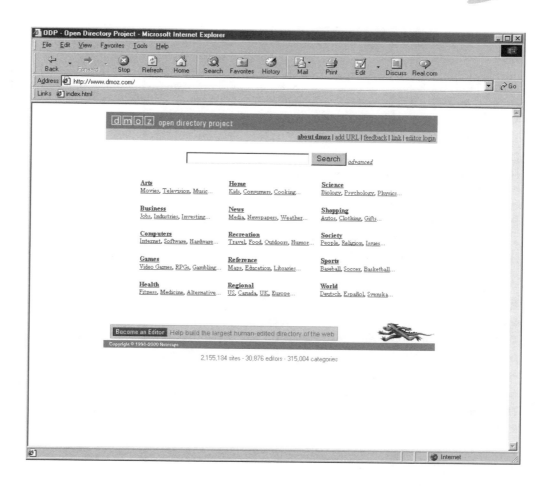

Facts about This Engine

The Open Directory Project is owned by Netscape Communications, which is in turn owned by America Online. The irony here is that while America Online is the king of proprietary content, the Open Directory Project sees itself as an extension of the open source movement. The Open Directory is staffed by nearly 30,000 volunteer editors.

The Open Directory is not really as important to a search engine positioning campaign as a standalone search engine; however, it provides its data to many other search engines including Lycos, America Online, Direct Hit, Google, and many other engines.

1. **Web address:** http://www.dmoz.org

2. **Type of engine:** Directory

3. **Partnerships:** Owned by Netscape, which is in turn owned by America Online. The Open Directory data is freely available to anyone who abides by the terms of an open license. Many other search engines, including Ask Jeeves, Google, and AOL, use this data.

4. **Total documents indexed:** Over two million.

5. **Total page views per month:** 84,522,000 (Source: Alexa Research, Feb. 2001)

6. **E-mail support:** staff@dmoz.org

7. **How to confirm listing:** Either browse to the category you submitted to or search for words in your description.

8. **Obtain link popularity information:** Not applicable; directories do not spider sites.

9. **Result returns:** Returns categories first, then individual listings.

10. **Receive higher rankings for link popularity:** Not applicable

11. **Additional off-the-page considerations:** The Open Directory is made up by scores of volunteer editors. As of September 2000, there were over 29,000 editors. These editors have full control over their categories, including the site title and description.

12. **Rankings influenced by after-the-click behavior:** No

13. **Recognition and utilization of META tags:** Not applicable

14. **Consideration of META tags for relevancy:** Not applicable

15. **Importance of Title tag keyword prominence:** Not applicable

16. **Importance of <ALT> tag:** Not applicable

17. **Importance of multiple occurrences of keywords in Title tag:** None

18. **Maximum length of Title tag:** While actual META tags are not used by Open Directory, when you submit a site you may suggest a title. The title you suggest will be edited, especially if it is long. Open Directory guidelines state that the title should only be the official name of the site — no keywords; however, this rule is not strictly enforced.

19. **Maximum length of keyword META tag:** No relevance

20. **Maximum length of description META tag:** As with the Title tag, you may suggest a description. This description should be short, between 25 and 30 words. It will be edited.

21. **Comment tags considered for relevancy:** No

22. **Frame support:** Not applicable

23. **Image map support:** Not applicable

24. **Accepts automated submissions:** No

25. **Indexes submitted pages only or conducts deep crawls:** Not applicable

26. **Instant spidering of submitted page:** Not applicable

27. **Number of pages that can be submitted per day:** Appears to be unlimited as long as you are submitting different sites to different categories. However, many of the editors are very picky about allowing sites into their categories, so be prepared for a lot of rejections.

28. **Word stemming and plural sensitive:** Yes

29. **Case-sensitive searches:** No

30. **Alphabetical page listings:** If you browse through the categories instead of using the search features, the page listings are alphabetical.
31. **Time to index page:** 4 to 6 weeks
32. **Spam penalties:** Banishment
33. **Refuses pages with META refresh:** Not applicable
34. **Refuses pages with invisible text:** Not applicable
35. **Refuses pages with "tiny text":** Not applicable
36. **Remove URL:** None

This information may be out of date by the time of publication. Because search engines frequently change their ranking algorithms and other page scoring variables, we have posted updates and revisions to these chapters on our Web site: http://www.iprospect.com/search-engine-chapters.htm.

Understanding the Results

As you can see in the figure on the following page, the results are broken into two sections. The first section is Open Directory Categories. This section displays categories that match our query. Note that no matter how many categories match the query, only five will be shown. Below the category listings are Open Directory Sites. These show individual Web sites that match the query. The sites are displayed according to a simple relevance score.

Recommended Site Optimization Tactics

The first step is just to get your site into the Open Directory. This is not always easy. The submission of your main page, that is http://www.yoursite.com, should be approached with great care. Find the category that best describes your site and look at the titles and descriptions in that category. A good strategy is to use the same style of language for your title and description suggestions as the editor of that category has used to describe other sites.

Off-the-Page Factors That Influence Success

The best way to be successful in the Open Directory is to build an informative, attractive site with valuable content. Then submit this site to an appropriate category with a good title and description.

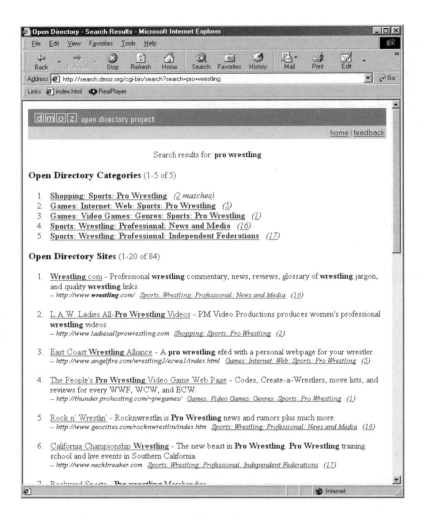

How to Submit a Site to This Engine

Information about submitting a site to the Open Directory can be found by clicking on the "Add URL" link of the home page.

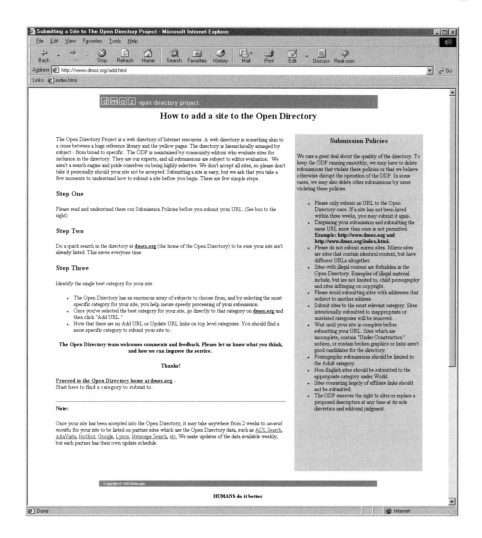

How to Build Informational Pages for this Engine

Do not build informational pages for Open Directory. Submission policies can also be found at http://www.dmoz.org/add.html.

How to Know If Your Site Has Been Spidered/Listed

Search for your URL.

Indexing Timetable

As the Open Directory is a human-edited directory staffed by volunteers, there is no set schedule for indexing. It can take four to six weeks to get into the Open Directory and even longer — up to several months — for your submission to get picked up by other search engines that use Open Directory data.

What to Do If Your Rankings Disappear

If all your rankings disappear at once, it is likely that the Open Directory has determined that you violated their submission policies in some way. If you lose all your submissions across multiple categories with different editors, then you have probably been banned. If this happens, you can try to appeal your banishment to Open Directory staff at staff@dmoz.org. However, if you have violated the submission policies it is extremely unlikely that the staff will reinstate you.

If you lost just a few rankings, then there are several different things that may have happened. An editor of one of your categories may have decided that your site was no longer relevant and deleted it. Or periodically, the Open Directory goes through reorganization on different levels. Depending on the level of reorganization you may lose rankings temporarily or permanently. The best thing to do is to wait a week or two and resubmit any purged sites.

Special Tips and Tactics for This Engine

The best advice when dealing with the Open Directory is to follow the submission policies outlined at http://www.dmoz.org/add.html.

In a recent interview graciously granted to the author, one of the Open Directory founders noted that primary consideration is given to the quality of the editor application. When you are ready to submit your site to the Open Directory, be sure that the site is ready for visitors; the worst possible mistake would be to have an editor visit a site under construction or that does not load. Then, make sure that you carefully select where your site best fits. Don't shoot for the top-level category if a subcategory more accurately reflects your site.

One of the best tactics for getting your site listed is to become a volunteer editor. To do this, navigate to the category you are interested in editing and hit the "become an editor" link. This will bring up an application form. See http://dmoz.org/cgi-bin/apply.cgi?where=Home/Urban_Living for an example.

The form asks you to explain your expertise and interest in the chosen category as well as your business affiliation with the category. You cannot expect to become the editor of a category that directly relates to your business, so choose a category that genuinely interests you. You should also begin by seeking to edit a subcategory and should not try to move too quickly to the top category level. Concentrate on doing a good job with your initial subcategory, and you will advance.

The editor's application form also asks you to provide two or three URLs, with titles and descriptions, which you think should be added to the category. This is the most important part of the form. Think of this as a job application and really put some effort into it. My experience suggests that you should always suggest three URLs. This improves your chances of being selected as an editor. Once you have been an editor for a while, you can ask to edit additional subcategories or categories. Additional categories are granted on the basis of your editing history. If you put in enough time and effort and you don't garner too many complaints, you may become a high-level editor, a "meta-editor," or even an "editall." It takes a lot of devotion to achieve this status. However, as an editor of multiple subcategories or categories, you have some input into the sites that are included for the topic and how they are represented. This gives you significant power over how the listings for your category will look in the future. Being an Open Directory editor gives you control and input into how your category develops. This can be particularly important if you have a keen interest in the performance of specific sites in the category.

Responsiveness and Help Provided

The Open Directory can be very responsive and helpful, or not. It depends on the editor you've contacted. If you need help and the editor of your category won't respond, go to the parent of that category and ask an editor there for help.

Chapter 30:

Raging Search

Raging Search
1040 Arastradero Road
Palo Alto, CA 94304
(978) 247-5500

Free updates to this book are available via e-mail newsletter
by visiting: http://www.iprospect.com/book-news.htm.

Raging Search is a trademark of AltaVista Company.

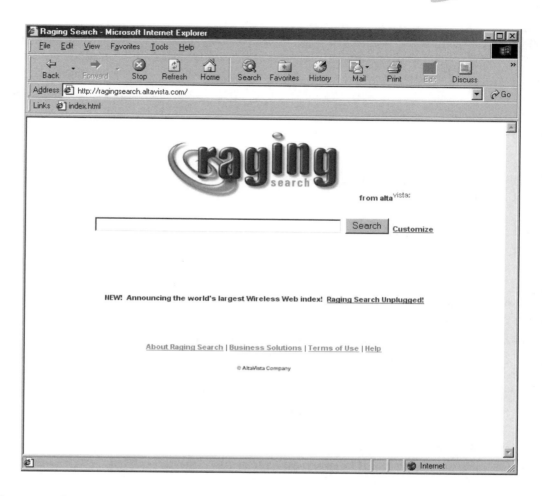

Facts about This Engine

AltaVista created the Raging Search engine in May 2000. Raging Search was billed as a simple search engine that would provide fast and relevant results. This form of simple search was designed to capture a growing number of users who are increasingly using engines such as Google because of the easy-to-use interface and relevant results. In essence, Raging Search was designed to remain free of the clutter and spam that is increasingly haunting search results.

Fredrick Marckini – iProspect.com

It is interesting to note that searches for numerous phrases produce the same results on AltaVista and Raging Search. Yet, on other phrases, the results are different. Raging Search uses AltaVista's database and submissions. However, it appears that some additional factors are being considered on some searches.

1. **Web address:** http://www.raging.com
2. **Type of engine:** Spider
3. **Partnerships:** Owned by AltaVista
4. **Total documents indexed:** Over 350 million unique Web pages
5. **Total page views per month:** 243,000 (Source: Alexa Research, Feb. 2001)
6. **E-mail support:** feedback@raging.com
7. **How to confirm listing:** host://www.yoursite.com
8. **Obtain link popularity information:** link://www.domain.com
9. **Result returns:** All from own database.
10. **Receive higher rankings for link popularity:** Yes
11. **Additional off-the-page considerations:** None
12. **Rankings influenced by after-the-click behavior:** No
13. **Recognition and utilization of META tags:** Yes
14. **Consideration of META tags for relevancy:** Yes
15. **Importance of Title tag keyword prominence:** Yes
16. **Importance of <ALT> tag:** Unconfirmed
17. **Importance of multiple occurrences of keywords in Title tag:** Yes
18. **Maximum length of Title tag:** 417 characters
19. **Maximum length of keyword META tag:** 1,017 characters
20. **Maximum length of description META tag:** 1,017 characters
21. **Comment tags considered for relevancy:** Unconfirmed
22. **Frame support:** Yes
23. **Image map support:** Unconfirmed
24. **Accepts automated submissions:** No
25. **Indexes submitted pages only or conducts deep crawls:** Accepts no submissions
26. **Instant spidering of submitted page:** Accepts no pages
27. **Number of pages that can be submitted per day:** None
28. **Word stemming and plural sensitive:** No
29. **Case-sensitive searches:** Yes
30. **Alphabetical page listings:** No
31. **Time to index page:** Serves AltaVista database
32. **Spam penalties:** Banned URL

33.   **Refuses pages with META refresh:** Unconfirmed
34.   **Refuses pages with invisible text:** Yes
35.   **Refuses pages with "tiny text":** Unconfirmed
36.   **Remove URL:** None

This information may be out of date by the time of publication. Because search engines frequently change their ranking algorithms and other page scoring variables, we have posted updates and revisions to these chapters on our Web site: http://www.iprospect.com/search-engine-chapters.htm.

Understanding the Results

Raging Search displays 10 search results per page. These results are all served by AltaVista.

Notice that directly below the search box, Raging Search lists the number of pages returned. This information is important for determining how many other people are competing for the number one placement of the phrase you're targeting. Certain phrases might be too competitive, and therefore you will benefit from more clearly defining your audience.

Each of the 10 results contains a title, description, and URL listing. Most of the results also show "More like this" and "Results from this site only" links. The "More like this" link leads you to pages that either link to that page or are deemed by Raging Search as associated pages. The "Results from this site only" section shows pages from the same URL as the one that achieved a ranking.

Below the search results, Raging Search displays a list of related search terms. These are searches that also contain the words for which you searched. It is helpful to examine this list of words, as you may find phrases that you did not think of or that are capable of bringing a more defined audience to your site.

At the bottom of the search results page, Raging Search shows a list of additional resources. These include the option to search for the item you queried on several of Raging Search's affiliate sites. You can also jump to AltaVista to conduct your search.

Site Elements That Can Cause Problems

Since Raging Search uses AltaVista's spider, problems arise with frames, cookies, broken links, user input pages, page redirects, and graphic-intensive pages. It is best to avoid these elements altogether. However, for a more detailed discussions of the problems caused by these elements, see Chapter 13 on AltaVista.

Recommended Site Optimization Tactics

Raging Search has its own algorithm to determine relevancy. It is safe to say that words in the Title tag and on the viewable page will attain the greatest results. See the chapter on AltaVista for more detailed instructions about achieving rankings.

Off-the-Page Factors That Influence Success

Again, Raging Search has followed AltaVista and implemented link popularity as an element in determining rankings.

How to Submit a Site to This Engine

See the section in the AltaVista chapter about how to submit your site. Sites added to the AltaVista search engine are listed in Raging Search, so submit to AltaVista.

How to Build Informational Pages for this Engine

The chapter on AltaVista shows how to build informational pages geared for AltaVista. Please refer to the Chapter 13 for tips on how to build informational pages for Raging Search.

How to Know If Your Site Has Been Spidered/Listed

Please refer to the AltaVista chapter for information regarding the names and IP numbers of their spiders.

Indexing Timetable

It typically takes two to four weeks to get indexed by AltaVista and a few more days to become searchable in Raging Search. As is the case with AltaVista, you can actually hurt your rankings by submitting too often.

What to Do If Your Rankings Disappear

Refer to the chapter on AltaVista.

Special Tips and Tactics for This Engine

Refer to the chapter on AltaVista.

Responsiveness and Help Provided

Raging Search contains a useful help section located at http://ragingsearch .altavista.com/cgi-bin/query?pg=acc&v=help. This page offers numerous tips about searching on Raging Search. The e-mail support is feedback@raging.com. We received adequate help. However, it is difficult to reach a human.

Chapter 31:

WebCrawler

Excite@Home
450 Broadway Street
Redwood City, CA 94063
(650) 556-5665
Fax: (650) 556-5006

Free updates to this book are available via e-mail newsletter
by visiting: http://www.iprospect.com/book-news.htm.

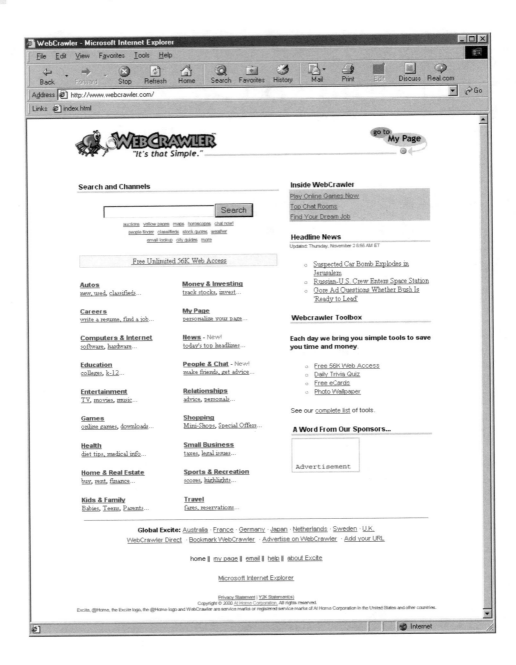

Facts about This Engine

WebCrawler is historically regarded as the first "true search engine." Ironically enough, it began as what essentially was a homework project at the University of Washington. In 1994, computer science and engineering students and faculty at UW held a seminar to talk about the inception and future potential of the Web. This led to the generation of several small project assignments. A student named Brian Pinkerton came up with a small application project called "The WebCrawler." Pinkerton's classmates, impressed by the project, encouraged him to build a more usable interface. That interface debuted on April 20, 1994; at the time, it contained information drawn from over 6,000 different Web servers. By October 1994, WebCrawler was receiving an average of 15,000 search queries per day.

As WebCrawler continued to expand, a Seattle company called Dealernet offered it sponsorship, donating a server in exchange for the display of the Dealernet logo on WebCrawler's home page. Also at this time, the company Starwave signed on as an additional sponsor, offering to financially support Brian Pinkerton in his effort to promote and expand WebCrawler's presence and capabilities.

By early 1995, WebCrawler was in dire straits: It was so massive and so popular that it was rapidly exceeding the resources available to it. Pinkerton had a goal of reaching out to one million Internet users, but his dream proved too much to be contained merely within a university's research department. WebCrawler was sold to AOL and relocated to San Francisco in March 1995.

Although myriad competitors quickly emerged, WebCrawler remained successful, and is regarded today as the first full-text search engine on the Internet. In November 1996, WebCrawler was purchased by Excite, Inc. The primary difference between Excite and WebCrawler is the interface. Despite Excite's heavy influence on the engine, WebCrawler's site and search box remain distinctly different in appearance and functionality.

1.   **Web address:** http://www.webcrawler.com

2.   **Type of engine:** Hybrid

3.   **Partnerships:** Now owned and operated by Excite. Excite also has ties to the LookSmart Network through a submitting option called Express Submit. This option provides access to several partner sites in addition to LookSmart itself, including Excite, MSN, AltaVista, Time Warner, CNN, Net Zero, and over 370 other ISPs.

4.   **Total documents indexed:** 2 million

5.   **Total page views per month:** 47,220,000 (Source: Alexa Research, Feb. 2001)

6.   **E-mail support:** http://www.excite.com/feedback

7.   **How to confirm listing:** Type in your full URL.

8.   **Obtain link popularity information:** No

9.   **Result returns:** WebCrawler Directory matches from LookSmart, Web Results from Excite (up to 25), then News Stories, followed by a link to Excite Search with the invitation to try a "more comprehensive search."

10. **Receive higher rankings for link popularity:** Yes

11. **Additional off-the-page considerations:** Directory listings are controlled by human editors.

12. **Rankings influenced by after-the-click behavior:** No

13. **Recognition and utilization of META tags:** Yes, emphasis on the Title and description META tags.

14. **Consideration of META tags for relevancy:** Yes

15. **Importance of Title tag keyword prominence:** Yes

16. **Importance of <ALT> tag:** No

17. **Importance of multiple occurrences of keywords in Title tag:** No

18. **Maximum length of Title tag:** None specified. However, it is a general assumption that Excite crops any Title tags longer than five or six words.

19. **Maximum length of keyword META tag:** Unconfirmed

20. **Maximum length of description META tag:** Unconfirmed

21. **Comment tags considered for relevancy:** No

22. **Frame support:** No

23. **Image map support:** No

24. **Accepts automated submissions:** No

25. **Indexes submitted pages only or conducts deep crawls:** Accepts submitted pages, but rarely crawls other pages

26. **Instant spidering of submitted page:** No

27. **Number of pages that can be submitted per day:** No published limit

28. **Word stemming and plural sensitive:** No

29. **Case-sensitive searches:** No

30. **Alphabetical page listings:** Yes, for category listings.

31. **Time to index page:** Uses Excite's index (4-6 weeks).

32. **Spam penalties:** None listed

33. **Refuses pages with META refresh:** Unconfirmed
34. **Refuses pages with invisible text:** Unconfirmed
35. **Refuses pages with "tiny text":** Unconfirmed
36. **Remove URL:** Either remove the page and resubmit the URL (when spidered your page will be removed) or add a robots.txt file to exclude spiders (your page will not be crawled again and the listing will be removed).

This information may be out of date by the time of publication. Because search engines frequently change their ranking algorithms and other page scoring variables, we have posted updates and revisions to these chapters on our Web site: http://www.iprospect.com/search-engine-chapters.htm.

Understanding the Results

WebCrawler presents its return results in a manner decidedly unique from other search engines. The first option you will see at the top of the results page (shown on the following page) is "Directory Matches for: *Your Topic*." These matches appear as links to relevant WebCrawler directory categories, with brief descriptions in the format "Includes: keyword phrase, keyword phrase, keyword phrase."

The next option on the page is "Web Results for: *Your Topic*." Typically, WebCrawler will return 25 results, showing the full number of matches found in parentheses. You will also have the option of viewing summaries for these Web results, which occur as different Web sites within the Internet. You will be able to click through additional return results in series of 25.

Finally, at the bottom of the page is the heading "News Stories about: *Your Topic*," featuring links to major newspapers with stories including the phrase for which you have searched. And, if you are still not satisfied, you have the option of clicking on "For More Comprehensive Results, Try Excite Search," leading directly to Excite's return results on the same phrase.

It is believed that recently Excite stopped maintaining a separate database at WebCrawler. Currently, it appears that search results at WebCrawler are identical to those at Excite. As such, optimization techniques applied for Excite translate into rankings at WebCrawler.

Site Elements That Can Cause Problems

Excite and WebCrawler will not accept, spider, or list any sites containing frames. If your site must contain frames, be sure to implement a

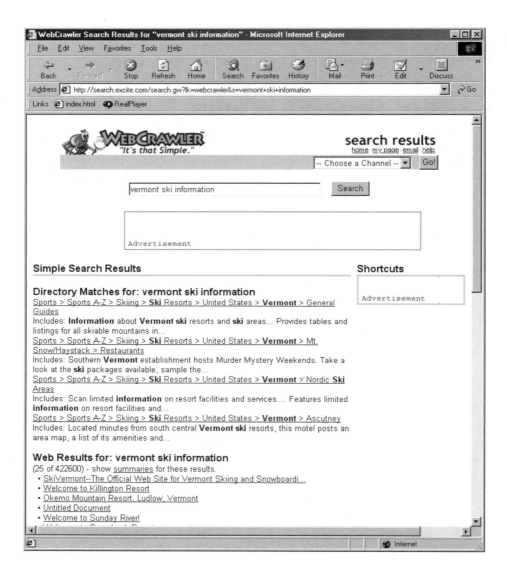

<NOFRAMES> tag somewhere within your source code. Redirects and other similar stealth tactics, while not explicitly mentioned in Excite's terms of service, are extremely risky, and should be avoided at all costs in order to ensure a clean and successful submission attempt.

Recommended Site Optimization Tactics

Remember that Excite (and, consequently, WebCrawler) places considerable importance upon keywords, particularly those in the description META tag. Make certain you include meaningful keywords in that tag in order to optimize your site to its fullest potential. In contrast, the keyword META tag has almost no relevance — concentrate on your description tag, and you can leave out the keyword tag altogether. Also, pay attention to your Title tag. Place the most important keywords near the beginning of your title.

To give site owners more say in how Excite Search represents their pages in its result returns, the Excite indexing process first looks for the presence of a description META tag before trying to generate its own summary, which is usually drawn from page content. If a document has a description META tag, Excite Search will use its contents as the summary of that document when the page shows up in search results.

If you'd like to write your own summary instead of having Excite generate one for you, you can specify your summary in the header of your page as follows:

```
<HTML>
<HEAD>
<TITLE>Buy Yellow Umbrellas</TITLE>
<META NAME="DESCRIPTION" CONTENT="Locate yellow umbrellas for rain
protection, comfort in inclement weather, and trendy fashion statements.">
</HEAD>
<BODY>
</BODY>
</HTML>
```

This way, when your page shows up in Excite Search results, a potential yellow umbrella purchaser will see the summary for it just as you intended them to see it.

Off-the-Page Factors That Influence Success

WebCrawler also values link popularity, i.e., how many sites link to you, and how many sites in turn link to those sites that link to you. It is therefore vital to the success of your search engine campaign that you improve your link popularity. See Chapter 5 for more on link popularity.

How to Submit a Site to This Engine

To submit a site to the Excite database, which powers WebCrawler, go to the "Add Your URL" page off the home page. You will have the option of submitting via Express Submit or Basic Submit, or to Excite. The Express Submit will send your listing to LookSmart's editors for inclusion into the entire LookSmart network of sites. There is a $199 charge for each Express Submit (up to five URLs per domain can be submitted via this method). LookSmart makes no guarantee of inclusion or a preferential description; you are paying for a 48-hour review. Basic Submit costs $99 and offers review within eight weeks. The third option is to simply submit your site to the Excite and WebCrawler databases. Again, acceptance is not guaranteed. Indexing usually occurs in four to six weeks, although long blackouts have been known to occur. It is also important to note that WebCrawler claims that any submissions over 25 pages will result in human review to determine if the pages should be added.

How to Build Informational Pages for this Engine

Excite places significant importance upon keywords found in the URL. If at all possible, create informational pages on domain names consisting of at least two keywords strung together. Also, consider registering numerous domains to allow yourself to maximize your real estate.

Excite values keywords in the Title and description tags. Make certain to provide your own description META tag which contains keywords, or a description will be automatically created for you. Keep in mind that there is no substitute for content so make your pages talk about your keywords.

How to Know If Your Site Has Been Spidered/Listed

Please refer to Excite's list of spiders in Chapter 16.

Indexing Timetable

Uses Excite's database, which typically indexes sites within four to six weeks.

What to Do If Your Rankings Disappear

Industry insider information suggests that Excite's spider cycles through recently submitted sites, as well as existing sites in its database, every couple of weeks. Typically, it will begin by spidering the home page, and will follow links from there. As soon as Excite has located approximately 25 pages, it will add them to its index; the rest are then removed from Excite's database.

The downside of this seemingly random strategy is that vital pages can disappear, leaving relatively unimportant pages to stay, become indexed, and garner rankings. One solution is to add the following tag to those pages which you do not feel need to be indexed (as opposed to those that you consider essential to the success and promotion of your site):

```
<meta name="robots" content="noindex">
```

This tag is placed in the head section, along with the Title, description, and other tags. It simply lets Excite know that this page should not be indexed. This will allow the pages you want to stay to be indexed.

Unfortunately, there is a downside to using the <NOINDEX> tag: You can also only add 25 pages to every other engine that processes <NOINDEX> tags. This means that other search engines reading the tag — including those that might let you have far more than 25 pages ordinarily — will throw out all but 25 pages. It is up to you to determine whether this sacrifice is worth it in the long run.

Bear in mind that Excite has been known to experience "indexing blackouts," most recently in 1999, when it did not add new sites for over six months. Patience, continual reassessment and reoptimization of your site, and careful contemplation of the keywords in your description will allow you to overcome any such blackouts and remain consistently indexed.

Special Tips and Tactics for This Engine

When trying to achieve excellent real estate in WebCrawler, it is important to use the same tactics favored by Excite. See Chapter 16 for tips and tactics.

Responsiveness and Help Provided

Excite offers a fairly high level of interaction and information for search engine positioning professionals. Calls and e-mails to Excite are generally responded to quickly and thoroughly. Rather than contacting WebCrawler and having responses deferred to Excite, your best bet is to contact Excite directly.

Chapter 32:

Metasearch Engines

InfoSpace, Inc.
601 108th Ave. NE Suite 1200
Bellevue, WA 98004
Phone: (425) 201-6100
Fax: (425) 201-6150
E-mail: http://www.infospace.com/info/about/feedback.htm

Mamma
388 St. Jacques Street West
9th Floor
Montreal, QC
H2Y 1S1, Canada
Phone: (514) 844-2700
E-mail: search@mamma.com

Facts about Metasearch Engines

I had originally planned to discuss each metasearch engine as its own unique entity. However, after careful consideration I have decided that the concept of what a metasearch engine is and discussions regarding their general functionality is more important than specifics regarding each of the META engines. This chapter first discusses metasearch engines in general and then covers the four major players — Mamma and three properties owned by InfoSpace, Inc., Go2net.com, MetaCrawler, and Dogpile.

The idea behind metasearch engines is quite simple. If each of the major search engines is able to provide relevant content for a vast range of user queries, then logic would dictate that gathering up the results for several other engines and compiling them into an "all-star team" of results would produce more relevant returns. This is the very belief that engendered metasearch engines. By pulling information from numerous engines on the Web, metasearch engines claim to be most able to satisfy users' requests. There are many times when the results from engine to engine can vary and could contain a lot of irrelevant information. By using a metasearch engine, these problems are avoided. All of the results you want are available at one site, which avoids the tedious task of querying several search engines. However, the downside is that an individual search often takes much longer than a typical search engine query.

Operating a metasearch engine also has numerous benefits. First, since results are pulled from the provider engines at the time of a user's request, there is no database to maintain, and no spiders are needed to crawl content. Standard Web search engines use substantial storage space to store Web pages in their indexes. This need for storage does not exist at metasearch engines.

However, the very nature of a metasearch engine makes it impossible to focus on attaining results in specific metasearch engines. It has already been mentioned that there is no specific database to submit to. The use of multiple data sources also makes it difficult to determine exactly what tactics will result in rankings in metasearch engines. In fact, many metasearch engines now also use directory results. In short, while no metasearch engines are among the top dozen engines, gaining rankings in them should naturally result from successful strategies in the provider engines.

Results from numerous providers will be returned in a variety of orders. That is to say, two different queries will almost always return results from different engines in different orders depending on the quality of matches gathered from each engine. None of the metasearch engines show a preference toward any specific provider.

Charting your results is further complicated by the fact that almost none of the rank-checking software programs report results from these metasearch engines. Therefore, all reporting must be manually generated. Next, given the volatile nature of rankings in any one of the major search engines, one can only imagine the week-to-week changes in results on metasearch engines. The best recommendation would be to avoid getting caught up in targeting any metasearch engines. Rather, focus on gaining significant rankings across the board in all major search engines, and success in metasearch engines will follow.

Understanding the Players

Now that you know what metasearch engines are in general, we'll briefly discuss four important metasearch engines: Dogpile, MetaCrawler, Go2Net, and Mamma. Although the page layout and manner in which results are displayed varies widely, it is important to discuss the providers for each of these engines. Each of the four main metasearch engines displays the name of the engine along with the result.

Dogpile is a metacrawler that simultaneously searches a multitude of individual search engines and directories including AltaVista, GoTo, FindWhat, LookSmart, Yahoo!, and many others. Because the results are collected from these outside sources, Dogpile cannot maintain control over the content that a given search engine provides. This also includes the Dogpile Web Catalog and Dogpile Open Directory. As a result, all Dogpile search results are collected from entirely separate resources. In short, Dogpile does not maintain its own, personal database.

Dogpile's metacrawl system does prove to be an efficient time-saver in that it goes to a number of the major search engines for you, all at the same time. A drawback to this system is that the more engines a metasearcher queries, the longer the search may take. Each time a user issues a query, the metasearcher has to then pass the information to the other sites, obtain the results, and combine them into a single page of relevant results. A metasearcher can, however, decrease time spent searching and retrieving by reducing the number of engines it searches.

From the home page, when conducting a search, a user is also able to choose which **type** of database they'd like Dogpile to query. For example, when a user types the keyword phrase in the search box and clicks Fetch, they are automatically choosing The Web option from the pull-down menu beneath the search box to access the standard Dogpile metasearch results (including Dogpile's Web Catalog). If a user would like to query Dogpile's graphic links, he or she need only choose the second option from the pull-down menu, Images. The results display a set of graphics provided by Ditto.com that relate to the user's query. Clicking on the thumbnail will direct the user to the image's source. Choosing the Audio/MP3 option from the pull-down menu will direct the user to MP3 links that relate to the keyword searched. MP3 results are provided by Astraweb, AudioGalaxy, and MP3 Board. The Auctions option allows users to search 200 auction sites including eBay, Amazon, Haggle Online, and Yahoo!. There are a number of selections to investigate; choose additional search options including News, FTP, Discussion, Small Biz, and Streaming Media. The overall benefit with Dogpile is, perhaps, the fact that it is possible to query a considerable number of sources all from one place.

Dogpile also provides a Custom Search page. This page presents pull-down menus of the 14 search engines that Dogpile utilizes for its metadata. A user can set the order in which Dogpile's metasearcher will display search engine results. Once users make their initial choice, they can save the settings so that metasearch results will always be rendered in the order they originally chose. If they do not want a particular engine's results to be rendered at all, they can choose to skip those results altogether.

From the home page, Dogpile also provides access to the Marketplace area, which features quick links to other online services including online banking, discount airfares, job postings, and Dogpile's own online radio. In addition, users have access to Dogpile's convenient shopping section. Dogpile's associate online shopping destinations include such retailers as Gap.com, Amazon.com, uBid.com, Camera Club, and many others. There is also a What's Hot area that includes links to special deals and hard-to-find merchandise.

MetaCrawler uses multiple search engines including: About, AltaVista, Direct Hit, Excite, FindWhat, Google, GoTo, Infoseek, Kanoodle, LookSmart, Lycos, RealNames, Sprinks, Thunderstone, and WebCrawler.

MetaCrawler was developed at the University of Washington in 1994. In November 1998, Go2Net acquired the metasearch provider. MetaCrawler remains one of the oldest and most prominent metasearch engines available. In 1997 and 1998, *PC Magazine* voted MetaCrawler "Best Search Engine." Currently, MetaCrawler powers the search function at Go2Net.

MetaCrawler was originally developed at the University of Washington by then-UW graduate student Erik Selberg and UW Associate Professor Oren Etzioni. It was first released to the Net in June 1995, then licensed to Netbot, Inc., which Etzioni co-founded and where he served as the company's chief scientist. Go2Net took over exclusive operation of MetaCrawler from Netbot in February 1997. In October 1998, Etzioni joined Go2Net's board of directors and in May 1999 came on board as the company's chief technology officer.

Go2Net utilizes the search function provided by MetaCrawler. The new Go2Net.com portal offers a best-of-breed navigational component that makes finding great content easy and fast. In addition, the portal features metasearch technology from Go2Net's MetaCrawler, financial information and discussion from Go2Net's Silicon Investor, along with an expansive directory and other resources such as news, weather, games, and a full suite of integrated communications services.

For major corporations that wish to create and manage their own premium, branded portal, Go2Net now offers company-branded, customized versions of the Go2Net.com portal. This enables external organizations to enjoy the benefits of having a fully functional, custom-branded portal, without having to commit to the necessary development and maintenance resources.

Go2Net.com also provides easy access to a co-branded version of AskMe.com's person-to-person expert advice service, where Go2Net users can ask questions directly to more than 50,000 online experts on more than 2,000 topics.

Mamma uses a process involving two steps that results in a user-friendly listing of relevant resources for the user to navigate through. The two steps involved in this process can be broken down as follows:

1.   When a user enters a query at the Mamma.com search engine, nine search engines are queried — Yahoo!, Lycos, GoTo, Infoseek, LookSmart, MSN, NBCi, Kanoodle, and Ask Jeeves — in addition to five lesser-known search engines — FindWhat, 7 search, Epilot, Savvy, and Bay9.

2.   For each search engine being queried, Mamma's proprietary filtering software takes out words and phrases irrelevant to the user's search query.

Mamma creates a virtual database, organizes the results into a uniform format, and presents them by relevance and source. In this manner, Mamma.com provides the user with a highly relevant and comprehensive set of search results. This is a feature that is meant to distinguish Mamma.com from other metacrawler/hybrid search engines. Unlike other metacrawler/hybrid search engines that display results in descending order for each search engine (according to relevancy), Mamma combines the results from all the search engines it scans, and gives an "all in one" listing in descending order. For example, if a user searches on tire companies, they will notice that the first five results come from Yahoo!, GoTo, Ask Jeeves, LookSmart, and NBCi. The results are sorted using Mamma's proprietary technology.

Site Elements That Can Cause Problems

As a metasearch engine, all elements that cause problems are dictated at the base search engine level.

Recommended Site Optimization Tactics

Please see the specific chapters on the queried engines for optimization tactics.

Off-the-Page Factors That Influence Success

Please see the specific chapters on the queried engines to determine which use off-the-page factors.

How to Submit a Site to This Engine

Metasearch engines pull results from other search engines and do not maintain their own databases that receive submissions. Please see the related chapters on each engine or directory for specific submission procedures.

How to Build Informational Pages for this Engine

Informational pages built for specific engines should be addressed toward the underlying search engines.

How to Know If Your Site Has Been Spidered/Listed

Please see the chapters on the underlying engines.

Indexing Timetable

Conforms to the rules of the underlying engines.

What to Do If Your Rankings Disappear

Please see the chapters on the underlying engines.

Special Tips and Tactics for This Engine

The nature of metasearch engines requires that the individual underlying engines be targeted and metasearch engine rankings will result.

Chapter 33:

Paying for Placement

Pay-for-placement search engines can be a very efficient source of supplemental search engine referral traffic — but they are no substitute for a thorough search engine positioning campaign. Business models of pay-for-placement search engines are built on the premise that people will pay for high rankings. This model also assumes that people will pay only for rankings on those keywords that are most relevant to their Web site. After all, if they pay to be in the top search position and someone clicks on it, they will be billed — who would pay for a click-through on a keyword phrase that is irrelevant to their Web site? In these search engines, the Web marketer can decide where they want to be in the rankings according to how much they're willing to pay via a bidding process.

By nature of this bidding model, someone must agree to pay a higher price per click if they hope to be placed higher in the search results. You can then return and raise your bid, thus moving up a position ahead of your competitor. Bids on some keywords have been bid up so high that there appears to be a disconnect between what is being paid and the value of being found on the search term — this will always be an issue for these types of search engines. If you offer the highest bid for a certain keyword or phrase, you are automatically placed at the top of those search results. Subsequent listings are ranked by decreasing bid amount.

Now pay close attention. While all other forms of online marketing, including banner ads, are facing downward price pressure, pay-for-rankings search engines are set up to produce ever-increasing prices. Uninformed companies and companies that cannot determine the value or yield of a click-through should proceed with caution. Sure, it might seem great that you can attain a top ranking on a search for "online casinos" but at $3.52 per click-through, what value is there if you don't sell or offer online gaming?

It is important to note that pay-for-placement systems are not in place on all or even most major search engines. GoTo.com is the dominant pay-for-placement search engine, but GoTo.com has a little secret: More than 80 percent of its click-throughs and traffic are not people who visited GoTo.com, but rather people who view GoTo.com listings as they are displayed on other Web sites. Most people who click on pay-for-placement search engine listings are not actually using the search engine that operates the service. Instead, these paid listings are distributed, syndicated if you will, across other major search engines. For instance, GoTo.com displays between three and five of its rankings across AOL, Netscape, Lycos, HotBot, and others. And, in each of these situations, the GoTo.com "sponsored" search results are easily identifiable as advertisements, not search results.

As such, GoTo.com is really more of an advertising network than it is a search engine. But that doesn't mean it's wrong, bad, or inappropriate to pay for high rankings in GoTo — it just means you have to recognize that you're making a media buy, understand what it is that you're buying, and determine how it will supplement your search engine positioning campaign. To treat pay-for-placement listings as a substitute for a complete search engine positioning program is like launching a national radio campaign using only ads in one small regional market instead of running them nationwide. Search engine positioning is a global campaign and should cross all major search engines. More importantly, when search results from these pay-for-placement engines are distributed across other search engines they are clearly set apart as "advertising" and users know they're not "editorial" content or "actual search results."

The major advantage of pay-for-placement is the amount of control you have over your rankings, budget, and keyword phrases or search terms for which your site is returned. This allows you to target a specific audience and make the most of the money you spend on promoting your site or products — but don't confuse it with a search engine positioning campaign.

Pay-for-placement search engines usually have one of two different payment systems. The first is click-through: For every click on a keyword that leads to your site, you pay the amount that you bid in advance. With a fee-based system, you pay a set fee for your ranking regardless of the number of click-throughs. In both of these cases, the price you pay is directly proportional to the amount of traffic the search engine receives.

Pay-per-placement search engines offer three things that others don't:

■ As an advertiser, you get complete control over your placement in the search results (at least until someone outbids you). You will need to check back with the search engine daily or weekly to ensure you have not been outbid and your position lowered. Companies with larger budgets can request an automatic increase in their bid to sustain their ranking if they work directly with a GoTo.com salesperson. And, you only pay GoTo when customers click on your listings.

■ In theory, users' search results are highly relevant; you don't get the mess of unrelated sites that often accompany major search engines' results. Why is this? Advertisers are much more strategic in pay-per-placement engines, because they're directly paying for it. So they have incentive to bid for top placement only on search terms that will enable them to meet consumers who are looking for exactly what they have to offer.

■ You pay only what you want for each visitor who clicks on your listing. You have complete control over the dollar value of the bid you decide to place. If being at the top is worth it to you, you can pay for it. If not, you don't have to, and you'll be listed below.

Pay-for-placement search listings do have some limitations. Currently, you cannot determine which partner sites your search listings are displayed on if you advertise at GoTo or any of the other pay-for-placement services. If you bid for a ranking in position one, two, or three, your listing will be displayed as a sponsored link in AOL, Netscape, AltaVista, Lycos, and HotBot as well as the many other search partners. If your audience doesn't use HotBot, for instance, and you would never pay for a banner in this search engine because your customers' demographic is so different than what HotBot reaches, you're just out of luck. Your listing will appear there, whether or not you want it to appear on that engine.

GoTo — The Pay-For-Placement Leader

The largest pay-for-placement search engine and the current market leader is GoTo. GoTo was started in late 1997 in Old Town Pasadena, California, with the novel premise that advertisers would pay only for the rankings that served them and that this phenomenon would produce a relevant search engine. GoTo and all the engines like it really pretend to be search engines but are actually an advertising vehicle — kind of a hybrid between eBay, the DoubleClick advertising network, and an actual search engine. In reality, GoTo has thrived financially, but not because it's a valuable search tool that produces relevant search results. As we've stated earlier, the Web site advertiser who pays the most per click appears first in the search results.

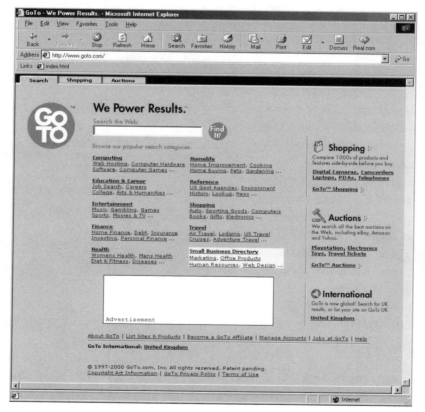

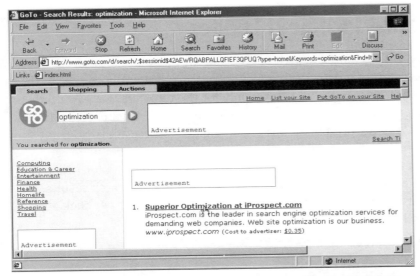

Whenever a consumer clicks on an advertiser's listing in the search results, the advertiser pays GoTo the amount of its bid, which is clearly displayed next to the listing.

This site may have started out as a small search engine with a very specific agenda, but it's rapidly expanding in a number of different areas, including venues for shopping and auctions.

GoTo recently expanded its business model into the international arena by establishing and building a presence for advertisers, consumers, and affiliates throughout the world. GoTo starts with a simple home page that is clean and viewer friendly. There's no clutter, and banners are displayed only at the top of the results pages (integrated

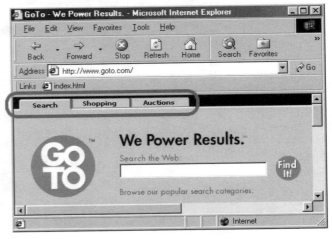

into the GoTo site nameplate), making for a pleasant search interface that's also easy to navigate.

GoTo has enjoyed phenomenal success since its inception. It currently processes more than 100 million searches each month. In recent studies conducted by NPD Online Research, this site ranked ahead of Yahoo!, Excite, Lycos, and Disney-owned Go Network in frequency of finding information sought every time. GoTo also services other search engines, including Ask Jeeves, Dogpile, MetaCrawler, AOL, Netscape, Lycos, HotBot, and AltaVista.

How to Enroll in GoTo

You can sign up easily by calling 1-877-WWW-GOTO (999-4686). Express service, which costs $99, includes one-on-one consultation with GoTo experts, 20 relevant search terms, professionally written search listings, and $50 worth of clicks (up to a maximum of 5,000 targeted visitors). Along with this express service, GoTo has an additional offer. If you pay $50 more, you get double the number of search listings, bringing the total to 40. Advertisers can start receiving targeted traffic in less than five business days, and you have direct access to your account 24-7.

Shopping at GoTo

GoTo launched its shopping venue in January 2000 when the site acquired Cadabra, an online shopping guide and comparison engine.

This shopping guide uses Dynamic Data Integration technology that enables GoTo to gather product information from a variety of different sources and organize it in an easy-to-understand fashion, thus allowing consumers to compare products and pricing. If you want to list your products on GoTo, just fill out their online form that requests information including your site URL, e-mail address, type of product sold, and monthly advertising budget. Again, you have complete control of how much you want to spend on your advertising.

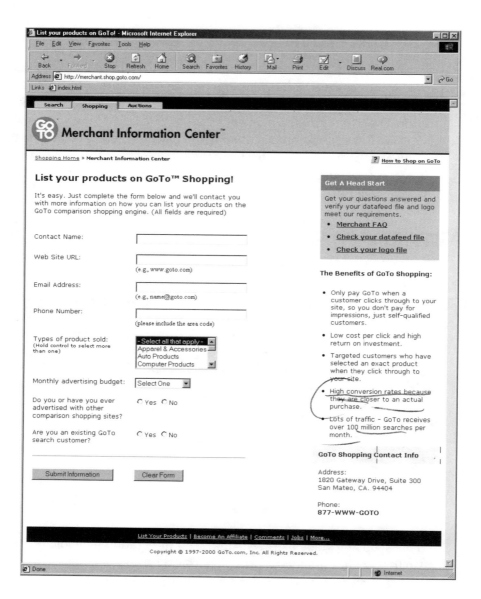

Auctions at GoTo

You can offer GoTo's auctions right at your own Web site via two different methods. Both methods earn commissions for you and are easy to install.

■ Integrated auction search (IS). In this case, customized results are integrated into your Web site. You have three search boxes to choose from, and installation time runs about one to two hours. It's free to join and you'll earn $10 for every 1,000 searches performed via your site. The key benefits to this type of auction are that you can earn money for searches and your visitors will stay longer on your site.

■   Search-in-the-Box (SIB). It's free to join, and installation time is less than one hour. In this case, results are displayed on the GoTo auction site, not on your site. You'll earn $0.04 for every click-through. There are more than five search boxes from which to choose.

The Downside of Pay-For-Placement

While the advantages offered by pay-for-placement search engines seem promising, the disadvantages are far greater. The pay-for-placement search engines' tendencies to draw results from a smaller, commercially skewed index emphasizes the necessity of smart search techniques on an algorithm-based search engine.

Disadvantages for Users

When you do a search on a specific subject, you're not necessarily getting a wide variety of results, and they're not guaranteed to be the best results. You're simply getting the advertisers who paid the most money. A search engine such as Google has well over a billion Web sites at its disposal when a search is conducted. This offers a huge pool from which to draw results. With a pay-for-placement search engine, this pool is substantially smaller.

Then there's also the "commercialness" of the results. When you conduct a query for information on a medical topic, for example, you'll get tons of commercial sites in the results as opposed to information about clinical studies published by universities or research papers. There is no commercial motive for paying advertising fees or for paying by click-through for some types of Web sites and so they don't show up in GoTo.

Commercial sites are more likely to use pay-for-placement search engines because they're trying to sell their product and are usually more likely to invest in the purchase of high rankings.

Disadvantages for Advertisers

Another disadvantage affects the advertisers. GoTo may very well be a large site that receives a lot of traffic and it may be worthwhile to pay for rankings there. However, many other pay-for-placement engines vary tremendously in quality and content; placing a bid on some of these could be a gamble.

If paying for rankings is something you really want to do, be sure to thoroughly check out the site with which you're dealing. If the search engine offers great prices, there is a good chance it gets very little traffic or it would be charging a lot more. If you are performing search engine positioning services for a client, monitor the click-throughs from both GoTo and the lesser known pay-for-placement search services. Make sure your client is getting value for the investment.

Other Pay-For-Placement Engines

Besides GoTo, there are numerous other pay-for-placement engines out there. Here's a list for your reference. Please note that these engines vary widely as far as start-up costs and enrollment procedures.

Site Name	URL	Company Name	Address
FindWhat.com	http://www.findwhat.com	FindWhat.com	FindWhat.com, 121 W. 27th St., 9th Floor, New York, NY 10001
Kanoodle	http://www.kanoodle.com	Kanoodle.com	Kanoodle.com, 260 Creekside Drive Suite 200, Amherst, NY 14228
RocketLinks	http://www.bay9.com	Bay9.com	Bay9.com, 450 7th Ave. Suite 1605, New York, NY 10123
SimpleSearch	http://www.simplesearch.com	SimpleSearch.com, Inc.	SimpleSearch.com, 3690 N. Rancho Drive, Las Vegas, NV 89130
Ah-ha.com	http://www.ah-ha.com	Ah-ha.com, Inc.	Ah-ha.com, Inc., 3521 North University, Suite 100, Provo, UT 84604
OneSearch	http://www.onesearch.com	Knew Technologies	OneSearch.com, P.O. Box 670, Beavercreek, OR 97004
7search.com	http://www.7search.com	EMERgency 24 family of Internet Service	Chicago Headquarters, 3950 Avondale Ave., Chicago, IL 60641
CleanSearch.com	http://www.cleansearch.com	CleanSearch.com	Entertainment On The Web, Inc., 38423 9th Street East, Palmdale, CA 93550
Sprinks	http://www.sprinks.com	About.com, Inc.	About.com, Inc., 220 E 42nd St., New York, NY 10017
SearchHound	http://www.searchhound.com	SearchHound.com, Inc.	SearchHound, 1700 Wyandotte, Kansas City, MO 64108
Win4Win	http://www.win4win.com	Win4Win.com	Win4Win.com, P.O. Box 10879 Steenberg Estate, Cape Town, 7945 South Africa
Searchgalore.com	http://www.searchgalore.com	Allegiant Marketing, Inc.	Allegiant Marketing, Inc., 702 W. Bloomington Road, Suite 101, Champaign, IL 61820
3apes.com	http://www.3apes.com	Bornis, Inc.	Bornis, Inc., 3585 Hancock Street, Suite A, San Diego, CA 92110

Site Name	URL	Company Name	Address
Zcoolweb.com	http://www.zcoolweb.com	Prima Internet, Inc.	ZCoolWeb.com, P.O. Box 43, Carencro, LA 70520-0043
Net-buster.com	http://www.net-buster.com	Net Buster	Net Buster Internet Services, 18 Kathleen Avenue, Wembley, Middlesex UK HA0 4JH
Godado.co.uk	http://www.godado.co.uk	Godado.com Ltd.	
Netflip.com	http://www.netflip.com	NetFlip	NetFlip, 860 E. Charleston Road, Palo Alto, CA 94303
Zeedee.com	http://www.gabagob.com/main/index/asp		
Searchcactus.com	http://www.searchcactus.com	SearchCactus, LLC	SearchCactus, LLC, 1729 Larchwood Drive, Troy, MI 48083
Colorstamps.com	http://www.colorstamps.com/index.phtm	Colorstamps, Inc.	Colorstamps, Inc., 2 North Second Street, Suite 900, San Jose, CA 95113
Sabril.com	http://www.sabril.com	Sabril.com	Sabril.com, P.O. Box 561, Huntington Station, NY 11746
Efind.com	http://www.efind.com	eFind, Inc.	eFind, Inc., 1816 Lincoln Ave., San Diego, CA 92103
Ustarthere.com	http://www.ustarthere.com	MPC Internetworks, Inc.	MPC Internetworks, Inc., P.O. Box 5782, San Bernardino, CA 92048
Findit-quick.com	http://www.findit-quick.com	Findit-Quick.com	Findit-Quick.com, 1817 Saunders Settlement Rd., Niagara Falls, NY 14304

Site Name	Contact Information	Cost to Purchase Ranking	Information Page URL	Ranking
FindWhat.com	T: 1-800-823-3477 T: 1-212-255-1500 F: 1-212-989-4392	Open bidding	http://www.findwhat.com/static/ab_promote.html	*****
Kanoodle	T: 1-877-526-6635	From $25, open bidding process	http://www.kanoodle.com/about/about/html	*
RocketLinks	T: 1-212-244-3312 F: 1-212-244-5662	Bidding	http://www.bay9.com/promotesite.cgi?link=&clicktrade=#pay	**
SimpleSearch	T: 1-702-307-4636 F: 1-702-307-4640	$20 deposit for account (min. amount), bidding	http://www.simplesearch.com/advertise/simpleclick.shtml	****
Ah-ha.com	T: 1-801-418-1111 F: 1-801-418-1110	$25 activation fee, bidding	http://secure1.ah-ha.com/logolink/default.asp?JAVA=1	****
OneSearch		Minimum $25	http://www.onesearch.com/mediakit/mediakit.html	***
7search.com	T: 1-800-577-1165 T: 1-773-283-0086 F: 1-773-283-0170	Minimum $25 deposit, bidding	http://www.payperranking.com	*
CleanSearch.com	T: 1-661-274-0729 marketing@cleansearch.com	$25 nonrefundable account bal., minimum bid $.05	http://www.cleansearch.com/advertising/bfp-terms.html	**
Sprinks	sprinks@about.com	$25 start and valid credit card	http://sprinks.about.com	****
SearchHound	T: 1-816-960-3444 info@searchhound.com	Minimum $100 total spending	http://www.searchhound.com/Pages/bids.htm	****
Win4Win	T: 27 21 712-5920 F: 27 21 712-5932	Minimum $25, bidding	http://www.win4win.com/Promote/p_index.asp	**

Site Name	Contact Information	Cost to Purchase Ranking	Information Page URL	Ranking
Searchgalore.com	T: 1-217-359-1627 info@searchgalore.com	$50 to start account, bidding	http://www.searchgalore.com/add/htm	**
alpha3apes.com	T: 1-619-296-1732 advertising@bornis.com	Bidding	http://www.3apes.com/a/traffic/ ?p=none	*
Zcoolweb.com	support@zcoolweb.com	$25 start, bidding	http://www.zcoolweb.com/add.shtml	***
Net-buster.com	T: +44 208 795 1307 F: +44 845 638 2906	$99	Under Web promotion	**
Godado.co.uk	infouk@godado.com	Minimum £50	http://www.godado.co.uk/ promote_i.vep	***
Netflip.com	T: 1-650-812-3260 info@netflip.com	Nonrefundable $25 enrollment fee	http://www.netflip.com/advertiser/ signin.jsp	****
Zeedee.com				*
Searchcactus.com	T: 1-248-689-9961 F: 1-248-689-9964 info@searchcactus.com	Open an account for $25	http://www.searchcactus.com/ advertiser	**
Colorstamps.com	T: 1-408-298-1000 F: 1-408-298-1010			****
Sabril.com	T: 1-914-555-2134 contact@sabril.com	$25 deposit	http://www.sabril.com/ ads2.htm	**
Efind.com	T: 1-888-909-Find (3463) T: 1-619-725-3130 F: 1-619-725-3139 feedback@efind.com	Bidding	http://www.efind.com/ asp/sitepromotion.asp	**
Ustarthere.com	T: 1-909-888-5500 webmaster@nomonthlyfees.com	Free sign-up	http://www.ustarthere.com/get_ visitors.htm	*
Findit-quick.com	T: 1-716-297-5292	$25 deposit	http://www.findit-quick.com/aboutus. html	***

Ranking is based on relevancy of results, lack of clutter, ease of bidding on keywords, and ease of signup.

Part 4:

Tools and Resources

Part 4:

Chapter 34:

Submitting and Rank-Checking Tools

here are a variety of tools that search engine positioning professionals can employ to submit your Web site to the major search engines as well as measure your Web site's ranking in the search engines. Each of these tools has their benefits and failings, and each is appropriate for different applications.

For the most part, serious search engine positioning pros use WebPosition Gold. It is the standard by which other search engine positioning software is measured. The software is, in fact, a suite of tools. It contains a rank checker to measure your Web site's rank in search engines, a submitter that submits to the major search engines based on their rules and limits, a page critic that gives specific advice for optimizing your page to rank well on the major search engines, and a traffic measurement tool. It is the all-in-one search engine positioning software suite.

Checking the success of your submissions and seeing where you placed in the engines is of the utmost importance. A one-time mass submission may help you get traffic to your site in the short term, but if you don't consistently track your placement to see where you rank, your rankings will eventually slip. Software with a detailed rank-checking feature allows for constant monitoring of rankings, so that you can work on maintaining and improving your placement.

Although this chapter will provide you information on a variety of tools for submissions and ranking, detailed information is given on just two major products: WebPosition Gold software and Position Technologies' online tools. These two tools represent different approaches. WebPosition Gold is a suite of software tools that you can purchase and use for all of your campaigns. WebPosition will automatically update as needed, if you set the feature in place, so that you will never need to purchase an upgrade.

Position Pro, from Position Technologies, Inc., uses a different model. Position Technologies is a Web-based applications services provider (ASP). You create an account, pay a fee, and then use the tools directly from www.positionpro.com. There is no software to install on your computer. Position Pro is not a rank measurement tool, although it will perform limited rank measurement for you. It should be noted that as an ASP it includes a pay-as-you go component. Your fees are based on the quantity of submissions that you perform.

Investing in search engine positioning software is a worthwhile endeavor — it can save you hundreds of hours of time, while accomplishing things that are not humanly possible. (Imagine the time you would spend searching for every keyword you attained a ranking for, for every page, in 20 search engines!)

Before spending your money, however, it is critical that you know what products are available, and what would be the wisest investment for your needs.

WebPosition Gold — The Leading Software Tool

WebPosition Gold is made up of integrated modules that assist users in performing these important search engine promotion steps:

- ▪ Generating optimized Web pages
- ▪ Optimizing those pages to target a specific keyword and search engine
- ▪ Uploading the newly optimized pages
- ▪ Submitting to search engines
- ▪ Reporting the pages' search positions or rankings
- ▪ Measuring how much traffic the pages receive

The software functions as an integrated suite of tools with each easy-to-use tool selectable from an icon palette. Although the tools are integrated into a single suite, you can use each separately. So that you can fully appreciate how powerful and comprehensive WebPosition Gold is, each tool is discussed separately.

Page Generator

This module creates an HTML page based on the keywords and details that the user supplies.

 CAUTION   Some search engines will penalize the use of doorway type pages so this tool should be used with caution.

Page Critic

This tool provides expert advice on how to optimize new or existing pages. It employs an expert system with its own knowledge base. This base contains accurate definitions of each search engine's algorithm. These are constantly updated and the information is part of the automatic updates users can elect to receive each time they open WebPosition Gold. The knowledge database contains information about how each search engine measures and ranks pages including many page definition variables such as:

- Keyword weight
- Keyword frequency
- Prominence
- Repetition limits
- Page layout preferences
- Spam penalties
- Partial and exact match preferences
- Case sensitivity

Page Critic will also dissect the page and provide information on how to improve the page's performance. This tool will also compare the Web page to:

- Any specified HTML page on the Web
- Any Web page stored on the user's hard disk
- Any top-ranking page for a keyword search in any search engine
- The statistical averages of a group of top-ranking pages for a keyword search

Because search engine algorithms are complex and never disclosed to the public, the WebPosition Gold knowledge base represents highly educated guesses supplemented by ongoing data analysis. It is as accurate as possible, but it cannot measure off-the-page metrics such as link popularity or click-through behavior such as measured by Direct Hit.

Upload Manager

This module tracks the pages created, changed, or added and ensures that pages get uploaded to the Web site.

Submitter

Users can submit their Web site's pages to the important search engines using this module. Because resubmitting can often provide an extra boost in rankings,

Submitter can be scheduled to resubmit pages regularly. It will even verify if a site was indexed by the expected date.

Reporter

For many search engine positioning experts, this is the most valuable component of the WebPosition Gold suite, because it is invaluable for checking a site's position in the major search engines to determine their ranking. It even provides an Alert Report about pages that have declined in rank or have been dropped entirely. Armed with this information, you can keep track of your positions and will know when you should resubmit or reoptimize your pages.

Scheduler

This lets the user set up the program to recheck the site's rankings automatically on a self-determined schedule. With regular statistics, it is easy to track a site's long-term performance and determine the success of optimization tactics. Not only will the scheduler automate rank checking, it can also be set up to handle automatic site submissions.

Traffic Analyzer

With this module, users can find out what keywords visitors used to find their site without downloading and analyzing log files. By providing some information, the user can receive statistics and origins for all visitors, page by page.

There are two versions of the software. The Standard Edition ($149) supports up to five different Web sites, and unlimited keywords and pages. The Professional Edition ($349) includes all the same features as the Standard Edition but also supports an unlimited number of Web sites. It will also provide output to ASCII so that the data can be used in spreadsheets or databases.

Position Pro — The World's Best Submitter

Position Pro (www.positionpro.com) is a suite of online tools from Position Technologies designed for the search engine optimization professional working with a number of sites or with a single large Web site. The user does not download or buy a program like WebPosition, but instead logs into www.submit-director.com (for small sites of less than 50 pages) or www.positionpro.com (for

sites over 50 pages). Each tool provides access from the browser to a service that allows the user to optimize and submit some or all of their spider-friendly pages.

Submit Director guides the user through the process. It begins with an initial spider crawl of the site with Position Technologies' spider to find the site's pages that are acceptable to search engines. Then, the application guides the user through the process of optimization and on to submissions and monitoring of the site's presence in the search engines. When Submit Director crawls a site, it scores each page and provides a list of words deemed relevant to it. It will also suggest keywords for inclusion in the Title tag. The application will even produce META tags that can be copied and pasted into Web pages. For the novice working with a Web site of less than 50 pages, Submit Director is an excellent online option. It is available by annual subscription for $149.

However, Position Pro is an advanced suite of tools designed for the professional working with a group of clients or on behalf of a large organization. Position Pro offers users access to all of the same features as Submit Director; however, the interface is more geared for the professional inasmuch as it gives less information to guide the process.

With Position Pro, the user can mark optimized pages for "priority submit," which means that the submitter will place them in a 24-hour queue of revolving pages. The queue is designed to submit in an orderly fashion that avoids exceeding the submission limits imposed by the search engines. Because Position Pro's fee structure is based on the number of pages in the site, it can be a costly alternative to a standalone program such as WebPosition.

Both Submit Director and Position Pro have access to the Inktomi Inclusion program. Position Pro, along with Network Solutions, is an Inktomi Submission partner. Through these partners, site owners can pay for inclusion in the Inktomi Web database. This database has a presence in the AOL, MSN, About.com, HotBot, GoTo, and iWon search engines, and with other portals. Site owners pay for each URL included in the Inktomi database. The fees are $30 for the first URL and $15 for each additional URL. For this fee, the site is listed in the database for a full year. URLs are re-spidered every 48 hours to ensure that the content stays up to date. This is an alternative form of submission to the Inktomi database. Other products, such as Web Position, submit to Inktomi through the free interface, which offers no inclusion guarantees.

Other Considerations

Following the success of WebPosition Gold, many companies have entered the market offering software or online services to aid in the process of achieving high rankings. Manually submitting URLs and searching for attained rankings is an extremely tedious and time-consuming process, especially when dealing with a large number of URLs and keywords. It is evident that there is a necessity for software and services to assist in the search engine positioning process. There are many products now on the market, and the tools offered within these applications can vary greatly.

The ability to submit URLs to search engines is one of the primary tools that nearly all products offer. The submission process can normally be readily automated. It is quite tedious and a main reason for seeking search engine positioning software. With these submission products, the user simply fills out a form detailing the site name, keywords, contact e-mail, etc., then selects the engines to submit to, and lets the program take it from there. It is important to note here that submitting to more search engines is not necessarily better. More than 95 percent of the traffic generated to Web sites from search engines comes through the 20 main search engines. Programs claiming to submit to hundreds of search engines mislead the consumer. Only a tiny fraction of these sites are true search engines or directories. The rest are simply FFA (Free-For-All) sites, which are designed solely to gather e-mail addresses for Webmasters so they can send users junk mail.

Submitting to the lesser engines truly is a waste of time and a cause for needless aggravation. Oversubmitting is a potential problem that can occur when using search engine positioning software and services. Many of the submitters on the market do not have any safeguards in place to prevent the user from exceeding the search engines' submission limits. Most search engines limit how many URL submissions they will accept from one site. For the best chance at getting indexed, any submission software should warn consumers of the average indexing time for each engine and the daily URL submission limits, as well as keep track of which URLs have already been submitted (WebPosition and Position Pro both offer these features). Many contenders in the market have overlooked this vital feature.

Many of the search engine positioning software packages available vary greatly in the quality and accuracy of reporting of rankings. Some programs do not even offer a rank checker, while others offer a very basic and limited report.

Almost all of the products listed in the following chart are "newcomers" to the search engine optimization genre.

Product Name	URL	Company Name	Submitter or Rank Checker	Available as Software or as an Online Service	Number of Search Engines Utilized	Key Notes	Price
Add Web 4	http://www.cyberspacehq.com/addweb	Cyberspace Headquarters	both	Software	500,000 including directories and link sites	May be one of the best software programs	$69-$299
Dynamic Submission 2000 6	http://www.submission2000.com	Apex Pacific Pty. Ltd.	both	Software	1000+	Generates doorway pages and contains a keyword builder	$49.95-$199.95
Exploit	http://www.exploit.net	Exploit Information Technology	Submitter	Software	1000+	Very fast and efficient	$30/month, $135/year
PositionAgent	http://positionagent.com	Microsoft	Rank checker	Online	Not applicable	Graphical reports with results via e-mail	Starting at $19.99/ month
Submit-it	http://www.submit-it.com	Microsoft	both	Online	Up to 400	Utilizes automatic submissions	$59/year
Submit Spider	http://www.submitspider.com	Submit Spider	Submitter	Online	Not available	Sends submission reports	$29.95-$89.85
Submit Wolf 4	http://www.submitwolf.com	Trellian Software	both	Software	3500, including directories and link sites	Concurrent submissions and detailed reports	$95
Swiss Army App	http://www.swissarmyapp.com	Aesop Marketing Corporation	both	Software	22	An exceptionally complete tool	$99.90-$149.95
Top Dogg 5.8	http://www.topdogg.com	DC Micro Development, Inc.	both	Software	239	Very easy to use	$179
Web Site Traffic Builder 4	http://www.websitetrafficbuilder.com	Intelliquis International, Inc.	both	Software	4200	Automatically fills in the submission form	$199-$349

FirstPlace Software pioneered search engine positioning software with WebPosition and has built a reputation for being the best. All others joining the market have been trying to emulate what FirstPlace Software created as the standard. Other software packages may have a few extra "bells and whistles" in certain areas, but the consumer should determine whether they are worth the extra frustration of dealing with a product that is less proven.

After thorough use and testing by search professionals and testing organizations (such as HyperGalaxy), WebPosition has proven to be the most stable during the URL submission process and the most accurate in detecting rankings (other packages with features very similar to WebPosition were found to miss out on reporting many rankings that actually existed).

Before buying any product, it is important to determine how you might answer the following questions. Have you been frustrated with companies that offer products that don't work as advertised? If so, make sure they have a rock-solid, money-back guarantee. If the company doesn't offer a guarantee, then you must ask yourself why not. Once you own the product, do they offer free, quality support or do they charge you $50/hr or more for phone calls? If you pay just $149 for a product, how many phone calls before you find the price of your product doubling? Also, make sure the company you choose offers fast, quality service. The previous table offers a comparison of the search engine positioning software and services currently available. For more information on any specific product, please visit their respective Web sites or contact them directly.

Chapter 35:

Building Informational Pages

he goal of informational pages is building additional Web site content with the express purpose of attaining higher rankings in the major spider-based search engines. If there's one thing to remember it's this: Any content that seeks to gain a ranking in spider-based search engines based on keyword on-the-page placement and strategy will not influence a Web site's ranking in human-edited directories. In other words, the human editors who review Web site submissions at the Yahoo! or LookSmart directories are not particularly interested in viewing your META tags, Title tag, or clever keyword placement in the first 25 words of your Web site copy. The purpose of keyword placement tactics is to ensure that a Web site is properly indexed and catalogued by the automated search engine spiders that visit Web sites, and download and index Web pages.

Pure spider-based search engines no longer make up the majority of the search engine landscape. The landscape has evolved, and directories currently dominate. A properly constructed informational page, while coded in a way that is friendly to search engine spiders, is in and of itself informative and visually appealing to visitors. Such well-constructed informational pages may be eligible for Yahoo! or one of the other major human-edited directories, but informational pages are primarily a spider-based search engine strategy, **not** a directory strategy. And when you remember that spider-based search engines make up less and less of the search engine landscape, you must adjust your strategy accordingly. Focus your efforts first and foremost on your directory submission, and then on optimizing your actual Web site (Title tags, META tags, etc.). Only after those have been completed should you worry about informational pages. The only exception to this prioritization is if your Web site is unindexable due to some site design issue, at which point the informational page strategy would increase in importance.

As of the date of this publication, informational pages are of most help in attaining top 10 to top 30 rankings in these major spider-driven search engines:

- AltaVista

- Excite

- Google

- HotBot (powered by Inktomi which powers several important search engines)

While Raging Search, Northern Light, Direct Hit, WebCrawler, and FAST (alltheweb.com) are also "pure" search engines populated by spiders, they are not considered major search engines and don't deliver very much traffic to Web sites (see StatMarket data for information on search engines and their ability to refer traffic to Web sites). AOL, NBCi, Lycos, Yahoo!, LookSmart, Netscape, and MSN are primarily human-edited directories. GoTo.com provides its primary search matches from a system where people/companies bid for a top ranking. GO.com, formerly Infoseek.com, no longer displays its spider-populated search matches first. Instead, GO's site redesign features pay-per-placement listings, as we covered in detail in Chapter 33.

Having made the point about search engines becoming less important, though, here's an interesting fact: A spider-based search engine partner supplements each major directory — even Yahoo!. If you target an obscure search term, even Yahoo! will default to Google, so if your informational page is listed there and ranking well, you will appear to attain a ranking in Yahoo!.

So, while people obsess over informational pages and spend their time tweaking keyword concentrations and page metrics for major search engines, we see that informational pages have their limits, in terms of reach and value. This is not to say that you should skip building informational pages. Even one first-page ranking in AltaVista on an important keyword can drive hundreds, if not thousands, of visitors a month. The point is that if you are either too busy or too inexperienced to build a high-ranking informational page, don't worry about it. You can achieve success by optimizing your existing Web site so that it will attain rankings in the spider-based search engines and by properly submitting to the major directories.

Building successful informational pages is difficult. Many pages are built, few attain high rankings. You could categorize building them as an advanced search engine positioning tactic.

That Plane (er, Page) Just Won't Fly

There can be any number of reasons why you would build an informational page, but most often it is due to some problematic site design issue that prevents the "actual pages" of a Web site from being indexed or attaining a high ranking in a major search engine. You can't always trash a Web page and start over. Sometimes you have to go with what you've got, and produce "fixes."

Here are a few design failures that may call for an informational page solution:

Graphics Without HTML

I've said this elsewhere, and I'll say it again (with my apologies to those who've read it already): Since search engines can't optically recognize text contained within graphics, they have nothing to index when they encounter a Web site entirely made up of graphics instead of HTML text; therefore, the Web site receives no rankings. In such a case, a Web site designer might construct an informational page to address any of the important keyword phrases that the site covers, and then link the visitor to the other areas of the Web site that the search engine could not index.

Not Enough Text

Here is one place where the saying "less is more" doesn't necessarily apply. Unfortunately, search engines need a reasonable amount of text to analyze to determine the content of a Web page. If you only throw 10 or 20 words into the mix, your site is unlikely to be a winner in the rankings. Some search engines have even stated that they won't index Web pages containing less than 250 words of copy (sometimes more, sometimes less). One thing you can do is construct your informational pages to cover various topics in more detail and link to pages that are full of dazzling graphics.

Too Many Topics

Ever eat a dish that tasted like the cook threw in every spice at hand? If so, you know that not all flavors combine well. When a Web page covers several unrelated topics, search engine algorithms have trouble classifying it. For instance, a Web page that discusses "dashboard mounted cellular telephones," "global positioning satellite navigational devices," and "bulletproof glass" (all high-end automobile after-market accessories) may have difficulty attaining rankings on any of those phrases. Remember, one of the search engine's ranking criteria is "keyword weight." If a Web page contains 1,000 words of copy and only one paragraph dedicated to each of those items, the page is unlikely to reach the critical keyword weight for any one of those keyword phrases. Additionally, if a search engine is applying a term vector measure, the term vector for any one of the targeted keyword phrases may be skewed by the presence of the other phrases. In our case of the auto accessories, you might construct informational pages that address each topic individually, so that the theme of the page is more focused and has a better chance of attaining a top ranking for the targeted keyword or phrase.

Dynamically Generated Web Sites

Search engines seek to index Web pages that exist. That sounds like an overly obvious statement, right? But what if the Web page does not, in fact, exist until it is "called" by a program? Dynamically generated Web sites present a challenge to search engines, both technically and philosophically, because until the user clicks on a particular link, that page may not actually exist or have been built. Philosophically, the search engine does not want to index a Web page that's not actually there, one that doesn't, in fact, "exist." Technically, many platforms that produce dynamically generated content produce URL strings so long and complicated that some search engine spiders are unable to read or comprehend them. Worse yet, depending on how the dynamically generated site has been programmed, that same URL can launch a completely different page the next time it is selected, though the URL appears identical. Hence, the search engine indexes and describes a Web page, but the searcher clicks through to find an entirely different page.

More and more search engines are improving their spiders and search algorithms so they can index and include more dynamically generated Web content. Recently, we've been pleased to see URLs containing question marks (e.g., www.domain.com?929-2-i322) showing up in Google. In our recent interview with Google, they indicated that they are moving toward indexing more dynamic content.

In July 2000, BrightPlanet.com released a white paper that suggested that the "deep Web" contained some 550 billion unindexed Web pages as compared to the known indexable Web, which is believed to contain about 1 billion total documents (though Google now boasts 1.3 billion indexed pages). Search engines are always in a race to claim the largest database. Each time a study reveals a new size leader, the others race to increase the size of their databases.

As you can see from the BrightPlanet estimate, search engines have a tough time indexing the "deep Web." If your Web site is served dynamically and the URL contains unusual ASCII characters such as question marks, tildes, multiple commas, exclamation marks, etc., there is a good chance those pages will be unindexable by most search engines. In these cases, there is significant value in creating informational pages that summarize some of the contents of those unindexable pages and that lead visitors to other areas of your site.

Requiring Cookies

Several of our pharmaceutical clients face this dilemma: The Federal Drug Administration (FDA) requires that pharmaceutical companies not dispense information about drugs in countries where those drugs may not be approved. So what happens when you visit a drug product Web site? You are served a "splash page" that asks you to indicate whether you are accessing the Internet from within the United States or from another country. If you click the Yes button, indicating that you are in the United States, you are served a cookie that allows you to visit and view the rest of the Web site. If, however, you click the No button, you are served a different cookie, which prevents you from accessing the Web site.

Search engine spiders do not accept cookies. Sometimes, the only page that is indexed is the "We're sorry, you cannot access our Web site" notice. In such cases, there is value in creating an informational page that discusses some of the relevant terms and doesn't require the user to accept a cookie to view it. These pages might discuss the highlights of a drug product, its specific use, and indications for treatment without touching that legal threshold requiring the warning splash page.

Using Frames

As we've stated throughout this book, search engines don't do a good job of indexing framed content, and they don't understand Flash. Despite the many workarounds, such as the <NOFRAMES> tag, framed pages just don't consistently rank well. In these cases, the developer might build an informational page that discusses or summarizes specific content of a Web site and that is more inviting and indexable to the search engines. Even the best efforts by the largest companies do not produce good outcomes with framed Web sites or Web sites that use Flash.

Hallway Pages

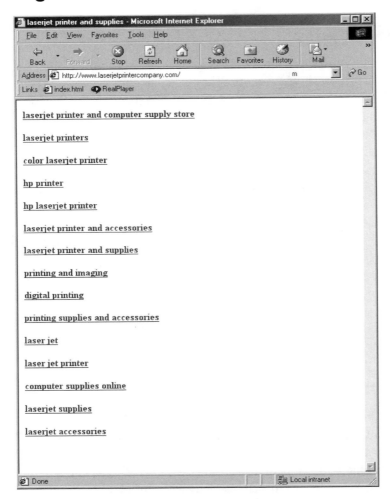

What is a hallway page? It's essentially a site map, or Web page that contains links to all of the pages you'd like a search engine to index. Someone discovered that pages that search engines "found," as opposed to those that were directly submitted to the search engine, seemed to rank higher. One person discovered that you could build a Web page that includes only links to all of your external pages and submit just that page. When this page is submitted, the search engine indexes it and then follows all the links on the page, thereby finding all the informational pages and indexing them. This also saves time in the submission process, since the Webmaster can submit just one page instead of every page.

Techniques for Building Informational Pages

The informational page is your chance to make up for all of the sins of your Web site. If some important keyword was created in a graphic, here's your chance to reproduce it as an <H1> headline. If the body copy of the actual Web site didn't use the keyword near the top of the first paragraph, the informational page can feature that keyword or phrase, front and center.

Given that search engines favor the simplest Web pages, informational pages should be designed to contain only the bare minimum of HTML. Frames should be avoided at all cost, as should tables, though often tables are necessary to match the look and feel of the Web site in question. You can custom tailor the META tags, body copy, and everything else on the informational pages to gain an advantage for individual targeted keywords in any particular search engine. This is your chance to compose body copy that is about a particular topic (read: keyword or phrase) and expands on that topic in such a way as to create a Web page that contains a good weight for that targeted keyword.

Try to fit other keywords into your sentences, but keep the primary emphasis of the page on a single topic. You will want to add links from that informational page to the other pages of your Web site that discuss that topic, keyword, or phrase.

Generally speaking, without targeting a specific search engine, an informational page should include:

- Between 250 to 1,000 words of legitimate body copy and/or navigational instructions

- A Title tag that contains at least one occurrence of the targeted keyword or phrase

- A description META tag that includes at least one occurrence of the targeted keyword or phrase

- A keyword META tag that contains at least one but no more than three repetitions of the targeted keyword or phrase

- A headline that contains at least one occurrence of the targeted keyword or phrase

- A keyword weight of between 2 and 15 percent
- A keyword in an activated link

An informational page that your Web site hosts internally, or even one that is hosted externally (on a separate domain) should have links to it from the main Web site. The mistake many make when building informational pages is to make them exist as islands: Nothing links to them — they only link to destination pages. Remember, most of the major search engines now consider link popularity as a component of their ranking algorithm. They maintain a "connectivity server" or other topographical map of Web site interconnectivity. If a Web site has links to resources but not from other sites, it's unlikely to attain a high ranking on any competitive keyword. If your informational page is devoid of valuable content, nobody will want to link to it. If your informational page is rich with interesting and relevant content, others will establish links to the page and your rankings will rise. Link popularity is becoming as important as tweaking those page variables.

Note that simply building a Web page containing all the elements listed above is no guarantee that your informational page will be a winner. The page must have very simple HTML and certain keyword concentrations, or weight values, of your different targeted keyword phrases in order to ace the rankings. Informational pages evolve over time and respond to the different ranking algorithms at each search engine. A winner today may not rank well in a few months. It also may decline in ranking for a month or two, only to rise again when a particular search engine tweaks its algorithm. Most search engine positioning services companies have built dozens if not hundreds of different informational page templates. Staff members continually toss older, nonfunctional pages on the discard heap, while building newer, more successful templates to take their place.

Some SEP professionals claim to have templates that work well in all of the major search engines. Depending on the difficulty or competitiveness of the keyword or phrase they target, their "tried and true" templates may work well. For more competitive keywords or phrases, however, even the best pages have to be tweaked.

iProspect.com has developed several informational page templates that rank well across most of the major search engines, depending on the keyword. During our five years of practice we have crafted pages that have remained very successful for long periods of time, but we fully understand that we cannot rest on our laurels. We develop and refine new pages constantly. More importantly, even our best, most successful informational page templates experience performance problems when we modify them to match the look and feel of a client's Web site. Remember, the goal of an informational page is to be indistinguishable from the rest of the Web site. iProspect works primarily with Fortune 500 accounts that require a higher level of branding consistency. In our efforts to match these companies' "brand standards" it's often necessary to build additional tables or other elements into their informational pages that, to some extent, reduce the pages' effectiveness. Usually, in spite of page changes for branding considerations, our informational pages will garner a spate of top search engine rankings; yours should too. Just remember that search engine positioning is an iterative process. It is not about finding or building the perfect informational page template on your first try; it is about writing solid, valuable copy about the product or service you're promoting and then testing the first page you build. Once the page has been submitted and indexed by a particular search engine, you measure your ranking, make any necessary improvements to the page, and resubmit it. Hopefully, your search engine position improves, or at the very least you record the change you made and its outcome. Using this process, you continually tweak your pages and learn how to cause their rankings to climb over time.

You Can't Satisfy All of the Engines All of the Time

The techniques that get you a high ranking in one search engine can get you penalized or even removed from the index of another search engine. Surprised? This is because it's difficult to design a single page that will rank well for all of your chosen keywords in all engines, though a good informational page will sometimes rank well in more than one search engine.

Since there are so many sites indexed, you must focus the content of your page to rank well in today's overflowing engines.

Most companies want their Web sites to be found under several keywords that their prospects are likely to query in search engines. For this reason, you'll want to create separate pages that emphasize each of those keywords. Look at an example of a Web site of a company that would like to rank well for searches on keywords related to horses. This company would like its site to rank well under three keywords in particular:

1. horse
2. performance horse
3. equine

The following Web page naming convention illustrates how you might name the individual informational pages optimized to achieve a high ranking for each keyword:

http://www.horsesite.com/a-horse.htm
(optimized for the keyword "horse" for AltaVista)

http://www.horsesite.com/a-performance-horse.htm
(optimized for the keyword phrase "performance horse" for AltaVista)

http://www.horsesite.com/a-equine.htm
(optimized for the keyword "equine" for AltaVista)

You can create several of these informational pages, each optimized to rank well for a different keyword in a different engine.

You should keep in mind, however, that most search engines consider the act of creating dozens of near-identical pages as "spamming" their index and might remove your pages altogether. This is most dangerous when you either inadvertently (or intentionally) cause dozens of your site's pages to rank well for one keyword search. The search engine user is returned 30 matches, all of them leading to one of your informational pages and looking identical or very similar! If your competitors see this, you can bet they'll inform the search engine in hopes of getting your Web site permanently expelled.

This form of spamming devalues the search engine. Nobody wants to scroll through dozens of duplicate sites to locate the information they need. Unless you run the CNN Web site or some other huge content-based site, you probably don't have something to please everyone.

You can avoid potential problems by creating informational pages with different content that describes your product or services briefly and then linking them to different pages within your Web site. If the content that these informational pages link to involves different topical information or products, and you don't create more than a couple pages for each keyword, no one is likely to complain. Vary the content on each informational page, and you won't be breaking any rules.

> **CAUTION**   Some search engine "experts" have long advised that you simply create copies of your index page (and make changes to the page to emphasize different keywords) and name them index1.htm, index2.htm, index3.htm, etc. Doing this only asks for trouble, since anyone seeing index10.htm is going to know immediately that you've got at least nine other copies of your home page out there. If one of your competitors complains to a search engine, you then run the risk of getting dropped from the index. The search engine could easily red flag pages that are named this way in order to spot potential troublemakers.

> **TIP**   Some techniques work better than others, depending on the engine. Sometimes a shorter, more concise page will rank higher on AltaVista than a longer one. You could create alternate shorter pages and name them accordingly:
> http://www.horse-web-site.com/horse-short.htm
> http://www.horse-web-site.com/performance-horse-short.htm
> http://www.horse-web-site/equine-short.htm

Experiment with different pages and page names to describe these experiments, but be careful. Don't go overboard!

Further Warnings about Naming Pages

After several tests, we believe that GO.com may have implemented a penalty to combat potential spam for pages that contain the name "index" after the root domain. And while this data was gathered from GO.com, most of the other search engines have followed suit. In this example, the "is" stands for pages submitted to GO.com, and the next word is the keyword for which the pages are optimized.

http://www.party-web-site.com/index-is-balloons.htm
http://www.party-web-site.com/index-is-singingtelegram.htm
http://www.party-web-site.com/index-is-magician.htm

After being in the index for two weeks, several pages that we created using this naming convention were dropped even though they contained nothing that would otherwise red flag them as being unacceptable. Based on feedback from readers of this report, we believe that GO.com now searches their database for pages using this sort of naming convention (specifically the word "index") as the first part of the page name.

To verify, we submitted different pages containing the word "index." In this case, two of three pages were immediately ignored and not added to the database at all. However, we did manage to get the two pages with the "index" prefix accepted into the database after several tries.

It would seem that the unwritten rule is not entirely consistent, or perhaps GO.com was simply losing pages at random recently. If that's the case, make sure all your pages are actually being added to the index and staying there. To be on the safe side, we suggest you avoid naming multiple pages with "index" as the prefix.

This type of penalty is probably in response to unethical marketers who create dozens of duplicate pages targeting one or two keywords. Some of these spammers are trying to get their pages to occupy all of the first 20 to 30 matches returned for a particular keyword search. This almost ensures that someone searching for that keyword will visit one of their sites (or doorways to their one main site). And this technique infuriates searchers and other Web site owners alike.

We recommend naming your pages after the keyword you are targeting, such as "balloons.htm." If you create a page designed for a specific engine, you might designate it "all-balloons.htm" for AltaVista (choose a random prefix word that contains the letter "a"; we used the word "all" but you could just as easily use the word "always" or "any"). However, avoid numbering pages such as "balloons1.htm" and "balloons2.htm." Even if the information on each page is unique, you might draw attention to yourself by numbering pages. It's better to choose safer filenames for Web pages created for the different engines.

How to Optimize Your Informational Pages

I've read countless articles online that seek to advise Web marketers on the specific fine-tuning of page elements that help an informational page attain a top ranking in a specific engine. Many people obsess too much about these fine points. These folks seek to split the proverbial hair over and over again in search of an "ideal page" for one search engine or another.

Remember this about informational pages: The most important goal of an informational page is to focus on one theme, which typically will build the page around one to three keywords or keyword phrases. When you build an informational page, it is likely that your reason for building it is that your existing Web site doesn't address a particular topic in sufficient depth to achieve a top search engine ranking, or your Web site has some technical issue that prevents your other Web pages from attaining a top ranking. So, the most important goal of that informational page is to cover the topic and weave a "keyword theme" throughout the page. Refer to the image and code in the figure on the following page as an example of how to tune an informational page for a particular search engine.

The truth is, the "perfect page" depends to some extent on these variables:

- The current algorithm at use in a particular search engine

- How well optimized the pages are that rank near the top for a particular keyword or phrase search in a particular search engine

- How many Web pages there are that target the keyword phrase you're targeting (a search for one keyword in AltaVista can yield three million matches, while a search for another keyword or phrase will yield just a few thousand. Fewer are usually better.)

- How many editor-reviewed pages dominate the top spots. If your page hasn't or won't be reviewed by an editor, you may not attain a ranking no matter how well you tweak the keyword concentrations and placement on the page.

- How many links the top-ranking pages enjoy, and how much weight a particular search engine places on link popularity

- The popularity or frequency of the individual keywords that make up the phrase you're targeting. If your keyword phrase is "car parts," the word "car" may appear in 3 million Web pages and the word "parts" may appear in 10 million Web pages (lots of things have "parts," including stereos, electronics, games, chickens, etc.).

If you're targeting the phrase "radioactive isotope spectrometer," each word of the phrase is probably seldom used in Web documents. It is much easier to attain a ranking on that phrase than on the phrase "car parts." The most basic of informational pages will likely help you gain a ranking on that phrase, and there will probably be no need to build one page per engine and tweak each page toward each engine's algorithm.

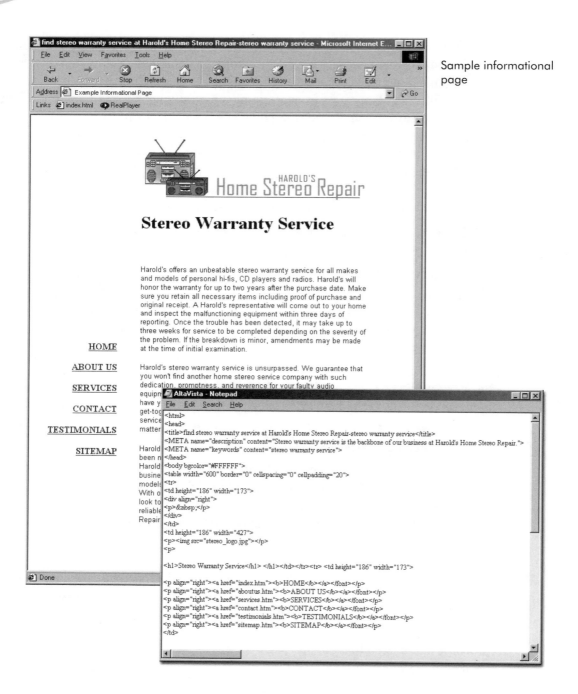

Sample informational page

But for the more competitive phrases — those that are made up of commonly occurring words with millions of associated documents — you need to refine your page as carefully as you can.

As a general rule of thumb, a basic Web page that contains a keyword theme and keywords in the Title tag, keyword META tag, headline, first 25 words, last 25 words, and an activated link will get the job done for most people and most keyword phrases. If you find yourself competing for a more popular keyword, here are steps you can take to tweak your page and further optimize it to best your competition.

1. Measure a page in one of the top-ranking positions and match their keyword concentrations

The oldest tactic in the book is to find a top-ranking page and simply make yours match it keyword for keyword — this does not mean you copy the page or reuse even one of their sentences. We are not condoning or recommending copyright infringement. Instead, evaluate the page ahead of yours. Make your Title tag the exact same length in terms of the number of words in the title. If this page has a keyword in the third position, make sure your Title tag has a keyword in the third position. If their page has the keyword twice in the title, in position three and seven, you do the same — without copying their Title tag. If their page has 264 words of copy, write 264 words of copy for your informational page. If their 264 words of copy contain three occurrences of the targeted keyword, yours should have three, and so on. In theory, you can build a page that is identical to theirs in format. However, the search engine will treat the two pages differently depending on what other ranking factors the engine considers.

2. Use WebPosition Gold's Page Critic

WebPosition Gold includes a very powerful tool called Page Critic which allows you to evaluate an individual Web page against each search engine's algorithm (or even compare your page against a top-ranking page). Of course, WebPosition Gold does not know with complete certainty what each search engine's algorithm is, but it is the best tool available for the job.

WebPosition Gold performs thousands of searches on dozens of keywords in each search engine and then sends its own spider to visit and measure each Web page that was found in the search results. It captures all those pages, thousands of search matches to each query, and then evaluates the pages, looking for

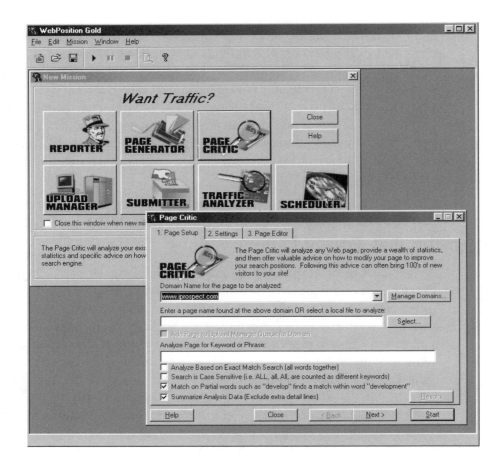

discernable trends in each engine's search results. For instance, it may discover that pages with more than 500 words are all grouped in the top search matches at AltaVista in a given month, or that all top-ranking pages in Excite have the targeted keyword in two headline statements, or that HotBot (Inktomi) is favoring pages that have a 15 percent keyword weight. It takes this information and creates what it calls a knowledge base.

All you need to do is launch WebPosition Gold, select the Page Critic, and input your page's filename and location, and WebPosition Gold will produce a report that advises you on changes you should make to your page to improve its rank in each of the search engines. A trial version of WebPosition Gold is included on the companion CD.

3. Increase the keyword weight, prominence, and frequency

Often, simply increasing the total number of occurrences of the targeted keyword phrase on the page by one will help you improve your ranking. By doing this, you're not just increasing frequency, you're also increasing the keyword weight. Other times, you have to increase the prominence or position of the keyword in a particular HTML element, such as the title. In other words, moving the keyword in the site's Title tag from the third word to the second word can improve your ranking. Another tactic that has worked is to add another headline tag (an <H1> through <H6> tag) containing the targeted keyword phrase. If there are three paragraphs of text on the page, perhaps another headline that introduces one of the paragraphs of copy is warranted.

4. Increase the occurrences of the most unique keyword phrase but not the entire keyword phrase

If you're targeting the phrase "whitewater rafting," query each word of the phrase individually in AltaVista and watch how many Web pages are returned for each search. To illustrate:

> AltaVista search for "white" produces: 9,971,765 pages
> AltaVista search for "water" produces: 8,853,475 pages
> AltaVista search for "rafting" produces: 326,995 pages
> AltaVista search for "whitewater" produces: 279,320 pages

Chances are that one of the words in your keyword phrase has fewer total associated Web pages. In this example the word "whitewater" has the fewest total Web pages — less than 300,000 associated documents, as opposed to more than 8 million for "white" and "water." If you build an informational page with five occurrences of your targeted keyword phrase, try adding additional occurrences of the keyword that contains the least frequently occurring word to your page to improve its ranking.

This is called Term Frequency Inverse Document Frequency (TFIDF) relevancy scoring, and many search engines employ it as part of a term vector approach to relevancy. The premise behind this relevancy criterion is that keywords that have fewer associated documents must be more specific than those that have more associated documents and as such, are weighed more heavily by the search engine's relevancy algorithm. The "term frequency" in the expression is the occurrence frequency of the term in the Web page and is usually reflective of the importance of that keyword or phrase. The "inverse document frequency" is a factor that enhances terms (keywords or phrases) that appear in fewer total documents while simultaneously de-emphasizing terms that occur in many documents. Hence, a search for "Edelbrock intake" would place more emphasis on "Edelbrock" (a popular brand of high-performance auto parts) than the word "intake" because the brand name Edelbrock occurs in fewer documents.

5. Increase the Number of Links to Your Web Page

Keyword placement on your informational page alone will not ace the rankings. Even if you copied (stole) a competitor's page and uploaded it to your Web site, it would rank differently from that competitor's page. Why? Because search engines count the number of links to a page. You must match not only the competing page's content or keyword metrics, but also its link popularity. Go to AltaVista and type link: www.competitor-domain-name.com (whatever your competitor's domain name happens to be).

AltaVista will return a list of all the pages that link to your competitor's page, including all of the pages of their Web site that link to that page. This is where most people's informational pages fail. They link the pages to their Web site, but don't link their other pages to their informational pages. When a search engine finds a Web page with links in only one direction, it becomes suspicious. Link to your informational pages from your other site pages. If you've done a good job on your informational pages, they provide valuable information about a product or service, so why not link to them? Solicit links to your informational pages from other Web sites. The importance of link popularity can't be underestimated.

Targeting Specific Search Engines Using the Robots.txt File

How do you build informational pages that are so focused that they target a specific search engine, without allowing those pages to be picked up and indexed by another search engine? This is an important question because you don't want to have several Web pages show up in the search results in a particular search engine. You can literally build informational pages that target search engine A, while directing search engine B to ignore the page.

You accomplish this feat by using the robots.txt file. To create a robots.txt file, open Window's Notepad or any other editor that can save plain ASCII text files. (Note: For the purpose of this example, the terms "spider" and "search engine" are used interchangeably.) Use the following syntax to exclude a file-name from a particular search engine:

```
User-agent: {SpiderNameHere}
Disallow: {FilenameHere}
```

For example, to instruct Excite's spider, named ArchitextSpider, to ignore your Web pages named contact-information.html, services1.html, and services2.html, include a robots.txt file with the following content:

```
User-agent: ArchitextSpider
Disallow: /contact-information.html
Disallow: /services1.html
Disallow: /services2.html
```

To exclude an entire directory, use this syntax:

```
User-agent: ArchitextSpider
Disallow: /directory-name/
```

To disallow a particular file within the above directory, use the following syntax:

```
User-agent: ArchitextSpider
Disallow: /directory-name/file.htm
```

Once you create and then save this as a text file, simply upload the file to the root directory of your Web site. The search engine spiders will open and read this file, and ignore those pages you've asked it to ignore. That way, your AltaVista pages will find their way into AltaVista but not into Excite, and vice versa. A simpler solution for those of you who are not comfortable writing a robots.txt file is to create a site map or hallway page that links only to your informational pages that target a particular search engine. If these pages are not interlinked with informational pages that target other search engines, you'll have some separation without the robots.txt file. Remember, though, that just because you did not submit a Web page to an engine is no assurance that the page won't be found by another engine if someone links to it. That's why the robots.txt file is the more desirable solution.

Get a Grip: Make Them Click

Don't forget to tell visitors to your informational pages to "click here" for additional information or to "learn more." All the research on banner advertising extols the virtue of asking the visitor to take a specific action. Don't question this wisdom; just use it. Make the phrase "click here" a part of your marketing practices.

External Domains Provide Added Traction

For many engines, including Excite, HotBot, and AltaVista, you will find it easier to get high rankings on your site's home page than on internal pages. For some reason, these search engines tend to favor the "default page" of the Web site, often thought of as the "home page" and usually containing the index.html or default.asp filename. Additionally, some search engines favor Web sites that include the targeted keyword in the domain name, so consider this when you're considering what domain name to register.

Your home page is the page displayed when someone visits your Web site's root domain, e.g., www.yourcompany.com. The page they actually see is:

http://www.yourcompany.com/index.htm

The index.htm page name is usually not displayed in the browser window.

To take advantage of this effect, you may choose to register additional domain names on which you'll host your informational pages or other related Web site content. There's no reason why your Web site should be hosted on only one domain name. Think outside the box! Domain names are cheap, and you may benefit by having more than one. Informational pages aside, if you sell camping gear, hiking gear, and rafting gear, your Web site could be made up of three domain names that cover all the topics.

No matter which page your visitor enters through, the look and feel should be consistent with your other pages, and the surfer may not even notice that the domain name has changed from one section to another. You'll have the benefit of an additional default or home page for each of your domains, and each area of the Web site gains the benefit of the targeted keyword appearing in the root domain. As we discuss in Chapter 7, having a keyword in your top-level domain name sometimes will improve your Web site's ranking in certain search engines.

Try to select and register domain names that include your targeted keywords. For instance, if you're targeting "whitewater rafting" and you find that "whitewaterrafting.com" is taken, you may be able to register "white-waterrafting.com" or "white-water-rafting.com" or perhaps "i-love-white-water-rafting.com" or even "white-water-rafting-is-fun.com." Be creative! You'll find a way to register a domain name with a keyword or phrase in it.

Expect that your hosting provider will not add a domain name for free. You'll be looking at $25 per domain name per month, at least, even if you're only putting up static informational pages. But this additional cost is well worth it for the high rankings it may generate.

> **REMINDER**   On the CD is a link to a low-cost domain name registration company, BulkRegister.com.

The Doorway Page: Another Option

A doorway page, or gateway page, is an alternate entrance to a Web site created in the interest of attaining a top ranking on particular keywords or keyword phrases in a major search engine. Unscrupulous Web marketers are known to hide their doorway pages.

Doorway pages are often hosted externally to the Web site. In other words, a domain name is registered (usually one that includes the targeted keyword phrase) and the doorway page is erected on that domain name, with links to a destination page on another Web site. Informational pages can be hosted externally, too, but typically, these pages match the look and feel of the actual Web site and are more often hosted on that Web site instead of externally.

Doorway pages have been very controversial due to their misuse by spammers. As stated previously, many engines require a minimum of 250 words of body copy to index your site. Someone discovered that if you wrote (or stole) 250 words of copy — about anything — but changed the keyword in the Title tag, the headline, and just the keywords that appear in the copy, the pages would all attain high rankings in several of the major search engines. Then, someone discovered that you could simply take one of your successful doorway pages and duplicate it, thousands of times. If you were proficient in programming, you could write a script that would go through and replace the targeted keywords. Suddenly, one person could build thousands and thousands of doorway pages, each one targeting a different keyword, with the touch of a button. Instant spam. Reams of it.

Search engines became inundated with gazillions of near-duplicate pages. Typically, these pages would have little, if any, content. A page designed to attain a ranking for "laserjet printer" might have 250 words of copy stolen from Shakespeare! The link above the body copy might read: "Click here for information about 'laserjet printers'" (the keyword phrase would be the activated link). The Title tag would contain the phrase "laserjet printer," the headline (<H1> tag) above the 250 words of Shakespeare copy would contain the keyword phrase "laserjet printer," and the first 25 words of the copy would have the keyword randomly inserted. There would be text links on the page that contained the targeted keyword phrase.

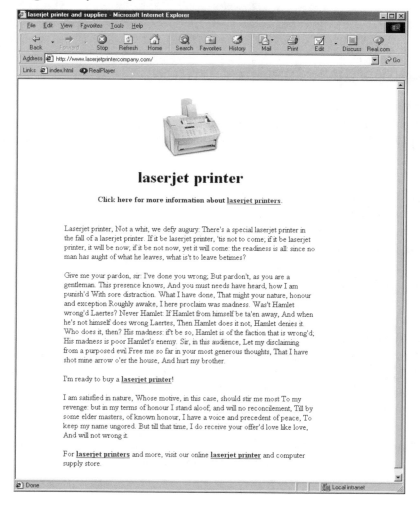

When someone stumbled across one of these pages, they might find them odd, but they'd simply click the link that promised to provide information about the search term, and hopefully, they'd enter a Web site that sold laserjet printers. Of course, most of the time the search engine user would never see this page, because they would be instantly redirected to the destination Web site through a fast redirect script. One trusted that the owner of the doorway page hadn't sought a ranking on "laserjet printer" and then sent the person to an adult sex Web site instead — but it did and does happen.

NOTE   Doorway pages, when used properly and when they contain relevant informative content, are a perfectly legitimate ranking tool. However, you should avoid registering a large number of domains for this tactic as it could be considered spam by the search engines.

Chapter 36:

Assessing Your Performance

T here's more to assessing a Web site's performance than checking ranks. In addition to rank checking, two of the most important capabilities are log file analysis and link checking. Using these tools, you can develop a comprehensive picture of a site's overall performance. In the case of large sites, you can mine the data provided by your analysis to create decisional information for marketing purposes. What is this data and why is it so important? Identifying and retracing the "steps" of visitors to Web sites are the meat and potatoes of search engine positioning. But how can we do those tracings quickly and get the information we need? Read on.

Log File Analysis: Searching for Buried Treasure

First, a few basics. Every request made to a Web server is logged in its access, or transfer, log as a new line. These requests are commonly known as hits. At a minimum, the data on each hit includes the Internet Protocol (IP) address of the resource making the request, the date and time of the request, and the actual request. Most Web servers also record any errors, but we'll leave that subject for later. Another type of log — the one we're most concerned with — is called the referrer (sometimes misspelled as *referer*) log. This log shows the page the surfer was on before they came to your site. The number and quality of links to your site is key here.

Unfortunately, many common Web servers allow their administrators to disable referrer logging, sometimes even disabling it as a default. Since most server administrators are more concerned with minimizing file size than marketing, many of them choose this option. This is a major mistake from the standpoint of the SEP professional, because you can mine a lot of useful data from referrer logs.

Many Web servers use combined logs that include the referrer log (there is a "referrer" field within the log). The combined log also shows a status code, such as 404, and the number of bytes transferred.

There are numerous formats for log files. Here is a brief list of log formats supported by WebTrends software:

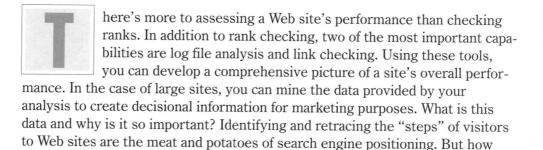

Apache
Apache Common with Cookies
Apache Extended
Apache Extended with Cookies
Best Internet

CERN
Cold Fusion
Emwac
HP
IBM Internet Connection Secure Server
Lotus Domino
Market Focus
MCI
Microsoft Extended Log File Format v3.0 (MS IIS — produced using WebTrends plug-in)
Microsoft IIS International Date Format (MS IIS)
Microsoft Internet Information Server 3.0 (MS IIS)
Microsoft Internet Information Server 4.0 (W3C Extended format)
Microsoft ODBC
NCSA Combined (Extended) Log File
NCSA Common Log File
NCSA Common Multi-Home
Netscape Enterprise Server
Netscape FastTrack
Netscape NSAPI Extended Format
Open Market Log File
Oracle
Purveyor Extended Format
Purveyor Multi-Home Format
Real Audio Log File
Spry
WebSite Combined Multi-Home Format
WebSite Common Multi-Home Format

Notice that just about every server on the market has its own log file format. Don't panic! It gets better. When you get down to the nitty-gritty, you only need to remember that there are two major log file formats: common and extended. The extended format is the one we are concerned with here. Now, there are a lot of people out there who are going to read this and scream, "That's not true!" Let me explain. I'm not talking about the exact structure of the log file — I'm talking about the **fields** contained in the file. The common log file format contains only five fields: the Internet Protocol (IP) address of the resource making the request, the date of the request, the time of the request, the status code, and the number of bytes transferred. Before you get a headache, let's postpone the detailed discussion of these.

Flexing Your Log File Muscle

The extended log file format, probably the most common in use today (in one version or another), is thoroughly described in World Wide Web Consortium (W3C) Working Draft WD-logfile-960323, titled *Extended Log File Format*. This document was authored by Phillip Hallam-Baker and Brian Behlendorf and can be found at http://www.w3.org/TR. Microsoft Internet Information Server 4.0 (IIS 4.0), in the list noted above, explicitly uses this format.

Hallam-Baker and Behlendorf describe the extended log file format as *extensible*, meaning that the server administrators can customize captured data. The document defines several aspects of capturing, which we'll discuss briefly here.

A few more basics (be patient!): As I said previously, a Web server records each HTTP request, or hit, on a new line. Each line may contain either an entry or a *directive*. A line that begins with the # character is a directive, of which there are seven: version, fields, software, start-date, end-date, date, and remark. *Version* describes the version of the extended log file format used. (As far as I know, version 1.0 is the only one to date.) *Fields* specifies the fields recorded in the log. *Software* identifies the program that created the log. *Start-date* and *end-date* record the dates and times the log began and ended, respectively. *Date* is the date and time that the entry was added. *Remark* contains comment information. WD-logfile-960323 defines a large group of *field identifiers* that are allowed as values of the fields directive. Although a detailed discussion of these field identifiers is beyond the scope of this book, I've taken one example from WD-logfile-960323:

```
#Fields: time cs-method cs-uri
00:34:23 GET /foo/bar.html
12:21:16 GET /foo/bar.html
12:45:52 GET /foo/bar.html
```

In this case, the field identifiers specify that each entry must contain a time, an HTTP method, and the file requested. What you need to learn from all this is that the ability to specify the fields makes this format extremely flexible. Any other log file format can become compatible with the extended log file format by using the fields directive.

How to Decipher Log Entries

One of the first steps toward unraveling the mystery of site performance assessment is learning the parts of a combined log file. Take a look at this typical entry:

```
209.192.223.180 - - [07/Dec/2000:05:56:15 -0800] "GET /images/inc.jpg
HTTP/1.1" 200 20291 "http://4advertisingontheweb.com/incorporate_
your_internet_business/" "Mozilla/4.0 (compatible; MSIE 5.01; Windows NT 5.0)"
```

In the raw log file, this paragraph would all be run in a single line. At first glance, this line appears about as clear as mud. But wait! Everything in this entry has a meaning. Let's look at the pieces individually.

The first part of the line, "209.192.223.180", is the Internet Protocol (IP) address of the machine that issued the request. Most of the time this is a server owned by one of the many Internet service providers (ISP), such as America Online. This subject is covered in more detail later.

The next section of note, "[07/Dec/2000:05:56:15 –0800]", is the time stamp. This section is mostly self-explanatory. The part before the dash is the date and time the request was made, in Greenwich Mean Time (GMT). The offset "0800" tells us that the server is located on the West Coast of the United States, eight hours behind GMT.

The third important section is the actual request the server received. This example, "GET /images/inc.jpg HTTP/1.1", is a request for an image: inc.jpg. The last part is the protocol, HTTP 1.1.

The example brings up an important topic: There's a big difference between hits and page views. This user is asking for a specific image on the site, but people don't see raw images when surfing the Web. Images are embedded in Hypertext Markup Language (HTML) pages. The request for this image counts as a hit, but not as a page view. A page view only includes those requests that include document-type files, dynamic pages, or forms.

The next piece of the log entry puzzle is a rather mysterious number: 200. Have you ever clicked on a link and seen "The page cannot be found"? On the page it says "HTTP 404 — File not found." Well, I can guarantee that you'll never see a page with "HTTP 200" on it. That is because 200 is the status code for success, meaning that the request was successfully answered. The next number, 20291, is simply the number of bytes transferred.

Things start to get interesting in the next section. This is the Uniform Resource Locator (URL) for the referring page. Since this request was for an image, this line, "http://4advertisingontheweb.com/incorporate_your_internet_

business/," shows the page within which the image is embedded. It gets far more exciting when the referrer is a search engine. In that case, the URL looks something like http://www.altavista.com/cgi-bin/query?pg=q&stype=stext &Translate=on&sc=on&q=starting+Internet+business&stq=10. This informs us that the search engine is AltaVista, and the user searched on "starting Internet business."

How do you separate AltaVista search results from drill downs into the AltaVista Directory (powered by LookSmart)? This is easier than you might assume. If the user had come to us from the AltaVista Directory, the referrer field would look something like http://looksmart.altavista.com/cgi-bin/query? pg=dir&tp=Work_.26_Money/Small_Business/Products_.26_Services/ Business_Incubators&crid=579127. Look closely. The domain looksmart.altavista.com reveals the fact that this surfer indeed came to us from the directory, and we can even tell that the site is listed in the Business Incubators category. We discuss the referrer in much greater detail later on.

The last field in the log entry simply indicates that this Web surfer was using Microsoft Internet Explorer 5.01 on a machine running Microsoft Windows NT 5.0, also known as Windows 2000.

Retracing the Visitor's Path

Now that we know the fields in a combined log file, the next step in solving our mystery is analyzing logs. Do we have to buy a really expensive piece of software to conduct rudimentary log file analyses? No! Log files are actually ASCII text files, and can be opened by a program as simple as Notepad or WordPad. Neither of these is very good at manipulating data, though, so I use Microsoft Excel. In this case, I've imported a sample log into Excel as a delimited file, with spaces as the delimiters. Here's an example of what I ended up with:

24.16.141.26- -	[23/Nov/2000:20:49:20	0800]	GET /starting_an_online_business/ HTTP/1.0	200	8221	http://www.altavista.com/ cgi-bin/query?pg=q&stype= stext&Translate=on&sc= on&q=starting+Internet+ business&stq=10	Mozilla/4.76 [en] (Win98; U)
24.16.141.26- -	[23/Nov/2000:20:49:20	0800]	GET /images/inc.jpg HTTP/1.0	200	20291	http://4advertisingontheweb .com/starting_an_online_ business/	Mozilla/4.76 [en] (Win98; U)

24.16.141.26- -	[23/Nov/2000:20:49:21	0800]	GET /images/spacer.gif HTTP/1.0	200	51	http://4advertisingontheweb.com/starting_an_online_business/	Mozilla/4.76 [en] (Win98; U)
24.16.141.26- -	[23/Nov/2000:20:49:21	0800]	GET /images/inc_bottomline.gif HTTP/1.0	200	871	http://4advertisingontheweb.com/starting_an_online_business/	Mozilla/4.76 [en] (Win98; U)
24.16.141.26- -	[23/Nov/2000:21:00:12	0800]	GET /starting_an_online_business/index.html HTTP/1.0	200	8221	http://www.altavista.com/cgi-bin/query?pg=q&stype=stext&Translate=on&sc=on&q=starting+Internet+business&stq=10	Mozilla/4.76 [en] (Win98; U)
24.16.141.26- -	[23/Nov/2000:21:00:13	0800]	GET /images/inc.jpg HTTP/1.0	200	20291	http://4advertisingontheweb.com/starting_an_online_business/index.html	Mozilla/4.76 [en] (Win98; U)
24.16.141.26- -	[23/Nov/2000:21:00:13	0800]	GET /images/spacer.gif HTTP/1.0	200	51	http://4advertisingontheweb.com/starting_an_online_business/index.html	Mozilla/4.76 [en] (Win98; U)
24.16.141.26- -	[23/Nov/2000:21:00:13	0800]	GET /images/inc_bottomline.gif HTTP/1.0	200	871	http://4advertisingontheweb.com/starting_an_online_business/index.html	Mozilla/4.76 [en] (Win98; U)

Notice that Excel has done a very good job of placing the fields in columns. Now, how do we interpret these entries? The first thing to notice is that all the entries in the example come from the same IP address: 24.16.141.26. Using a reverse DNS lookup tool (see http://www.dns.net/dnsrd for more information), we find that the block of IPs from 24.0.0.0 to 24.23.255.255 are registered to the @Home Network, a broadband ISP. The example shows eight hits from this same IP address. Since all eight hits occur on the same day, starting at 20:49:20 and ending at 21:00:13, we'll assume that all of them came from a single user, constituting a single user session, or visit. All but two of the eight hits were requests for images: Six of them asked for and received either a .gif or .jpg file. The two requests for HTML files are referred to as page views.

The next field is the status code field. All eight examples have the 200 code for success. The link to W3C's RFC 2616 is http://www.w3.org/Protocols/rfc2616/rfc2616-sec6.html#sec6.1.1. Section 6.1.1 of RFC 2616 describes all the recognized status or response codes allowed by the HTTP 1.1 standard, including the 200, the dreaded 404, "Page not found," and others that you probably don't want to hear about.

The next field gives us the number of bytes transferred. This is a very important field, but not for our purposes.

Now, the referrer field becomes very important. The referrer here is the search engine AltaVista. Let's just copy that URL directly into the address bar of our browser. The best thing about seeing a search engine as a referrer is that you know immediately that you must have a ranking on some keyword or phrase. Why else would a search engine be a referrer? In this case we can see that the user was searching on the words "starting Internet business" in AltaVista.

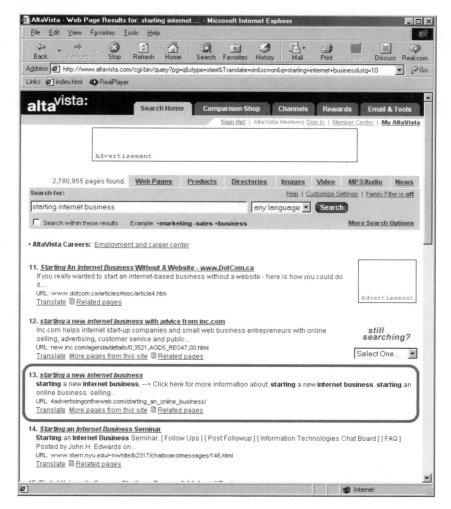

Once we drop the referring URL in our browser, we see that we are in a rather disappointing 13th position. Thirteenth isn't so bad when you consider two things, however. One, AltaVista claims to have indexed 2,780,955 pages relevant to "starting Internet business." Two, the user clicked-through to our page. That's pretty important in and of itself.

The other thing we should notice in this entry is the user agent field. Notice that our surfer was using something called "Mozilla 4.76," with their language set to English (en), on a machine running Microsoft Windows 98. The "U" is code for United States. That doesn't identify the country the user is in, though; rather it indicates the level of encryption on the machine. In this case, "U" means that the machine is running strong encryption that cannot be exported. The other possible value is "I", for international, meaning that the machine is running weak encryption that may be exportable. Do we really need to know this? Probably not, but it's an interesting tidbit to share with friends.

Let's try to reconstruct this visitor's actions on our site. I have to admit, this user's path drove me nuts. The first GET occurred at 20:49:20 GMT and the last image GET occurred at 20:49:21 GMT. Since one of the images on the site, the JPEG, is fairly large (20,291 bytes), we can be fairly sure that the user was on some type of broadband connection, probably a DSL or corporate T1. Then what did our user do? Well, there are a couple of possibilities. It is pretty obvious that they didn't click onto another page on the site, since if they had we would see another GET with the user's entry page as the referrer, much as we see the entry page as the referrer for the image GETs.

Another very real possibility is that they clicked on a link on our site to another site, since the request for any pages on another site would be logged in that site's log files, not in ours. In this case, though, I'm fairly sure the user hit the Back button. Why do I say that? Because our user came back to the site ten minutes later with the same referring URL. Now we get to the part that drove me nuts. When the user came back to our site they came from a different link. I know this because the first entry has "GET /starting_an_online_business/ HTTP/1.0" and the second entry has the string "GET /starting_an_online_business/index.html HTTP/1.0". You get a gold star if you happen to know that both of these requests are asking for the same page, since any HTTP request for a directory — i.e., a folder on the server — is answered with the default page for that directory, usually "index.html" or "default.asp" or something similar. If our visitor had clicked on the same link to come **back** to the page, however, the requests would be logged identically.

So now we go back to the referring page, http://www.altavista.com/cgi-bin/query?pg=q&stype=stext&Translate=on&sc=on&q=starting+Internet+business&stq=10, to find the second link. Here's what I found frustrating. At the time of this writing, there is no second link to our site on this page. So how did this user get referred to another page on our site if there's no link? We know what the link must have been: http://www.4advertisingontheweb.com/starting_an_online_business/index.html. And we know what the referring URL was: http://www.altavista.com/cgi-bin/query?pg=q&stype=stext&Translate=on&sc=on&q=starting+Internet+business&stq=10. But there is no link! Have you figured it out yet?

The answer lies in the fact that the user made these requests on 23 November 2000, and I'm writing this on 12 December 2000. One thing that you've probably learned from reading this book is that search engines and their results are like shifting sands: in constant flux. Currently, there's no link to http://www.4advertisingontheweb.com/starting_an_online_business/index.html from http://www.altavista.com/cgi-bin/query?pg=q&stype=stext&Translate=on&sc=on&q=starting+Internet+business&stq=10, but there had to have been one on November 23, 2000. If we go to http://www.altavista.com/cgi-bin/query?pg=q&stype=stext&Translate=on&sc=on&q=starting+Internet+business&stq=20, we see that the first link on the page, position 21, is the link we're seeking. Make sense? The lesson to learn from this is that log files do not lie. Unless something is grievously wrong with your server configuration, there must be a logical explanation for every single thing you see in the log file. If you see 404 errors for a page you know is up and running, then that page wasn't up and running at the time the request was made. **Log files do not lie.**

Log File Analysis

At this point you must be saying, "This is all great and very interesting, but it just took me ten minutes to look at eight lines of a log file. My site gets a thousand hits a day! Isn't there an easier way?"

Well, where there's a need, there's somebody willing to sell you something to fill it. Actually, there are a number of commercial log file analysis tools on the market, as well as quite a few shareware programs. A recent search in Google on the words "shareware log analysis" returned about 25,000 documents. And the Open Directory category Top: Computers: Software: Internet: Site Management: Log Analysis contains about 100 listings for noncommercial log analysis software. From what I've seen, most of the noncommercial software tools out there share a few specific problems. First, many of these tools are available only as C source code or Perl scripts, meaning that you have to be a fairly advanced programmer to install them and use them. Second, many of them only output to an HTML document, viewable using a browser. That's fine for somebody who's just fooling around with a small site, but to perform any type of serious analysis you need to output to a spreadsheet or a format that can be opened by a spreadsheet program. If you are a skilled administrator with knowledge of C or Perl, you can probably find some source code that you can alter to fit your specific needs.

For the rest of us there is quite a large selection of commercial log analysis software. In fact, the array is huge, with an equally amazing price range, from $99.95 for Mach5's FastStats Analyzer to over $100,000 for WebTrends' CommerceTrends 3.0 platform. The real question is, what do you need the software to do and what kind of site are you running? If you are running a single-server Web site for a local florist shop, you probably don't need CommerceTrends. If, however, you are running a complex Web site hosted on multiple servers and are responsible for reporting ROI on numerous online advertising campaigns, then perhaps FastStats won't quite cut it. Decide what your individual needs are, and then buy the solution that comes closest to meeting those needs.

That said, there are definitely a couple of major players to be aware of. The biggest heavies are probably Accrue Software, Sane Solutions, NetGenesis, and WebTrends. All of these companies offer high-end products for managing complex, multiserver, e-commerce Web sites, but be prepared to part with some cash! The only two that really offer a broad range of software (in terms of price) are Sane Solutions and WebTrends. Sane Solutions' NetTracker 5.0 comes in three different flavors — Professional for $495, Enterprise for $995, and eBusiness Edition starting at $9,995. WebTrends has similar offerings, with their Log Analyzer starting at $499 and, as already mentioned, Commerce-Trends 3.0, which starts at $100,000. Again, the most important thing is to find a solution that works for **your** site. Most of these companies have sample reports on their Web sites, so you can find the software that provides the information you really need.

Using Log File Reports

The commercial log analysis software package I'm most familiar with is WebTrends' Professional Suite. The base package costs about $1,000 and includes a year's worth of full support and upgrades. It's a fairly flexible tool that offers the option of exporting the report to Microsoft Excel format, a feature I absolutely love. A detailed discussion of how to configure WebTrends' reporting is beyond the scope of this book, but here's one tip: Be sure to set any reports detailing search engines, phrases, or keywords to full depth.

The following four "clues" tell you a great deal about how your site is performing in the search engines and where there is room for improvement: the number of unique visitors, the number of unique referring URLs, the number of referrals from searches, and the top phrases and keywords. If you are getting 25,000 visitors per month and only two of those are from Yahoo!, take another look at your Yahoo! listing. You can use the top phrases to help choose keywords to target in your site's META tags.

Another thing to look at is the top entry pages report. This list of pages should correlate fairly well with the list of pages you've optimized and submitted to the search engines. If it doesn't, something may be wrong. If there are pages on that list you haven't optimized, you should optimize them. If they're driving traffic now, just imagine what some META tags and targeted search engine submissions could do! If some of your optimized pages aren't appearing on the top entry pages list, a couple of things may be happening. Perhaps not many users are seeking the keywords you're targeting on that page. Perhaps the pages don't have enough content and are getting tagged as spam. Either way, you need to make some changes. Some people say that you should analyze the least-requested pages to pick what areas of your site to cut. I don't quite agree with that. The problem there is that the report is titled "Least Requested Pages." That means the report shows only the pages that somebody actually requested. What about all the pages that haven't been requested at all? Consider cutting some of them instead!

Understanding Links

As pointed out in the previous section, most referrals to your site come initially from two sources: searches and links. Once people have found your fantastic Web site, they most likely will bookmark it and return often. But first they must find it. Therefore, one of the most important things a Webmaster should be on top of is the status of their links, both internal and external. Links are, in many ways, the "killer app" that allows the Internet to exist. They are becoming more important every day. Why are they so important to SEP? External links from high-quality, well-traveled sites spread the word that your site is of high quality and deserves to be well traveled. And internal links indicate user friendliness. New search technology, such as Google's, actually rates a site by the number and quality of the links pointing to it. Google was the first search engine to use link popularity to rank results, and others have followed suit.

How to Manage and Maintain Your Links

Links do not just exist — they are created and controlled. Link analysis tools are intended primarily to ensure that all the links on a site are still active, but you can use most of them to develop a site map as well. These tools give you an idea of how a spider "sees" a Web site. They can be used, indirectly, to find "orphan" Web pages, i.e., pages that are hosted on your site but aren't linked to by any other pages on the site. The following table lists a number of tools that allow you to accomplish this quickly and easily.

Application	Cost (basic ver.)	OS req.	Max. # links checked	Report format
InfoLink	$49.95	Windows	over 10,000 pages	html
LinkAlarm	$0.10/page $10 min.	none	none	html
Linkbot	$295	Win 98, 2000, NT	1000	html
LinkScan	$300	Linux, Unix, Windows	500,000+ pages	html
NetMechanic	$35/yr.	none	400 pages	html
Thesus	$49	Mac only	not tested	not tested
WebAnalyzer	$419.95 CA	Win 3.X, 95, NT 4.0	based on memory	html
Xenu	Free	Windows	based on memory	html, tab separated text

Xenu is my personal favorite — and it's free to boot! Xenu is available for download at http://home.snafu.de/tilman/XENU.ZIP. **Xenu's Link Sleuth** (TM)

Work Those Search Engines!

Most of the tools check not only internal links but outgoing, or external, links as well. This is very useful in ensuring that a site is well maintained and user friendly, but doesn't tell you who is linking to you. The only way to get that information is — you guessed it — from the search engines. Many of the engines have a feature, usually hidden in their advanced or "power" search areas, that allows you to find out how many sites link to your site. This only tells you the pages that are indexed by the search engine you are using. For example, if you go to AltaVista and search for the exact phrase "+link:www.iprospect.com –www.iprospect.com," you get a list of sites, excluding the target, that link to the target. If you don't include the "-www.iprospect.com" portion you get a larger number of incoming links, but many of them are internal links on the target site. AltaVista isn't the only search engine that allows you to conduct this type of link check. The following table shows some of the search engines that expose this functionality and how to access it.

Search Engine	URL	Find internal and external links to a page on your Web site	Find external links only to a page on your Web site
alltheweb.com	http://alltheweb.com/cgi-bin/advsearch	Change the word filter to "must include," put the target in the text box, and change "in the text" to "in the link to URL."	Do the same thing as for internal and external query, but add the target URL to the "exclude" text box.
AltaVista	http://www.altavista.com	link:www.company-name.com	link:www.company-name.com -www.company-name.com
GO	http://www.go.com	link:www.company-name.com	link:www.company-name.com -www.company-name.com
Google	http://www.google.com/advanced_search	link:www.company-name.com	none known
HotBot	http://hotbot.lycos.com/?MT=&SM=MC&DV=0&LG=any&DC=10&DE=2&AM1=MC&act.super.x=61&act.super.y=5	Change the "all the words" drop-down to "links to this URL" and search for "http://www.company-name.com."	Do the same thing as for internal and external query, but add company-name.com to the word filter and select "must not contain."
Lycos	http://lycospro.lycos.com/?tab=mylink&aloc=sb_tab_mylink&lpv=1	Put "www.company-name.com" in the "Your URL" text box.	Same as before, but put the target URL in the "Exclude this host" text box.
MSN	http://search.msn.com/advanced.asp	Change the find drop-down from "any of the words" to "links to URL" and search for http://www.company-name.com.	none known

Summing Up the Mystery of Performance Assessment

The three major tools at the disposal of the search engine positioning professional are rank checking, log file analysis, and link checking. If the mystery to be solved is how a site is functioning within the Internet environment, then using these tools the professional can build a comprehensive picture of a site's current performance. More importantly, these tools can provide valuable decisional data to use in the improvement of the site's performance in the search engines.

Rank checking and log file analysis may indicate that a site is performing poorly in Google. What can you do about it? Well, you can check and see how many sites Google shows as linking to the site. Most likely, if the site is performing poorly, there aren't many. Based on your own analysis, you might then solicit links to the site and even submit sites to Google that link to it.

The Ultimate Goal: Visibility Leading to Qualified Traffic

Qualified traffic is the natural outcome of a successful search engine positioning campaign. The goal of search engine positioning is visibility on the universe of keywords and phrases in all of the major search engines. When search engine positioning has traffic as its goal, the practice is perverted to achieve an end that is not necessarily related to the potential of a relevant set of keywords. Each different keyword universe that each different Web site targets will have its own potential. For one client in a niche industry, a fully optimized Web site with rankings on every targeted keyword in every search engine will drive just a few thousand visitors a month, where for another client with a different keyword universe, similar rankings will drive hundreds of thousands or perhaps millions of visitors a month. To expand the keyword universe with the aim of increasing the Web site's traffic produces little value. Broader, less relevant keywords may be queried with greater frequency but the quality of the click-through declines. This strategy will surely increase the site's traffic but the increased numbers will do nothing to improve the quality of the outcomes that the site produces.

In essence, you can succeed at increasing your traffic and fail in the success of your campaign at the same time. The quality of outcome, the richness of the visitor's interaction with your Web site, the conversion rate of visitors into customers, the subscription rate, quantity of page impressions, or length of time on the Web site should be considered depending on a company's site and the goals of their online marketing program. To increase traffic without consideration for how that traffic interacts with the Web site is folly, but worse, it wastes time and your search engine positioning agency's bandwidth on an endeavor that will yield little if any improvement in your outcomes.

Worst of all, it inappropriately wastes your search engine positioning agency's resources and staff time in pursuit of the wrong goal when the time could and should be devoted to retargeting, revising, and optimizing to gain rankings in every engine on the most effective keywords.

NOTE   Still need help? Provide us with a detailed description of your Web site challenge. We'll be pleased to help in any way we can, or will refer you to any number of high-quality search engine optimization specialists whom we know and trust. Feel free to e-mail us at: sales@iprospect.com, or visit our quote request page at: http://www.iprospect.com/book-quote.htm.

Fredrick Marckini – iProspect.com

Chapter 37:

Buying Advertising on Search Engines

This chapter contributed by Catherine Seda,
vice president of online promotions, SiteLab International,
San Diego, CA

Special guest author: Catherine Seda, vice president of online promotions, SiteLab International, San Diego, CA

kay, SEP is a lot of work. Isn't there any other way to get close to the top rankings? Well, there is. You may not be able to get the #1 ranking in the search engine you choose, but you can purchase advertisements located directly next to the top rankings in your keywords of choice! Or, you can attain prominent placement via other banner advertising and content sponsorships.

Even if you are achieving top rankings, you should also consider purchasing text links as a part of your total SEP strategy. By offering users several places to access your Web site, you increase your odds of attracting a targeted audience. It's a complementary strategy designed to get you even more traffic. This chapter will outline the steps involved to help you get started.

Keyword Links

When you run a keyword search, do you ever notice how much information is presented to you besides the ranked sites you requested? If you look between the banner ad and the automated search results, you may see text links that appear to be editorial recommendations — all related to the search you just performed. Besides text links, you'll also see strategically placed "sidebar ads" alongside the search engine's automated results. Many of these are available for purchase. This area of the page is a blend of editorials and advertisements, creating "advertorial" opportunities not normally seen in the print world.

Purchasing text links instead of banner or sidebar ads can be a strategic move for three reasons:

■ They often appear more "editorial looking" than banner ads, enticing users to click on what they think is objective information.

■ They can help you reach more users since some users choose to hide all Web graphics (for faster surfing or because their companies require it), and thus will not see banner ads.

■ They are often a more cost-effective buy than banner ads since the text link cost is usually much less than banner ads, and the click-through rate may only vary slightly (some venues even claim a significantly higher click-through rate on links than banners).

Most portals sell these links based on a cost-per-thousand (CPM) impressions served for selected keywords. A few are based on a cost-per-click (CPC) model. Full or partial "inventory" of available impressions may be bought for each keyword to meet the program's cost minimum.

If you're responsible for online media buying in your company, here's how to get started:

1. **Set a budget.** You'll generally need $2,500 to $7,500 per contract, depending on the venue. A targeted online campaign can run $40 to $100 CPM. (General retail rates of top portals are included later in this chapter.)

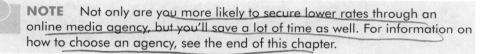

NOTE   Not only are you more likely to secure lower rates through an online media agency, but you'll save a lot of time as well. For information on how to choose an agency, see the end of this chapter.

2. **Choose your 15 to 20 keywords.** These will likely be the same keywords you chose for your SEP campaign. Refer to Chapter 4 for detailed instructions and recommendations on how to select them. Also, ask each portal's media department for other ideas — they know their venue best.

3. **Compile your information.** Assemble a list of the portals you want to target, your site's traffic reports, and/or customer surveys for the search engines most used by your target audience. Then, put the portal cost and traffic information into a spreadsheet. Here's an example:

Venue	Keywords	Approximate Inventory	Rate (CPM/CPC)	Cost
Lycos	"used cars"	500,000 impressions/month	$60 CPM	$3,000
	"sports cars"	25,000 impressions/month	$60 CPM	$1,500
GoTo	"used cars"	40 clicks	$2.50 CPC	$100
	"sports cars"	200 clicks	$0.50 CPC	$100

4. **Review your link placement.** Where are these links placed on the search results page? Are they close to the search results, or above a banner where nobody will notice? How many other advertising links are you competing with? Portals may launch a new interface every few months, and sometimes placement of the advertising links is less than ideal. Run a keyword search on each portal to test your potential link placement. (This is also a good time to look at keyword phrases your competitors are using.)

5.   **Secure the deal.** Provide your finalized budget and campaign elements to your portal sales representative, and you will receive an insertion order. If your budget and selected venues are approved, you can purchase long-term contracts to "lock up" the inventory and your rates for competitive words. However, recent changes in the Internet economy are increasing competition, making negotiations more possible. Sometimes it's good to wait for end-of-the-year "blowout sales" as the portals scramble to reduce rates to attain next year's contracts. One thing is certain: The best Internet advertising space is limited, and competition is fierce.

CAUTION   Once advertising contracts are signed, they are generally not cancelable, even if your ads haven't run yet. Make absolutely sure the contract is agreeable to you before you sign. Consider short-term contracts (quarterly or monthly) if you are unsure of the venue. You'll get better prices with long-term contracts, but if it turns out to be a poorly performing venue, you may lose more money overall!

Keyword Link Buys — A Portal Overview

Listed in the following sections are many of the top portals that offer keyword text link purchases, along with their estimated retail costs. As Internet advertising costs constantly vary due to demand, mergers, and acquisitions, please note the following rates should only be used for general information. (And remember, by hiring an interactive agency, you should be able to receive better rates.)

Cost-per-Impression Models

An advertising pricing model based on cost per impression charges the advertiser a cost per thousand user impressions or page views. A person only has to load the page in their browser for it to count as one impression. Current CPM rates are typically around $30 per CPM based on the site.

AltaVista

Type in "spas" on AltaVista, and you may notice two or three small ads to the right of the first ranked site. These are usually logos with text links.

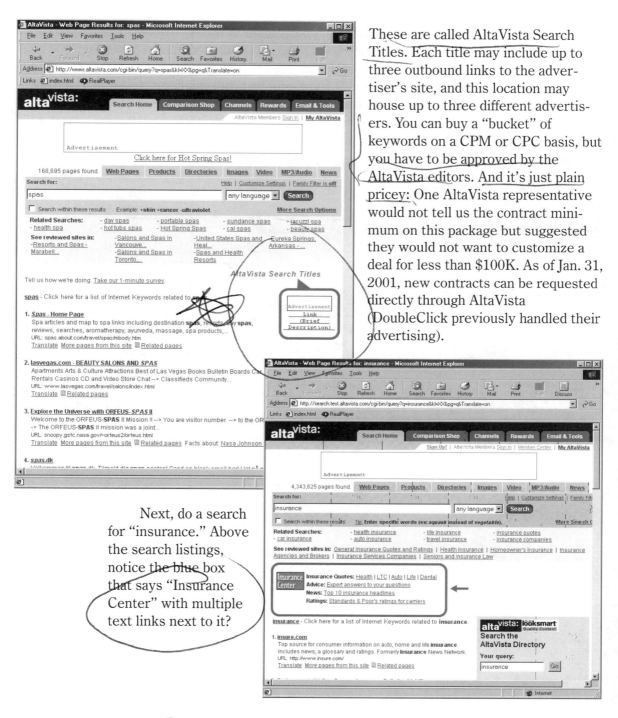

These are called AltaVista Search Titles. Each title may include up to three outbound links to the advertiser's site, and this location may house up to three different advertisers. You can buy a "bucket" of keywords on a CPM or CPC basis, but you have to be approved by the AltaVista editors. And it's just plain pricey: One AltaVista representative would not tell us the contract minimum on this package but suggested they would not want to customize a deal for less than $100K. As of Jan. 31, 2001, new contracts can be requested directly through AltaVista (DoubleClick previously handled their advertising).

Next, do a search for "insurance." Above the search listings, notice the blue box that says "Insurance Center" with multiple text links next to it?

These links are powered by ebix.com. This is an example of text link and content integration since the links don't just take you to the advertiser, but instead link you to relevant, sponsored content. The elements of these deals are more negotiable than a simple keyword text link campaign, since they're more similar to a content sponsorship than just advertising.

Now, look right below the Insurance Center links. See the line that says, "Insurance — Click here for a list of Internet Keywords related to insurance"?

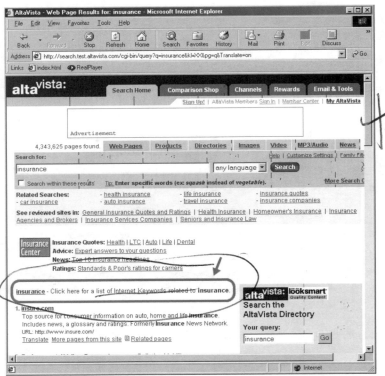

This is an option to run an additional keyword search for the term you used, powered by RealNames, from whom you can purchase Internet keywords.

When you purchase keywords through RealNames, you will also see your listings integrated with search results on portals such as MSN. RealNames also gives you visibility via certain browsers. For example, if you use Microsoft's Internet Explorer 5.0 browser, and instead of typing in the full URL of a site you enter a keyword, you may be automatically directed to the advertiser's site. This is a good idea since many people try to use the URL locator as a search application, and can forget or misspell the full path of the Web site address. Costs for RealNames keywords start at $100 per year for at least 1,000 visits (redirects to your site). Pay-per-performance or larger traffic accounts are negotiable.

AltaVista has recently added GoTo as provider of its "Sponsored Listings" which appear below the result pages. As with several top portals listed in this chapter, buying a top link on GoTo will give you automatic (and free!) visibility on AltaVista. For more information on GoTo, see Chapter 33.

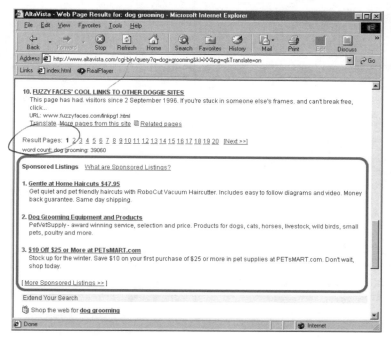

General Costs:

Search Titles: $10 CPM, three-month contract minimum

Editorial Links: $1-$2 CPM or $0.15-$0.30 CPC, $100K+ minimum

Excite

Similar to AltaVista, Excite offers sidebar text links in a box format to the right of ranked sites, which they refer to as "Search Sponsor Boxes."

These, too, are less expensive than banner ads, and can be bought for select keywords or channels (categories). Excite now also offers a larger and more prominent "Enhanced Sponsor Box" that is right under the "Search Sponsor Box." Within the "Enhanced Sponsor Box," there are three types of ads, each with varied pricing. One style allows for a larger graphic display, another offers multiple text links, and the grandest of the three may house a search function within the box.

General Costs: $25 CPM for Search Sponsor Boxes
$35-$65 CPM Enhanced Sponsor Boxes
$5,000 contract minimum

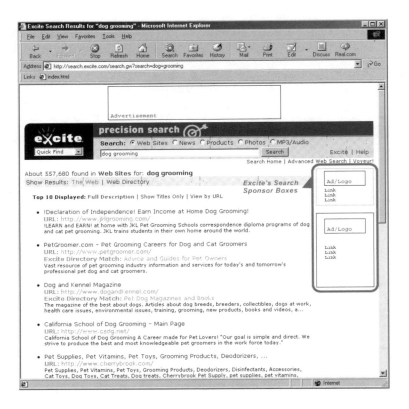

Ask Jeeves

Ask Jeeves is a portal that deserves some special attention for its myriad of keyword content and text link advertising options, in addition to its unique approach to search. Ask Jeeves, with its memorable butler mascot, utilizes natural language queries for its question style search engine. A user can type a keyword and will receive a set of questions back to help refine their search. The most obvious keyword advertising campaign is the text sponsorship which allows you to have your site appear in one of the top three positions across a network of sites including Ask Jeeves, Direct Hit, MSN, Bomis.com, and SuperCyber-Search. Similar to the GoTo model, you can set up an account online and select your keywords/description, charge a specific amount to your credit card, and update your keyword bids any time (look for the "Visit These Sponsors" link to the right of the search results).

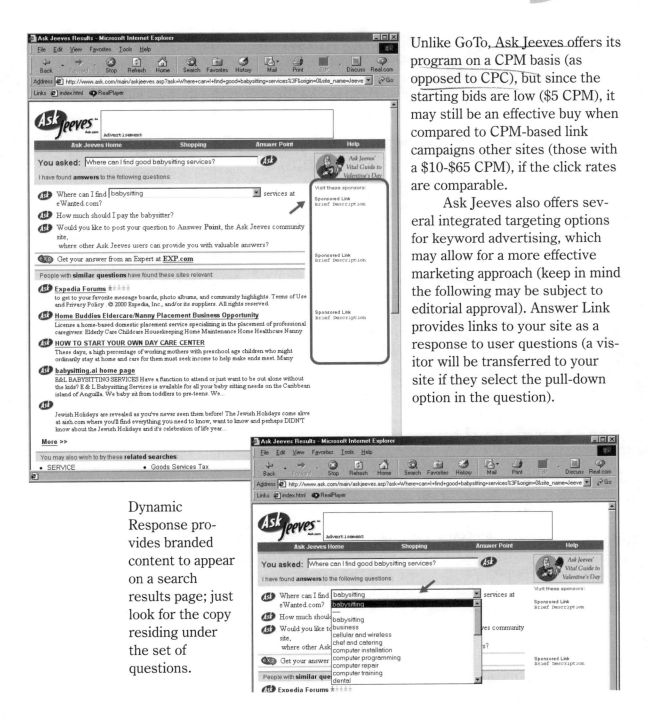

Unlike GoTo, Ask Jeeves offers its program on a CPM basis (as opposed to CPC), but since the starting bids are low ($5 CPM), it may still be an effective buy when compared to CPM-based link campaigns other sites (those with a $10-$65 CPM), if the click rates are comparable.

Ask Jeeves also offers several integrated targeting options for keyword advertising, which may allow for a more effective marketing approach (keep in mind the following may be subject to editorial approval). Answer Link provides links to your site as a response to user questions (a visitor will be transferred to your site if they select the pull-down option in the question).

Dynamic Response provides branded content to appear on a search results page; just look for the copy residing under the set of questions.

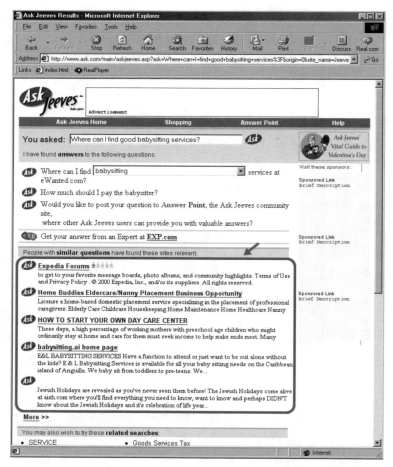

Ask Jeeves' keyword advertisements are one of the best editorial-looking campaigns available, and a CPC program makes this a very cost-effective buy.

General Costs:

Text Sponsorships: $5 CPM bid minimum

Answer Link: $0.75-$1.00 CPC, $5K/mo. minimum

Dynamic Response: $0.40 CPC and $60 CPM, $5K/mo. minimum

GO.com

GO offers three types of advertising links: banner links, spot banners, and active ads. Banner links are placed to the left of banner ads (up to two advertisers may be presented).

Spot banners are placed to the right of the search result sites in outlined boxes containing the advertiser's logo and multiple links (look for the word "advertisement" written across the right side of the ad).

The additional benefit of the GO spot banner is that multiple links are allowed. So for the price of one impression, you may be able to highlight three different messages or areas on your site.

The active ads are pitched by GO as the best-performing ad type. The chief benefits of these ads include position and content; they are positioned above the fold, offer a larger space than the spot ads, and allow for functionality such as a pull-down menu or search function.

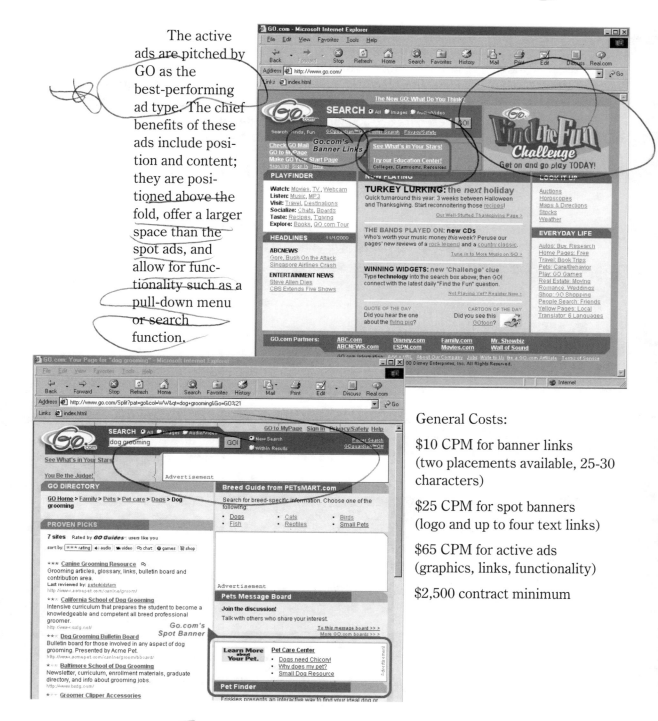

General Costs:

$10 CPM for banner links (two placements available, 25-30 characters)

$25 CPM for spot banners (logo and up to four text links)

$65 CPM for active ads (graphics, links, functionality)

$2,500 contract minimum

Google

Google is a hot newcomer in the portal field. Google ranked #2 as a search engine on January 11, 2001[1], right behind Yahoo!. Google's integration in powering top portals such as Yahoo![2] and Netscape[3] during the second half of 2000 has certainly bolstered its use and public recognition. If you buy text links on Google, your site will **not** appear on Yahoo! or Netscape; however, Google is worth considering since its public recognition will continue to grow. Since your keywords will also incorporate related keywords, use GoTo's Recommended Keyword search or a comparable program to eliminate any undesirable words from the grouping.

There are three sidebar positions available to the right of the search results, and all are very affordable. Or, you may prefer to own one of the text link descriptions that are above the ranked sites. For branding purposes, these may be better positions. However, since they're about three times as expensive as the right-side links — with only slightly better click rates (2 percent vs. 1.5 percent) — they may not be the more cost-effective purchase in terms of click results.

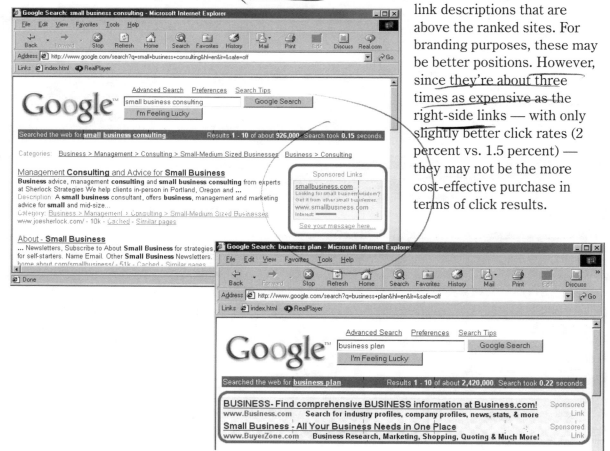

General Costs:

$10-$15 CPM (three placements available to the right of search results, title/description/URL included, positioning based upon popularity of the three sponsor sites)

$40-$45 CPM (one position available above ranked sites)

$50 account activation deposit (you must use a credit card for these campaigns)

Lycos

Go to www.lycos.com and type in a very popular keyword such as "insurance." Notice the "START HERE" text and message highlighted in red right above the numbered relevant sites.

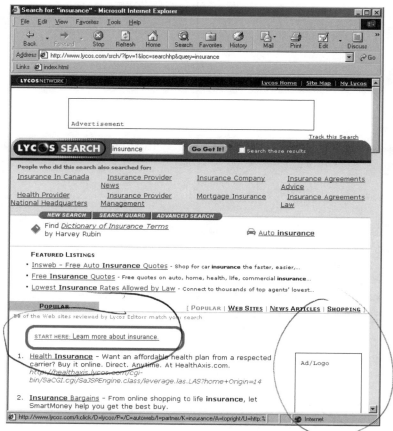

The "START HERE" link is well showcased and each advertiser can enjoy being the only "recommended" site in this area. Lycos' sidebar ads are to the right of the sites listed in the search result, and contain an advertiser's logo with a text description. However, these may sometimes be included in larger sponsorship deals (e.g., Barnes & Noble) and may not be purchased a la carte.

Right above the search results, you'll notice what Lycos calls "Featured Listings."

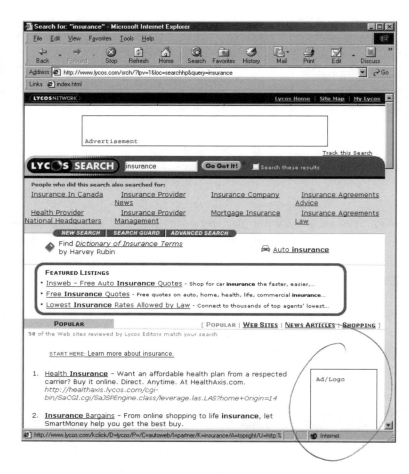

These are purchased listings — they're the top paid-for spots at GoTo.com! If you do the exact same search at both Lycos and GoTo.com, you'll see what I mean. Thus, if you want to be a featured site on Lycos, you need to go bid on a top spot at GoTo. (See GoTo under the "Cost-Per-Click Models" section below.)

General costs:

$60 CPM for single keywords

$2,500 program minimum

> **TIP**   Both Lycos and MSN's text links appear to the user to be editorial rather than advertorial, so use that valuable showcase to entice people to your site with a problem-solution situation. For example, "Buying a New Car? Click here first to lock in a low car loan rate." Sometimes, by not mentioning your company, it's more likely the user will assume this is a portal editorial link.

MSN

The "Featured Sites" placement on MSN is very well highlighted. Up to four featured sites are listed beneath the banner ad and search field, and before the ranked Web sites.

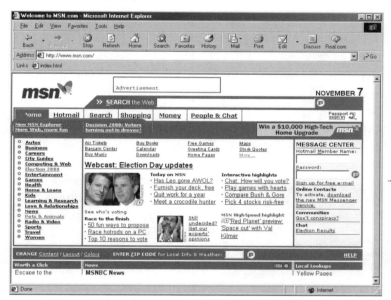

Although you can't buy keywords, you can buy an entire category that includes many keywords and phrases. One MSN rep quotes the click-through rate as substantially higher than banner ads — a 10 percent click-through rate on the keyword links is quite possible! But compared with other text link opportunities on portals, this may not be a first recommendation due to costs and some non-specific targeting requirements. The rates and total costs are high considering that half of the campaign must consist of run-of-site impressions, which are generally considered a "junk buy" for companies wanting to target a specific audience. If the packages are within your budget and you are also interested in general branding to Internet Explorer browser users (which loads MSN as the default home page), MSN may be a good choice.

General Costs:

$33-$43 CPM

$245K-$1.1M for a 12-month minimum contract

Cost-per-Click Models

Unlike the cost-per-impression model, an advertising pricing model based on cost per click (CPC) will charge the advertiser every time a user actually clicks on a banner or link. CPC rates typically range around $0.25-$0.40 per click based on the site.

GoTo

This was one of the first search engines to include CPC pricing. On GoTo, the coveted top spots are fee-based — no optimization headaches required. The idea is simple: The highest CPC bidder has the #1 position, and the following sites are ranked according to bid. Bids start at $0.01 per keyword and bids must be made in $0.01 increments (in the Shopping area, setup is $0.05 per keyword and bids are in $0.05 increments).

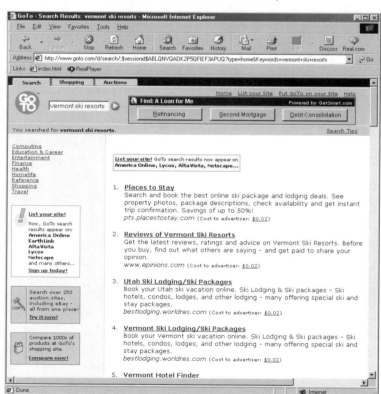

It's fairly easy to set up an account via their automated system, use their keyword suggestion tool, and select your keywords. You can also use their express service ($99) and have a consultant help you with keyword selection (up to 20 keywords per consulting fee), budget estimates, and program setup.

CPC search engines are inexpensive and results oriented, but there are a few major drawbacks: Bids can be entered at any time, so you must constantly check your keywords to ensure your site is still in a top spot. It's difficult to project how long a budget will last since there's no estimate for the number of clicks your links will receive. Once the budget has been exhausted, you'll need to renew the program. This program model is similar to the ones used by FindWhat and Mamma.com.

> **NOTE** GoTo is also the premier provider of paid listings to several other major search engines, so if you secure a top position here, you will likely be featured prominently on Netscape Search, AOL Search, Lycos, HotBot, and AltaVista. This list is sure to grow as the year progresses. For the full scoop on GoTo, see Chapter 33.

General Costs:

$0.01 CPC per keyword minimum, $25 account activation minimum

Flat Fee Models

Flat fee pricing models are usually based on large retainers paid by the advertisers to secure priority placement on the tops of select pages.

AOL

Can you call an AOL rep and buy text links based on AOL Search or categories? Not at this time. If you spend enough money on a sponsorship (content integration), can you negotiate a few? Maybe. There have been less than a handful of advertisers that spend millions of dollars (AOL could not disclose how many) who have been able to secure keyword-related text links. Still coveted, but with slightly higher availability, are text links within the AOL.com Web Centers or within content — if the price is right, of course. The bottom line: Leave the amount blank on your check when entering sponsorship negotiations with AOL!

At the very top of AOL search results, you'll notice AOL's "Sponsored Links." Just as with Lycos, these are simply the top paid-for spots at GoTo.com. At least AOL gives a disclaimer and doesn't mislead the users into thinking these are true, ranked results: "The search results below are provided by a third party and are not necessarily endorsed by AOL." To appear here, you need to bid on your keywords at GoTo.com.

General Costs:

$1 million and up, may include keyword or category text link purchase opportunities.

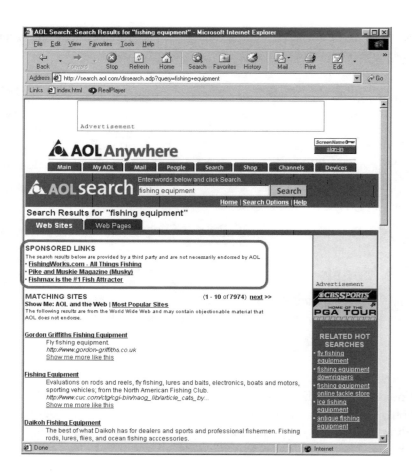

Netscape

Similarly to AOL, you can't go to Netscape and buy keyword text links. If you're a business-to-business company, the "no" may become a "maybe" if the price is right and the match makes sense. There are about six categories where links may be purchased on a CPC basis. This space is currently occupied by portals, and the monthly minimum may be $12K to $50K. Keep in mind that no matter how much money you may be willing to spend, most text links are considered editorial, so there must be a good match or reason for the venue to promote your site. Netscape may be offering additional areas for text link purchases in the near future.

Netscape has also jumped on the GoTo bandwagon. After you do a search, look at the "Partner Search Results" section at the top. These, again, are simply the top paid-for spots at GoTo.com. To appear here, you need to bid on your keywords at GoTo.com.

General Costs:

$1 million and up, may include category text link purchase opportunities

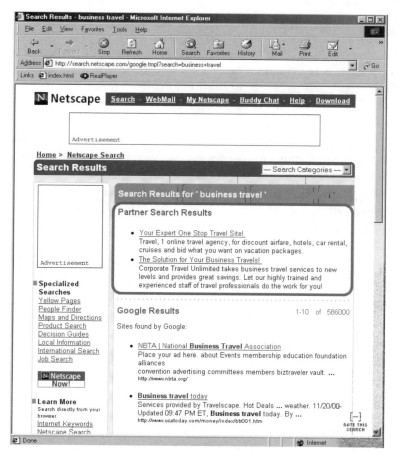

The Scoop on Content Sponsorships

To maximize the power of the portals, you need to go "beyond the banner and text link." Optimization and text link purchases are a necessary start, but they don't complete an online marketing campaign. Although portal partnerships have been criticized for being overinflated (million-dollar deals were hyped during the reign of the dot-com boom), strategic or time-specific content sponsorships with portals deserve more consideration.

Sponsorships are completely different from banner ads and text links. Everyone benefits from them: portals, advertisers, and users. For portals, valuable content is provided for their users, paid for by the advertisers. Advertisers are not restricted to branding their company or product in a 468x60 pixel ad, or having to entice people in five words or less. Users are happy with the relevant content presented. Sponsorships allow advertisers to educate consumers, collect data, and communicate with a targeted audience without leaving the portal. Most users are hungry for product or service information and use portals and vertical sites to conduct the hunt, so feed them!

What's in most sponsorships? Often they may include banner ads, text links, and opt-in e-mail, but the focus is on the relationship with the portal. A sponsorship will forge a rich experience between your company and site users. How? This is done through content integration and interactive feature development within the portal. To users, your sponsored features seem to be an extension of the portal's normal content. Look for some of the following elements to distinguish a sponsorship from an advertising campaign.

Sponsorships may include:

- Co-branded content or "advertorials" that are relevant to the site's content and audience (may also involve endorsement)
- E-commerce (storefront, special product offerings, or promotions)
- Live events or streaming content
- Right to use site's logos/trademarks in other promotional materials
- Access to site's database or research (opt-in e-mail, statistics)
- Custom interactive opportunities (surveys, polls, games)
- Flat fee cost or revenue sharing instead of traditional CPM/CPC

■ Advertiser approval by the venue

■ Longevity of content (may be archived)

An Illuminating Case Study

Illuminations, a candle and home decor company, is investing in content sponsorships with several top portals. Two years ago, it entered into its first sponsorship with AOL, and has been pleased with the results. Currently, it is an AOL Gold Level Sponsor, which includes advertising and special editorials throughout targeted channels within AOL, as well as product integration into the AOL merchandise database.

Lanya Havas, director of marketing at Illuminations, says the primary goal of generating enough revenue to cover the cost of the sponsorship was easily surpassed in 2000. This is good news for other retailers who may faint at the initial costs of sponsorships. In 2001, Illuminations will continue growing and improving its affiliate and e-mail marketing programs.

Most portals won't touch a sponsorship for less than $50K to $100K per month. Why? There is substantial effort and time required to integrate the advertiser's content into the portal database and site. AOL's Gold Level Sponsorship runs from $40K to $200K per month, which does not include integration into their merchandise database (add another $40K to $150K). According to AOL, the costs are based on the popularity of the channel in which your products/services would be featured. Expect to pay premium prices for clothing/accessories and home furnishings, while you may be able to breathe a sigh of relief if you are advertising auctions/collectibles or food.

Don't lose sleep over the high fees, as the branding value and sales potential may be well worth the initial chunk of cash. But don't just throw money at the portals and expect the campaign to fly. Sponsorships will require a lot more management on your part, too. Havas believes the AOL campaign performed significantly better in 2000 over 1999 due to a new AOL merchandising team assigned to its account. AOL continued to create innovative opportunities for Illuminations to market its products, and brought successful strategies for other promotions.

What You Should Consider

Hopefully, you're now ready to jump into sponsorship discussions with portals. The most beneficial, yet challenging, part of sponsorships is that they are customized. Do you want to showcase products through a showroom, video clips, or animation? Would you like to communicate with existing and potential customers through contests, newsletters, or site referrals? How about collecting marketing information via polls, surveys, collateral requests, and dealer/store locators? Any or all of the above may be integrated into a sponsorship, and portals will also look to you to provide your goals and content delivery. Expect to fork over at least $100K or more for any sponsorship or content integration. So, how will you know if you should be paying $250K or $1 million for this portal sponsorship? Here a few top issues you should ask your executive team and the portals to help you measure the sponsorship's viability and success:

- What features will be included under this contract? (monthly opt-in e-mail, survey)
- How will your sponsorship be promoted? (banners, text links, newsletters, offline promotions, and advertising)
- What results are expected? (traffic, participants in interactive features, sales)
- How will results be tracked? (portal reports, WebTrends, or deep tracking system)
- Who owns the data gathered? (can you export this information?)
- What technical issues do you need to be aware of?
- What guarantees are included? (specific number of impressions or actions)
- What are the terms and conditions? (payment terms, program length, cancellation policies)

Track Your Return on Investment

Executing an online media campaign is an admirable endeavor, but it's of no value unless you know what kind of results you're getting. **You must track your campaign!**

There are several ways to do this. One is through each portal from which you're purchasing ad space. However, engines don't track much more than simple impressions and clicks. They **can't** tell you, for example, which of your multiple text links directly resulted in more sales on your site. The good news is that there are third-party ad serving and tracking systems to help you calculate your online campaign's return on investment (ROI).

Third-party ad systems offer "deep tracking" that can help you manage, analyze, and optimize your campaign. Through centralization, targeting, and unparalleled detail in reporting, deep tracking enables you to measure your customers' responses and turn that information into useful knowledge. There are several programs out there — DoubleClick's DART, InterAdNet, AdKnowledge, MatchLogic, and AdForce, to name a few.

Here's an example of how third-party ad systems can work for you: Let's say you have a women's jeans company. You purchase a strategic banner ad to be placed on AltaVista's site, and you will track the campaign through DoubleClick's DART system. Your banner ad is assigned its own tracking code (or tag) that will follow each user when she clicks on it. When someone types in a query for "women's jeans" on AltaVista, the banner ad that appears is actually pulled in from DoubleClick's server — it does not reside on AltaVista. When the visitor clicks on the banner ad or text link, she's routed to your site and is tracked throughout her visit as to whether she hits any of the embedded "action" tags that you've predetermined. Your action tags can be assigned to sales transactions, completed information request forms, a ZIP-code-based search, file download, or any page on your site that would be valuable in determining your campaign's ROI. (A tracking code may be embedded on any page, but dynamic database pages are more difficult.)

Does your online campaign include multiple venues and advertising tools (banner ads or text links)? No problem. Deep tracking will tell you how they all stack up. For example, you can learn that your banner A resulted in 20 percent of last week's sales, but banner B resulted in 80 percent! Therefore, you know banner B works best. You also have 24-7 access to your analytical information — very valuable in determining your ROI on the fly.

Just as important as the reporting is the campaign management that third-party ad systems offer. It's much easier to manage banner ad campaigns on 10 different portals through one system than it is to manually submit your advertisement to each venue, test each venue, then cross-analyze each venue's reports. Using a third-party system can save you hours a week and give you instant, comprehensive reporting to help you make better and faster decisions about your campaign strategy.

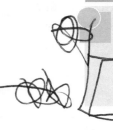

NOTE   The content for this chapter was contributed by Catherine Seda, vice president of online promotions for SiteLab International (www.sitelab.com), whom we wholeheartedly recommend. Or, for an exhaustive list of media buying agencies, visit: http://dir.yahoo.com/Business_and_Ecomony/Business_to_Business/Marketing_and_Advertising/Advertising/Media_Buying_and_Planning/.

[1] http://websnapshot.mycomputer.com/searchengines.html (Jan. 11, 2001)

[2] http://searchenginewatch.internet.com/_subscribers/articles/0007-yahoo.html

[3] http://biz.yahoo.com/bw/001004/ca_google_.html

Chapter 38:

The Sociology of Cloaking

The practice of redirecting search engine users to pages other than those used to attain the ranking is referred to by a variety of names, including "stealth scripting," "IP redirection," and most commonly, "cloaking." This tactic is prohibited by all of the major search engines and it's even been known to get Web sites banned for life.

This technology and practice was pioneered and is still used largely by pornographers and Webmasters who operate adult "triple-X" Web sites. The fact that the practice has become so widespread and that several SEP companies have based their business model on "fooling the search engines" is no excuse for credible companies to employ these tactics. It's a lot like a telemarketing agency promising its clients a higher sales rate because their reps call private homes between the hours of 9 p.m. and midnight — sure it's illegal and a violation of both good manners and FCC statutes, but they're getting away with it, lots of other companies are doing it, and heck, it's been working pretty well. So why not?

Even if cloaking is employed without detection, it's still an underhanded and unethical technique that does not and will not pass the "red face test" with most company investors or shareholders. The revelation that your company is cloaking can be hugely embarrassing, to say the least.

 CAUTION   Search engines do enforce their cloaking policy whenever they detect the practice or when it's pointed out to them by an interested party. Your site could be banned, so don't risk it!

What Industry Insiders Have to Say about Cloaking

SEP practitioners who employ cloaking are fond of advising clients that "the search engines don't really mind" its use. **This is false.** In a June 1999 article published in the SEP e-newsletter *MarketPosition*, I interviewed several executives from the major search engines for their opinions on cloaking. Here are some excerpts from that article:

A vice president at Lycos on IP redirection:

"Our policy is fairly strict: We blacklist the offending site. Lycos does consider the act of hiding pages via a stealth script to be 'spamdexing.' We remove these domains from our live search engine database, and the only

time we've ever put them back is if we get feedback from the site that, for instance, they fired the Webmaster or something and it was an honest mistake. Most of the time it comes up in porn [sites]."

Regarding indexing and blacklisting at Lycos, he continues:

"No search engine can logically endorse IP redirection since it completely undermines its ability to rank a page based on its content and the engine's ranking algorithms. This holds true even if the person employing the cloaking software targets only 'appropriate' keywords."

People who argue for using IP redirection scripts (usually those selling the software or making money from it) will often try to turn the tables when they find they're losing the ethical argument. However, other techniques such as "doorway pages" (pages designed to rank well in search engines, but which users actually see) use accepted methods and are ethically sound. The crucial difference is that a doorway page is simply "pleasing" to a search engine, whereas an IP-redirected page is a different page altogether. The search engines know you want to rank well and many even include Help pages with discussions on the proper use of META tags. Some include other general tips on optimizing your page. (This shows that simply trying to make your pages rank well is not wrong, even as defined by the search engines.)

NOTE   Don't confuse an IP-redirected page with a doorway page. Doorway pages are legit — users actually see them. IP-redirected pages are created to "fool" the search engines and are never seen by Web users.

I asked the VP at Lycos about their policy on doorway pages:

"If a doorway page promotes something accurate, then that's great. If you compose a page with some legitimate and accurate copy that describes the Web site that the page is leading people into, then that's perfectly legitimate. You should probably be encouraging people to do this, especially when dealing with a site that has frames, or some other problematic feature that makes properly indexing the page difficult. Lycos will ban pages or sites which intentionally misrepresent the information contained on the pages, especially when such pages or sites deal with common queries that lead people to an irrelevant site."

A principal at HotBot had this comment about IP redirection techniques:

"Our basic point of view is that, yes, if you show the indexer one page and the consumer another, even in good faith, you're spamming, and you're annoying us and our users."

An Excite representative on IP redirection:

"If the user of the search engine gets a page that's different than what we index, it is not good for our users. It's bad because it harms the user's experience. You could extrapolate from this. In turn, it trickles down to harm the company [Excite]. Excite does not have an official policy dealing with stealth scripting, though. So much of our stuff is automated, we can't go around checking everything."

While some may argue that the search engines do not seem to be vigilant in strictly enforcing their publicly stated prohibition against cloaking, it's clear they would if not for a lack of resources and technology.

Other search engine executives — who were informally interviewed by Marshall Simmonds, the director of search for About.com — had this to say about cloaking in a post to the I-Search Digest (the I-Search Digest is a popular discussion list moderated by Detlev Johnson, a well-known and respected search engine positioning practitioner):

"If we find out your page is cloaked, we will ban your URL and sites for life."

— Marc Krellenstein, Ph.D., CTO and senior VP of Engineering, and Mark Sprague, senior vice president of Product Design and Operations, for Northern Light

Executives at Inktomi and AltaVista agree that if you send an engine a page other than what the user actually sees, you are misrepresenting content and subverting the engine's database — by definition, that's spam. Proceed at your own risk.

How Cloaking Works

The technology involved in implementing a "stealth script" is relatively simple. Many off-the-shelf tools are freely available and the software itself is little more than a simple Perl script (in the case of Unix- or Apache-hosting servers) that references a list of search engine IP addresses that have been collected over time by the developer.

NOTE   An IP address is a designation for a particular location on the Internet, such as 140.23.719.6. IP addresses are associated with all domain names. While your Web site might be named www.company-name.com, this name was translated and mapped to a particular IP address by a DNS or domain name server at some point or another.

A spider has to originate from somewhere — and that somewhere is the unique IP address reserved by the engine for that spider. Engines can and do change the IP addresses of their spiders in an attempt to defeat SEP practitioners who employ these stealth scripts. (By the way, if someone tells you that search engines don't mind IP redirection so much, simply ask him or her why they constantly change their spiders' IP addresses to deter the practice!) The real value of these programs, then, is in the quality of that list of search engine IP addresses and not the quality of the software code underlying the script.

Cloaking requires the Webmaster to install a server-side script that references the database of known search engine IP addresses. That way, the program can serve a Web page that has been designed specifically to attain a high ranking in a particular search engine to just that engine. For example, when the stealth script detects Excite's spider visiting the Web site and requesting a page, it serves up a Web page that was specifically designed to attain a high ranking for a particular keyword phrase in Excite. It's important to note that this page is **different** from any other page in the actual Web site and will never be seen by anyone other than the Excite spider.

The Downside of Cloaking

What's most surprising about companies that hire SEP professionals who cloak is how shortsighted their decision will be regarded in the long run. Here are several of drawbacks of cloaking.

If You Rely on Cloaking, You'll Miss More Than 80 Percent of the Major Search Engines

Yep, that's right! Pages that are hidden or cloaked aren't eligible to be included in the major human-edited search directories such as Yahoo!, LookSmart (which powers AltaVista's directory, the MSN search engine results, Excite's directory, and others), Open Directory (the search database for AOL Search, Netscape, Lycos, HotBot, and many others), NBCi (formerly Snap), GO.com (formerly Infoseek), or any other directory-powered search portal.

While secondary search results at Yahoo! are supplied by Google, a true search engine where cloaked doorway pages or informational pages can gain rankings, the vast majority of queries result in search matches from the Yahoo! human-edited directory. MSN similarly serves search matches to most queries from its directory partner LookSmart. The vast majority of searches in Lycos produce search matches from the Open Directory and a lesser number from their secondary search partner FAST. While "technically," cloaked pages can show up in these directories for obscure keyword phrase queries that have no associated directory listings and that default to their search engine partner, the majority of queries produce directory search matches. When you engage in cloaking, you miss the majority of your audience in these directory-led search services as cloaked pages are ineligible to be included in human-edited directories. This means you could miss a significant portion of your potential audience.

You'll Achieve No Lasting Value and Will Have No Search Engine Visibility

SEP companies that cloak usually charge on a cost-per-click basis. This means the moment you stop paying for the traffic, those rankings and traffic are redirected to the next paying customer. Also, SEP companies that cloak usually don't allow you to take ownership of the cloaked pages after the campaign has ended. Even if the SEP company did turn over the cloaked pages to you, they wouldn't be suitable for viewing by the public. These people had no incentive to make them aesthetically pleasing because they were hidden behind a cloaking program anyway. Therefore, you'll need to invest in and build a significant infrastructure, including a hosting server and implementation of a cloaking script, as well as pay subscription fees for the frequent updates to cloaking software's ever-changing database of search engine IP addresses.

Furthermore, those pages would not attain the same high rankings for you either. Why? Because the provider usually executes an elaborate cross-linking scheme between thousands of unrelated client doorway pages, since most search engines consider "link popularity" (how many Web sites link to a particular Web site) as a consideration in their ranking algorithm. Unless you had a similar cross-linking capability between thousands of Web pages on hundreds of different domains, these pages will not attain the same, or even similar, rankings.

You Risk Being Banned for Life

If a search engine detects that you've employed the services of a cloaking provider, you risk having your site banned or blacklisted. Remember, a search engine has no way of knowing that you've employed a vendor. All they know is you submitted a "hidden" page for indexing and then redirected the search engine's end user. So what if you used a provider to help you? Search engines are not interested in exploring each violation case by case to determine which company employed which vendor. They're only interested in cleaning their index of hidden pages and penalizing companies that employ this tactic. If you take advantage of cloaking, you're a legitimate target.

You Get No Consultative Value

Cloaking companies strive solely for quantity of rankings and total referred traffic, since this is how they're compensated. They target any remotely related keyword phrase that you'll allow them to get away with. These companies have made no investment in research and development as it pertains to creating long-term value for your Web site, since they're only compensated for attaining rankings external to your site.

It Doesn't Directly Benefit Your Site

All cloaking companies work outside of their clients' Web sites. None of them will help you write one META tag or prepare one directory submission. After all, a high ranking listed in a directory or attained by your site itself will steer visitors to the actual client site — not to the cloaker's intermediate page where additional traffic can be counted, referred, and ultimately billed to you. There is no incentive for the cloaking provider to help you attain rankings in these directories or for your actual Web site pages.

Cloaking is Not a Necessary Measure to "Protect" Your Site

While the most commonly stated defense of employing cloaking technology is that it "prevents competitors from stealing your high-ranking code," experience has taught us this is merely a red herring. In fact, although page-jacking (the unauthorized copying and use of another Web site's pages for the purpose of attaining higher rankings) and META tag theft do occur, they're not as widespread as cloakers would lead you to believe. They're a nuisance more than anything.

High-ranking pages often have more to thank for their prominence than just cleverly placed keyword META tags. Search engines employ a variety of off-the-page metrics to rate pages including the number of links that point to a particular Web site, editorial reviews of that site, where searchers go after performing a query and how long they stay, and a host of other elements that have little to do with the site's HTML code.

However, while cloaking companies argue that they fear others stealing their HTML code, several recent high-profile debacles have shown that some of these companies actually stole high-ranking pages belonging to others and hid them behind their cloaking script. If you employ a vendor who uses cloaking technology, you may be unwittingly sponsoring copyright infringement and page-jacking. You risk a very embarrassing situation if your vendor steals Web pages from others — worse yet, you have no way of knowing it's happening!

Okay, Is Cloaking Ever Legit?

There are a few, **very** few, legitimate uses of cloaking technology — but they are never employed by the kind of SEP companies who charge clients by the click-through. The only time a cloaking script can be legitimately employed is if the user gets **the very same content** presented to the search engine.

We at iProspect have used cloaking software on behalf of one client, but only in what we considered a "completely defensible implementation" — using the software only to facilitate proper site spidering and only to display **the exact same page** to the search engine that we display to the user. We do not need to hide any part of our optimization from the search engines or a Web site's visitors in order to achieve results. We serve the search engine and the search engine user the **exact** same page content.

For example, some Web sites require each visitor to accept a browser "cookie" in order to gain entry so they can track that user's purchases and progress through the Web site. Search engines, however, will not accept these cookies. In such a situation, a Webmaster could choose to employ a stealth script or cloaking software to identify an incoming search engine and serve it the exact same Web page the user would see, minus the requirement that it accept a cookie. The technical requirement of accepting a cookie has no bearing on the content of the site nor the relevance of that site to a particular search engine query.

For these types of implementations, we use and recommend a tool called Food Script, which was written by a company called Beyond Engineering. It can be found at www.ip-delivery.com. Regrettably, many companies use this script to hide their source code, which is also known as cloaking your pages. However, Food Script has worked flawlessly for us, and we recommend it to anyone who needs to use it **for a legitimate purpose**.

The only time that a cloaking script can legitimately be employed to show a user a **different** Web page than the one indexed is if both the user and the search engine view the very same text content but different graphical content. Search engines don't make any relevancy judgments about a Web page based on its visual appeal. Their spiders have no way of interpreting the contents of a graphic or any text contained in a graphic — they simply don't optically recognize text.

Here's an example: It's conceivable that a Web site built with Flash, the popular Web graphic and animation design tool, could not be indexed by some search engines. A Webmaster serving the search engine a text-only version of the Web page containing **exactly the same text** as the Flash site would be legitimately applying cloaking technology. After all, sites built with Flash cannot be viewed by people using some older browsers, so Webmasters often make links to text-only or older browser-friendly versions of a Web site available to people who cannot view Flash pages. Serving a text-only version of a graphically intense Web site to a search engine is perfectly legitimate, so long as the text-only version contains **the exact same content** as the animated or graphical version of the site.

A Final Word on Cloaking

SEP gained through the practice of cloaking is, quite possibly, fraud. What else can you call the process of fooling one corporation and then deceiving the end user for the benefit of a client? If you have a credible company, don't take a chance with cloaking. If you have doubts, just ask your shareholders or the search engines themselves.

If you wish to manipulate how high your Web pages rank, visit GoTo.com. This search engine operates via open auction, allowing companies to bid for the rankings they seek. (See Chapter 33 for the full scoop.) The highest bidder is granted the highest ranking. The other major search engines have not opted to offer such an open-market approach.

Companies that cloak will sooner or later be forced to change their business model. The only question yet to be answered is how many of their clients will be tarnished because of this passing fad.

Chapter 39:

Case Studies

ntentionally launching a Web site that can't be found by any of the major search engines could hardly be the goal of any Web site owner. That would be akin to opening a mail-order business and not sending out a catalog, or opening a store and not publishing your phone number or address — or even forgetting to unlock the front door! On the Internet, the major search engines such as Yahoo!, AltaVista, and NBCi are the equivalent of the Yellow Pages, and the listings on search engines are just as valuable for garnering new business. No matter how pretty and interactive your firm's new Web site is, if it can't be found in one or more of the major search engines, then you might as well have put a billboard in the woods.

This chapter chronicles the experiences of several Web sites and how thoughtful SEP led to positive results. Each of these companies represents a different scenario, but each strongly benefited from a search engine positioning program. The first is a lovely Web site launched by a professional copywriter. This site exemplifies the importance of addressing SEP while the site is being designed. In the second case, an e-commerce site illustrates how rankings lead to traffic and how traffic increases in proportion to the growth in a site's search engine visibility. The third case study focuses on an unusual business that uses SEP as its sole form of site promotion. The client has gone all the way from startup to public offering using just SEP to garner customers, and the site was able to generate sales without absorbing huge marketing expenses. And finally, we examine how a drug company has used SEP to increase brand awareness for one of its products.

Case Study 1: Lovely to Look At, but Rarely Seen

A professional copywriter, a good friend of mine, launched a great-looking Web site — AKBWriting.com. She spent months preparing the right words to describe her services. She solicited testimonials from her satisfied clients. She sent out broadcast e-mail to everyone with whom she had ever come in contact. There was just one problem: Her site was practically invisible to search engines. Because of its design, the search engines — and by extension, potential customers — ignored it. I discuss a few of the problems here, namely, how it uses graphics, frames, and keywords.

Search Engines Can't Read Graphics

The first page of the Web site describes the service that is offered and lists contact information. Unfortunately, the Web site designer chose graphic representation of this key message and did not use HTML text. Since search engines look for HTML text and can't read text contained in graphics, the search engines found no content to index. The Web designer sought to overcome this problem by including copy in a <NOFRAMES> tag — a useful tactic but not as valuable as making text readily available.

Don't Use Frames

The remainder of AKBWriting.com uses frames, meaning that the site displays in a split screen. Most sites use frames to keep links, and navigation and contact information static on the left side of the screen as visitors scroll through. Search engines still have problems with frames, however. First, only about half the search engines even get across to the right side to index the entire site's "real" content. Second, frames prevent users from setting a bookmark in their browser to a particular page within the site. By the same token, major search engines often are unable to link to internal pages.

While an increasing number of search engines now claim to support framed pages, most SEP professionals agree: Don't use frames in your Web design unless you absolutely have to. If you insist on having a framed Web site, the <NOFRAMES> tag is your best hope for getting listed.

Trap 404 Error Messages

Web pages change. Site owners add pages to their Web sites and remove pages they've changed. What happens to the high ranking of an internal page that is taken down at a later date? It remains, and anyone who visits that page from the search engine is served a "404 NOT FOUND" error. Sooner or later, the search engine's spider revisits the page to see if it still exists. When it gets a 404 error, it instantly drops the page listing and ranking from its index. You can use a switch at the server level to ensure that instead of a 404 error, the visitor is delivered a predetermined page. To determine if a site has this trapping enabled, put the site's URL into your browser followed by a nonsense string (www.myprettysite.com/nonebetter.htm). If you are trapping 404s, you'll receive the predetermined page instead of the annoying 404 error message. A quick check showed that my friend's Web site was not trapping these errors.

Pay Attention to Keyword Format

The keyword META tag on the AKBWriting.com Web site is:

The keywords themselves are good, but separating them with commas is not the best strategy. This makes search engines consider them individually, but most people do not search on single-word phrases anymore. If the commas are left out of the keyword META tag, the search engine will consider several possible combinations of keywords. These combinations could generate unanticipated traffic. So, AKBWriting.com would likely get more mileage out of the following:

From my brief review, it is easy to see that many well-intentioned designers make beautiful sites that are, in fact, invisible. A lack of attention to some very small details, such as the 404 error trapping and commas in the META tags, adds to a site's visibility problems.

You may have noticed that AKB & Associates was thanked in this book's acknowledgments section. They performed the copy editing for much of this book and we were thrilled with the quality of their work. I wholeheartedly and enthusiastically endorse them as a vendor and encourage you to contact them for copywriting and editing assistance. We gratefully acknowledge and thank them for not changing and optimizing their Web site so that readers of this book could review it as they read this chapter. Rest assured that when the time is right, AKB & Associates will surely optimize their Web site and take advantage of the search engine positioning techniques they helped us describe.

The following example explores how increased rankings on a widening range of keywords lead to improved search engine visibility and increased traffic.

Case Study 2: How to Increase Traffic

One of the basic assumptions of SEP is that increased search engine visibility will lead to increased traffic. The real objective is actually yet another step further along the same continuum, that is, that SEP leads to capturing the right visibility that will drive the most qualified traffic to the client's site. Then, the true measure of success can, in fact, be stated in terms of the search engine optimization campaign.

Make Yourself Seen

At one time there was an iProspect.com client with a retail site targeting college students. The baseline was established for the client's site immediately after the keywords were agreed upon. Immediately after choosing the keywords and before optimizing the site, developers set the baseline by rank checking on those keywords with WebPosition Gold. This baseline makes it possible to measure growth against a real yardstick.

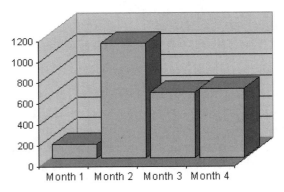

Top 30 search engine rankings

When the baseline was established at Month 1, the site had 131 rankings in the top 30 positions across the top search engines on the targeted keyword list. By the end of Month 4, the client had close to 600 rankings. This translates into a rankings increase of over 400 percent, in just four months! Clearly, aggressive optimization of a site can increase search engine rankings.

Rankings are just one key element of the visibility equation. The diversity of keyword phrases that have rankings is another. If a site has hundreds of rankings on just a handful of keywords, visibility will be limited to searches for those keywords. A small number of keywords doesn't necessarily mean that the site will have no or little traffic; a site with a number one ranking on a high frequency keyword may, in fact, net more traffic from this lone keyword than it might from a handful of low-traffic keywords. For most sites though, the optimal situation is to have a number of top rankings on a broad universe of keywords that accurately define the site's contents. Then, the offering of the site will appeal to a broader base of searchers using a broader search vocabulary.

When the baseline was taken, there were 47 unique keywords ranking from the site's selected keyword universe. These 47 keywords were drawing 131 rankings, or 2.8 rankings per keyword.

Keyword ranking

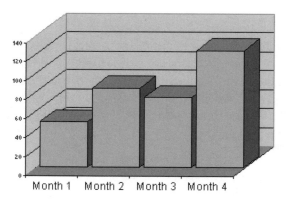

Four months into the campaign, 123 keywords were drawing almost 600 rankings, or 5.7 rankings per keyword. This represents a 162 percent increase in the diversity of keywords ranking within the top search engines.

The client's footprint in the major engines increased dramatically during the campaign. With more keywords ranking, the site has a much more diverse target audience and many more rankings to draw the attention of surfers and searchers. One question still remains: Did these results increase search engine referrals and qualified traffic? Let's find out.

Big Foot Means Big Traffic?

To test the assumption that a larger footprint in the search engines and higher rankings on a more diverse keyword list lead to more referrals and increased qualified traffic, it is necessary to review the site's performance in the logs over the duration of the campaign. Take a look at the following illustration. In Month 1, the site was receiving just 620 visitors from search engines.

Search engine traffic

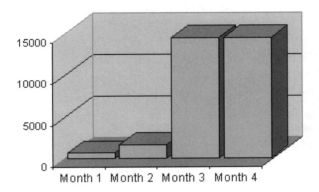

By the end of Month 4, however, the number of search engine referrals had risen to 14,500 visitors, an increase of 2,243 percent. As rankings increased and more traffic-driving keywords attained prominent positions on major search engines, referrals increased exponentially.

Increased referrals from search engines are a major component — but not the totality — of the traffic equation. A successful search engine optimization campaign should result in an increase in the number of visitors who find the site from a search engine the first time and return a second or third time from a bookmark or a remembered URL. If your content is engaging or your business proposition worthy, your increased referrals will translate into increased monthly unique visitors.

The client site in this second case study truly exemplifies this phenomenon. In Month 1 the site was attracting 50,000 monthly unique visitors. As this illustration shows, by the end of Month 4 the site was receiving over 700,000 monthly unique visitors.

Monthly unique
visitors

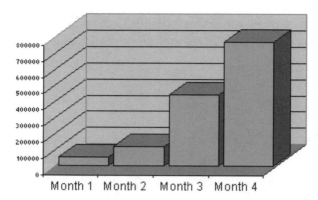

This is an increase of more than 1,400 percent, a tremendous growth in visitors. As this case clearly demonstrates, it is vital to focus on these key components of traffic in your development of an SEP campaign.

Case Study 3: SEP as an Exclusive Marketing Tool

Carpartsonsale.com is an e-commerce retailer in the $4 billion performance car parts market. Steve Newmark and Scott Hudson developed the site in March 1999, using SEP to fuel its growth. They thought the Web might provide an avenue for the distribution of performance parts to auto enthusiasts.

Unlike many Web site owners who have tried to develop a new business without an understanding of the market and its dynamics, Newmark and Hudson were already familiar with the performance car market through Lone Star Classics, Newmark's replicar business. Lone Star Classics is a leading manufacturer of replicas of Mercedes roadsters and Ford street hot rods. Through Lone Star Classics, they had already developed relationships with a number of manufacturers. Their Web site enabled them to expand into e-commerce. Let's see how they used SEP to drive enthusiasts to the site.

Playing the Name Game

There is no mistaking what Carpartsonsale.com sells. In purchasing a domain name that contains their most important keyword, "car parts," the site owners gave themselves a huge boost toward a successful SEP campaign. Google, AltaVista, and Inktomi have all shown a preference in ranking for keywords that are in the domain name. By registering carpartsonsale.com, the site received a boost in ranking preference for this highly competitive keyword. A recent search on "car parts" using AltaVista yielded over 3 million pages. With competition so fierce, site owners should carefully consider any extra boost they can legitimately get.

When the site launched, it was among the first to offer performance car parts on the Internet. Car enthusiasts could readily remember the URL's catchy name or, having once found the site, return to it with ease. The SEP campaign focused on bringing traffic familiar with performance cars to the site through the use of keywords that these enthusiasts use in their queries.

Most searchers query search engines looking for an answer to a specific problem. Car enthusiasts are no different; however, they are usually seeking a very specific part or solution. The keywords used in the campaign focused on the parts that the site offers. They included "Borla exhaust systems," "Holley carburetor," and "Edelbrock part," as well as a number of keywords that might address, for example, an enthusiast's need for "performance brakes" or "race car parts." Through its distribution agreements, the site was able to include the names of brands that are well known among auto enthusiasts.

Knowing Your Market

The owners recognized that the site would appeal to a very specific type of auto parts buyer — a buyer who would very likely know exactly the part needed right down to its make and even its part number. These hard-core enthusiasts aren't attracted to a lot of glitz and glamour that doesn't deliver. Just how many slick pictures of exhaust systems have you seen? Performance car enthusiasts were used to purchasing parts from catalogs printed on low-grade newsprint decorated with few, if any, pictures. Recognizing the market's dynamics, the site owners opted to add features over time, and didn't initially provide a lot of functionality. The site owners put their efforts into making sure that the performance car enthusiast, whether a professional or a hobbyist, could find the site on a search engine, find and order the part on the site, and receive it promptly. The site was not designed for the "tire kicker" who likes to browse.

The site owners chose to spend no funds on marketing other than for SEP. The search positioning campaign was a success. The site achieved strong visibility with over 2,000 rankings across all of the major search engines for the keywords that performance car owners and mechanics often use. With around 10,000 searchers per month finding the site from queries in the search engines, its clientele and sales grew rapidly. Once performance car enthusiasts found the site, they frequently bookmarked it and became regular clients. By July 2000, the owners had filed with the SEC to conduct a direct public stock offering.

This successful case history points out the value of knowing your market and how your purchasers will refer to the goods and services that you plan to offer before developing a Web site. This is just common sense, but it is often neglected. Knowing their business is one of the reasons for the success of click-and-mortar vendors. They are already experts in selling to their market.

Clearly, our study of Carpartsonsale.com demonstrates that a solid SEP campaign can serve as the sole marketing vehicle for a growing business. It's important to note that the campaign, in this case, was greatly helped by the fact that the site fulfills the specific intent of a searcher's query. If you are looking for performance car parts, a search engine may lead you directly to this site.

Case Study 4: How SEP Increases Brand Awareness

The Internet provides excellent opportunities for businesses to make the Web-using public aware of their brand names. Manufacturers of prescription drugs, however, face a unique set of challenges. They operate in a heavily regulated environment that prohibits the use of e-commerce and constrains how they market to consumers. Developing a new drug costs millions, which a drug company must recover from its sales. There is also fierce competition among drug companies offering competing remedies for the same malady.

An SEP campaign undertaken by one major drug company has yielded some remarkable results. The firm was able to attain, through SEP, visibility in 16 major engines in under a year, including 118 rankings in the #1 position, 262 rankings in the 1st through 10th positions (first-page listings), and 319 rankings in positions 1 through 30 (first three pages, beyond which few users will scroll). The promotion was for a drug that targets baldness.

Research done by the Pew Internet & American Life Project (www.pewinternet.org) has shown that Americans are using the Internet for health information. According to this organization, 70 percent of the 21 million health information seekers indicate that Web information has influenced their decisions about how to treat an illness or condition. Most health information seekers use the Web to obtain reference and background information. Men, the group more likely to suffer hair loss, look for information about their own conditions and are likely to make health decisions based on their Web research.

Because of the demographics, a Web site addressing the male problem of baldness has a significant chance of influencing the target market's behavior. This is an opportunity that the SEP campaign addressed.

By attaining rankings in every major search engine on iterations or phrases containing the keyword or phrase of the drug name and "hair loss" or "baldness," the site obtained a significant share of attention. A brand impression in the form of the site's name and search description information was delivered whenever a searcher made a query about the condition. This represents a major capture for the cost of an SEP campaign.

A World of Many Colors

Apropos of this chapter, a final thought: Keep in mind that no two sites are alike. Each Web site and each SEP campaign present a different set of exciting opportunities and challenges. As these case studies illustrate, site owners can take advantage of the benefits that search engine positioning offers only if they're careful about the details of site construction and how it suits marketing of their particular product or service. As in everything else, take nothing for granted.

SEP Campaign Potential and Limitations

iProspect has attained thousands of top 10 rankings for clients, many of which resulted in huge site traffic gains, but raw traffic volume is never the goal of an SEP campaign, just a natural outcome. Visibility that leads to qualified traffic must be the only goal. Each Web site and each different kind of company will have its own targeted keyword set. The targeted keyword set alone will determine the amount of traffic that your search engine positioning campaign will yield when properly executed. The goal of driving traffic perverts the proper aim of search engine positioning which is visibility. Qualified traffic simply follows.

Chapter 40:

The Future of Search Engine Positioning

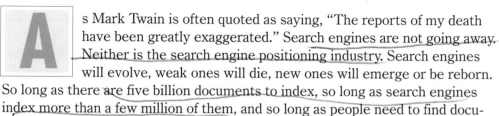

s Mark Twain is often quoted as saying, "The reports of my death have been greatly exaggerated." Search engines are not going away. Neither is the search engine positioning industry. Search engines will evolve, weak ones will die, new ones will emerge or be reborn. So long as there are five billion documents to index, so long as search engines index more than a few million of them, and so long as people need to find documents on the Internet, there is a bounty to be had by those companies and individuals who can cause their Web site to place high in the search rankings. That much will remain the same. What will change are the search engines that we will target, how they rank and sort Web pages, and the fees they charge to advertisers and promoters.

The "Monetization" of Search

The biggest change in search engine positioning is the trend toward what is being called "monetization of search." Our nation's little experiment in capitalism without profits hit a brick wall recently. Lo and behold, the world discovered that a company must reach profitability if it intends to survive. Many of the search engines are still struggling to reach that illusive goal of profitability and they are looking everywhere in pursuit of revenues. One untapped revenue source is you — search engine positioning practitioners, their clients, and Web marketers.

A recent article by a reporter at a respected trade publication has raised some interesting questions about what the search engine landscape will look like in the coming months and years. The reporter proposed that search engine optimizers could fall on hard times as many of the companies who would hire them would opt instead to "cut out the middleman" and elect, instead, to deal directly with the search engines.

While a titillating premise and controversial fodder for an article, the reporter came to the wrong conclusion and missed the more important component of the story. Namely, that search engines that charge for the privilege of submitting and being added to their index make absolutely no assurance that those Web sites will be displayed in the search results — exactly as it was before the fees were instituted. Now there's just a tollbooth on the add-URL interface.

These fees are a good thing. I know that sounds antithetical to the search engine positioning practitioner, but I assure you, these fees are the best thing that could possibly happen to our industry. They make it cost prohibitive for spammers to submit, and they make all of us Web marketers customers of the search engines who must be recognized and dealt with as such. Suddenly, the search engine positioning profession is not a thorn in the side of the search engines, but a significant revenue stream. Suddenly, we're important to the search engines and our voices are heard. Suddenly, when we pay them and nothing happens, we have recourse, and perhaps more importantly, we have grounds and standing in their minds. These are good things. These are things that improve the quality of the work we can provide to customers and the quality of the outcomes we can produce.

Therefore, the primary trends we see impacting the search engine positioning space reflect the monetization of search, namely:

- Paying for consideration but not ranking
- Paying for inclusion but not ranking
- Paying for placement and click-throughs

Paying for Consideration but Not Ranking

Pay-for-consideration fees are present only in human-edited directories. Under this system, a directory such as Yahoo! or LookSmart charges a $199 fee to "consider" or review your requested submission but is under no obligation to add your Web site after you've paid the fee. More troubling, however, is that in spite of the fact that you become a customer by paying their fees, they reserve the right to edit or change your submitted description, removing any and all keywords you may have included, or they can elect to reject you entirely. This seems highly offensive, but instead, think of the fee as an "application fee." Often in life we are asked to pay an application fee, only to be rejected. Remember, Yahoo! and LookSmart promise only that your submission "will be considered" — they make no promise that your Web site will ultimately be added to their database if you pay their fees! I cannot stress this enough: **None** of the search engines that have implemented these submission fees promise that if you pay them your site will show up in search results or attain rankings on important keywords, or even that you'll be added to their index!

However, these fees have significant benefits to the Web marketer. First, submitting to Yahoo! used to take upwards of eight weeks, and if your submission had been rejected, ignored, or lost you'd have no way of knowing. At least now with the fees there is an "appeals process" where you can plead your case in the event that your submission was edited or ignored. And now you can gain entry into the most important search directories in days, not months. This is a good development which we hope continues. I'd rather pay a fee for something I used to receive for free if I also gain some level of service and the vendor accepts some level of accountability.

What's most important to remember with the paid Yahoo! or LookSmart submissions is that even if you succeed, you could ultimately fail. I've seen companies pat each other on the back when they get added to a directory only to discover that their submission resulted in no rankings on any of their important keywords. I've known companies to attain rankings on their important keywords only to find that they had the keywords all wrong and although they enjoy rankings, those rankings deliver little traffic. Worse still is when they attain rankings and lots of traffic but no sales or qualified leads. What happened? They succeeded in getting listed, they succeeded in attaining rankings, they succeeded in generating search engine referral traffic, but they targeted the wrong group of keywords and did not effectively target their audience. The outcome is hordes of visitors, but nobody is interested in their wares. This is the reason there is significant value in working with an established search engine positioning company. Search engine positioning companies bring experience from dozens of campaigns to bear on your project. Search engine positioning companies can tell you from experience which keywords will drive traffic and which will drive qualified traffic.

One of our newer clients was already listed in Yahoo!. We resubmitted their site to Yahoo!, requested a change in their listing, and increased their Yahoo! referral traffic by over 85 percent — conversions and on-the-site behavior improved dramatically, too.

Now that many of the directory services have implemented these pay-for-consideration programs, there is value in retaining the counsel of an expert before you invest those fees. Most importantly, read and then reread our chapters on selecting keywords and submitting to Yahoo! and LookSmart if you still plan to go it alone. Be aware that it is difficult even for a professional SEP company to get a listing changed in Yahoo! or LookSmart. Do it right the first time or work with a search engine positioning company.

Paying for Inclusion but Not Ranking

Inktomi was the first search engine (as opposed to a directory like Yahoo! or LookSmart) to charge a submission fee. This means a Web site must pay for every page submitted. This fee ensures only that the submitted page will be visited by the search engine's automated robot or spider and added to the database. There is no promise, implied or inferred, that the submission will result in a ranking.

Here again, having a qualified search engine positioning company working on your behalf is important. Submission fees for this type of engine can run upwards of $6,000 for a Web site of a thousand pages. However, not all pages that make up a Web site will ever attain rankings or should be submitted. A search engine positioning expert will know which pages of a Web site are unlikely to attain rankings under different algorithms. Most Web sites contain Web pages that one search engine or another will not like. Any number of issues can prevent a particular Web page from attaining rankings, from having little indexable text to problematic HTML construction that will interfere with proper search engine spidering. Regardless, in very few cases should all or even most of the pages that make up a Web site be submitted to any given search engine. And, when a page is submitted for a fee, you want to make sure it counts.

It's a bit like going out and buying a lottery ticket and then making a down payment on a big house you expect to buy with the winnings. However, the odds of winning the lottery are greater than the odds that your Web page will be displayed simply because you paid a fee to ensure that your Web site was added to a search database — unless, of course, you've optimized the Web page first.

Think about it: Lottery odds are usually one in a few million. Inktomi, the search engine that started the pay-for-submission model and that powers HotBot and others, contains more than 500 million Web pages. If you pay to submit just one page of your Web site, your odds of being found could very literally be one in 500 million unless you're working with a search engine positioning company that properly optimizes that page before it is submitted.

We've discovered that there are many benefits for our clients in Inktomi's new paid-submission program. In the past, Web site owners were forced to submit to HotBot or any of several search portals that used the Inktomi database in order to gain entry into this important database. Submissions to Inktomi through partners could take months to be added. Under the new paid-submission system, submissions are accepted in 24 hours. If we've done our job and properly optimized the submitted pages, rankings materialize almost overnight.

iProspect was among the first to use Inktomi's paid submission interface and has had time to learn its intricacies. We've achieved rankings increases in all Inktomi-powered search engines for all of our clients under the new system, and we've discovered that Inktomi seems to love our optimization techniques because our client's pages score very high. We're very encouraged by the results thus far and we encourage you to take advantage of this interface.

We know that at least two other search engines have plans to follow this paid-submission model, and we believe it will only make search engine positioning services more valuable by enabling professionals to achieve results more quickly. Without paid submission, search engines take their time in updating their databases. When search engines charge for submission, they must add their customers' pages more quickly. That benefits the search engine positioning industry a great deal.

The primary Inktomi submission partner is Position Technologies of St. Charles, Illinois. Their Web site is www.positionpro.com. While Network Solutions has recently been made an Inktomi submission partner, we have no experience with their interface. iProspect.com uses and recommends Position Technologies' submission service based on our successful experience with their tool.

Paying for Placement and Click-throughs

Sooner or later someone had to think, "Hey, what if we charge everyone who wants to be in our search engine and then make them pay every time someone clicks on their listing in the search results? Why are we just serving search results for free, anyway? We can make money with these search results!" And a couple of search engines did just that, namely LookSmart and GoTo.

LookSmart is a human-edited directory service and a competitor to the Yahoo! directory. While not an important search engine on its own, LookSmart's search index is distributed on several more important search portals. For example, a search conducted at MSN.com displays search results derived from LookSmart.

LookSmart, unlike Yahoo!, also has begun to offer a "sub-site" listing program. LookSmart editors will visit a Web site and review it to determine how many other subcategories or additional listings it may qualify for. They state publicly that they will only list or propose content that meets their strict editorial standards, but the additional listings a site can be granted can be significant. After they've listed your Web site under additional content areas, you would pay for any resulting click-throughs on that content. Note that while LookSmart agrees to list you in these additional categories, and while they profit only if lots of people click on your new listings, they make no promise that any of the new listings will result in increased rankings or visibility. However, if you work with LookSmart through an SEP service, you can propose additional categories and possibly better site titles and descriptions that will result in more click-throughs. The involvement of an SEP service can often mean the difference between additional listings that result in significant traffic and rankings or just an average outcome. Regardless of whether or not you work with a search engine positioning company, we encourage everyone to take advantage of the LookSmart sub-site listing program. We think it's a great tool to incrementally increase search engine referral traffic.

GoTo.com is the "search engine" that most people think of when they talk about pay-for-placement search engines. As we discussed in Chapter 33 on pay-for-placement search engines, GoTo.com operates an escalating bidding system that continually causes prices to increase. If you wish to rank higher in the search results, simply raise the amount you pay when someone clicks on your listing and you'll move right to the top. The reality of this model is that it works well as an ad network but hasn't attracted a following as a search engine. GoTo is now really an ad network that syndicates its paid search results across a number of other search engines and Web sites.

The trend to watch is that paid rankings, pay-for-placement, and pay-for-click-through models will continue to prosper, though they will never replace traditional search. Likewise, they will never replace search engine positioning, but instead remain an integral, though merely incremental, component of some types of search engine positioning campaigns. The reason I say that this makes sense for only some kinds of campaigns is simple: Many Web sites do not sell anything or have any way of determining the yield or value of a visitor. Paying for each visitor for these types of sites makes little sense and therefore, they may elect not to participate in a pay-for-placement or pay-for-click-through program.

Who Loses in the Future?

There are a number of search engine optimization companies that have written elaborate scripts to build thousands and thousands of nearly identical doorway pages targeting thousands of keywords at a time. They submit these to all of the search engines with the hope that some will "stick" and attain rankings. That practice is considered spamming because it adds unwanted overhead in the form of storage costs for the search engines, not to mention thousands of pages with little value that searchers might find in the search results.

By adding a fee to the submission interface and charging Web sites for every page that is submitted, companies who employed the "throw it against the wall and see if it sticks" strategy are locked out in the cold. We believe this was at least a small part of the goal of these pay-for-submission models.

In the long run, we believe this will be good for the search engines and for high-quality Web sites. As more search engines adopt these pay models, high-quality Web sites will not have to compete with millions of machine gener-ated doorway or gateway pages for rankings in search engines because employing such strategies will be cost prohibitive.

Summary

Currently, only three of the major search engines have moved to a paid-submis-sion model. There will be more, but we feel this is a good development in the long run. These added fees amount to a toll on what used to be the free "add-URL" link. For the most part, all that has happened is that the free process of submitting to a search engine now incurs a fee. That's it. Pay for inclusion? Yes. The end of the need for search engine positioning? Hardly.

A Web site must still be optimized in order to attain a top ranking. Every submitted Web page must still be revised and tweaked whenever a search engine's algorithm changes, as they do every few months, in order to maintain top rankings.

Now that a tollbooth has been placed in front of the submission interface to a few search engines, it is even more important that the content submitted is properly optimized before that toll is paid. Otherwise, those fees are truly wasted.

Most importantly, the search engine landscape has always changed rapidly. Consider that in 1996 there were just eight major search engines worth target-ing. A year later there were 10, then 15, and now 18 or possibly 20 (with two more that we're watching). In 1997, all search engines were just that — search engines. They considered only keyword placement on the page to determine a Web site's ranking. Today, most search engines are hybrids and display human-edited directory content supplemented by spider, or robot-populated

(constant process)

search engine results, a trend we call "Directory Nation" because all search engines formed partnerships with human-edited directory services.

In the last two years we've witnessed new search technology that considers link popularity, or how many Web sites established links to yours as a component of their relevancy algorithm. We've witnessed search engines that track click-through behavior to determine relevancy and a Web site's popularity. Excite purchased WebCrawler, Lycos purchased HotBot, and AOL purchased Netscape. Yahoo! dumped Inktomi, its supplemental search engine, and replaced it with Google. Lycos ditched its own search database and replaced it with the Open Directory. Currently, when you perform a search in Lycos, it displays up to five search matches from Direct Hit (the search partner that tracks click-through behavior to determine which sites are "most popular"), then Open Directory categories, and then Web sites from within Open Directory categories below those. If that's not enough, all of those search results are supplemented by search matches from FAST (alltheweb.com). It's a mess, really.

But if anything should be clear after reading this advisory it is this: Search engine positioning is a quickly and continuously changing space. These latest trends may catch on and evolve, but search engine positioning professionals will continue to help companies make sense of the changes and leverage those changes into optimal results.

NOTE   Still need help? Provide us with a detailed description of your Web site challenge. We'll be pleased to help in any way we can, or will refer you to any number of high-quality search engine optimization specialists whom we know and trust. Feel free to e-mail us at: sales@iprospect.com, or visit our quote request page at: http://www.iprospect.com/book-quote.htm.

So, what's the best search engine?

Which search engine do I use personally? I use two regularly — Google and AltaVista — and like them both immensely. I find Google to be the most relevant today, but on other days AltaVista is truly impressive. FAST (alltheweb.com) is surprisingly good and the best "up and comer." I use Google for one- and two-word searches and AltaVista for multiple word searches. I also spend quite a bit of time searching Yahoo!, Lycos, and MSN. I'm a really big fan of LookSmart and the engines it powers. I've met or interviewed executives at most of the search engines. I was particularly impressed with the people I met at LookSmart, AltaVista, and FAST — genuinely brilliant people with incredible insights into the future of this space. About the only search engine I don't use is iWon.com, not because it's weak or bad, but just because I don't like the concept of a lottery or a contest.

I'm like everyone else. More often than not, I use several search engines to find what I'm looking for and use different search engines for different kinds of searches. And that, my friends, is yet another reason why the search engine positioning industry will continue to thrive. To succeed on the Web, a Web site must be found in several search engines for multiple search terms and phrases. As the complexity increases (because it never decreases), search engine positioning companies will remain a valuable resource to help companies navigate and succeed on an ever-shifting playing field.

Appendix A:

Words That are Commonly Misspelled

absence	attendance	colossal
abundance	attorneys	column
accelerate	auxiliary	coming
accessible	balloon	commitment
accidentally	bankruptcy	committee
acclaim	barbecue	comparative
accommodate	barbiturate	competent
accomplish	bargain	completely
accordion	basically	compromise
accrued	beggar	concede
accumulate	beginning	conceive
achievement	believe	condemn
acquaintance	benefited	condescend
across	biscuit	conference
address	bouillon	congratulate
advertise	boundary	conscientious
advertisement	bouquet	consciousness
advisory	Britain	consistent
affiliate	bureau	continuous
aggravate	business	control
airport	calendar	controlled
alignment	camouflage	controversy
alleged	campaign	convenient
alphabetize	cancellation	coolly
analyze	cantaloupe	corollary
annual	casualty	correlate
annulment	cemetery	correspondence
apiece	chagrined	counselor
apostrophe	challenge	courteous
apparent	changeable	courtesy
appearance	characteristic	criticize
archives	chief	cynical
argument	chosen	deceive
article	cigarette	defendant
assessed	climbed	defense
assignment	collateral	deferred
atheist	collectible	delegate
athletics	colonel	dependent

descend	excellent	guaranteeing
description	excitable	guerrilla
desirable	exhaust	guidance
despair	existence	handkerchief
desperate	expense	happily
develop	experience	harass
development	experiment	height
difference	explanation	heinous
dilemma	extremely	hemorrhage
dining	exuberance	heroes
disappearance	fallacious	hesitancy
disappoint	fallacy	hindrance
disastrous	familiar	hoarse
discipline	fascinate	hoping
disease	fascinating	humorous
dispensable	February	hypocrisy
dissatisfied	fictitious	hypocrite
dominant	finally	ideally
drunkenness	financially	identical
easily	fireproof	idiosyncrasy
ecstasy	forcibly	ignorance
efficiency	foreclosure	imaginary
eighth	foreign	immediately
either	forfeit	implement
eligible	formerly	incidentally
embarrassing	forty	incredible
enemy	fourteen	independence
enforceable	fourth	independent
entirely	fulfill	indicted
equipped	fundamentally	indictment
equivalent	gauge	indispensable
escape	generally	inevitable
especially	genius	influential
everyday	government	information
exaggerate	governor	inoculate
exasperated	grateful	installment
exceed	grievous	insurance
excellence	guarantee	intelligence

intercede
interference
interpret
interrupt
introduce
irrelevant
irresistible
island
issuing
jealousy
jewelry
judicial
knowledge
laboratory
lacquer
legitimate
leisure
length
lenient
liaison
license
lien
lieutenant
lightning
likelihood
likely
liquid
loneliness
losing
lovely
luxury
magazine
mailbox
maintain
maintenance
manageable
maneuver
marriage

mathematics
medicine
mediocre
merchandise
millennium
millionaire
miniature
minutes
miscellaneous
mischievous
missile
misspelled
mortgage
mosquito
mosquitoes
murmur
muscle
mysterious
narrative
naturally
necessary
necessity
negotiate
neighbor
neutron
nickel
ninety
ninth
noticeable
notifying
nowadays
nuisance
obedience
obstacle
occasion
occasionally
occurred
occurrence

offense
official
omission
omit
omitted
opinion
opponent
opportunity
oppression
optimism
optimistic
ordinarily
origin
outrageous
overrun
oversight
panicky
parallel
parliament
particularly
pavilion
payroll
peaceable
peculiar
penetrate
perceive
percent
performance
permanent
permissible
permitted
perseverance
persistence
personnel
phenomenal
physical
physician
picnicking

piece
pilgrimage
pitiful
planning
pleasant
policyholder
portray
possess
possessive
postgraduate
postmortem
potato
potatoes
practically
prairie
preferable
preference
preferred
prejudice
preparation
preponderance
prescription
prevalent
primitive
privacy
privilege
probably
procedure
proceed
professor
prominent
promissory
pronounce
pronunciation
propaganda
psychology
publicly
pursue

quandary
quarantine
questionnaire
quizzes
realistically
realize
really
recede
receipt
receive
recognize
recommend
reference
referred
referring
regrettable
relevant
relieving
religious
remembrance
reminiscence
repetition
representative
resemblance
reservoir
resistance
restaurant
rheumatism
rhythm
rhythmical
roommate
sacrifice
sacrilegious
safety
salary
satellite
scenery
schedule

secede
secretary
seize
separate
sergeant
serviceable
several
shepherd
shining
similar
simile
simply
simultaneous
sincerely
skeptic
skeptical
skiing
soliloquy
someday
sophomore
souvenir
specifically
specimen
sponsor
spontaneous
statistics
stimulus
stopped
strategy
strength
strenuous
stubbornness
subordinate
subsidiary
substantial
subtle
succeed
success

succession
sufficient
supersede
suppress
surprise
surround
susceptible
suspicious
syllable
symmetrical
synonymous
tangible
tariff
technical
technique
temperature
tendency
themselves
theories

therefore
thorough
though
through
till
tomorrow
tournament
tourniquet
tragedy
transferred
truly
twelfth
tyranny
unanimous
undoubtedly
unnecessary
until
usage
usually

vacuum
valuable
vengeance
vigilant
village
villain
violence
visible
warehouse
warrant
Wednesday
weird
welfare
wherever
wholly
worthwhile
yacht
yield
zoology

Appendix B:

Common Stop Words

a	because	down	further
about	become	due	furthermore
above	becomes	during	get
across	becoming	e.g.	give
adj	been	each	go
after	before	eg	got
afterwards	beforehand	eight	had
again	behind	either	hardly
against	being	eleven	has
all	below	else	hasn't
almost	beside	elsewhere	have
alone	besides	empty	having
along	between	enough	he
already	beyond	etc.	head
also	bill	even	hence
although	both	ever	her
always	bottom	every	here
am	but	everyone	hereafter
among	by	everything	hereby
amongst	call	everywhere	herein
amoungst	came	except	hereof
amount	can	few	hereon
an	cannot	fifteen	hereto
and	can't	fifty	hereupon
another	co	fill	herewith
any	come	find	hers
anyhow	computer	fire	herself
anyone	con	first	hi
anything	could	five	him
anyway	couldn't	for	himself
anywhere	cry	former	his
are	de	formerly	how
around	describe	forty	however
as	detail	found	html
at	did	four	hundred
back	do	from	I
be	does	front	i.e.
became	done	full	ie

if	namely	rather	them
in	neither	re	themselves
inc	never	really	then
indeed	nevertheless	said	thence
interest	next	same	there
into	nine	see	thereafter
is	no	seem	thereby
it	nobody	seemed	therefore
its	none	seeming	therein
itself	no one	seems	thereupon
just	nor	serious	these
keep	not	several	they
last	nothing	she	thick
latter	now	should	thin
latterly	nowhere	show	third
least	of	side	this
less	off	since	those
like	often	sincere	though
ltd	on	six	three
made	once	sixty	through
many	one	so	throughout
may	only	some	thru
me	onto	somehow	thus
meanwhile	or	someone	title
meta	other	something	to
might	others	sometime	together
mill	otherwise	sometimes	too
mine	our	somewhere	top
more	ours	still	toward
moreover	ourselves	such	towards
most	out	system	twelve
mostly	over	table	twenty
move	own	take	two
much	part	ten	un
must	per	than	under
my	perhaps	that	until
myself	please	the	unto
name	put	their	up

upon	whatever	whether	with
us	when	which	within
very	whence	while	without
via	whenever	whither	would
viz.	where	who	yet
was	whereafter	whoever	you
way	whereas	whole	your
we	whereby	whom	yours
well	wherein	whose	yourself
were	whereupon	why	yourselves
what	wherever	will	

Index

iProspect.com™

Industrial Strength Search Engine Positioning

Need Search Engine Positioning Help?

We can help your customers find you --
and help you find new customers.

High rankings in the major search engines and directories are *essential* for any business that wants to thrive on the Web.

iProspect has grown to become the leading search engine positioning consulting services agency, with the largest full-time staff of search engine positioning professionals. Founded in 1996, iProspect represents traditional brick-and-mortar firms and the most successful companies on the Web.

You've just invested millions of dollars developing a sophisticated Web site to pursue your slice of the $1.3 trillion market. You're waiting for customers to flock to the site...but they don't. Why?

Maybe no one knows you're open for business.

In cyberspace, like on Main Street, *location is key.* If your customers can't find you, you're out of business. We can help you stake out prime real estate on the Internet.

www.iprospect.com

We can develop a search engine positioning campaign for your Web site.

T: 800.522.1152
T: 781.641.5700
F: 781.641.5755

iProspect.com, Inc.
5 Water Street
Arlington, MA 02476

About the CD

The companion CD contains links to all of the major search engines and directories discussed in the text. In addition, there are links to the following:

- Position Technologies' Position Pro Web site management service
- BulkRegister.com, the leading provider of wholesale domain name registration services
- SubmitWolf Pro, a professional Web site promotional tool

A trial version of WebPosition Gold, the leading search engine positioning software, is also included.

The CD should auto-run when you insert it into your CD drive. If it does not, double-click on index.htm in Windows Explorer.

Warning: Opening the CD package makes this book non-returnable.

CD/Source Code Usage License Agreement

Please read the following CD/Source Code usage license agreement before opening the CD and using the contents therein:

1. By opening the accompanying software package, you are indicating that you have read and agree to be bound by all terms and conditions of this CD/Source Code usage license agreement.

2. The compilation of code and utilities contained on the CD and in the book are copyrighted and protected by both U.S. copyright law and international copyright treaties, and is owned by Wordware Publishing, Inc. Individual source code, example programs, help files, freeware, shareware, utilities, and evaluation packages, including their copyrights, are owned by the respective authors.

3. No part of the enclosed CD or this book, including all source code, help files, shareware, freeware, utilities, example programs, or evaluation programs, may be made available on a public forum (such as a World Wide Web page, FTP site, bulletin board, or Internet news group) without the express written permission of Wordware Publishing, Inc. or the author of the respective source code, help files, shareware, freeware, utilities, example programs, or evaluation programs.

4. You may not decompile, reverse engineer, disassemble, create a derivative work, or otherwise use the enclosed programs, help files, freeware, shareware, utilities, or evaluation programs except as stated in this agreement.

5. The software, contained on the CD and/or as source code in this book, is sold without warranty of any kind. Wordware Publishing, Inc. and the authors specifically disclaim all other warranties, express or implied, including but not limited to implied warranties of merchantability and fitness for a particular purpose with respect to defects in the disk, the program, source code, sample files, help files, freeware, shareware, utilities, and evaluation programs contained therein, and/or the techniques described in the book and implemented in the example programs. In no event shall Wordware Publishing, Inc., its dealers, its distributors, or the authors be liable or held responsible for any loss of profit or any other alleged or actual private or commercial damage, including but not limited to special, incidental, consequential, or other damages.

6. One (1) copy of the CD or any source code therein may be created for backup purposes. The CD and all accompanying source code, sample files, help files, freeware, shareware, utilities, and evaluation programs may be copied to your hard drive. With the exception of freeware and shareware programs, at no time can any part of the contents of this CD reside on more than one computer at one time. The contents of the CD can be copied to another computer, as long as the contents of the CD contained on the original computer are deleted.

7. You may not include any part of the CD contents, including all source code, example programs, shareware, freeware, help files, utilities, or evaluation programs in any compilation of source code, utilities, help files, example programs, freeware, shareware, or evaluation programs on any media, including but not limited to CD, disk, or Internet distribution, without the express written permission of Wordware Publishing, Inc. or the owner of the individual source code, utilities, help files, example programs, freeware, shareware, or evaluation programs.

8. You may use the source code, techniques, and example programs in your own commercial or private applications unless otherwise noted by additional usage agreements as found on the CD.